PENGUIN HANDBOOKS

THE DEFINITIVE
WORD-PROCESSING BOOK

Jonathan Price got his first typewriter when he started ninth grade, and he's been typing ever since. He has taught writing, worked as a word-processing operator, helped companies choose word-processing systems, created manuals about computer networks and word-processing programs, and written ten other books, including *Life Show* (with John Lahr), *Video Visions, The Best Thing on TV, Classic Scenes, Thirty Days to More Powerful Writing,* and *Put That in Writing.* He likes cooking Hunan-style, making video art, and going to the drive-in. He lives in Berkeley, California, with his wife, Lisa, and son, Ben.

Linda Pinneau Urban learned word processing the hard way—as a user. Since then, she has trained scores of people on word-processing systems and other business applications. She has helped design software, and has documented a dozen major programs. She is now at work on manuals for one of the most advanced word processors in the business. In her spare time she likes to garden and read science fiction. She lives in Berkeley, California, with her husband, Greg, and son, Nick.

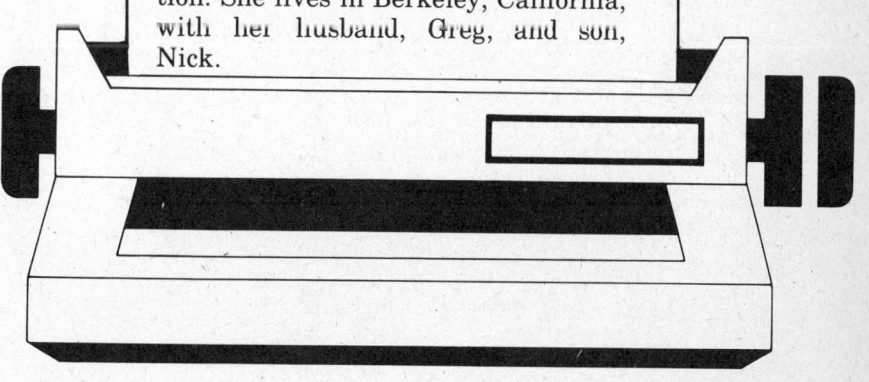

THE DEFINITIVE WORD-PROCESSING BOOK

by
Jonathan Price
and
Linda Pinneau Urban

PENGUIN BOOKS

PENGUIN BOOKS
Viking Penguin Inc., 40 West 23rd Street,
New York, New York 10010, U.S.A.
Penguin Books Ltd, Harmondsworth,
Middlesex, England
Penguin Books Australia Ltd, Ringwood,
Victoria, Australia
Penguin Books Canada Limited,
2801 John Street,
Markham, Ontario, Canada L3R 1B4
Penguin Books (N.Z.) Ltd,
182–190 Wairau Road,
Auckland 10, New Zealand

Copyright © Jonathan Price and
  Linda Pinneau Urban, 1984
All rights reserved

First published in 1984 by
Viking Penguin Inc.
Published simultaneously in Canada

Library of Congress Catalog Card
Number: 84-42858

Printed in the United States of America by
Fairfield Graphics, Fairfield, Pennsylvania
Set in Century Schoolbook

Except in the United States of America,
this book is sold subject to the condition
that it shall not, by way of trade or
otherwise, be lent, re-sold, hired out, or
otherwise circulated without the
publisher's prior consent in any form of
binding or cover other than that in which
it is published and without a similar
condition including this condition being
imposed on the subsequent purchaser

Advice to Readers

Word-processing technology constantly changes, and possible uses and adaptations for individual needs are almost infinite. Therefore, although we have made every effort to supply the reader with complete and accurate information, responsibility for its use must rest with the reader, with the sources of particular equipment or systems, or with training services used by the reader. We do not recommend any particular word-processing system, equipment, or services. Selection of equipment and services will always require individual assessment of needs and personal evaluation of different products. We make no representations, either express or implied, with respect to this book, to the products described in it, or to the uses which may be made of such products. In no event will Jonathan Price, Linda Pinneau Urban, or Viking Penguin Inc. be liable for damages of any kind or nature resulting from or arising in connection with this book or any use which may be made of it by the reader or anyone who discusses the subject with the reader.

Acknowledgments

First and foremost, thanks to Greg Urban and Lisa Price for their encouragement, patience, and advice. They've cheerfully endured hundreds of phone calls, late-night printing, piles of manuscript. And they've given us lots of good ideas.

We would also like to thank the many friends, old and new, who contributed their time, knowledge, and stories to the writing of this book.

Special thanks to Dotti Sauer, Marty Downey, Roslyn Heimberg, Sonya Johnson, Mary Molloy, Alan Cooper, and Judy Dohn.

In addition, many people across the country in word-processing, computer, and software companies went out of their way to help us gather the most accurate information available on word-processing products. Thanks to:

Steve Abbott, Data Processing Designs
Frank Abbruscata, Exxon Corporation
Richard Adams, Algorithmics
Donatta Anderson, CPT Corporation
Sharon Anderson, Information
   Unlimited Software
Linda Barber, ATV Jacquard
Lisa Bell, Lanier Business Products
Peter Belvel, Itek Graphic Systems
John Bintz, Lexisoft
Mark Bovino, Northern Telecom
Ken Bright, Dictaphone
Arthur Burns, Wang Laboratories
Bruce Camber, Para Research
Julia Case, Datapoint
Mary Lou Close, Radio Shack
Andy Czernek, Zenith
Les Dace, Philips Information Systems
Jan Desjarden, Toshiba
Steve Eames, IBM Corporation
Ken Edoff, Exxon Corporation
Trudy Edwards, Syntrex
Carole Ely, Vector Graphic
Maureen Emberly, Algorithmics

ACKNOWLEDGMENTS ‖ vii

David Eyes, Hayden Publications
Bob Farkas, NCR Corporation
Linda Franka, Royal Business
  Machines
Marlan Gilbert, Rothenberg
  Information Systems
Rick Goldstein, Microdata
Kathy Hahn, Burroughs Corporation
Kathy Hansen, Raytheon
Paul Harris, NBI
Neil Helm, Peachtree Software
Don Holcomb, Designer Software
Neil Holzman, Prolink
Lucille Hunt, ATV Jacquard
Peggy Hyndeman, NBI
Mitch Kadish, Compal
Trish Kalkhof, Basic Four Corporation
Cynthia Karban, Olivetti
Geof Karlin, Applied Digital Data
  Systems
Elaine Kauffman, Scientific Data
  Systems
Donna Keeling, Durango
Claudia Koehler, Monroe Systems for
  Business
Patrice Lantier, Megadata
Barbara Lee, Microdata
Diane Leeds, NorthStar Computers
Peter Leimpeter, Compugraphic
Dick Lockman, Toshiba
Bill Lohse, Information Unlimited
  Software
Theo Loster, Nixdorf Computers
Alan Macher, IBM Corporation
Pam Madelena, Prime Computer
Glen Malmquist, ATV Jacquard
Brenda Mannos, Prime Computer
Beverly McDonald, Peachtree
  Software
Jim McKenzie, Sperry Univac
Jua McSween, NCR Corporation
Richard Menneg, Savin Corporation
Linda Merrill, Apple Computer
Adrienne Miller, Exxon Corporation
Elaine Millspaugh
Wendy Mitchell, MicroPro
  International
Donel Moss, Sperry Univac

Richard Mumper, Raytheon Data Systems
Len Myers, Ontel
Renee Olson, Apple Computer
Abraham Ostrovsky, Savin Corporation
Rosemary Peat, Burroughs Corporation
Harvard Pennington, IJG
Donna Perrone, Intelligent Systems Corporation
Ruth Porter, Digital Equipment Corporation
Shelley Potter, Honeywell
Ann Prine, Basic Four Corporation
Zev Rettet, Select Information Systems
Nelson Riegel, Point Four Data Systems
John Risken, Sofsys
Joan Roden, Barrister
Alma Rodoni, Hewlett-Packard
Susan Rosanberger, Texas Instruments
Steve Rothenberg, Rothenberg Systems
Steve Rothenburger, Wordplex
Susan Rubin, Xerox Corporation
Ronni Sarmanian, Data General
Gerald Schacter, Lexor
Carl Schmaedig, AM Varityper
Tom Scornavacca, Delta Data
Dave Scott, IBM Corporation
Don Shaw, Monroe
Ron Smebye, Xerox Corporation
Bill Smith, Structured Systems Group
Kim Speer, AB Dick
Don Stanfield, Radio Shack
Tracy Strickland, Technology International
James Sweeney, Lexor
K. Terhorst, Compucorp
Dave Wadman, Cado
Mr. Walker, XMark
Nancy Webb, MicroComputer Service Center
Teresa Welsh, ABC Sales
Stefan Zimberoff, Fortune

Trademark Acknowledgments

Please note: The companies listed below hold trademarks on the following products mentioned in the text.

ABC Sales, Inc.: LazyWriter
AB Dick Company: Magna SL, Magna III
Apple Computer Inc.: Apple, Apple Writer III, Lisa, Macintosh, Apple IIe
Applied Digital Data Systems Inc.: Multivision
ATV Jacquard Inc.: Jacquard, Jacquard Systems, Account-Rite, Type-Rite, Data-Rite
Basic 4 Corporation: Dataword II
Burroughs Corporation: Ofiswriter
Cado Corporation: CAT III
Compal Computer Systems: Compal, EzType
Comptek Research Inc.: Barrister
Compucorp: Compucorp
Compugraphic Corporation: Compugraphic
CPT Corporation: CPT, MathPak, CompuPak
Data General Corporation: Eclipse, Nova, MicroNova, Comprehensive Electronic Office
Data Processing Design, Inc.: Word-11
Datapoint Corporation: Datapoint, ARC, ISX
Datasoft: Text Wizard
Delta Data Systems Corporation: Easyone
Designer Software: Palantir
Dictaphone: Dual Display
Digital Equipment Corporation: Decword/DP, Decmate, RSTS/E, RSX, VAX/VMS
Digital Research Corporation: CP/M
Durango Systems, Inc.: Durango, Star Text
Fortune Systems Corporation: Fortune 32:16, For:Word
Hayden: Pie Writer, Pro/Format
Hayes: DC Hayes MicroModem
Hendrix Corporation: Teletypereader
Hewlett Packard: HP Word
Honeywell Information Systems: Infowriter
IBM Corporation: Displaywriter, MTST, Selectric, MagCard
Itek Corporation: Quadritek
Lanier Business Products: Ez-1, No Problem, No Problem Shared System
Lexisoft Inc.: Spellbinder

Lexor Corporation: Lexor, Lexoriter
Microdata Corporation: Wordmate, Reality, Sequel
MicroPro International: WordStar
Mohawk Data Sciences: Series 21, MDS
NBI: Oasys
NCR Corporation: Worksaver
North Star Computers, Inc.: Northword, Horizon, Advantage
Northern Telecom: Omniword
Para Research Inc.: Para Text
Peachtree Software Inc.: Peachtext
Perfect Writer Inc.: Perfect Writer
Prolink Corporation: Prolink, ProWord
Raytheon Corporation: Lexitron
Royal Business Machines, Inc.: Royal
Savin Corporation: Savin
Scientific Data Systems: SDS
Shasta General Systems: Parrot
Sorcim/IUS Micro Software: Easy Writer, Easy Writer Professional
Select Information Systems Inc.: Select
Tandy Corporation: Radio Shack, Scripsit, TRS-80
Wang Laboratories, Inc.: Wang Writer
Xerox Corporation: Xerox, Xerox 820, Xerox 800, Xerox 850, Xerox 860

Contents

ACKNOWLEDGMENTS *vi*
HOW TO USE THIS BOOK *xv*
INTRODUCTION: WHY WORD
   PROCESSING? *xvii*

1. WHO USES WORD PROCESSING? *1*

2. HOW IT WORKS *11*

   The Basic Word-Processing
     Functions *13*
   Editing and Formatting Features of
     a Word Processor *22*
   Other Features of a Word
     Processor *30*
   Functions Checklist *42*

3. WHAT MAKES UP A WORD
   PROCESSOR? *54*

   The Human Connection: Screens
     and Keyboards *55*
   A Computer at Heart: The CPU *65*
   Memory *68*
   Disk Storage *69*
   Software *73*
   Printers *82*
   Photocomposers *93*
   Modems *96*
   Optical Character Readers *101*
   Components Checklist *105*

4. NARROWING THE FIELD *114*

   Electronic and Memory
     Typewriters *116*

Dedicated Word Processors *118*
Hybrid Systems: Word Processing Combined with Data Processing *125*
Microcomputers as Word Processors *131*
Word-Processing Software for Existing Computers *136*
Total Office Systems *140*
Your Needs Checklist *141*

5. MAKING THE CHANGE EASIER *144*

The Effects on Health *144*
The Effects on Your Office Society *148*
The Effects on Your Company *154*

6. SHOPPING FOR A WORD PROCESSOR *172*

Support *184*

7. WHAT IT'S LIKE TO START *204*

Before the System Arrives: Preparing Your Office and Staff *204*
When the Equipment Arrives: Installation and Training *210*
Procedures for Long-Term Successful Use of Your Equipment *216*

8. THE OFFICE OF THE FUTURE *226*

What's Possible Now *232*
Buying an Automated Office *235*

APPENDIX A
LIST OF WORD-PROCESSING PRODUCTS *259*

Key to the List of Word-Processing Products *262*
Complete Systems *274*
Software *403*

APPENDIX B
JOBS IN WORD PROCESSING *434*

APPENDIX C
WHAT TO READ *441*

APPENDIX D
  DIRECTORY OF VENDORS *444*

GLOSSARY *450*

INDEX *481*

How to Use This Book

If you're new to word processing... | Start at the beginning. You'll see why the industrialized world is tilting toward word processing: who uses it and what it can do for you.

If you wonder how other people use word processing... | Read Chapter 1, "Who Uses Word Processing?"

If you know something and want to know more... | You could jump to components—Chapter 3, "What Makes Up a Word Processor?"

If you are ready to buy... | Use the checklists in Chapters 3, 4, and 5. Read Chapter 4, "Narrowing the Field" and Chapter 6, "Shopping for a Word Processor." Then turn to Appendix A for a comparison of word processors on the market today.

If you're worried about support... | Find out about training, advice, and repair in Chapter 6, "Shopping for a Word Processor."

If you want to know what it's like to bring in word processing to your workplace... | Read Chapter 7, "What's It's Like to Start."

If you want to know how word processing will fit into an automated office . . .

Turn to Chapter 8, "The Office of the Future."

If you want to compare word processors . . .

Turn to Appendix A, "List of Word-Processing Products."

If you're thinking about a job in word processing . . .

Read Appendix B, "Jobs in Word Processing."

If you want to read more . . .

Turn to the section on books and magazines, Appendix C, "What to Read."

If you want to know what a particular term means . . .

See the Glossary.

If you want to read about a particular topic . . .

Please look it up in the Index.

Introduction: Why Word Processing?

This book will help you decide if you need word-processing equipment, and if so, what kind will work best for you. You've probably seen word processors in advertisements, heard about them from friends, maybe even tried out a few. But still you may wonder: why word processing?

Since 1975 a majority of American wage earners have put in their days as clerks, secretaries, writers, systems analysts, middle managers, bosses, or professionals; most of us work in offices now. And every day we turn out about 600 million pages of computer printout, 234 million photocopies, 76 million letters. On average, each of us produces 45 new sheets of paper a day.

However, we don't handle all that paper too well. While the productivity of American factory workers soared 80 percent from 1960 to 1980, white-collar productivity crept up a mere 4 percent, and even started downhill in 1980. Offices are not assembly lines. "Henry Ford never said, 'Hey, let's design an efficient office.' He brilliantly conceived of mass production and industrial efficiency, and as an afterthought, got a couple of desks and chairs to run the operation," says David Elovitz, a real-estate consultant with Jones, Lang, Wooton, Inc.

And since office costs have been rising 12 to 15 percent a year, it is possible we will see the $800 billion spent on office operations in 1978 multiply to $1.5 trillion by 1990. Eighty percent of these costs reflects wage-and-benefit packages. But the age group that supplies the cheapest labor, 15- to 24-year-olds, will decline some 20 percent by 1987, while the need for office workers will keep on growing.

Looking at these figures, thousands of companies—from one-woman law practices to Fortune 500 corporations—are automating their offices. The three Generals (Mills, Electric, and Motors) have all instituted major studies of ways to increase white-collar speed and efficiency.

Central to these studies is a new idea of the office. "It's a clearinghouse for information," says Randi Goldfield, president of the Gibbs Consulting Group. Information has now been recognized as a corporate resource—one that does not wear out, and even grows more valuable when used. As office workers, then, our job is to accumulate, create, record, organize, display, store, retrieve, transmit, interpret, and weed out information. And according to one research organization, Data Pro, only 10 percent of most information is numbers—the rest is text.

So whatever kind of information you handle, you're probably going to have to learn word processing. The first tool most of us look to for help in handling information is the electric typewriter—and the next is the computer. Word processors combine these two familiar machines. And that may be why word processors are leading the trend toward the automated office. In 1979, about a hundred vendors sold $1.1 billion worth of word-processing equipment; in 1980, that volume doubled. By 1985 sales should reach $7.3 billion, according to Charles Norris of International Data Corporation. Word-processing trade shows have started to tour America and Europe. Professional associations have sprung up, trailing hundreds of consultants, who give $600 weekend seminars, teach community college courses, and contribute articles to ad-heavy trade journals with headings such as, "Word processing—it's a lot more than automated typing."

By 1990 you'll have to understand word processing to work in most offices. Half of the companies that have bought word processing are large corporations. They need 50 to 100 terminals in each department, linked by phone lines, so that reports can be sent back and forth. These organizations (most are in banking, insurance, consulting, law, and government) may also buy optical scanners to read old documents into the word-processing system; attach high-speed ink jet printers to turn out a hundred letter-quality pages a minute; transmit copies electronically to be turned into micrographic records; and zip other information to a photocomposition machine, to be set in cold type for use in a printed brochure. That's a fully automated office.

But the other half of the market for word processing is much simpler—small businesses, individuals who work out of their homes, freelancers, consultants, solo professionals. Basically anyone who uses a typewriter—or has a secretary—will find that a word processor pays for itself in a year or two.

These are some of the benefits of installing a word processor in your office:

- Faster output of better-typed material.
- Easier and faster revision of materials.
- Less proofreading.
- Less paper (documents can be stored electronically).
- Greater volume of output (increases threefold or more).
- Instant originals printed at speeds of 450 words per minute, or faster.
- Direct links with mainframe computers, optical scanners, high-speed printers, phototypesetters, and other peripheral devices, to send and receive data.
- Cost savings (reported by 85 percent of users).
- Fast and accurate calculations.
- Quick access to records for updating information.

"A secretary's productivity can be increased by 25 to 200 percent with a word processor, depending on how much typing she does," says Dan McGlaughlin, a vice-president at IBM. With an electric typewriter, a secretary types an average of 50,000 lines a year; with a word-processing system, that average rises to 150,000. Costs per page drop to a third or less (from a $3.25–$5.25 range to $1.00–$1.50 per standard one-page letter). And prices for word processing will be coming down even more, since the costs for computer logic and memory are dropping 25 to 40 percent a year. You can expect to spend an average of $6500 per workstation today—and that will certainly shrink over the next few years, when every office acquires a system as it once did a typewriter.

You'll reap the most benefits if you usually work on long documents, make numerous revisions, or need many original copies. You won't get such big savings if all you write are short memos and telegrams. And you'll lose money if you pick the wrong system—one that won't fit your particular needs.

Randi Sacha, assistant editor of *Administrative Management* magazine, warns, "If you haven't jumped on the word-processing bandwagon, then before you do, take the time to do it right. Any major mistake is bound to be a costly one." So you should find out first what you really need—and what word processing can or cannot do for you. That's what this book is designed to help you do.

No one word processor is right for everyone. If you write long manuals and update them regularly, you'll want one system; if you send out lots of short memos, you'll want another; if you write complex chemical and mathematical formulas, and derive lengthy calculations from a large computer, you'll want still another. Some people use the cathode-ray-tube display all day long, so they're willing to pay extra for a low-glare surface; this wouldn't matter so much at an office in which four or five people take turns entering data and calling up reports to be printed. Some people need letter-quality printing equal to that of the best electric typewriter; others settle for the much cheaper—and fuzzier—dot matrix printer. One person wants a system just for herself; another needs to hook up seven terminals to one central processing unit, so that seven people can all use the same reference material. Some people want a system that's easy to learn, even if it's not very flexible; in other situations, where just a few people will use the system all the time, they accept a more complicated system that can do more.

The headquarters of a major bank, for example, has a dozen word-processing centers spread out through its different departments. Several of these generate form letters, connecting up to a huge data base to add the customer's name, date of last payment, amount owed, and so on. The training department manager keeps her manuals on such topics as "The New Cashier" and "Electronic Funds Transfer" on another word processor, so she can update a few pages here and there, then get a freshly typed copy of the whole. And the advertising department creates brochures, placards, and signs using a word processor that feeds the perfected copy to a photocomposition machine, which then produces type ready to go to the printer.

In contrast to this, one lawyer has her secretary type up a letter, and then a request to the word-processing center. There the letter is read by an optical scanner, which enters the text into the word processor's memory for storage. And following the request, the word-processing operator calls up a standard partnership agreement, enters the names given, and prints it out on a high-speed (but not-so-sharp) printer. Then the lawyer marks up the pages, tailoring this agreement for her clients. The operator revises the document on-screen, then prints it out again. Sometimes the lawyer goes through 15 revisions before getting a letter-quality copy that is ready for signature. In the meantime, three other lawyers in the firm have used the same stored format to create their own customized versions of the agreement. And the accountant has updated his general ledger, accounts receivable and payable, based on time sheets filled out by the lawyers. In one week, this small word-processing center has turned out 2000 pages of text.

Writers and other people who work alone at home have bought themselves word processors, too. Alvin Toffler, author of *Future Shock*, says, "I'm a perfectionist; I don't like to work on sloppy copy. I spent half of my adult life retyping. And when somebody came up with a machine that was going to do that retyping for me, terrific!"

History. When Remington introduced the first commercial typewriter in the 1870s, offices began to "automate" their correspondence, which until then had been written and copied by hand. In the 1930s International Business Machines introduced the first electric typewriter. And close on their heels, the M. Shultz Company developed an automatic typewriter that could record text on paper rolls—much like those used on player pianos—to produce repetitive copies and fill-in form letters. Soon after came paper tape recording devices.

IBM's MTST (Magnetic Tape Selectric Typewriter) had the first reusable storage medium for text produced on a typewriter. (Photo courtesy of International Business Machines Corporation)

Then, in 1964 IBM brought out the first *reusable* storage medium for a typewriter—magnetic tape—on their MTST (Magnetic Tape Selectric Typewriter). Their regular Selectric typewriter had already become a standard item in offices, but with MTST's magnetic tape the operator could store information, replay it, make corrections and deletions, reprint as many copies as desired, then reuse the tape for another project. With MTST modern word processing was born. It took approximately 94 years for the evolution from typewriter to MTST. Less than 20 years later, the MTST seems almost as archaic as early upright typewriters.

In 1969 IBM introduced MagCards—magnetic cards that were slipped in a box beside the typewriter. The operator typed both on paper and on the card, then used the card to recall the text. A lot of companies that send out form letters bought MagCards, and many such systems are still in operation. But one MagCard can remember only about one full page of text.

INTRODUCTION: WHY WORD PROCESSING?

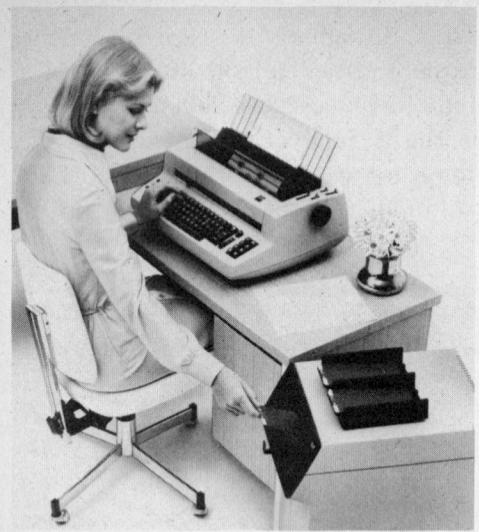

The IBM MagCard/A Typewriter shown here has both an internal memory of 6,000 characters and the ability to store text on magnetic cards. (Photo courtesy of International Business Machines Corporation)

In 1972 Lexitron and Linolex added two things to a similar word processor: video display screens and tape cassettes for storage. A year later Vydec produced a system using floppy diskettes, circles of magnetic tape that look like flimsy 45 rpm records and hold 80 to 100 pages of text. Word processors began to look like the systems we know today. With a screen to display the information, we can now make corrections and changes faster, and most important, we don't need to print a copy until it is correct. Thanks to the larger memory on the diskette, we can create multipage documents and work on all the pages at once, instead of being limited to a page or two at a time.

Since 1973 more and more companies have brought products to the word-processing marketplace. The hot competition for sales has helped speed the development of features that help an inexperienced user. As vendors fought to provide the best and most saleable systems, these "feature wars" generated systems to meet the needs of almost any writer or typist.

We've seen improvements both in hardware—the physical machine—and in software—the programs that tell the hardware how to handle the information and text that we input. Originally programs were almost exclusively "hardwired" into the systems, making them part of the hardware—so you had a rough time upgrading or changing the system. When software became available on disks that could be "loaded" into the system, vendors just released updates and improvements on new disks; all you had to do was pull out the old disk and put in the new. Nowadays you can upgrade your system by adding hardware—more terminals, memory, or disk space—or by multiplying features through fancier software. And by mounting a word-processing program on a large computer, you gain the ability to store massive amounts of text instead of a few pages, and you can plug in a lot of terminals to the same system, so that dozens of users can share the same files of documents.

In the last five years, many of the advances in computer technology have increased word-processing power, making systems physically smaller, faster, and cheaper. The advent of microcomputers and computers-in-a-chip has shrunk the size and price of cheaper systems. In 1976, for instance, a stand-alone word processor cost approximately $15,000 to $25,000. Today a comparable system with the same power (and often more) can be had for as little as $5000 while bare-bone systems are available for less than $1500. Recent developments in telecommunications allow many large and small systems, thousands of miles apart, to link forces and send files to one another, or even share files in a central data bank.

For a long time word processing was divorced from the word *computer,* which implied that you might have to memorize strange codes and understand programming languages. Sales pitches encouraged prospective buyers to think of the word-processing system as an office tool, not a computer. But as the so-called "Word-Processing Revolution" absorbs such tasks as computerized bookkeeping and inventory management, and as companies put word processing on even the biggest computer systems (which continue to do other functions as well), word processing has become part of the "Computer Revolution."

As word processing uses smarter computers, it becomes simpler. Instead of memorizing intricate codes and learning computer-ese to operate a system, it is possible now just to think in terms of ordinary office chores. For instance, a few years ago Xerox introduced the Star Information System. With most word processors, you work on one document at a time, making additions and changes, moving text up and down on the screen, then filing it away when you are finished. But the Star screen is set up as a desktop, where you can set out various files or reports you want to work on. "File folders" are displayed as pictures on the screen. You move a pointer to the folder you want to work on, and "open it"; the page you want is then displayed on the screen, without obscuring the rest of your "desktop." You can work on that first project, pull out another and set it on top, return to the first project, or pull in a paragraph from a third. You set the pace of work, just as you would with paper, pencil, and file folders on your desk. Xerox is aiming their Star at the professional—not just the clerk-typist, secretary, or administrative assistant. And their publicists don't even like to call the Star a word processor; your terminal is part of a vast "information system."

Apple Computer has popularized this approach in its Lisa and Macintosh computers. These perform word processing, graphics, accounting, filing, and hundreds of other "computer chores." And many other companies are upgrading their programs to mimic this "visual" approach.

In the past companies have focused on improving secretaries' productivity. Now they are turning to the manager as well, and we are seeing the boss's desk turn into an "executive workstation."

Today there is a wide range of word processors. For instance, you can buy:

- A one-user system, dedicated just to word processing. (No other computer programs will run on this system.)
- A system that can expand to allow many users, with access to hundreds of documents.
- A system that can do your bookkeeping, inventory, or other data processing, in addition to word processing.
- A system with a one-line display, a half-page display, or a full-page display.
- A system with a display of your whole desk, with several folders and pages showing at once.
- A word-processing software package that can be used on a variety of different computers.

If you suspect you could benefit from word processing, read on. The following chapters will help you decide which functions you need and which system to choose. Amid hundreds of word processors on the market today, we'll help you find the one that's right for you.

Who Uses Word Processing?

Hundreds of thousands of people are using word processors today. Some are dentists, doctors, lawyers, architects. Others are clerks in large companies, secretaries in small offices, writers alone at home, or technicians in special word-processing centers. If you ask around, you'll find dozens of people who have had some experience—brief or intense, pleasant or horrible, well-planned or crazy—with word processors.

Their experiences may not be a perfect guide to your own, but they can tip you off to important benefits—and problems. It's tempting to assume that a system that worked well for a friend will be just right for you, but that's not often true. You'll need to think through exactly what kind of work you want the word processor to perform before you pick one of the hundreds of different systems available. But first, here is what some fairly typical users might tell you about their experiences. Browse through their stories to see how word processing has helped out—or hurt.

A Secretary in an Engineering Firm

"Three years now, I've worked for engineers. Not one of them writes so you can read it. Scrawls and scratchings, and lines here, and lines there. Arrows, and 'Put this in here.' And they have these formulas with eight lines, up and down, and it isn't good enough to use English letters, so they have to put in all these Greek letters. So we guess a lot—and then we redo it, and redo it again. I call myself the Rewrite Queen.

"This is a small firm. I mean they just do contract drilling, and a little exploration, but for any contract, they've got to have these tables, with not just five or six columns, but some of them are a hundred or more. We had one we had to do sideways on computer paper—it was six feet long.

"The work all has to be done at the last minute. Those proposals! Before we got this cluster system in, we had five secretaries, and every time there was a deadline, there we'd be, working all night. And the next morning, some engineer would say, 'Oh, I didn't mean that, I meant this,' so we'd have to retype a whole page. And like as not, it would be a chart. You could only get away with, you know, half a dozen white-outs before you had to retype the whole sheet. Now, with word processing, it's a snap. Nobody stays late but the engineers."

A Medical Assistant

"Reports! I don't mind cutting them. I just don't like writing them up. We've got two pathologists, and two pathology residents in here, and together we do about 200 to 400 pathology reports, and maybe half a dozen autopsy reports every month. Now, sure, a lot of what you say gets to be a routine. So we had the word-processing center put the standard stuff on the computer. We just fill in the blanks. Used to keep three or four secretaries busy all the time. Now we just need somebody to print the stuff out for us, and send it along. Takes him a few hours a day. We keep the old reports on disks, so if we ever have to look one up, we can resurrect it. Each disk has a directory at the start, so you know what's in it, and we've made a master directory—everything that's in every disk. That's how we find Juan Alvarez, DOA, gunshot wound in abdomen, brought in from ER last November 3rd. We can look up the case by name, date, or cause of death. I think the cops ought to get something like this. They are always coming back to us for 'just one extra copy.'"

An Accountant

"I say we're our word processor's best advertisement. When the boss told me to go ahead and pick a word processor with those special accounting packages, I thought that we'd about cut our time in half, on most ledgers and wills and leases—almost anything that's got a set format and a lot of stuff you can repeat from the last one. We got an extra-wide printer to handle the statistical stuff—and it can keep up with the pace.

"We have most of the federal and state tax forms on the word processor, so we can take the penciled-in version from the CPA and simply fill in the blanks. Then we feed the right form into the printer, and we've got it. The printer has a mechanism that skips anywhere it's not going to print, so it zips down a form, types something in, then zips down to the next slot. Just changing printers has meant we get forms out faster.

"We did a before-and-after study. We're using five people to do what ten secretaries couldn't handle before. Three times the work from three years ago. And our average turnaround time is less than a day.

"The boss started telling his clients about how great the word processor is, and about a dozen of them have bought the same system. Now I get calls from their people, saying 'Thank God you put that in. We'd been telling him to get word processing, but he wouldn't believe us. He had to see his accountant using one first. Well, it's a business expense.'"

An Insurance Agent

"We bought a word processor that was specifically designed for insurance. It handles expiration dates, next-call dates, proposals, and property appraisals. It lets us keep an up-to-date file of all our clients, with their addresses, phone numbers, insurance classes, and total premiums, so we can see who's a prospect for some extra life coverage. We just tell the machine, 'Take the name of everyone we've marked, and send them letter 28'—that's already written; it's on another file, a kind of collection of form letters and pat paragraphs. It puts the two together and prints out a letter ready for me to sign. We've got all our forms dummied up on them, so my secretary can just type right onto the screen and be sure the words come out in the right boxes. I've kept track, and we're sending out four times as many letters—and we've done that without adding a secretary. And I did a little study on how long it takes us to answer a client. That used to take five days; now it's a day or two.

"When we call someone, we just punch the person's name in, and the screen shows us a profile of his policy. I also have a prospect file, and we bought the general ledger package, so every check we write and every bill we get goes automatically into the right slot. And our word processor talks to the carrier's computer—we send client data and they send back a policy—over the phone. I can get a new policy out in the morning mail."

A Subscription Manager

"Boy did we get stung! We have hundreds of letters we need sent out every day—almost all of them are form letters. But the post office gave us a hard time because we weren't responding to subscriber complaints. So we have to show we can turn around a question in a week. That's why we bought the word-processing system in the first place.

"The salesman told us that the stand-alone unit would be perfect for merging names and addresses from our subscription list with the different canned letters. Well, it turned out that you can merge two lines, but not three. So we got hundreds of letters with no city, state, and zip code. We called the salesman and asked him what happened. He said maybe we needed a different program. Where is it? They haven't written it yet.

"We asked the salesman to take the machine back, but he said what we needed was the shared logic system. That gave us two terminals—they took the stand-alone back on credit. The new system could handle addresses with three lines, but its printer couldn't handle descenders. It could print only upper-case letters, and it couldn't handle anything below the line. So everything looked like a telegram. Then the new printer wouldn't accept any text at all. It just printed and froze.

"Meanwhile, letters were piling up. Our clerks were getting a lot of training at entering new material, but none of it was being printed out. Then someone had the bright idea that since all the subscribers' names are stored on another computer, maybe we could just draw the information directly from there, without having to key it in every time. Wrong. Our computer doesn't talk to that computer. For about $4,000 we could have all the disks altered, so our word processor could read the current list. But we'd have to spend that every month or so, to keep up. So we discarded that idea.

"Then our clerks told us that it was hard to change text we had already stored. We had to do it line by line. We couldn't change the margins. Basically, we had to delete the old and type in the new. Evidently the programmer never thought we'd change the boilerplate paragraphs.

"I know that word processing can work, but we didn't take enough time to find out exactly what we needed, and then we let the salesman fast-talk us into buying the wrong system. We found out too late that it's designed for memos and letters—lots of fast, short, original material. But this system can't handle form letters.

"It's been nearly three months, and the backlog is worse than before we brought in word processing, and we've already spent $35,000 just on the equipment. We're beginning to lose subscriptions, and the post office is on our back again. We'd have been better off buying quill pens."

A Technical Writer

"When I came to work here, they already had a word-processing department. They did memos, and large statistical charts—the sort you have to unfold to read. But they didn't do many of these three-hundred-page manuals we turn out. My group was typing them and copying them, and that was that. But I'd used word processing at my last job, and I knew that we could turn out these manuals much faster with word processing.

"First we write up what we think the program does. Then we show that to the programmer, and he makes a few changes. Then the boss changes his mind, and the programmers have to change the screens, so we redo the page again. But then some other programmer does something, and that means that where we told people to enter '1B,' they now have to enter, say, '4C.' These revisions can go on for months.

"So we asked for our own word processors. But the person in charge of buying the word-processing system didn't listen to what we told her about our needs. We produce long documents—three to five hundred pages. And when I want to change an abbreviation to the spelled-out name throughout, I want to have the machine make the changes. But with this memo-oriented word processor she bought, you have to do it page by page.

"That's what we got stuck with. We've got enough terminals for half the writers, but it's the wrong system for the work. And it breaks down. And it doesn't have enough disk space to store all our current work. We told them what we needed, and they didn't listen. In a few years, it'll be obvious that these clunkers aren't helping—they're slowing us down."

A Teacher

"I use it like a typewriter. Whatever I'm going to hand out in class, I work up on the screen. I like being able to change it right onscreen, without retyping. I'll intend to fill a whole page with quiz problems, then I'll realize that the first three are hard enough. Then with the word-processing software that came with it, I can reformat the page and move the problems down, with two keystrokes.

"The dean's office has the same system. I can take the diskette in and use his printer to run off enough copies for class. Each student gets an original. It looks better—and it's a lot faster than waiting in line at the copier.

"I bought my own computer when we put a dozen of them in the math room. I use it to test out computer-aided instruction before we buy it for school. The word processing is an extra I hadn't really thought about. My husband uses it to prepare all his seminar papers. He usually gets an A on a B paper, because the system makes him look so good. On the dean's printer, of course."

A Bookseller

"Every book in this store is on our computer. I've got real-time inventory control, and any time stock on a title falls below our prearranged minimum number of copies, the system reorders the book automatically. I just added a word-processing software package, so we can do our billing and correspondence without having it look like some computer did it. The biggest expense was a printer that made the lower-case letters. My computer only talked in capitals before. And every line was fuzzy, like they'd used up the ribbon years ago. Dot matrix they call that—too many dots, and not enough ink, I say. But this daisy wheel printer can crank out a letter a minute, and it can justify the right margins when I want something to look like it's been printed. I use that when I announce our poetry readings."

A Policeman

"Six cops, and not one of them likes paper. You should have seen this place before we got the micro. They'd come in and write up their notes on any slip of paper they could find, cram it in under the wrong heading, wrong date, wrong spelling of the perpetrator's name. It could take days to find anything, and often the trial'd have to be bound over.

"So I asked the mayor to buy some portable dictating machines—tape recorders. Then, when we're out in the field, we can just sit in the car and talk our reports. At the end of the shift, we turn in our car—and the tape.

"And then I used a micro to test out three or four different computer programs that do word processing and filing. Now I can type up a barking dog report, or a breaking and entry, and when I'm through, select some key words that I might want to search for later, like *dog*, and *Maple Street,* or the date. And then I file it. To save it on paper, I have the printer run off a second copy, for the master file. And I just make a copy on a duplicate disk.

"We took out one of the file cabinets, since there's not much paper around here anymore. Just me and my micro."

A Lawyer

"Before we bought the word-processing system, we'd have a real-estate deal, and the attorneys would scribble up paragraphs and then change their minds, and the whole offering and partnership agreement would run to 150 pages—and every page had to be an original. When an attorney changed his mind on the morning of the offering, that meant that someone had to retype 18 copies of the same page, just to change one word. Now something like that can't happen. We've got boilerplate partnership agreements, wills, estate plans, pensions, all on the word processor. And each attorney has a copy of the standard form, so he can make changes on it and write in names. We have the attorney come in and talk with the word-processing operator so she will know who to call with questions. Our error rate has gone down, and our productivity has gone up."

A Personnel Secretary

"I used to work at a company where they did the whole application process by hand. It took days, and we lost forms, and some interviewers stuck them in their desk drawers or poured coffee all over them.

"But here we use the word-processing system to do a lot of that. As soon as we get a job request from someone upstairs, we put it on the computer, with information like the hours, salary, do you have to be a union member, what the requirements are. Then when someone calls to ask about that job, we just type in the title, and the system flashes the information on the screen.

"Then when we get an application for that job, we enter the person's name there, so we always know how many people have applied, and then when they get turned down, we record that too.

"The application form is already on the computer, so I can call it up and fill in the blanks with whatever the applicant says. We save the application form itself, in a paper version, to prove they signed it, but for our purposes, we use the electronic version. I just send it to the manager's terminal, and she can print it out there. And we've always got a copy on file, in case the original gets lost.

"Usually I send the application upstairs, and if the manager wants to talk to the applicant, I set up an appointment. When it's set, I type the time and date onto the word processor and send the information to the manager's terminal. If she wants a paper copy, she can print it out for herself. And I automatically add the interview information to the file in the computer, so if the applicant brings suit and says he never got an interview, we have the time and date right there."

A College Dean

"We've tied every phone into the university's central computer. We use the word-processing program there to write the catalog and update it, then send text over to the print shop, where they have one of those super-fast printers. They can print a draft at a hundred pages a minute. Or they can put it into the photocomposition machine and give us camera-ready copy the next day.

"It takes us about two months of fussing—lots of second thoughts, cancellations, rewrites—to get the catalog ready. With the catalog, I approve copy that's already been entered on the computer by department chairmen, and the copy is transferred from their files to mine, then moved into the right section. But we set the type for the whole thing in two or three days. We can prepare special bulletins in a week. Those used to take us a month, and by the time they came out the faculty would have changed its mind.

"My office is in charge of keeping the phone directory up to date. But faculty are moving around all the time, and we have a ten percent turnover every year. That means we have to send out a correction sheet almost every week and a whole new directory about every three months. But since it's all on the computer, we just make the changes as we go, then have the printer run off 500 copies—each with a person's name on the front, so it can go through interoffice mail.

"We prepare our budgets the same way. The chairmen or chairwomen update their own budgets weekly, and I can call up any budget on my screen, to see how it's going. And if I have any questions, I just type them into this space at the bottom, where it says 'COMMENTS.' The chairperson can answer me there, or send me a regular letter.

"It takes everyone a while to learn this word-processing system, but it can do a lot if you know all the commands."

A Librarian

"We have our card catalog on disk, so we can call up a card, make a change, and send it back to memory, without having to collect cards for a week, then go out with a drawer and pull the old ones, and mark where we've taken one out, and then make up new ones, and go back, and pull the pins out again, and fit the card in, and then push the pins back, to hold them. I sometimes thought I was going to throw out the whole drawer and run out screaming.

"I use word processing for letters, too, and weekly reports, interoffice memos, and subscriptions. And now that we have a modem, I can call the computers in other libraries and see how they handled a tricky problem, make a copy of their card, edit it, and have my printer run that off too."

An Architect

"We have a port proposal that has dragged on for three years. We're dealing with the state, the federal railway people, the feds, three local chambers of commerce, and two dozen officials high and low—and everyone wants a few changes. Every few months, we get a little farther—but they want the rail lines eighteen feet closer to the wharf, or the highway administration says we can't have an overpass at this point, or the container derricks have to carry a few more tons. The same proposal has been through two dozen major changes.

"We did the first draft on one of the first electronic typewriters, but it couldn't remember enough information—only a few addresses, half a page. Basically, we had to retype, and retype, and retype. So that's when we got a real word processor, because our secretary thought it was really designed for typing—not just a computer that could also do some word processing. We can change text right down to the Federal Express deadline and still get out a clean original of 150 pages—that looks like we spent a week typing it.

"The best feature is the way it handles the budgets and statistics. We change a few figures, and the machine recalculates the totals. We can switch columns, knock out a row, and the system recalculates the other figures.

"We can change typefaces in the middle of a page, and print a simplified version of our logo. We can do graphs and bar charts, pie charts, and critical path diagrams. It is not as sharp as printing, but it gives us an edge over firms that have to do all that by hand, paste it onto the page, and then Xerox it to make it look like it's all together.

"The equipment paid for itself in the first year and a half. We took out a maintenance contract, but we haven't had to use it. The Mr. Coffee machine breaks down more often."

And What About You?

In the next chapter, we use case histories to show how specific word-processing features are put to use, so you can see what word processing can do for you.

How It Works

This chapter will give you a feel for what it's like to use a word processor. If you pick up a word-processing brochure, or go to see a demonstration of equipment, you'll hear many different functions discussed—moving a word, say, or deleting a sentence. Each system you see will do the same job a little differently, with its own series of keystrokes. But basically, all word-processing functions do things that get done in every office; the job has just been automated. In word processing you may find special names for steps that are so routine when you type that you don't think of them as distinct tasks—like putting the same heading at the top of each page of a report, or setting a tab stop. Other tasks take so many steps manually—like editing a rough draft by cutting and pasting parts of it and then retyping it—that it's hard to believe that the same function can be completed in two or three quick steps on a word processor.

Each word-processing system has its own way of accomplishing a task, and may have its own term for it as well. "Cut and Paste" on one system is called "Move" on another. One system asks you to set margins and tabs on a "Ruler"; another has you do it on the "Format Line."

Despite the different labels on keycaps and the varying names given to functions, all word processors are similar. They have the same basic components: a workstation (keyboard and screen), a processor, some kind of storage drives (disk, diskette, tape, or cassette), and a program that makes all the parts work together. (Although technically electronic typewriters and memory typewriters without screen displays may be considered "word processors," they are not included in our discussion. Our main emphasis is on screen-based word processing. You will find some of them listed in the comparison tables in Appendix A, "List of Word-Processing Products," and a brief discussion of them in Chapter 4, "Narrowing the Field.")

When you sit down at a word processor, you work primarily with the keyboard and the screen. Word-processing keyboards look like typewriter keyboards, with some extra keys at the sides and/or above the row of number keys. These extra keys are "function keys," and are used to tell the system what to do. Often the function keys are labeled (CUT, PASTE, DELETE, etc.).

When you type on the keyboard, characters appear on the screen at the "cursor," a small square or line that marks your position on the screen. The cursor moves to the right as you type, much as the typing position on your typewriter does.

Many programs first display "menus" on the screen, which list the tasks you can perform and tell you how to pick one. As in a restaurant, a menu offers you a list of choices. On most systems you can ask for menus when you want them and suppress them when you don't need them.

Screens vary in size. The most common sizes display either a half-page of text at a time (24 lines), or a full page (66 lines). The page we're talking about is an ordinary 8½ × 11 sheet of typing paper. A width of 80 characters is the norm, although on some screens you can see 132 or more, and on some you are limited to as few as 40.

To help you get a sense of what it's like to use a word processor, this chapter gives specific examples of how the main functions might be used by a range of people, from professionals to secretaries to managers. We have combined elements of several of the most common word-processing systems in these examples. We have made up our own screen displays and labeled keys, borrowing approaches and terms from a variety of equipment available on the market. Our sample word processor does not exactly match any system you will see. All of our examples assume a word processor with a half-page display, a square cursor, and a double floppy diskette drive. Over the years we've worked with many people learning to use word processors, from lawyers, accountants, and bankers, to freelance writers and clerks in government offices. These scenarios are composites based on interviews with many people using similar features on different systems. The characters and companies are fictitious.

On some systems certain functions will turn out to be more complicated than others. When you look at equipment, keep in mind that the same functions will probably be performed differently on different systems. You will need to try out the functions that are most important to you, to see how they work.

HOW IT WORKS || 13

At the end of the chapter we've included a checklist for you, to note the functions you require in a system; you may want to mark those functions with high priority for you.

THE BASIC WORD-PROCESSING FUNCTIONS

Here's how word processing is used by one professional writer:

Sharon Gallagher composes most text on a word processor in her office at home. A long table takes up one wall of the room and holds the equipment she works on. She works at a keyboard, much as she used to work at a typewriter, but the characters appear on a screen in front of her that looks something like a black-and-white television. As she enters new text, it's as if there were an endless scroll of paper inside the television screen. Actually, inside the box with the screen are the electronic circuits and chips that make this equipment a computer. To her right is another box with two slots: the disk drive. The word-processing-program disk goes in one slot, and a disk to store her documents goes in the other. "Document" is the term used for each clump of text that Sharon enters into the computer. Her documents may vary from 5 to 20 or even 40 pages.

When Sharon writes, her first concern is with content—putting the words on "paper" (on the screen) and keeping a copy of them (on a disk). She makes some corrections as she goes, but she doesn't worry about format until later. Here's a typical writing session:

Creating a New Document

To start a document, Sharon turns on the computer, inserts the program disk and a document disk, and presses a button labeled START on the side of the computer. A "menu" of choices appears on the screen and looks like this:

```
        C   =   Create
        E   =   Edit
        P   =   Print
        D   =   Delete
        Q   =   Quit
        M   =   More Menu Items
        I   =   Index

    Type the letter of the option
    you want and press RETURN☐
```

In response to the instruction on the screen, Sharon types a "C" for create and then presses the RETURN key. Pressing RETURN signals the computer that her entry on the menu screen is complete. A new instruction replaces the menu on the screen, prompting Sharon to supply a document name:

```
Type a name for the document you
are creating and press RETURN☐
```

Typing in response to the instructions on the screen, the characters appear where the bright square, or "cursor," is, which then moves to the right. After Sharon names her new document "Chapter 1," the prompts disappear from the screen, and Sharon has an open window into the system's equivalent of a long piece of paper:

```
    Chapter 1    Page 1
    _____

    L----T-----------T---------R
    ☐
```

At the top of the screen is the name Sharon gave the document and the page number. Below that is a line showing the current lefthand margin (L), tab settings (T), and righthand margin (R), and then the cursor, marking her position in the new document.

Entering Text

As she types on the word processor, Sharon uses the same skills as in typing on a typewriter. The characters show up on the screen, and a lighted box (the "cursor") moves across the screen just as the typing position moves across on a typewriter, marking the place the next keystroke will appear.

When Sharon first learned to use a word processor she had pretty good typing skills—60 words per minute. Within a few weeks she was whipping out text almost twice as fast as before. Although many facilities on the word processor helped with this, most of the increase in speed came from two very basic functions, found on almost every system today—"word wrap" and "rub out."

Word Wrap

Word wrapping speeds up typing, simply by wrapping text around the end of one line and onto the beginning of the next—an automatic equivalent of a typewriter's carriage return. On a word processor, when the text reaches the right margin, it appears for a few characters to be going past it:

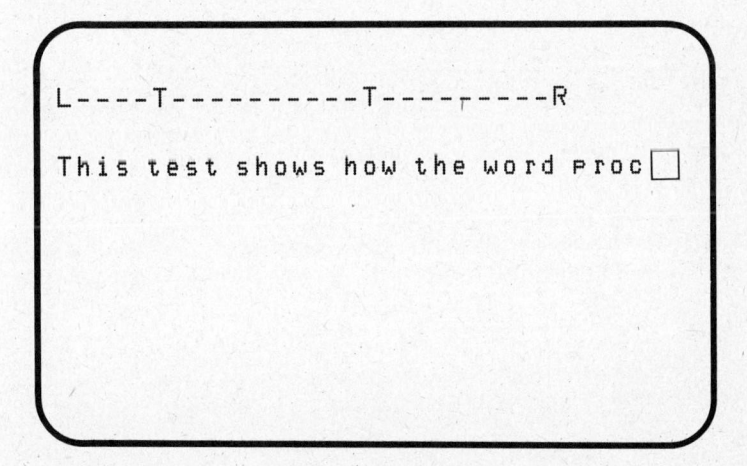

```
L----T-----------T-----r----R
This test shows how the word proc☐
```

But as soon as the word crossing the margin is ended, the system "wraps" the word around to the beginning of the next line:

```
L----T----------T----------R
This test shows how the word
processor handles□
```

"Word wrap" usually works backwards, too—when changes are made that allow a word to fit on a previous line, it moves right back up.

Rub Out

"Rub out" is one of the most useful features of word processing. Studies show that when using a word processor instead of a typewriter, the person entering text doesn't slow down toward the end of the page, increasingly wary of making mistakes and having to retype the whole thing, because corrections are so easy. Although self-correcting typewriters have helped, it still takes a lot of time and it's clumsy to correct mistakes.

On a word processor, if Sharon's right hand gets positioned just one key off on the keyboard, she might look at her input to find:

```
    If Sharon's right hand gets
positioned one key off on the
keyboard, she might kiij at ger
ubout ti fubd□
```

To correct this, all she has to do is locate the RUB OUT, DELETE, or BACKSPACE key. Pressing RUB OUT once moves the cursor backwards and erases the character to the left. Holding the RUB OUT key down erases back repeatedly. In a few seconds, the whole line is erased and the cursor is back where she wants it to retype the phrase.

```
       If Sharon's right hand gets
    positioned one key off on the
    keyboard, she might▯
```

Scrolling

When she's filled up the screen with words, the top lines move off the screen, and new lines appear at the bottom. The screen display serves as a window through which Sharon can see part of her text. When she writes, she likes to look back and forth at the text to review what she's said so far. To do this, she uses keys that "scroll" the text back and forth. She can scroll the text up and down one line at a time, a screenful at a time, or she can go directly to the top or bottom of the document.

When her screen is filled with words and she wants to see the text that precedes it, she presses the SCROLL DOWN key. For example, see the following screen:

```
    A̲lthough many facilities on
 the word processor helped with
 this, most of the increase in
 speed came from two very basic
 functions, found on almost every
 system today--"word wrap" and
 "rub out."

 WORD WRAP
    Word wrapping speeds up typing,
 simply by wrapping text around the
```

Pressing the SCROLL DOWN key once moves the text down so that the preceding line appears. Holding the key down longer repeats this action, until the preceding paragraph comes into view on the screen:

> When Sharon first learned to use a word processor she had pretty good typing skills--60 words per minute. Within a few weeks she was whipping out text almost twice as fast as before.
>
> [A]lthough many facilities on the word processor helped with this, most of the increase in speed came from two very basic functions, found on almost every

Going to Top or Bottom of Document

After reviewing the text, Sharon returns to the end of her document to keep writing. On the face of the "B" key is the word BOTTOM. She holds down a key labeled FUNC SHIFT while she presses the "B" key. This tells the system to activate the function named on the key instead of inserting the letter "B" in the text. The word processor moves the text up on the screen so that she sees the bottom of the document. The cursor is automatically placed at the very end of the text, so she can start typing immediately. Sharon can move to the top of the text in a similar way. The "T" key has the word TOP on the face of it. Pressing FUNC SHIFT plus the "T" key takes her directly to the top, where the material starts.

Ending a Document

When she's satisfied with the text and ready to put it away, Sharon finds the word END on the "E" key. She holds down the FUNC SHIFT key while she presses "E" for END. This activates the function END instead of adding the letter "E" to the document, and "closes" the file.

A slight *whirr-clunk* sound assures Sharon that the word processor has filed her document away on its storage disk. The menu of choices reappears on the screen, ready to accept another instruction:

```
        C  =  Create
        E  =  Edit
        P  =  Print
        D  =  Delete
        Q  =  Quit
        M  =  More Menu Items
        I  =  Index

    Type the letter of the option
    you want and press RETURN☐
```

Copying a Document

Sharon works at home, and she has cats. They're fascinated by the word processor and the diskettes on which she stores her text. Although she's careful and has been lucky so far, she has nightmares about one day discovering that a much-needed diskette has become a well-gnawed cat toy. So she makes a regular practice of storing her work on yet another diskette, and keeping the copy in a safe place. She just can't afford to re-create pages and pages of text.

It takes only a minute or two to copy a document. Another menu shows Sharon these options:

```
    DOCUMENT FUNCTIONS MENU

         COPY = Copy a Document

       RENAME = Rename a Document

       DELETE = Delete a Document

    Type the option you want and
    press RETURN☐
```

Sharon types COPY and presses RETURN. The display on the screen changes and asks her some questions:

```
DOCUMENT TO BE COPIED:☐
COPY TO DISK:
NAME FOR COPY:
```

Sharon types in "Chapter 1" as the name of the document she wants to copy, and presses RETURN. The cursor moves to the next question. She types the letter "B" and presses RETURN, indicating that she wants the copy to go onto the disk in drive B. (The two disk-drive slots in her word processor are labeled "A" and "B." Typing in the letter lets her specify which disk should receive the copy.) With the cursor next to NAME FOR COPY, she then just presses RETURN. This tells the word processor to insert the same name.

```
DOCUMENT TO BE COPIED: CHAPTER 1
COPY TO DISK: B
NAME FOR COPY: CHAPTER 1☐

Press RETURN to begin the copy
```

Sharon makes sure her backup diskette is in drive B, and then just presses the RETURN key to begin the actual copy. The drives make a *whirr-click-whirr* sound as the copying takes place. Depending on the length of the work she's copying, it takes anywhere from a few seconds to a minute or two. Sharon often takes a break and gets a cup of coffee while copying. When the duplicate disk is complete, the main menu reappears on the screen. She removes the backup diskette, labels it, and puts it away in a safe place.

Printing a Document

As a final step, after Sharon has entered the entire text, she prints it. Seeing words on the screen hasn't dampened her desire to see a printed copy of what she has written. So she types "P" for Print in response to the main menu. The screen changes and shows the standard print instructions automatically stored with each new document:

```
PRINT SETTINGS FOR DOCUMENT
NAMED CHAPTER 1

1. Number of Copies: 1

2. Extra Page Offset: 0

3. Start with Page: 1

4. Pitch: 10 cpi

5. Continuous Sheets: Yes

6. End with Page:

Press RETURN if settings are OK,
or type the number of the option
you want to change the setting
for, then press RETURN▯
```

The print settings let Sharon print multiple copies, indent the left margin by specifying extra page offset, specify page numbers if she wants to print only part of a document, choose the pitch (number of characters per inch) to be used, and specify the type of paper she's using in her printer. The standard settings that show up when she creates a new document are almost always what Sharon wants, especially when she's printing a new draft, so she just presses the RETURN key. Her document starts printing right away.

EDITING AND FORMATTING FEATURES OF A WORD PROCESSOR

As secretary for the marketing department of Electronic Innovations, Martha Greene types a wide range of correspondence and reports for the department staff. Press releases, marketing analyses, and product specification lists are some of the types of documents she produces on her word processor. Since many of these documents go through multiple drafts, Martha relies heavily on the editing capabilities of her system—the features that let her make changes in the content and format of each document.

Editing an Existing Document

A common task for Martha is to answer requests for information about the company and its products. She keeps a standard letter on file in her word processor and "personalizes" it by making a few changes before sending it out. She makes pencil notes on a printed copy and then edits the original on the screen. Here's an example of a basic letter that she's marked up:

```
Dear Mr. Reese

  Thank you for your interest in
Electronic Innovations. I am
enclosing (what?) I believe
these will answer your initial
questions.
  Please let me know if you would
like additional information.

          Sincerely,


          Martha Greene,
          Marketing Secretary
          enc.
```

(handwritten annotations: *Mr. Reese*; *annual Report + product specs*)

To edit the letter on her word-processing system, Martha turns on the system, loads her diskettes, then types the letter "E" and presses RETURN in response to the menu of options.

```
C = Create
E = Edit
P = Print
D = Delete
Q = Quit
M = More Menu Items
I = Index

Type the letter of the option
you want and press RETURN☐
```

A message appears, asking what document should be edited. Martha types STANDARD LETTER and presses RETURN.

Moving the Cursor to Make Changes in a Document

After a second or two, the beginning of Martha's standard letter appears on the screen. The cursor is at the letter "D" in "Dear." Since the first thing Martha wants to do is add the customer's name to the salutation line, she moves the cursor just past the word "Dear." (The keyboard on Martha's word processor has four keys marked with arrows, pointing up, down, left, and right, to control the movement of the cursor.) She presses the RIGHT ARROW key four times, until the cursor moves to the spot where she wants it:

```
STANDARD LETTER    PAGE 1

Dear☐
   Thank you for your interest in
Electronic Innovations. I am
enclosing (what?) I believe
these will answer your initial
questions.
   Please let me know if you would
like additional information.
```

Then she types "Mr. Reese:"

Deleting a Word

For the next change, she moves the cursor to "(what?)" by pressing the DOWN ARROW key twice to move the cursor down two lines and then holding down the RIGHT ARROW key to move the cursor along the line to the right. When the cursor appears at the opening parenthesis mark, Martha releases the RIGHT ARROW key, then presses a key labeled DELETE WORD. All characters from the cursor to the next space disappear. After the deletion, her screen looks like this:

```
STANDARD LETTER     PAGE 1

Dear Mr. Reese:
   Thank you for your interest in
Electronic Innovations. I am
enclosing  □I believe these
will answer your initial
questions.
   Please let me know if you would
like additional information.
```

Adding a Few Words

After "(what?)" is deleted, the beginning of the next line wraps back up to fill in the space where the word was deleted. However, when Martha presses INSERT, then types in "our Annual Report and some product specifications," it wraps back down to the next line. Her edited letter now looks like this:

```
STANDARD LETTER     PAGE 1

Dear Mr. Reese:
   Thank you for your interest in
Electronic Innovations. I am
enclosing our Annual Report and
some product specifications.□I
believe these will answer your
initial questions.
   Please let me know if you would
like additional information.
```

Making Major Changes

Although many of Martha's tasks involve simple editing, as in the letter, often she has to make major changes in much longer documents. For example, here's a list of changes her boss wants made in a proposal going out to a major customer:

1. Insert A on page 2. (See attached.)
2. Change all occurrences of "RFP" to "Request for Proposal."
3. Indent and justify all paragraphs marked with an *.
4. Include page numbers in our standard heading.

The list of changes is attached to a printed copy of the proposal, which her boss has marked up.

Locating Text

"Insert A" is a handwritten paragraph attached to the list of changes. Page two of the document is marked with an arrow to show where the insert belongs—just before "In response to your second requirement, Electronic Innovations," in the middle of a paragraph.

Rather than scrolling through the document to find the sentence, Martha uses a feature that can locate it immediately. To move directly to the place the insert belongs, she presses the SEARCH key. The machine then asks, "Search for what?" She types "In response to your second," and presses RETURN. The system then locates the first place the phrase occurs and stops, the blinking cursor marking the beginning of the phrase, just where Martha needs to type in the new text.

Searching and Replacing

After inserting the new text, Martha moves on to the next change: turning each occurrence of "RFP" into "Request for Proposal." She starts by scrolling back to the top of her document and pressing the SEARCH key again. She types in "RFP," and then, instead of pressing RETURN, she presses REPLACE. Another question appears on the screen:

```
Search for what? RFP

Replace with what?▫
```

Martha types in "Request for Proposal" and then presses RETURN. Then the system asks whether she wants to make the change each time "RFP" appears in the document. Martha types in "Yes."

```
Search for what? RFP

Replace with what? Request for
Proposal

Replace globally? Yes

Replace without asking? No▫
```

But when asked if she wants the change made automatically, without her okay, Martha answers "No." She prefers to view each change as it is being made. So when the word processor finds the first occurrence of "RFP" in the proposal, it highlights it and asks her if she wants to make the change:

```
                Replace (Y/N)?☐
   We received your  RFP  on June
12, 1984, and are happy to be
able to respond with a solution
to your needs. The following
```

When she types "Y," "Request for Proposal" is substituted in the text, and the next occurrence of "RFP" is highlighted on her screen. This process is repeated for every occurrence of "RFP."

Safeguarding Work

Just as she finishes the search-and-replace function, Martha is called away from her desk. To make sure the changes won't be lost if the power should go down, or in case one of her "curious but uninitiated" fellow workers comes along and starts pressing buttons, Martha presses the SAVE key. This places a copy of the document, with the current changes included, onto the disk in her word processor.

When Martha returns, this message is showing on her screen:

```
Press RETURN to resume edit.

Press END to return to the menu.
☐
```

She presses RETURN and her document is redisplayed, ready for any additional changes.

Formatting Text

Martha's boss had marked several paragraphs throughout the document with asterisks—he wanted these indented and justified, for emphasis. To make these changes, Martha first scrolls the document until the first paragraph to be changed shows on her screen. Then she moves the cursor to the first character in the paragraph and presses FORMAT. A new line, showing the current margins and tabs, appears on the screen before the paragraph:

```
Innovation's response to item
number (1) one.
L----T-------------------------R
    Electronic Innovations
specializes in customizing
marketing programs to meet our
clients' needs. A glance at the
enclosed portfolio will show you
the range of new products we
have created images for over the
last ten years.
```

The cursor now appears on the format line. ("L" stands for the left margin, "R" for the right margin, and "T" for Tab.) Martha wants to indent the left margin, so she moves the cursor to the "T" and types "L." (The previous "L" automatically disappears.) Then she moves the cursor five spaces to the right and types "T." This new tab will maintain an indent for the paragraph when the margins move. Now the format line looks like this:

```
Innovation's response to item
number (1) one.
-----L----T□-------------------R
    Electronic Innovations
specializes in customizing
marketing programs to meet our
clients' needs. A glance at the
enclosed portfolio will show you
the range of new products we
have created images for over the
last ten years.
```

Then she moves the cursor a few characters before the "R" and types a "J." The "R" immediately disappears—while "R" stands for right margin, it also stands for ragged margin. The new "J" indicates that the right margin should be evenly justified between right and left margins.

Then Martha presses RETURN. The format line disappears, and the paragraph lines itself up with the new margins. Here's the result:

```
Innovation's response to item
number (1) one.

    Electronic  Innovations  spe-
cializes in customizing market-
ing  programs  to  meet  our cli-
ents' needs. A glance at the en-
closed portfolio will show you
the range of new products we have
created images for over the last
ten years.
```

Martha then scrolls to the other paragraphs to be reformatted and follows the same steps.

Entering Headers

Electronic Innovations uses standard header material at the top of each page of its proposals, starting on page 2. This time Martha's boss wants each header to include a page number.

Returning to the top of the document, Martha presses GO TO PAGE and 2. Then she moves her cursor to the top left of the page, presses HEADER, and types in the main header information, "Proposal from Electronic Innovations." She then spaces over close to the right margin and types "Page #" to put in the page numbers automatically in this slot. The result:

```
Proposal from Electronic
Innovations                          Page 2
```

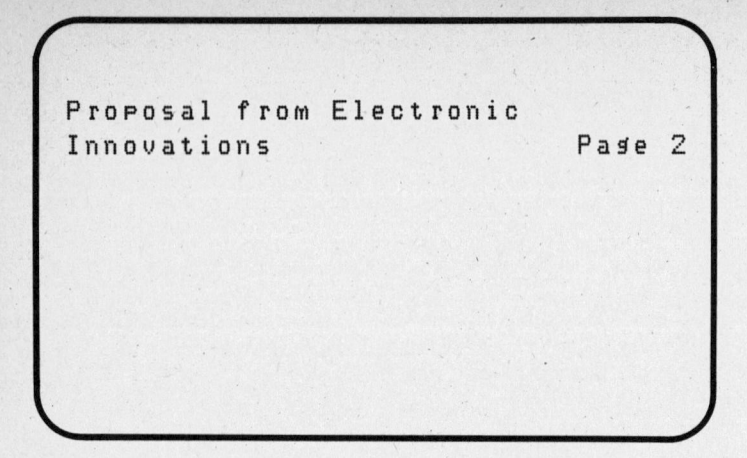

She presses RETURN four times, to separate the header from the text by four lines; then a special EXECUTE key to confirm that this is what she wants. The header disappears from the screen, but it will print at the top of each page of the proposal.

OTHER FEATURES OF A WORD PROCESSOR

Joe Crane, vice-president of marketing for a major variety store chain, has four assistants and two secretaries. Together they make up the marketing plans for the whole company, for specialty departments, and for the seasonal specials.

Joe bought a word-processing system for his department, with seven executive workstations—each with a keyboard and a video screen—and one communal printer. Two of his staff members started using the system right away to draw down information from the company's big computer and prepare proposals. When they give Joe a complete proposal on paper, they also give him the name of the electronic file at the same time, so that as he reads from the hard copy he can make the changes he wants onscreen, using the word-processing system.

Finding an Existing Document

Having read through his assistant Al Kramer's proposal for a calculator sale, Joe flips on his workstation, and this menu appears onscreen:

```
E = Edit
P = Print
C = Copy
D = Directory
R = Rename

Type the letter of the option
you want and press RETURN▢
```

He types "D" for Directory, and presses RETURN. The screen changes, displaying a list of the documents in the word processor's memory.

```
DOCUMENT DIRECTORY

▢Jones.let
 Store.let
 purchase 77.order
 Kramer.prp
 Lipsky.rpt
 Scan.rpt
 Churchill.rpt
 Gordon.let
 Allman.prp
 Cantor.prp
 Harris.let
 Stern.let

Press SCROLL to scroll up more
document names.
Press RETURN when the cursor is
next to the document you want.
```

When he spots "Kramer.prp" in the directory, Joe presses the DOWN ARROW key three times; the cursor moves three lines down the list of documents until it is positioned next to "Kramer.prp." Joe presses RETURN to tell the system to remember the document name.

The main menu returns, and Joe presses "E" to Edit. The word processor now knows which document he wants, so it brings that directly to the screen.

Kramer's proposal for a calculator sale in September has a working title, "Calculator Salathon—Ideas and Possibilities." Looking at it onscreen, Joe browses through the ten-page proposal, which he and Kramer have revised previously half a dozen times. It still looks good. Joe thinks about a title, then presses FUNC SHIFT, and "T" for top, and the screen jumps back to the very beginning of the text.

Centering

Whatever the title will be, Joe wants it centered. So before he begins typing it, he moves his cursor to the left margin, and presses the key marked CENTER. The cursor floats to the center of the screen, halfway between the left and right margins. Then he types in a title, and it centers automatically. He repeats the procedure for the subtitle and credit lines. Result:

```
         SEPTEMBER CALCULATOR SALE

               A PROPOSAL

                   BY

               JOE CRANE

       Prepared with the assistance of
                Al Kramer☐
```

Moving Text

Then Joe looks at the cover letter Al Kramer has made up. Since this is going to the boss, they have revised it six times.

TO: Bill Topke
FROM: Joe Crane
DATE: June 8, 1984

CONCERNING: Calculator Sale in September

Here's a great idea for our back-to-school sale: take advantage of the price war on low-end calculators and show prices slashed in our newspaper ads, as per attached copy.

   Please OK the ad budget (Page 10), and we'll start printing the in-store Take One's and six-by-eights.

   We figure we should be able to sell 100,000 units in September, for a net profit of $156,000. Pretty good.

Joe decides to move the last sentences to the end of the first paragraph. On his paper copy he draws an arrow, like this:

Here's a great idea for our back-to-school sale: take advantage of the price war on low-end calculators and show prices slashed in our newspaper ads, as per attached copy.
   Please OK the ad budget (Page 10), and we'll start printing the in-store Take One's and six-by-eights.
   We figure we should be able to sell 100,000 units in September, for a net profit of $156,000. Pretty good.

He moves the cursor to the space at the beginning of the last paragraph. Then he presses the button marked MOVE, and the screen flashes the question, "Move what?" The space above the cursor becomes highlighted.

He then presses the period button, indicating that he wants to move everything up to the next period. Highlighting now appears over the first sentence. He presses the period key again, and the highlighting spreads over the second sentence too.

To show this is correct, he presses RETURN. Now the system wants to know: "To where?"

So he moves the cursor up to the end of the first paragraph, and presses RETURN again. The highlighted text moves into place, realigning itself to fit into these lines, and the second paragraph drops down a line to leave room. Result:

```
TO: Bill Topke
FROM: Joe Crane
DATE: June 8, 1984

CONCERNING: Calculator Sale in
September

   Here's a great idea for our
back-to-school sale: take
advantage of the price war on
low-end calculators and show
prices slashed in our newspaper
ads, as per attached copy. We
figure we should be able to sell
100,000 units in September, for
a net profit of $156,000. Pretty
good[.]

   Please OK the ad budget (Page
10), and we'll start printing
the in-store Take One's and
six-by-eights.
```

Joe saves that new version, and sends a message to Al Kramer's terminal, "Please print calculator proposal and letter, and send to Bill." When Al comes back, he'll find the message, and the sale will be on.

Inserting

Now Joe turns his attention to a subject he loves to lecture his store managers about—window displays. He calls up his letter to them, and looks it over. Having warned store managers against "prettiness for prettiness' sake," he stresses the need to show high-profit items. As typed by his secretary, and printed out for him to correct, his letter ends:

```
   I've been in stores where the
jewelry and the wood bowls were
covered with dust. Clerks told
me: "Oh, those don't sell. Don't
send us any more of those."
   I cleaned up the counter and put
bowls of necklaces in the window.
Sales went up 300% the next day.
   Don't get mesmerized by fancy
"holiday" articles. Read
our merchandise reports and
pick out the high-profit items.
Put them in the window.
```

But then Joe gets an idea. He remembers a letter written by the grandfather of variety stores, Frank W. Woolworth. Joe looks it up in a book on the history of American marketing, circles the paragraph, and puts a big arrow on his letter, just before "Read." He scribbles in "Remember what F. W. Woolworth said:" And he makes a new paragraph after this insert, beginning, "So read . . ."

When his secretary gets the book and the paper copy back, she calls up the letter from the computer, positions her cursor under the "R" of "Read," and presses INSERT. The "R" and everything following it drop to the bottom of the screen, leaving room for her to type in the new material. She adds that, then presses RETURN. After adding "So," the letter ends this way:

> I've been in stores where the jewelry and the wood bowls were covered with dust. Clerks told me: "Oh, those don't sell. Don't send us any more of those."
> I cleaned up the counter and put bowls of necklaces in the window. Sales went up 300% the next day.
> Don't get mesmerized by fancy "holiday" articles. Remember what F.W. Woolworth said:
>
> > Glassware and crockery are holiday articles. I am convinced that some of the stores pay too much attention to these goods. Bear in mind, there is not so much profit in these. Profit is what we are working for, not sales or glory.
>
> So read our merchandise reports and pick out the <u>high-profit</u> items. Put <u>them</u> in the window. ☐

And that's the way Joe's secretary sends the letter out.

Calculating and Deleting

Joe's secretary brings in a number of purchase orders for him to sign. The first one is a purchase order for 600 six-by-eight-foot posters, advertising the back-to-school sale. Something looks odd about the figures, so Joe calls up the file for the purchase order onscreen. The middle section looks like this:

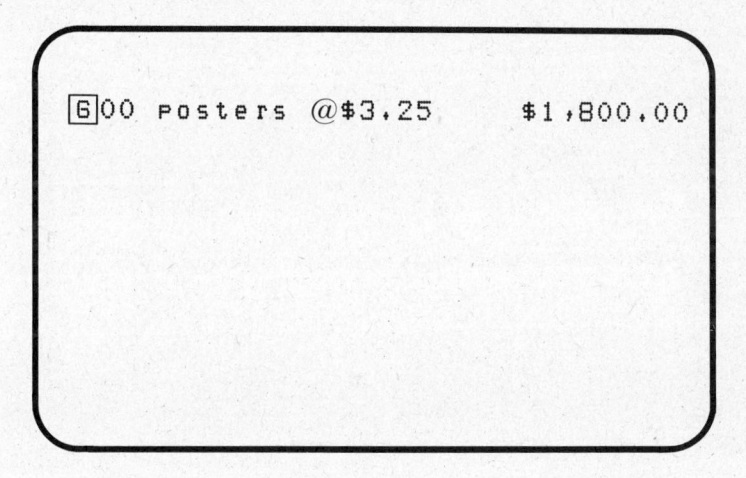

```
6 00 posters @$3.25      $1,800.00
```

This looks like a $150 discount, but Joe knows it is an error. And since he won't be allowed to spend more than the purchase order, he wants to be sure he has the right figures here. He presses the CALC key, which means that the numeric keypad on his right can now act as a calculator. The screen clears, except for the cursor.

He then types "600×3.25=" and presses ENTER. The answer appears in a second: 1,950.00.

He presses RETURN to signal that he is through with the calculator. The text of the purchase order returns.

Now Joe moves the cursor over the dollar sign and presses the DELETE key, to indicate that he wants to rub something out. Then he presses the RIGHT ARROW key and wipes out the figures "$1,800.00." To indicate he is through deleting, he presses RETURN.

Then he moves the cursor back to the spot just to the right of the dollar sign, presses INSERT, and types in the correct amount, $1,950.00. He tells his secretary, "Now print that out, and I'll sign it."

38 || THE DEFINITIVE WORD-PROCESSING BOOK

Copying Text from Another Document

For the Long-Range Planning Committee, Joe had assigned his assistant, Bill Lipsky, to research the census figures to learn how the age of the population would change over the 1980s and 1990s. He calls up Bill's report. One paragraph reads like this:

> [B]abies will peak in 1990, slough off after that; the boom will mean bigger sales in the 10-to-19-year-old market. There will be a big drop in the number of 20- to 34-year-olds. From 1990, almost every category over 34 years swells. So despite the teen boom, the nation as a whole will be getting older, on average.

Joe decides to add some statistics from another document here. He leaves his cursor on the line after "on average" and presses SHIFT and COPY.

The system prompts, "Document——?"

Joe keys in the title of the document he wants to take statistics from, "Overview of Census Figures," and after a few seconds, the first page comes onscreen. He scrolls through to find the table he is after, puts the cursor under the first letter, and presses RETURN.

The system asks, "Copy——?"

Joe runs the cursor down the table to its last line, highlighting the whole, then presses RETURN. The system copies the table into the text he was working on:

```
Babies will peak in 1990, slough
off after that; the boom will
mean bigger sales in the 10-to-
19-year-old market. There will be
a big drop in the number of 20-
to 34-year-olds. From 1990,
almost every category over 34
years swells. So despite the teen
boom, the nation as a whole will
be getting older, on average.

U.S. POPULATION BY AGE GROUP, IN
THOUSANDS
Age Group        1980    1990    2000
Under 5 years    16,020  19,437  17,852
5 to 9 years     16,096  19,040  19,000
10 to 14 years   17,800  16,718  20,153
15 to 19 years   20,609  16,777  19,727
20 to 24 years   20,918  17,953  16,898
25 to 29 years   18,930  20,169  16,469
30 to 34 years   17,242  20,917  17,981
35 to 39 years   14,033  19,261  20,435
40 to 44 years   11,688  17,331  20,909
45 to 49 years   11,030  13,899  18,99[0]
```

Paginating

The operations group in Joe's company decided to install scanning equipment in most stores. The laser scanner in the checkout counter scans the bar code on each product, identifies the product, and then consults the store computer for the price. But some customers are skeptical that they will be charged the right price.

Joe commissioned a public relations consultant to offer advice on how to present the new technology to the public. Joe rewrote the recommendations, and now wants to finalize the report.

Looking at the paper version, he decides that it looks too dense. He wants to add white space. For instance, his original runs like this:

> [S]o our customers react favorably to the installation of scanning equipment in your supermarkets because:
>
> - It's accurate. (59%)
> - It's fast. (83%)
> - It's high tech. (38%)
>
> Publicity Theme I Propose
>
> Stress the speed--that's what people like most.
>
> And the checkout clerks get to chat more, since they don't have to punch the register as much. So I'd show a cashier scanning with a balloon over her head saying, "I let the computer figure the bill while I talk to Maude."
>
> Mention accuracy and high technology later in the copy.

Moving the cursor to the spot after the third bulleted item, Joe presses the PAGE button and creates a page break. Nothing happens onscreen, but the computer will remember to stop typing on that page and to move on to a new page.

To see what this will look like printed out, Joe presses DISPLAY. So now one page ends like this:

> [S]o our customers react favorably to the installation of scanning equipment in your supermarkets because:
>
> - It's accurate. (59%)
> - It's fast. (83%)
> - It's high tech. (38%)

And the next begins:

```
[P]ublicity Theme I Propose

   Stress the speed--that's what
people like most.

   And the checkout clerks get to
chat more, since they don't have
to punch the register as much. So
I'd show a cashier scanning with
a balloon over her head saying,
"I let the computer figure the
bill while I talk to Maude."

   Mention accuracy and high
technology later in the copy.
They're important, and they
deserve several paragraphs in a
long-copy ad.

   We should probably show a
graph indicating the increase in
```

And of course now Joe has fouled up the old page numbering, but the word processor has already figured out how the pages would go, this way. So when he has the report printed out, he gets new page numbers, too.

FUNCTIONS CHECKLIST

You can use this list to check off the functions you need. On the right, you'll find an indication whether that feature comes with most word processors, some, or few.

DO I NEED THIS?	FUNCTION	FUNCTION OFFERED IN MOST SOME FEW SYSTEMS
☐	**ABANDON CHANGES** To erase the copy of the file being worked on, leaving any previous file, or to erase the changes you were making, leaving the text as it was	✔
☐	**BACKUP/RUB OUT** To move the cursor to the left and erase whatever character was there *Also known as* BACKSPACE, BACK DELETE	✔
	BOLD FACE To print text in extra-heavy type:	
☐	One word at a time	✔
☐	Line	✔
☐	Paragraph	✔
☐	Any amount you choose	✔
☐	On display	✔
☐	Printing only	✔
☐	**CALCULATE** To add or multiply a series of numbers, usually in a row or column *Also known as* MATH PACK	✔
☐	**CANCEL** Stop the current function	✔
	CENTER To center a word or phrase within right and left margins:	

HOW IT WORKS || 43

DO I NEED THIS?	FUNCTION	FUNCTION OFFERED IN MOST SOME FEW SYSTEMS

☐   In one line   ✔ MOST
☐   In line after line until you cancel   ✔ SOME
☐   On display   ✔ MOST
☐   Printing only   ✔ MOST

CHECK SPELLING
To check your spelling against a basic dictionary, highlighting errors for you to correct or let stand:

☐   Basic word list   ✔ MOST
☐   You can add your own special words for the system to check   ✔ MOST
☐   Highlights for you to act   ✔ MOST
☐   Corrects automatically without asking you   ✔ FEW
☐   On display   ✔ MOST

COPY
To copy text from one place to another, within one document, or from one document to another—without erasing it at the original spot:

☐   Less than a page   ✔ MOST
☐   More than a page   ✔ SOME
☐   Within one document   ✔ MOST
☐   From one document to another   ✔ SOME
☐   On display   ✔ MOST
☐   Printing only   ✔ SOME

Also known as WRITE TO

COPY A DISKETTE (BACKUP)
☐   To make a copy of all files present on a diskette onto another diskette or tape (copying usually formats at the same time)   ✔ MOST

COPY A DOCUMENT
☐   To place a copy of one document into another document on the same or another disk, with a different name   ✔ MOST

44 | THE DEFINITIVE WORD-PROCESSING BOOK

DO I NEED THIS?	FUNCTION	FUNCTION OFFERED IN MOST / SOME / FEW SYSTEMS

CREATE A NEW DOCUMENT
- ☐ To start inputting a new document — MOST
- ☐ To make a place on a disk for a new document to be stored in, name it, and put its name in the directory or index (these are usually actions that the *system* takes when you create a document) — MOST

Also known as: EDIT NEW DOCUMENT, OPEN FILE

CREATE FORMAT
To set page length, left and right margins, indentations, and tabs, so that when you enter new text it automatically falls into this format:
- ☐ Page length — MOST
- ☐ Left and right margins — MOST
- ☐ Indentations and tabs — MOST
- ☐ On display — MOST
- ☐ Printing only — FEW

DECIMAL TAB
To align a column of numbers on the decimal point:
- ☐ On display — SOME
- ☐ Printing only — SOME

DELETE
To erase a character, word, line, sentence, paragraph, page, section, or whole document:
- ☐ Character — MOST
- ☐ Word — MOST

HOW IT WORKS ‖ 45

DO I NEED THIS?	FUNCTION	FUNCTION OFFERED IN MOST	SOME	FEW SYSTEMS
☐	Line	✔		
☐	Sentence	✔		
☐	Paragraph	✔		
☐	Section		✔	
☐	Document	✔		
☐	Any amount you choose		✔	
☐	On display	✔		
☐	Printing only			✔

DOCUMENT INDEX
To list all the documents on a disk:

☐	Title only	✔		
☐	Date created		✔	
☐	Last date modified		✔	
☐	Operator name		✔	
☐	Author name		✔	
☐	Amount of time spent in document			✔
☐	Total time to date			✔
☐	Time spent on last edit			✔

DOCUMENT MERGE
To combine parts of two documents to create a third, as when you take an address from one list and a form letter from another:

☐	Automatic		✔	
☐	With pauses at each step for you to approve, onscreen		✔	
☐	Letter length		✔	
☐	On display			✔
☐	Printing only		✔	

FILE DOCUMENT
☐	To place all text onto diskette, clear the screen, and prepare to do another function	✔		

46 | THE DEFINITIVE WORD-PROCESSING BOOK

DO I NEED THIS?	FUNCTION	FUNCTION OFFERED IN MOST SOME FEW SYSTEMS

FOOTNOTE AUTOMATICALLY
To link the main body of the text to the footnote, so that if modifications are made that cause the text that is referenced to the note to move to another page, footnote will move too:

		MOST	SOME	FEW
☐	Automatic			✓
☐	With pauses at each step for you to intervene		✓	

FORMULA MODE
To input formulas that require many lines with characters sub- or super-scripted:

| ☐ | On display | | ✓ | |
| ☐ | Using special symbols on screen; actual formula formatted only in printing | | ✓ | |

GENERATE AN INDEX
To create an index to a document, based on a list of key words you prepare:

☐	Listing each page a given word or phrase appears on			✓
☐	Doing this in the background (off-screen)			✓
☐	On display			✓
☐	Printing only			✓

GLOSSARY
To call in prepared definitions, phrases, sentences, or paragraphs from a file called a glossary, or BOILERPLATE, collection:

☐	Phrases		✓	
☐	Lines		✓	
☐	Paragraphs		✓	
☐	Whole pages		✓	

HOW IT WORKS || 47

DO I NEED THIS?	FUNCTION	FUNCTION OFFERED IN MOST SOME FEW SYSTEMS

GO TO
To locate a specific page or section, and to have that displayed on screen:
- ☐ Go to specific page — SOME
- ☐ Go to section — SOME
- ☐ Go to end or start of document — MOST

Also known as LOCATE

HEADERS AND FOOTERS
To put running text on the top or bottom of the pages:
- ☐ To create — MOST
- ☐ To change — MOST
- ☐ To alternate left and right pages — SOME
- ☐ On display — FEW
- ☐ Printing only — MOST

HYPHENATE
To insert hyphens into words at line ends, so they do not run over right margin; used in right justification and partial justification:
- ☐ Automatic — FEW
- ☐ Highlights possible hyphenation for your OK — SOME
- ☐ On display — SOME
- ☐ Printing only — FEW

INSERT
To put new text into existing text:
- ☐ Less than a page — MOST
- ☐ More than a page — SOME
- ☐ On display — MOST
- ☐ Printing only — SOME

JUSTIFY
To make the text on the right margin line up evenly, as in a book:
- ☐ Perfectly even — SOME

48 || THE DEFINITIVE WORD-PROCESSING BOOK

DO I NEED THIS?	FUNCTION	FUNCTION OFFERED IN MOST SOME FEW SYSTEMS
☐	Within a few characters of even	MOST
☐	Using spaces between words to expand and contract lines	MOST
☐	Using spaces within and between words to expand and contract lines (less noticeable)	SOME
☐	On display	SOME
☐	Printing only	MOST

MAINTAIN AND UPDATE FILES
To keep files, such as the list of all documents on a diskette, and to update them from time to time:

☐	Create new documents on file	MOST
☐	Change and delete entries	MOST
☐	Preserve some files from unauthorized changes	SOME
☐	Create some data automatically (such as time this document was worked on by each operator)	SOME

MOVE CURSOR
To position the cursor or "location indicator" in the text:

☐	Move a character at a time	MOST
☐	Move a word at a time	MOST
☐	Move a line at a time	SOME
☐	Move a paragraph at a time	SOME
☐	Move a sentence at a time	FEW

(Some cursor movement also causes the text to scroll up or down)

MOVE
To move sections of text around within one document or from one document to another:

☐	Less than a page	MOST
☐	More than a page	SOME
☐	Within one document	MOST
☐	From one document to another	MOST

DO I NEED THIS?	FUNCTION	FUNCTION OFFERED IN MOST SOME FEW SYSTEMS
☐	On display	✔
☐	Printing only	✔

NONPRINTING COMMENTS

☐ Comments or "notes" typed into a document, but specified not to print out with the main text   ✔

PAGINATE

To divide the text into pages, assigning consecutive numbers:

☐   By numbers of lines on a page   ✔
☐   Allowing you to make a page break in the middle of a certain page, as when a chapter stops halfway down, and you want the next chapter to start on a new page   ✔
☐   Avoids leaving widows and orphans—isolated single lines at bottom or top of page   ✔
☐   On display   ✔
☐   Printing only   ✔

PRINT

To send text stored in a word processor to the printer and produce a "hard copy" of it on paper; print variables:

☐   Number of copies   ✔
☐   Continuous forms   ✔
☐   Single sheets   ✔
☐   Start printing with page number   ✔
☐   End printing with page number   ✔
☐   Pitch (10 or 12)   ✔
☐   Automatically paginate   ✔
☐   Break pages only at page markers   ✔
☐   Assign priorities to different documents, so one gets printed before another   ✔

DO I NEED THIS?	FUNCTION	FUNCTION OFFERED IN MOST SOME FEW SYSTEMS

REFORMAT
To change the format of existing text, without losing any:

☐	Left margins	✓
☐	Right margins	✓
☐	Tabs	✓
☐	Page length	✓
☐	On display	✓
☐	Printing only	✓

REMEMBER MULTIPLE FORMATS
To recall a number of formats you are using in one document, so you can switch easily from one to another, without pausing to create them new each time:

☐	Recalls one format (the "default" format)	✓
☐	Recalls two	✓
☐	Recalls up to ten	✓
☐	Displays the current one at the top of the page (or bottom)	✓
☐	Describes format within text	✓
☐	Shows only when printing	✓

RENAME A DOCUMENT

☐	To change the name associated with a document	✓

REPEAT COMMAND SEQUENCE

☐ To tell the system to repeat the last function you did, such as underlining a word, or searching for a specific word (on some systems this is done by allowing you to "define" a special key which will then repeat any series of keystrokes you want)   ✓

Also known as USER-DEFINED KEYS, USER-PROGRAMMABLE OPTIONS

DO I NEED THIS?	FUNCTION	FUNCTION OFFERED IN MOST SOME FEW SYSTEMS
	SCROLL TEXT To move the text up and down on the screen	
☐	Scroll a line at a time	✓
☐	Scroll a "screenful" at a time	✓
☐	Continuous scroll	✓
☐	Scroll a page at a time	✓
	SEARCH To find a given word or phrase within the text, and display it in context:	
☐	Only the way you type it in	✓
☐	All versions of the phrase (all capitals, say, even if you typed it in all lower case)	✓
☐	Keep doing this over and over	✓
	Also known as SEARCH AND RETRIEVE, FIND	
	SEARCH AND REPLACE To find instances of a given word or phrase within the text, and to replace it with a new word or phrase:	
☐	One at a time, so you can approve each change	✓
☐	Globally (throughout document)	✓
☐	On display	✓
☐	Printing only	✓
	SHIFT COLUMNS To shift columns of figures around within the text:	
☐	Right and left	✓
☐	In any direction	✓
☐	Within one page	✓
☐	Within one document	✓
☐	From one document to another	✓
☐	On display	✓
☐	Printing only	✓

52 | THE DEFINITIVE WORD-PROCESSING BOOK

DO I NEED THIS?	FUNCTION	FUNCTION OFFERED IN MOST / SOME / FEW SYSTEMS
	SORT	
	To sort text in alphabetical or numerical order:	
☐	By first letters or digits	MOST
☐	Including a line of accompanying text	MOST
☐	Including an accompanying paragraph	SOME
☐	Within a page	MOST
☐	Within a section	SOME
☐	Within any specified amount of text	SOME
☐	On display	MOST
☐	Printing only	MOST
☐	Performed in background, while you work on something else	MOST
	STRIKEOVER	
	To preserve one character while printing another on top of it, as when you need to show just what you are crossing out:	
☐	One character at a time	MOST
☐	One line at a time	MOST
☐	As long as you like	MOST
☐	On display	MOST
☐	Printing only	MOST
	SUBSCRIPT	
	To put a letter half a line down from the main line of text:	
☐	Displays on screen that way	MOST
☐	Special symbol displays on screen, actual subscript at printing only	MOST
	SUPERSCRIPT	
	To put a letter or number half a line above the main line of text:	
☐	Displays on screen	MOST
☐	Special symbol displays on screen; we see actual superscript at printing time only	MOST

HOW IT WORKS ‖ 53

DO I NEED THIS?	FUNCTION	FUNCTION OFFERED IN		
		MOST	SOME	FEW

UNDERLINE
To underscore individual characters, words, lines, paragraphs, or whatever you designate:

☐	One character at a time	✔		
☐	Word	✔		
☐	Line	✔		
☐	Paragraph	✔		
☐	Any amount you choose	✔		
☐	On display		✔	
☐	Printing only	✔		

UNDO

☐	To return the text to its status before you made the last change			✔

UPPER/LOWER CASE EXISTING TEXT
To change the text you have into all capital letters or small letters, without retyping the whole:

☐	One word at a time	✔		
☐	One line at a time	✔		
☐	Paragraph			✔
☐	Page			✔
☐	Document			✔
☐	On display		✔	
☐	Printing only		✔	

WORD WRAP

	To move a word crossing the right margin to the beginning of the next line (done automatically)	✔		

3

What Makes Up a Word Processor?

Like your stereo system, a word processor has a lot of components. You can buy a complete system with all the parts put together, or you can piece them together yourself. Choosing between whole word-processing systems and individual components, you need to know what your options are—and how they'll affect the basic job you want your word processor to do.

Picking the right components can help you avoid problems such as these:

- The system works well with just one person using it, but slows down with two or three.
- The screen reflects so much light you get a headache.
- The keyboard is so soft you want to pound it into a ball and throw it away.
- You bought your word processor and printer separately and the printer can't understand the formatting codes your word processor uses, so you get pages and pages of nonsense.
- The screen is capable of showing underlining, but the programmer didn't put that in the software, so there's no way to tell the screen where to show the underlines.
- You bought an Optical Character Reader to read all your company's financial records and turn each character into computer code, so your word processor can show them to you onscreen—but the OCR can't read the typeface you used a few years ago.
- You write hundred-page reports, but your word processor can process only one page at a time.

The more you understand about the way your word processor's components work, the more likely you are to avoid such problems. The basics of any word processor are the keyboard, screen, computer (hidden inside), disk drive (holding your text on disks), printer, and software (instructions that make the computer into a word processor). Then there are some extras such as modems (devices that let one word processor communicate with another over telephone lines or cables), and Optical Character Readers (machines that can read text into a word processor by scanning type). In this chapter, we discuss each of these components in detail.

THE HUMAN CONNECTION: SCREENS AND KEYBOARDS

The most obvious and familiar parts of a word processor are the video display screen and the keyboard. These are the parts you'll work with most frequently. The keyboard is your way of communicating with your word processor. It is your "input device"—you press keys to input text and to change it. The computer on the inside responds to the keys you press by displaying characters and messages on the video screen. The screen acts as an "output device," displaying information from the computer to you.

Since the keyboard and screen are your tools for interacting with the computer, they require extra attention. You will find some keyboards that feel finer than those on the best electric typewriters, while others seem to emulate the first manual ones. Some screens are easy on the eyes and pleasant to look at; others are blurry and can produce eyestrain.

Fortune's 32:16 system has three movable pieces, allowing maximum flexibility in a workspace. (Photo courtesy of Fortune Systems Corporation)

In looking at various word processors, the first difference you'll encounter is that in some systems, the video screen and keyboard are in one unit, à la typewriter and paper. Other keyboards are detached from the display screen, so you can move them around and position them separately. (A cable—or infrared beam—carries signals back and forth between them.)

We prefer the movable keyboards—they make most operations a little easier, as they are more flexible. You can pull the keyboard toward you and leave the screen further away. You can angle the two components apart, so that you don't feel as if you have blinders on—a sensation that can occur when you have to lean forward and "into" the screen all day. Some screens are movable, too, swiveling from right to left and tilting up and down to the most comfortable angle.

Here Fortune's 32:16 system is shown with the video display unit moved to the right of the keyboard. (Photo courtesy of Fortune Systems Corporation)

Whether or not the keyboard and screen are in the same box or are attached via cable, the combination of the two of them makes up what is known as "the terminal"; they are usually sold together as a unit. Of course, some personal computers come with just a keyboard; for a screen, you hook them up to your television set or purchase a separate screen unit called a "monitor."

VIDEO DISPLAY SCREENS

If you intend to use a word processor a lot, consider carefully the kind of display screen you want. One vendor we talked to about screens, eyestrain, and the hypnotizing effect of the video display if you work on it all day, said, "Well, you just have to take a break every two hours."

That's good advice. In fact, some studies on the effects of working in front of video screens suggest a 15-minute break every hour. Still, you want something as comfortable as possible to look at.

Colors

Display screens come in a range of colors. White, amber, or green characters on black, dark green, or gray backgrounds seem to be the most common color combinations. A few offer black characters on a white background, simulating paper in a typewriter. As more "ergonomic" studies of word processors are done, different color schemes are emerging. (Ergonomics is basically the study of how to make machines easy and pleasant for people to use.)

There are various opinions on how screen colors relate to eyestrain, general fatigue, and stress. It's hard to say what's true. We've seen green-and-black screens that were wonderful and others that were awful; the same with black and white. What does seem to be true is that the contrast between character and background and the clarity of the letters both make a difference. Most terminals have a brightness control (just like your television set), so that you can adjust the contrast for individual taste and different lighting conditions. If the sun shines in on your screen at three in the afternoon, the high contrast that was fine all morning may be suddenly too bright.

Size

Another difference in screens is size. For the most part, screens are either "half-page" or "full-page," denoting the amount of text that can be displayed on them at one time. Half-page screens have room to display 24 to 30 lines of text at a time; full-page can display 66 or 68. Most screens display 80 characters, or "columns," across. Some can show up to 132, by virtue of a wider screen or the use of a mode in which the characters can "shrink" and fit more on each line. A few personal computers still show only 40 columns of text—not enough for real writing.

Companies who offer word processors with full-page screens say that these are better because you can see a whole page at a time and really have an idea of how your document will look before it's printed. Manufacturers of half-page screens cite studies that the eye can't take in too many lines at a time, so full-page screens aren't really necessary. We find that it's largely a matter of personal preference and the kind of work you do. If you spend most of the day filling in the same one-page form, or writing one-page letters, you may prefer the full-page screen.

Gradually word-processing screens are getting bigger. The Xerox Star Information System, for example, has a light turquoise screen displaying more than a full page. In fact, there's room to lay several pages next to each other, as though you were working on your desk.

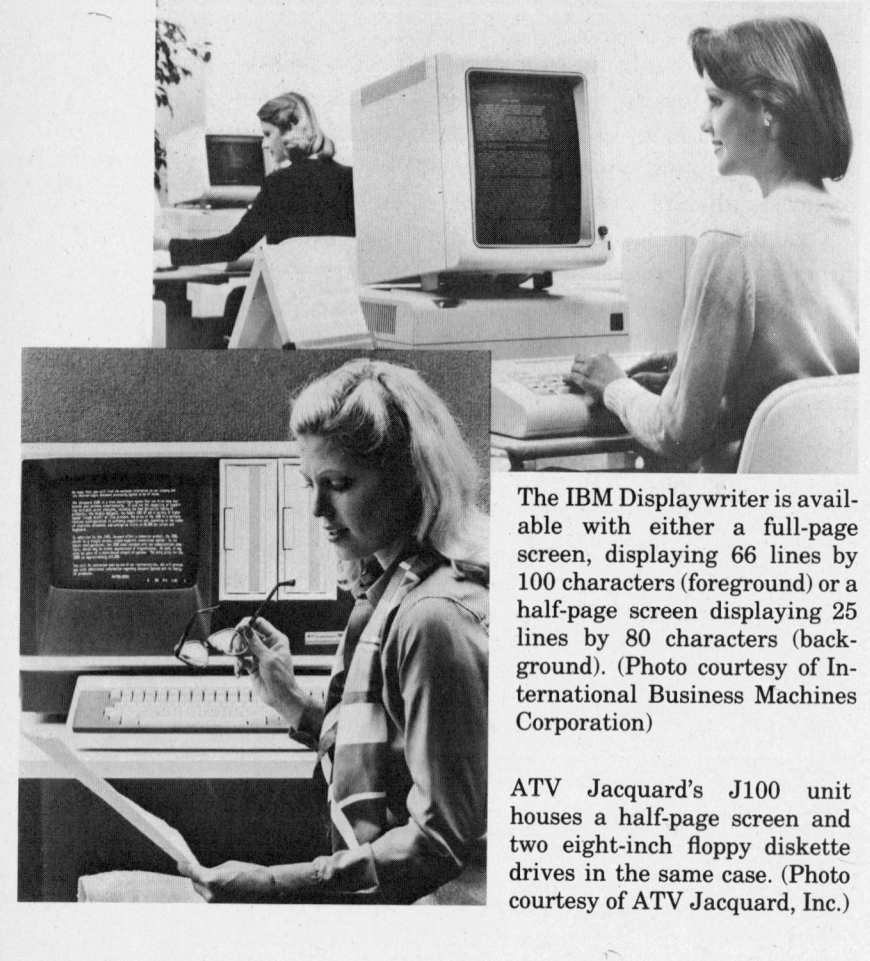

The IBM Displaywriter is available with either a full-page screen, displaying 66 lines by 100 characters (foreground) or a half-page screen displaying 25 lines by 80 characters (background). (Photo courtesy of International Business Machines Corporation)

ATV Jacquard's J100 unit houses a half-page screen and two eight-inch floppy diskette drives in the same case. (Photo courtesy of ATV Jacquard, Inc.)

Special Effects

Video display screen manufacturers have a term called "attributes." The attributes of a screen are its special display characteristics—how text can be marked or highlighted.

When you mark a portion of text to delete or to move it, it may appear on the screen in a variety of ways, depending on the screen's attributes. It may appear in "reverse video." If the screen normally displays white characters on a dark background, then reverse video will "light up" the marked text by displaying dark characters on a white background. Or the intensity of the selected characters may brighten or dim. The terminal that does this is said to have "high and low intensity." Such a terminal may be able to simulate **boldface** type by brightening and thickening the characters.

Screens that don't have reverse video or high/low intensity may have the ability to show specially marked characters as "blinking." This can be very disorienting. We had the blinking attribute active by accident while testing a business software package during development, and we can say we hope never to have to use it again with text that we're also trying to read on the screen. One-character blinking—to show the cursor position, for example—is fine, but a sentence or paragraph is unpalatable.

Underlining on the screen is a wonderful attribute, but unfortunately, it is not always used, even when it's available in the hardware of the terminal. Keep in mind that for your word processor to use any screen attribute, the software must provide the right instructions to the computer, and some programs don't.

Character Display

Most characters that you see on the screen are formed by dots, or "pixels." The size and number of dots per character determine the sharpness and clarity of the image. The fewer the dots, the fuzzier the character. The greater the number of dots shown in one character space, the clearer the character image. A high number of dots is called "high resolution."

When you use a typewriter, you make certain assumptions that you may never be aware of until you try out some word-processing screens. For example, think about lowercase letters that extend below the line of type, like "p's," "g's," and "q's." You probably haven't thought about extending them below the line since you learned to write in first grade. Well, it's time to think about them once again. The part of the character that extends below the line is called a "descender," and you may be surprised to find that these won't show up on some screens. If you try out a word processor, type the word "giggle," and if it looks more like "sissle," you're looking at a terminal that doesn't have descenders. If the rest of the system suits your needs, you'll probably find that you can get used to this; however it is one of those things that you'd think any self-respecting manufacturer would correct.

The Cursor

The cursor is the small line, rectangle, or triangle that indicates your position in the text on the screen. When you enter a character, it will appear where the cursor is. You'll move the cursor around to indicate where changes should occur, whether you're deleting a letter or inserting a new paragraph. The easiest cursors to use are the rectangles and triangles on screens that have the reverse-video attribute. When you move the cursor over an existing character, it appears to jump out at you; you see both the cursor image and the character clearly. Cursors that appear as underlines or blinking characters are not as easy to spot on the screen.

Alternate Character Sets

Some screens can display special characters, such as Greek or Arabic letters, or math symbols. The characters that can be displayed are determined by a "character generator," which translates keystrokes into character forms on the screen. It takes a special terminal and special software to display nonstandard characters.

Graphics and Color

Computer graphics—the ability to draw pictures on computer screens and print them out—are gradually entering the word-processing marketplace. Some word processors, such as CPT's, can draw boxes on the screen, interspersed with or surrounding the text—on organization charts, for example. If you want to use more graphics, such as colored pie charts, your selection of equipment is more limited, and will be more costly. The screen must have the ability to display the images and colors you want, and software must be available to make use of that ability. Word-processing equipment designed as an "executive workstation" is more likely to include graphics capabilities than equipment designed for a clerk's desk in the office. Interestingly, many micro-, or "personal," computers, such as Apple's Lisa and Macintosh, have graphics capabilities built in, or available at low cost.

Personal Preferences

What you like or dislike about a screen is often a matter of personal preference. Some people develop headaches and eyestrain from some screens; others don't seem to be bothered by them at all. How you use word processing may dictate how much you're affected, too. If you're a touch typist and spend most of your time looking at written material while your fingers transcribe it into the system, you may care more about the form of the original material than about how the screen looks. If you create text right on the system, however, or make a lot of editing changes on the screen, you're going to be staring at it a lot, so look it over carefully before you choose one.

KEYBOARDS

When you look at word-processing equipment, be sure to get your hands on the keyboard—don't settle for watching a demonstration by a trained specialist. There are lots of reasons for doing this. Word processing isn't always as easy as it looks, so you need to get a sense of how difficult it is to maneuver around the keyboard, and you also want to know if the touch requires sensitive fingers or elephantine pressure. If you're selecting equipment for someone else in your office, take him or her along to try out the keyboard before you buy it.

Touch

If you're the one who'll use the word processor and you type with only two fingers, you may not care about the touch of the keyboard. If you do know how to type, and especially if you're addicted to the feel of an IBM Selectric, flex your fingers. Most keyboards designed for word-processing use have tried to imitate or better the Selectric's touch. But some keyboards were designed for programming, data-processing, or business applications, in which the operator doesn't necessarily use touch typing. The cheaper computers sometimes come with "Chiclet" keyboards—okay for punching buttons, but uncomfortable and slow if you want to write. When a computer company adds word-processing capability to its line of products, the keyboard doesn't necessarily get redesigned, so try it out before you buy.

Lay-Out

MYTH: All keyboards have the standard letter and number keys in the same positions. REALITY: Watch out for extra keys in awkward places. Although the positions that letters and numbers occupy on typewriters is the basic standard used on terminal keyboards, minor changes can sometimes prove to be very clumsy. The most common change you'll find is an extra key inserted between the colon (:) key—on which a touch typist rests the right pinky—and the RETURN key. And we don't mean the quotation-mark (") key, which is often there; we mean an additional key. Although a regular user will adapt to having to stretch a little further than the typewriter requires, it's most frustrating for the new user, because it throws off the habitual "home" position of the hands.

Function Keys

A word-processing system is going to let you do wonderful things and save you time because you don't have to retype your entire text every time you make changes in it. How do these special things happen? You tell the system to do them, most often by pressing special keys or a special series of keys.

Take a good look at the keyboards you see on word processors. Sometimes you'll see how to do various functions immediately, by using specially labeled "function" keys. These may be separate keys, to the sides of the main keyboard, or they may appear above the number keys. Or you may see words engraved on the front of the letter keys on the main keyboard; when you first press a key named "ALTERNATE" and then the letter key, the system knows you mean the alternate (or front) function. Not "D," say, but DELETE.

Labeled function keys are a great boon to the word-processing user, especially while you're learning a system. When you see keys named DELETE WORD, CUT, PASTE, MOVE, SEARCH, REPLACE, and FORMAT, you know you're in the presence of a system designed with the word-processing user in mind. Separate function keys most often require that you press only one key to use a special function.

In a double-key system, the first key, sometimes called the "prefix" key, may be labeled something like ESC (for escape from the regular meaning of the key), CTRL (for control, meaning that what follows is not text, but a function that controls text), ALT (for alternate meaning of the key), or FUNC SHIFT (for shift to a special function).

When you activate a function by pressing a prefix key and then a letter or number key, the system is said to use "control keys." But when you hear vendors discuss "control keys," they often mean unlabeled keys. Good software designers who develop word-processing programs for terminals that don't have labeled keyboards try to keep control-key functions "mnemonic," i.e., easy to remember. This means that the letter key you press is the first letter of the function name. For example, CONTROL + "S" may be used to Save a document. CONTROL + "I" may activate Insert. When the software is designed to be used on a variety of terminals, however, as is often the case with software written for microcomputers, this isn't always possible. Thus the instruction sent to the computer when the control key is held down and the "A" key is then pressed may vary from one terminal to another. The plain letter "A" is the same, but CONTROL + "A" may be used to perform different functions on different equipment. We hope that someday a standard usage will evolve.

There's been a great deal of talk by word-processing vendors about saving keystrokes and therefore time. It's nice to have a function completed in one keystroke, but two isn't bad either. Three or four keystrokes is another story, especially when you have to remember the correct order of the strokes. Labels on keys that require a prefix go a long way toward keeping word-processing usage simple.

You'll see some keyboards with a long row of function keys across the top, labeled F1, F2, F3, etc. Personally, we've never understood this. Why go to the effort to provide function keys and then give them coded labels, forcing the user to memorize which function goes with which key? The rationale behind this is that the keyboard may be used for other tasks as well as word processing, so the meaning of the function will change with the program that is in use. Still, when companies have lots of customers who use their keyboards for word processing, it would seem worthwhile to provide specially labeled keycaps.

Smart software vendors whose products work on keyboards that don't have engraved function keys provide small labeled stickers that you can apply to your keyboard, creating the effect of labeled keys. If these aren't provided, you can certainly make your own.

Savin has developed a product with a unique approach to solving this problem. Above the row of numbers on their keyboard are two rows containing thirty-two touch-sensitive pads. Insertable Mylar strips come with each software package. These fit over the pads and label them. A word-processing operator uses the word-processing strip. An accounting clerk replaces it with an accounting strip. The function pads are used with a variety of applications and are labeled for each different one. Our compliments to the designers.

Savin's Information Stations come with a Touchpanel instead of function keys. Interchangeable Touchpanel strips allow the user to see quickly how to activate word-processing functions. (Photo courtesy of Savin Corporation)

Using a little forethought and ingenuity, vendors have arrived at other solutions for terminals that weren't originally designed for word processing. Shasta Business Systems sells Xerox hardware with specialized word- and data-processing packages. Their standard keyboard, designed initially for data processing, lacks special keys for marking portions of text directly, such as WORD and SENTENCE keys. Nonetheless, they arrived at another way to make deleting portions of text easy and intuitive for the user. To delete a word, you press DELETE and then the space bar. Then all characters from the cursor to the next space—a word—are deleted. To delete a sentence, you press DELETE and then type a period. Everything up to the next period—a sentence, usually—is removed.

Keys That Move the Cursor

The keys that move the cursor around the screen are a particular type of function key. They may be "amount keys," such as CHARACTER, WORD, LINE, SENTENCE, PARAGRAPH, PAGE, or they may be ARROW keys, which point in the direction they cause the cursor to move. Usually these keys are clumped together somewhere on the right of the keyboard. Since you'll use these almost as often as you use the space bar, make sure they're in easy reach, preferably toward the bottom of the keyboard.

Number Keypads

A pad with numbers sometimes appears to the right of the main keyboard. Duplicating the ten-key arrangement found on calculators, these pads were originally designed for data processing. With word processing, the number keypad may still generate numbers, allowing the easy entering of columns of numbers, or it may be used for word-processing functions.

Repeating Action

On a typewriter, the period (.), "x," and hyphen (-) keys often repeat if you hold them down a little firmer or longer. You'll find this repeating action on some word-processing keyboards, too. It may be restricted to a few specialized keys, or all keys on the keyboard may repeat if you hold them down. Some keyboards have a separate "repeat" key, which causes other keys to repeat if it is held down simultaneously. And you may find a few keyboards with no repeating action at all.

Caps Lock

On many video terminal keyboards the CAPS LOCK, UPPERCASE, or SHIFT LOCK key is not the same as on a typewriter. When "locked," letters may be shifted to uppercase, but numbers will remain their lowercase selves instead of becoming symbols, unless you use the regular shift key with them. This can be quite handy if you ever have to type a mixture of capital letters and numbers. When the CAPS LOCK key works this way, it is usually released by depressing it again; the lower-shift doesn't "unlock" it.

Keyboard Buffers

Despite the speed of the computer, it's still possible to type faster than the characters can be sent from the keyboard to the processor and interpreted. A keyboard buffer is a temporary storage area where your keystrokes are held if and when you get ahead of the computer. Different terminals have different buffers: some can hold only about eight characters; some can hold up to fifty or sixty. When you test a word processor, type as fast as you can on the keyboard and see if you lose any of your characters. This will give you an idea of how much of a buffer is available, and whether it's adequate for your needs.

A COMPUTER AT HEART: THE CPU

At the heart of every word-processing system is a computer. If you get a chance to look inside your word processor, it's well worth it. Have someone point out the "central processor" to you—it's amazing. The guts of the whole machine center around the CPU, or Central Processing Unit, which may be on a circuit board as small as a 3 × 5 index card. The processor chip itself may be the size of your thumbnail.

The central processing unit does the actual work of the computer. It processes instructions that have been reduced to simple on/off electrical impulses in its circuits. The computer is fed strings of 1s and 0s (ons and offs), and responds to them.

On most word processors, you never get to see the central processor. You may see a separate box that "houses" the central processor, or it may be contained with the disk drive, or even inside the video display terminal.

There are three main types of computers: mainframes, minicomputers, and microcomputers. We'll talk about them in order of size, from large to small, based on how much data they can work with at one time and how fast they can process it.

Mainframe computers were the first ones available. The word "mainframe" brings to mind a very large piece of equipment, and

Inside these chips is the operating system for your word processor. (Photo courtesy of Intel Corporation.)

major company names such as IBM. At one time mainframes used to fill entire rooms with tubes. As technology has advanced they've become smaller, but they're still pretty good-sized—as big as closets, with disk drives the size of filing cabinets. It's doubtful that you would buy a mainframe computer solely for word processing, so we won't dwell on them. If you have a mainframe, however, you might consider adding word-processing capability to it. We'll talk more about finding software for existing hardware in Chapter 4, "Narrowing the Field."

Mini-computers were developed as smaller alternatives to mainframes. Some of them are pretty large in their own right, sporting hundreds of terminals and good-sized cabinets. Some look like air-conditioning units for small buildings. They don't have to be big, however. Small mini-computers may have only a couple of terminals, or even one. Digital Equipment Corporation (DEC) brought mini-computers to the forefront in the sixties, and many other companies followed, including the giants who had introduced mainframes.

There are many word processors available on mini-computers; DEC, Wang, Nixdorf, MicroData, Datapoint, and Data General offer them, to name only a few companies. These computers can often be run as "hybrid systems," supporting both word and data processing, and almost all of them have multiple workstations and printers attached.

Micros are the smallest computers; they are the newcomers to the field. Although often thought of as single-user or "stand-alone" systems, some can handle several users. Many traditional word-processing systems are built around microcomputers bundled together with software, terminals, and disk drives, and sold as a complete system. They are not usually called "micros," however. The past few years have seen the popularization of the microcomputer as the "personal computer." Now you can select from a large group of micros in a computer store and pick out the software packages that you want.

Aside from the size of their systems, how do computers differ? You'll hear different computer processors described as having differences in power and capability. The nitty gritty of CPUs gets very technical. When you're looking for a business-application package such as word processing, you may not hear or understand much about them—who wants to know about megahertz? For the most part you don't need to. You should know, however, that the CPU dictates the speed at which the computer can handle data or text.

Computer processors respond to electrical impulses sent to their circuits and temporarily stored there. Each location in their memory circuit holds one "bit" of information. A bit is one "on" or "off" impulse, represented as a zero (0) or a one (1). The number of bits that the processor can use at one time determines the speed at which it can work. Each character entered in the computer is represented by a unique sequence of these on and off impulses (approximately 8 bits); CPUs are typically broken down into 8-bit, 16-bit, or 32 bit processors. Essentially, that means that they can handle one character, two characters, or four characters at a time. The smaller the number, the slower the computer processor, and the less it can handle at one time. Larger computers usually have faster processors.

In the microcomputer marketplace there has been a big stir recently over the arrival of new 16-bit and 32-bit processors. The standard for micros in the past has been 8-bit, while 16- and 32-bit systems were mini- and mainframe territory. With faster processors, micros become more powerful and flexible, while still costing significantly less then their larger cousins.

If you select a single-user system, the speed of the processor may not affect you very much. If you are looking for a larger system and want to attach a number of terminals to it, however, pay attention. Four operators using a word-processing system at the same time may find the computer's response to them much slower than one or two users on the same system.

MEMORY

When you press keys on your keyboard, the computer sends a picture of the characters to the screen; at the same time, it places them in its memory until told to take other action. The memory of the computer stores the word-processing program (the set of instructions that make the computer a word processor), as well as collecting the text you type in. The computer needs plenty of room to hold both the word-processing instructions and your text.

Types of Memory

On the insides of your word processor or computer are two kinds of memory: Read Only Memory (ROM) and Random Access Memory (RAM).

Read Only Memory (memory the computer can read from, but cannot send text to) contains instructions or "programs" that are "hard-wired" into your computer. They're present when you turn on the machine. These instructions include basic "foundation" information for the computer. Some systems contain more "firmware," as ROM is also called, than others. Some word-processing systems, such as the early Vydec models, hold most of their instructions in firmware. These systems have all their word-processing features present as soon as you turn them on. Read Only Memory is sometimes called "non-volatile," because its contents remain when you turn off the system and don't have to be loaded from disk each time you turn it on.

Random Access Memory, RAM, is the memory (or space) that you load your programs into from a disk, and which stores the text as you type it. This memory is sometimes called "volatile" because it is erased when you turn off the system. It's random because the computer can find what it wants fast, almost at random, anywhere in the memory.

How Much Do You Need?

When you hear terms like 128K, 256K, 512K, these amounts refer to the number of bytes, or characters, that can be stored in the computer's RAM memory. (A byte is eight on/off impulses, enough to code one character. The "K" stands for "kilobytes," or thousands of bytes. Actually, 1K is equal to 1024 bytes, but it's easier to think of them as rounded to thousands.)

You need enough RAM to be able to hold both your program and text. The size of your system, the word-processing program you use, and the size of the documents you create will dictate how much memory you need. A single-user stand-alone system may need only 48K, 64K, or 128K memory. A multi-user system usually requires more memory.

Adding More Memory

On some systems, in order to add another terminal or workstation, you'll need to add more memory. This is necessary when you need extra room for several users to work with programs and text simultaneously. Increased memory can allow the system to work faster, too. When there's room for more text in memory, information doesn't have to be transferred back and forth from the disks as frequently. The time the computer spends communicating with the disk can seem significantly slow once you're used to a fast response between keyboard and processor.

Different computers handle memory differently. Some treat the space on disks as an extension of internal memory, allowing you to work with programs and documents that are larger than would normally fit in the memory. The vendor should tell you how much memory you should have for your particular word-processing needs, whether more can be added, and what benefits you would derive from adding more.

DISK STORAGE

Since one of the reasons you buy a word processor is to be able to make changes to text later without retyping an entire document, you'll periodically "save" what you've typed—or perhaps the computer can do it for you automatically. "Saving" involves making a copy of whatever text you've typed; the copy is stored on some sort of magnetic medium, such as disk, cartridge, or reel-to-reel tape. Disks are the most common form of storage and come in two types: "floppy diskettes" and "hard disks."

When in use by the computer, disks spin around inside a cabinet called a "disk drive." A mechanism in the drive, comparable to the needle on a phonograph, reads information from the disks into the computer, or writes instructions from the computer onto the disks.

Floppy disks look somewhat like small records encased in square cardboard covers. They can be removed from the drive. You may or may not see hard disks, which are called "hard" because they're enclosed in a case that doesn't bend. Some are removable; some remain fixed inside the drive.

A hard disk drive; the eight-inch hard disk is capable of storing large numbers of characters. (Photo courtesy of Data Terminals Communication)

Disks are used as both input and output devices (I/O devices) to the computer. When you "save" a document, a copy goes from the computer onto the disk. That's output. When you start a software program, you often "load" (or copy) it into the computer from the disk. That's input. You'll also be loading in documents that you've previously saved and want to change.

Disks are your word processor's file cabinets. They store copies of your documents in magnetic form.

Floppy Diskettes

Floppy diskettes get their name because they're flexible to the touch. This doesn't mean that you can bend them without harm; it simply means that when you hold one, it feels somewhat limp. A floppy diskette looks very much like a 45 rpm record enclosed in a square cardboard cover. Part of the disk shows through the cover. When in use by your computer, the disk drive reads data from the exposed portion of the disk as it spins inside its case.

Sizes. There are two basic sizes of floppy diskettes, 8 inch and 5¼ inch. Eight-inch "floppies" were introduced by IBM in the 1960s. They were the standard disk for many small word processors for a long time, and hold at least 240K, or 240,000 characters. The 5¼-inch "mini-floppy," introduced in 1976 by Shugart, holds from 90K, or 90,000 characters, to about 600K. Some new versions of 5¼-inch diskettes can hold up to 600K.

Densities. To increase the amount of text that can be stored on diskette, different "densities" of floppy disks have been developed.

Standard 8- or 5¼-inch disks are now known as single-density disks. Double-density disks can pack twice the number of characters onto the same diskette. Some mini-diskettes are even "quad-density," allowing four times the usual number of characters to be stored on them.

Single-Sided or Double-Sided? Some floppy diskettes are single-sided. That means that they store data on one side only. On others you can use both sides, again doubling the usual amount of storage you can get with a diskette.

Just because a diskette can be double-density or double-sided doesn't mean your computer can use it that way. Be sure to ask if the disk drive, and the interface between the computer and the disk drive, can use double-density or double-sided disks.

How Is Density Determined? When you take a new blank diskette out of a box, it's not yet ready to be used by your word processor. It must first be "formatted" in such a way that your computer can communicate with it. Most systems have special programs for preparing diskettes. This process of getting a new diskette ready is sometimes called "formatting a disk," sometimes "initializing a disk."

Around the floppy diskette are "tracks," like the grooves in a record. Information can be stored and recalled from random places on the disk. To make this possible, each track is broken down into small "sectors." When you format, or initialize a diskette, your computer goes through the entire disk, sector by sector, erasing any current contents. Since diskettes are magnetized, they can sometimes pick up symbols that have nothing to do with what you want stored on them. (If you hear the term "garbage on the disk," this is what is being talked about.) Initializing a disk also lets the computer fill a few of the sectors with the basic information it needs to communicate with the disk.

On most systems, your disk will automatically be formatted to either single-density or double-density, according to what the system requires. A few systems can use both single- and double-density disks, and will ask which density you want to use.

Can You Use the Same Disks on Different Computers? With a phonograph record, you can play it on any equipment and hear the same music, but this is not so with most computer disks. You may be able to start with the same blank disk and format it for many different systems, but once it is formatted and used to store programs and text, you can't always insert it in different types of word processors and be able to read your text. The operating-system software, which communicates between your computer and the disks, formats your disk to store data its own way. Then the word-processing software inserts its own special characters into the text. Most word-processing manufacturers have developed their own operating systems and software, and there is little compatibility between equipment made by different companies. You'll find more compatibility in the microcomputer world, but if you want to use the same disk and data in different types of equipment, your best bet is to try it first.

Hard Disks

Hard disks hold much more information than floppy diskettes. While floppy disk storage is measured in "Ks," or kilobytes, hard disks are measured in "Mgs," or megabytes. Roughly, a megabyte can be considered a million characters. Hard disks are typically at least 5 Mg (with room for 5,000,000 characters), and may be 120 Mg, or even greater. (That would be roughly 3,330 to 80,000 pages of text, or more.)

Hard disks were originally used by the large mainframe and minicomputers to store millions of characters. Part of the drop in price of small computers has come with the mass production of floppy diskettes, because hard disks were very expensive—far too expensive for many small companies. As advances in technology and competition have brought the price of hard disks down, they've been made more accessible to many one- and two-user computers. Now it's common to be able to purchase a microcomputer-based system containing a hard disk, or to be able to add one later.

Fixed vs. Removable Hard Disks. Large computers often have both fixed and removable hard disks. Fixed disks come as part of the system and can't be taken out and stored until they are used later. Removable disks, sometimes called "cartridge disks," can be taken out of the computer. When a system doesn't have removable cartridge disks, you need some way to create a backup copy of the data stored on the disk fixed in the computer. On large systems, this may be done with reel-to-reel tape. On smaller systems, hard disks are usually fixed, and the backup copy is made on floppies.

Advantages of Hard Disks. In addition to having greater storage capacity, hard disks spin much faster than floppies. When the computer communicates with the disk, either to store information or retrieve program instructions, you may scarcely know it's doing it. The information appears almost immediately with hard disks. With floppies, there may be a pause while the exchange between computer and disk takes place, and you'll hear a kind of *k-klunk* from the floppy drives. Hard disks are usually quieter and faster.

You may or may not need a hard disk on your word processor. Even a single-sided, single-density 8-inch floppy disk can store a hundred pages or more of text. That number doubles if you have double-density floppies. If you're looking at a single-user system, and if most of your documents don't exceed ten or twenty pages, floppies may be all you will ever need. If you plan to add another workstation to your system and want more than one operator to share the same files, or if you constantly create hundred-page reports, you may find you want a hard disk immediately. Even if you don't think you need one now, your needs may change, so find out if hard disks can be added in the future.

Other Types of Disks

Although floppy diskettes and hard disks now prevail in most word processors, new types of disk drives and disks are being developed and used. Already 3¼-inch and 3½-inch removable cartridges are being used in some microcomputers. Small enough to be carried in a shirt pocket, the single-sided version of this cartridge can store 250,000 to 300,000 characters. The double-sided, double-density version can hold 600,000 to 800,000 characters.

SOFTWARE

By itself, a computer is a box of hardware—nuts, bolts, circuits, metal, and plastic. Before it can do anything, the machine needs instructions, and those instructions come from programs. Programs are actually groupings of instructions. Often a number of programs are used together to provide "applications software." "Application" is the task that the computer is being used for, or applied to, and "software" is a general term for programs. "Word-processing software," then, is a group of programs used to apply computer power to the task of processing words.

When you first turn on a word processor and it beeps or flashes a message on the screen, those reactions come from software. The software that is active as soon as the machine is turned on has already been "burnt in," as it is called, to circuits on the inside of the computer. Programs already present in the hardware circuits are sometimes called "firmware."

Other word-processing capabilities begin as special programs that are "loaded" (moved) into the computer's memory from a disk. Sometimes there is room in the computer's memory for only part of the instructions at one time. If you press a function key requiring instructions that aren't in memory, the computer may communicate with the disk to find them, and then bring a copy of them into memory, temporarily replacing some other instructions. How does the computer know to communicate with the disks and find the instructions? By using a program called an operating system. Operating systems tell the computer what to do with the word-processing program and how to communicate with all the computer "peripherals"—that is, all the pieces attached to the computer (terminal, disks, printer, etc.). Sometimes the operating system is resident, or hardwired, into memory. Sometimes it exists on disk and is the first thing the computer "reads in" to its memory when it communicates with the disk.

It used to be that when you bought a word processor, you paid one price for the entire system: computer processor, disk drive, video terminal, printer, and software. You can still buy systems bundled together like this, and many companies specialize in selling you complete packages, or "solutions." Increasingly, however, the application software is being "unbundled," or sold separately. This is particularly true when you look at systems that provide both word- and data-processing capability. You select the software you want, and each chunk of it is a separate item. Even when the basic word-processing capabilities are included in the initial price, "optional features" may cost extra. And although you pick out the software you need, you are limited to types that run on your hardware. Selecting software doesn't mean that you get your pick of any word-processing package on the market. Software must be able to run on the machine you want.

Since software is what makes a computer into a word processor, in many ways it is the most important item you're purchasing. The software dictates what word-processing functions are available and, ultimately, if the system will do what you need. When you compare capabilities from one system to another, you're mostly comparing software.

How Do Word-Processing Software Programs Differ?

In addition to offering different capabilities, word-processing software packages take different approaches as to how those capabilities are accomplished. We've touched on some of these approaches as we've talked about the hardware components. For example, it's the software that dictates how your characters appear on the screen. A screen may have the ability to display underlining or boldface, but it won't show unless the software is programmed to show it. It's also the software that lets you make use of special function keys. Your keyboard can conceivably have an extra row of keys with labels like CUT, PASTE, MOVE, INSERT, etc., that do nothing with certain software. The software interprets your keystrokes and tells the computer what to do with them.

Many factors that determine how easy it is for you to use a word processor depend on the interaction of the software with the hardware. Just as your terminal might have the ability to display underlining and your software not take advantage of it, the software can only work with what the hardware can do.

When you buy a word-processing system, you can expect it to have provisions for input, correction, storage, and printing of documents. You can also expect that it will be able to do what you can do on your typewriter: change margins and tabs, for example. Features such as automatic word wrap are now also standard. So, what will vary? Lots of things. We'll touch on a few.

Orientation. Does the system work with one page at a time, or with a whole document? Let's say you have a ten-page report. On some systems, each page of it is treated separately, and you work with one page at a time. You enter text on one page, file it away, and then enter the next page. To move a paragraph from one page to another requires calling up the page containing the paragraph, marking the paragraph, copying it to a temporary "page," putting the current page away, recalling the page you want to move it to, and inserting the temporary page. Now if the page you made the insert on is too long, you must "repaginate," or tell the system to shift the text around on the rest of the pages so that each page contains the correct number of lines.

On "document-oriented systems," you work with the entire document; the system treats it as one long scroll of text. As the text scrolls up on the screen, you may see lines appear to mark the ending and beginning of a new page. To move a paragraph, you scroll the text so that the paragraph appears on your screen, mark it, scroll the text to where you want to make the insert, press a MOVE key, and the text is moved. At the same time, the document may be automatically repaginated.

Document Size. Even when systems are document-oriented, the maximum possible length of each document may vary. Some systems have a maximum number of lines or pages per document. Others are dependent on the amount of memory in the computer. And some have no limit; as long as there's room on the disk, you can keep on writing.

Limitations in length are largely determined by where the text of the document is kept while you work on it. When you type in new text, it goes into the computer's memory. When the memory is full, something has to happen before you can continue entering text. Some systems automatically copy the text onto a disk, making room in the computer's memory for more. This may happen every few pages, or it may happen when the memory is full. These systems treat disk storage as an extension of their memory, moving text back and forth between them as needed. Other systems can work only with text that is in their memory; they don't talk to the disk while you're working on a document. You must specify when text should be transferred to disk, and when the memory is full, that's as large as your document can be. This limit may be the equivalent of five or six pages, or may be up to forty pages. Usually these systems have some way to link documents together when you print them so that they can be treated as one long document.

In addition to allowing longer documents, systems that automatically save your text on disk at various intervals help to protect your work. If the power in your building should suddenly go off, chances are that any text present in the computer's memory will be erased. When the system automatically copies to disk every few pages, you won't lose nearly as much work.

Where on the Screen Do You Enter Text? Where you can position your cursor on the screen dictates where you can enter text. Word-processing software uses one of two approaches: on the bottom line or anywhere on the screen.

When you use a typewriter, the typing position moves horizontally across the piece of paper. When you complete a line, you press the RETURN key, and the paper rolls up to the next line. If you want to add characters to a line you've already typed, you roll the paper back.

Some word processors use this same approach. The cursor imitates a typing element, moving across the screen. The characters that you type always appear on the same line, usually at the bottom of the screen, and the text scrolls up the screen as you complete more lines. To make an addition or change to text, you scroll, or roll it down to the entry line, just as you would with a piece of paper. Since this approach is similar to using a typewriter, a new user gets the hang of entering text onto a screen quickly.

Other systems have what is called a "floating cursor." This means that the cursor can be moved anywhere on the screen to enter text and make changes. Text can also be scrolled up and down, so you have two ways to get to the position you want. The main advantage of a floating cursor is in editing or changing text. If you're making changes to a paragraph, you can see the whole paragraph while you make changes to the beginning of it. You can view text above and below the change.

What You See Is What You Get—Or Is It? Ideally, the text you see onscreen should be displayed the same way it will print out. This feature is better on some systems than on others, and it depends on what kinds of special formatting you do. If most of your documents are general text in paragraphs, there's a good chance that what you see onscreen will resemble the way the text will print.

Here are some formats that you can often indicate in documents but won't always see onscreen:

Right margin justification
Sub- and superscripts
Varying line spacing
Underlines
Boldface characters
Italics and other typefonts
Special characters (such as scientific symbols)
Wide lines
Page numbers
Headers and footers

If you can't see these onscreen, what do you see? How do you know when you've requested a special format, and which text will be affected? Word-processing designers have found various ways to accomplish this.

Control Characters in the Text. Almost all special formats are indicated by inserting some kind of control, or special character, in your document. When you press an UNDERLINE key, and your text is displayed as underlined, a special character (invisible to you) has been stored at the beginning and ending of the underlined text. You see the results of the special characters in the form of the underlining. If the system cannot display underlining, pressing the UNDERLINE key may cause some other character to appear at the beginning and end of text to be underlined. The next line shows how one system indicates underlining onscreen:

```
The /\simportant/\s idea
```

When printed, the above line looks like this:

```
The important idea
```

The biggest problem with this method of indicating underlining or other formatting (aside from not being able to see how the printed result will look) is that it adds extra characters to the line of text. Within paragraphs this isn't necessarily a problem, but if you're working with columns of numbers, it becomes much harder to see if they're lined up the way you want them. For example, with this method of underlining, these following printed columns of numbers:

```
          JANUARY    FEBRUARY   MARCH      APRIL

          125.36     437.45     125.00     360.75
          175.34     132.30     350.50     450.30
          300.70     569.75     470.50     811.05
```

may look like this onscreen:

```
          /\SJANUARY    FEBRUARY    MARCH      APRIL/\S

          125.36        437.45      125.00     360.75
          /\S175.34     132.30      350.50     450.30/\S
          300.70        569.75      470.50     811.05
```

View Modes. One solution to the use of control characters is a "view mode." Systems that have view modes don't show any symbols within the regular text when you insert special formats. No matter how much underlining, bolding, or sub- and superscripting you do in a document, the characters appear the same onscreen. To see which characters or portions of text will be printed with special formatting, you can switch to a "view mode," which displays the text and the specially imbedded codes. This method allows you to see the spacing of your characters correctly most of the time, but doesn't clue you in if you've pressed a key by mistake. If you forget to check the view mode, you could conceivably underline an entire document without knowing it on some of these systems.

Dot Commands. Another favorite substitute for displaying formats, common in word-processing software developed for microcomputers, is "dot commands." Dot commands get their name because most of them start with a dot, or period (.). Some use an angle bracket (⟩) instead, but the effect is the same.

On the line preceding the text you want formatted, you type in a series of characters that tell the computer how to format. For example, to underline the word "memorandum" at the top of a page, you might type this:

```
                    .ul
                    memorandum
```

The ".ul" tells the system to underline the next line.

Dot commands can be very distracting when you aren't used to them. The page seems full of gibberish. But you can learn to ignore them when you're reading a passage for sense.

Dot commands can also make reformatting text easier. Let's say you want to change the right margin from 65 to 70 and reformat your document with slightly longer lines. Some word processors that format text onscreen require that you change the margin and then scroll through the entire document to realign the text. Since word processors that use dot commands for formatting don't actually format the text until you print it, all you have to do is change the line in your document with the dot command.

Optional Software Capabilities

On some systems, the more advanced or specialized word-processing functions are "optional"; that means that you pay an extra price to get them, because they are not considered standard word processing. Not all systems have them, and some systems do include them as part of their standard package. If you need these capabilities, be sure to find out if they're available, and if so, whether there is an extra charge for them.

Merge List. This option may be known as "mail merge," "mass mailing," or "list processing." It allows you to enter variable information, such as names and addresses, in one document, and merge them with the contents of another document, say, a standard letter or contract. You type the list once and the letter once, and the system combines the two and prints customized letters. Often you can select a part of the list. For example, say that you want to send a certain letter only to your customers in Los Angeles. The system can go through your name-and-address file and find all the entries for Los Angeles. When you want to do another mass mailing, you only have to type in the text of the new letter: your address list has already been created.

Sort. Sort capabilities often work with merge list capabilities. Sorting is the ability to organize a list of data in the order you want it. Sorting can be alphabetical, numerical, or both.

Math. Math packages allow you to perform calculations within documents. You might be able to total a column of numbers, for example, or create a new column next to the first, with an additional 10 percent added on.

Communications. Communications software allows you to send and retrieve information from other word processors or computers. Later in this section we'll be talking about the devices that let you communicate. Communications software is necessary to let you use these devices.

Spelling. A spelling-check program uses a dictionary of words on disk and, at your request, compares the text you've typed against the dictionary. Any unrecognized words are flagged for you to correct.

Index and Table of Contents Generation. This facility allows you to mark headings or words and phrases to be used to create an index and/or table of contents. The program will remember the page number of each item and be able to extract it along with the word or phrase, then alphabetize the entries.

Software for More Than Word Processing

Some word-processing systems allow you to use programs for other tasks on the same equipment. The manufacturer may have other software "packages" available (General Ledger or Accounts Payable and Receivable, for instance), or you may be able to use other companies' software with your equipment. We discuss this in detail in the sections on "Hybrid Systems: Word Processing Combined with Data Processing" and "Microcomputers as Word Processors" in Chapter 4, "Narrowing the Field," but we'll mention a few possibilities now.

Electronic Worksheets. What word processing does for writing and typing, electronic worksheets do for financial spreadsheets, calculations, and projections. These programs simulate a spreadsheet on the display screen, with rows and columns of boxes, or entry positions. You can enter headings with values under them, and then have the system do the required calculations.

Most electronic worksheets are designed to help you answer "what if" questions. If sales grow at 30 percent next year, how many units should be manufactured? What if sales grow at only 15 percent? Once you've entered the current year's figures (or week's or month's, depending on what you're projecting), you type in a "growth formula," and the result is displayed onscreen.

Electronic worksheets usually allow you to copy entries you've already made, change their positions on the worksheet, insert new rows and columns, and format your entries in various ways. For instance, you might want some numbers to be displayed with two decimal places and a dollar sign in front, for dollars and cents. You might want other numbers to be displayed as integers, or whole numbers. You might want some columns to be narrower than others. These formats are displayed onscreen and when the worksheet is printed out.

Data-Base-Management Systems. Like many people, you probably work with a great deal of information that you wish could be organized so that it is available to you at a moment's notice. Database-management systems (DBMS) help you do this. A "data base" is made up of many pieces of information that have been entered into a computer. For example, let's say you have a customer list. For each customer, you have:

- Company name and address
- Contact names
- Type of company
- Products they buy from you
- How many units they've purchased
- How often they purchase units
- Discount rate
- Identification number
- Balance due
- Last date paid
- Last date billed
- Back orders
- Special comments

Once you've entered information like this into a DBMS system, you can ask the computer to get various kinds of information for you. For example, you might want a list of all companies whose balance due is greater than $500. Or if one of your products is delayed in manufacturing, you might want a list of all companies who have ordered that product, so that you can notify them. Or you might want a list of all customers located in New Orleans who buy a particular product from you.

Data-base-management systems organize large amounts of information in one place and let you retrieve it according to your needs.

If this description reminds you of our discussion of mail-merge capabilities, it is indeed similar. Mail-merge or list-processing programs are limited types of data-base-management systems, tailored to address one type of office need. A true DBMS system gives you much greater capability and flexibility.

Calendars. Two types of calendar programs are now being provided by some word processing or information-processing equipment. The individual calendar simulates your desk calendar onscreen and helps you organize your time. You can enter appointments, "to do" lists, due dates, etc. You might be able to ask your computer to find the earliest two-hour slot available for a meeting. You might use a tickler file on your accounts, too, reminding you to follow up on important phone calls or projects.

Shared-calendar programs are also available, usually on multiterminal systems or networks of systems that can communicate with one another. Groups can schedule their time with this kind of a program.

PRINTERS

If you expect your word-processing system to turn out business letters, formal proposals, bills, reports, charts, or checks—in short, any item showing words typed on paper—you'll need a printer. Of course, you can "process words" onscreen, without a printer. And you can store your text, or send it over cables to another word processor, without a printer. That's why some computer people call a printer a "peripheral"—meaning that it is equipment on the periphery, far from the heart of the central processing unit. But to you, a printer may be central. When someone looks over your writing, they judge you, in part, by the quality of your printing.

So if you want to get your words on paper, you'll have to face the question: which printer is best for me?

The answer depends on what kind of printing you need. How sharp an image do you require? As clear as the one an office typewriter can produce? Or will fuzzy and pale be okay? Do you churn out hundreds of pages at a time so that you really have to have a printer that can spew out four pages a minute? Or would you settle for something that's only twice as fast as a human? Do you occasionally use Greek letters, or Chinese characters? While printing, do you want to be able to use the rest of the system for entering new material? Do you want a printer that can draw pictures, graphs, pie charts? And what about colored inks? Do you want 6, 16, or 64 colors? Do you prefer to print on your own letterhead, or is computer paper acceptable? How loud a printer can you stand, without going crazy? And how much control do you need over the various functions of the printer?

Clearly, the printer you hook up to your word processor is a lot more complicated than the letterpress you may have played with in school. Back then, you picked up wood blocks with metal letters on them, locked those in a form, inked it, laid paper on top, and pressed that down on the damp letters. The result—a slightly smeared message, smelling of oil of cloves and the intoxicating odor of fresh ink.

Now, with the printer linked to a computer, you can print things faster and cheaper, with less energy and with more control. And the printer itself has become intelligent—there's a microprocessor inside it to direct operations. So on some systems, you can change from English to Japanese characters, set many-layered formulas, or plot the three dimensions of a volcano—just by giving the command back at your keyboard.

But how do the new printers create letters on the page? There are a half dozen ways—and each technique affects the look of the page, the speed of the printer, and the range of characters or graphics available. Thus many of your most important choices will be based on the kind of print technology involved: dot matrix, thermal, electrostatic, ink jet, laser, full-form character, and plotter.

Dot Matrix

You've seen this style of printing on most computerized bills. Light gray and irregular, the letters seem to jiggle on the page, coming in and out of focus. That's because they're not made of continuous lines. They're really a series of dots, fitted into a grid known as a matrix. Here's the way a dot matrix printer breaks down the letter *K:*

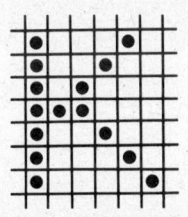

Now when it examines each box in the grid, the system will ask itself: on or off? If on, then it drives a pin against an inked ribbon, making a dot on the paper in the particular spot. In this illustration, we see there are 5×8 boxes, so for each letter the computer must make 40 decisions before the letter is complete. But since the computer can think quickly, and since the mechanical operation is simple, such dot matrix printers can create a few hundred letters per second.

The more dots, the sharper the letter will look. With a 9×11 grid, you'll find the dots get closer together, and the lines look more continuous—not smooth, but at least flowing. To make the image even more precise, some systems make repeated passes over the same area, shifting the printhead slightly on each pass to connect the earlier dots and darken the whole.

One of the advantages of the dot matrix system is that you can control each dot, so you can create characters beyond the traditional abc's. You can buy programs that will let you print out Japanese characters, Greek letters, French accents, and German umlauts. You can write your own program for new symbols. And you can use packaged programs to connect all the dots in drawings or abstract images—a company logo, or a chart, or a blurred photograph.

The dot matrix style of printer will be useful to you if:

- You don't care about "letter-quality" printing (printing that looks like an executive's correspondence).
- You want a lot of speed, because you have a lot of documents.

- You want to be able to create complex graphics.
- You want to create or use unusual character sets.

Beware of inexpensive dot matrix printers if you want to impress people with your neat reports and sharp-edged proposals. Some vendors will boast that with multiple passes, their dot matrix printer produces copy that looks "just like" a regular letter. That may be true if the reader has cataracts. But to anyone who can read street signs, most dot matrix printing looks fuzzy. Rule of thumb: it's fine for rough drafts, for your own use, or for bills and checks, for any use in which the reader doesn't care about the look.

Thermal. Used mainly on calculators and cash registers, thermal printing reproduces the dot matrix in a set of boxes held close to heat-sensitive paper; by heating the right boxes, the system burns squares onto the paper in those spots, creating a fairly jagged but recognizable letter. The result is a pale-gray message on smelly paper—tolerable in a sales receipt or calculation tape, but crude for correspondence.

Electrostatic. In electrostatic printing, the grid is placed behind the paper and charges the appropriate squares, so that flecks of dried ink are drawn electrostatically to the spot—just as in a Xerox. This means the ink's rich and black, though the letter "V" still looks like two staircases, and "O" hardly looks round. Quieter than any pin-thwacking printer, an electrostatic system can print five or six pages a minute. Like thermal printing, it is potentially a very fast system, but it isn't widely used for word processing, because it involves using toner, buying special paper, and doing frequent troubleshooting, as with a copying machine.

Ink Jet. This is a jet-speed system—it sets up a charged grid, just as electrostatic systems do, but instead of tossing bits of dried ink, it sprays the wet ink directly onto the paper. Since the droplets don't weigh much, they take off even faster than the powder—and much faster than metal pins. So you can print a hundred pages in three or four minutes. Of course, the basic equipment will cost a lot, but the results can be amazing. There are more dots on the grid, so the letters look more fully formed than on any other dot matrix system.

Laser. This is the most precise of all the dot matrix systems, since a laser can make a very fine dot. It is possible to have a lot of dots in the grid and come very close to a continuous line. The laser focuses on a tiny spot on a rotating drum; that becomes charged, and when paper lands on top of it, draws dried ink, as in a copying machine. The main advantage of the laser over other electrostatic systems is the precision and detail of the lines. Because of the cost of the optical equipment needed to direct the laser, this type of system has been even more expensive than the ink-jet system, costing as much as $400,000, but small models are available for less than $5000.

Fully Formed Characters

Some systems enable you to print a whole character in one stroke; your typewriter, for instance, slaps one key against the ribbon, and voila! You have a fully formed character. No dots, no boxes, no jagged edges.

Because this style of printing looks like what you're used to in business correspondence, it's often called "letter-quality," to distinguish it from the fuzzy dot matrix. It's also called "impact printing," which is a good description, since at some point in the process a raised metal or plastic surface hits against a ribbon, which bangs ink onto the page. Of course any dot matrix system that uses pins makes an impact, too—it's just much lighter, and not so obvious.

The simplest form of fully formed characters comes directly from an electric typewriter. For $500 or so, you can buy a conversion kit that will act as a computer for your typewriter, taking signals from your word processor and translating these into impulses to the six magnets that position the type ball. Or for about the same cost, you can buy a set of "magic fingers"—a microprocessor that activates levers pressing down on the keys from a box you lock on top of the keyboard of almost any electric typewriter. Or if you have an electronic typewriter—in which the keys send electronic, not mechanical, signals to the type ball—you can insert another black box, to take signals from your word processor and translate them into signals the typewriter recognizes. Some companies even sell the box already installed in the electronic typewriter (for around $1500). These attachments let you go on typing short memos directly on your typewriter, when you are not using it as a printer. You'll get first-rate printing, but you may wear the machine out if you keep it going steadily for a long time, because the computer pushes it to work at top speed all the time, whereas a human tends to type in bursts, resting in between. The speed of this kind of printing is about four seconds a line.

At least twice as fast—often four or five times faster—is the daisy wheel, or thimble. The daisy wheel is a circle of keys that has the ability to print 20 to 300 fully formed characters per second. (The more expensive ones move faster.) You can change the daisy wheel fairly easily, snapping in a new set of characters, provided that the manufacturer produces different typefaces. So as long as you don't need too many strange sets of characters, you'll do all right with daisy wheels. But you can't easily create graphics, unless you're willing to make them out of dollar signs and hash marks.

Daisy wheel printers usually cost more than dot matrix printers: starting at around $750, they quickly go up to $5000. For beautiful printing, then, you may pay more for the printer than for your word processor.

Plotter

A plotter uses one or more pens, controlled by signals from a computer, to draw charts, graphs, architectural renderings, and pictures. Sometimes you can just buy different-colored pens at a stationery store and put them in the plotter. In this way, you can create anywhere from 6 to 64 colors—and by putting one color on top of another, you can multiply that even farther. You may have to buy a new program, to translate your keyboard strokes into pictures; and you might even have to buy a new video screen, to handle the complex diagrams you want to create. Few screens can handle more than 16 colors now, so you may not be able to preview a drawing onscreen.

Deciding on a Printer

In deciding which of the preceding technologies would be best for you, you must select what you really need—and what you want to avoid—in several areas:

Quality of image—fuzzy or sharp	Paper handling ability
Number of character sets available	Ease of control and reliability
Speed of printing	Noise Level
Graphics ability	Cost

Quality of Image. Among the systems that cost somewhere in the range of $1000 to $6000, the sharpest letters come from typewriters, daisy wheels, and thimble wheels. If you've got a huge volume of work to do, and you want it all sharp, pick an ink jet or a laser system. However, these are expensive.

But if you're willing to settle for shakier images, any dot matrix system will do. For less than $500, you can get a very reliable, fairly fast dot matrix system—certainly faster than most daisy wheel systems or adapted typewriter systems. If you have a large volume of work, you can get a line printer, which prints a line at a time. If your printout's disposable, like sales receipts, you could get a very cheap thermal or electrostatic system; the look is terrible, but readable.

For smooth lines and multiple colors in your drawings, reach for a plotter. Not really meant for regular text, the plotter can generate large titles, company logos, and three-dimensional drawings, using pens you buy at your local stationery shop.

Character Sets. If you like using a number of different type fonts—Old Gothic, American Century, and Times Roman, say—or if you want to use the same typeface in various sizes and styles—sometimes italic, sometimes extra bold—then you'll want a system in which you can easily change character sets.

With an electric or electronic typewriter, you can quickly switch type elements; with any daisy wheel printer, you can snap in a new wheel fairly easily when you need it. But in both, you have to buy the particular element, and you have to put it on manually. You're also limited to those supplied by the manufacturer of your printer. You can't create your own characters, and you may not find the exact set of characters you want.

If you're after hard-to-find characters (Korean, say), or if you're making up new ones, you may want to look into a dot matrix printer that accepts various programs—including some you may have to create. Many dot matrix printers come with four or five different character sets already programmed and ready to go. Sometimes, for instance, a dot matrix system will offer you a draft, with fewer dots in the grid, and a letter-quality version, with more dots per grid; the draft version is faster, the letter-quality, sharper.

With many dot matrix printers, the programming lets you expand or condense the characters on any line, so you can cram 80 letters into a space you'd normally use for 60, say, or widen the characters, so they fill up the space of 120. With some dot matrix printers, you can tilt the letters, or rotate them around the points of the compass.

A few cautions: some dot matrix systems omit descenders—the part of the letter that descends below the line. This can make the lowercase versions of "g," "j," "p," "q," and "y" look very odd. Some avoid serifs, too—those little lines that extend from the main line of the letter in some typefaces. And some also run underlining straight through the bottom of the letters, rather than underneath them. If any of these matter to you, be sure to examine carefully a printout from any system you're thinking of buying.

In both dot matrix and letter-quality systems, you may be able to get proportional spacing—that is, when you justify text, lining it up on the righthand margins, the system doesn't just yank one word and place it over at the end of the line; rather, it inserts a little space between all the letters in the line, so your eye can't spot the way the line has been stretched to fit. Often this capability comes with more expensive printers.

Speed. Every time the printer has to make a move, it slows down the printing. That's why the typewriter and daisy wheel systems take the longest time to print copy, even though they produce the sharpest images. A whole type element has to lift up, shift around, pound through the ribbon, then settle back for the next letter. The usual speed for this kind of printing: 20 to 50 characters per second. Dot matrix systems that use pins work faster, because each pin is tiny—they tatoo the letters on. The average speeds are 100 to 200 characters per second. Even faster are electrostatic, ink jet, and laser systems, where you're just waiting for little bits of ink dust, drops of ink, and rays of light.

Another thing that slows down printing is the carriage return. If the type element has to race back to the lefthand margin every time it begins a new line, that adds seconds to the printing. So some systems teach the printer to remember the next line backward, and instead of returning to the lefthand margin, print the next line from right to left. That way all the type element has to do is drop down a line and continue. This two-way printing is called bidirectional—a sign that your printer will work faster than others, particularly if your text tends to go out to the margins.

Another waste of time is space blanks. Let's say you've got two words at the beginning of one line, then you skip three lines before beginning the regular text. A traditional system plods through every space in every line, expecting a letter. This takes time. Smarter systems feature short-line seeking. This means that the printer skips over the blank areas at top speed, slowing down to print again only when text is found.

Two other factors affect time—the time you want to spend at the keyboard entering new data. If you have a very basic system, you won't be able to type in anything new while it's sending text over to the printer. But with more memory in the printer, your word processor can send over a lot of text at once, storing it all inside the printer in something called a buffer (it acts as a buffer between the computer and the printer). Then the printer can draw text as fast as it needs, without making you wait to use the computer. The larger the buffer in the printer, the faster you can get back to work on your keyboard, while the printing takes place in the background. A small buffer might hold 2000 characters—about a page; a larger one could store as much as 100 pages.

And the wires used to send information from the computer to the printer can also affect the speed with which your computer clears out the text and frees itself up for your next ideas. Some systems use only one line and send one letter after another; this connection between computer and printer is called "serial interface," and it's slower than a parallel interface, in which half a dozen or more lines carry information at once.

If you have a lot to print every hour of the day, with tight deadlines to meet, you will probably want to go with a dot matrix system, with bidirectional printing, short-line seeking, a large buffer, and a parallel interface—even if the printing is somewhat inelegant. But if clarity and beauty are important, you may have to wait a few minutes while your daisy wheel thwacks away.

Graphics. Creating color graphs, drawing pictures, printing different text in six colors—these are possible now, but the technology's still going through growing pains. There are very few video screens that display more than 16 colors—and most of those are expensive. And to control color and line, you will probably have to buy a special program, called a graphics package, which may or may not run on your system, despite the claims of the dealer.

The crudest graphics come with daisy wheel printers, which you must switch into the "graphics mode." Speed may drop, and the resulting pictures will seem clumsy compared to what you're used to in books and magazines.

You'll probably have more control over the graphics in a dot matrix system, since there the computer can control each dot. The more dots, the sharper the picture. In some current "high-resolution" systems, you can control more than a million dots within an 8½ × 11" sheet of paper—and even so, the images are not super-sharp. To get control over those dots, though, you may well have to adapt your word processor and your printer, adding new boards, and buying new programs.

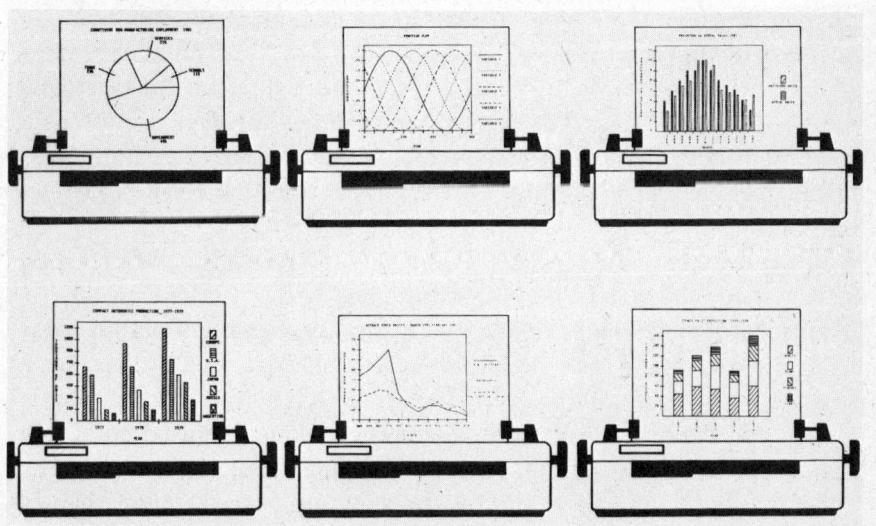

Graphics from a Vector software program called ACCUCHART produced on dot matrix printers. (Photo courtesy of Vector Graphic)

The same graph shows up on the Apple II screen and on paper, coming from Apple's low-cost, low-resolution thermal printer. (Photo courtesy of Apple Computer Inc.)

Don't take any dealer's word on these things. Try the whole system out first—with the graphics package installed. You may find that the page has the capability of including a million dots, but your computer can't remember that many—so you can't manipulate them, after all. Or you may find that your video screen can't really display the picture—or it has no color at all.

Some ink jet printers let you spray a lot of colors, but they may take a quarter of an hour a page to produce. For $30,000 you can buy a machine that uses dry toner to turn out foreground and background colors on almost 200 pages an hour. But the cheapest and most sophisticated current system for graphics involves a plotter—a computer-controlled set of pens, which sketch blue eyes, yellow hair, black glasses, red acne, orange tie, green shirt, and violet coat, in half an hour.

Some systems claim to offer graphics, but really don't offer much. You can draw horizontal or vertical lines with dots, dashes, or x's. You can tell the system to draw slanting lines from Point P to Point U. You can demand that the system create a circle, and inside that, a triangle. Or, if you add an optical scanner that can translate a photograph into dots, you can have this spotty version printed out. Only with a few microcomputers, such as the Apple IIe, can you get a pad and draw on it, and have the results show up onscreen, and then in printout—and even here, you'll get a jagged interpretation of what began as a smooth curve. What these systems do best, then, are graphs, pie charts, and statistical diagrams. Sophisticated graphics are now available on some systems, such as Apple's Lisa and Macintosh, thanks to a device known as a "mouse." You roll this small metal box around on your desk, making a line on the screen. At the click of a button, you get perfect circles, complex textures, multiple layers.

Paper Handling. Printers usually take only a few kinds of paper. Most accept the conventional wide fan-folded computer paper, with holes on either side; these holes fit into pins that move it into the printer, and then back out, on a tractor mechanism. If that's all right with you, you won't need any other gizmo for feeding the paper in—just a box on the floor and a light on the printer, to alert you when the paper runs out. Other systems expect you to use long rolls of paper; again, there's not much to putting the roll in. But do you want to cut it into pages?

Many systems also accept regular letter paper. But for that you may need a separate mechanism, known as a cut-sheet feeder. This takes a stack of separate "cut" sheets, and feeds them one at a time to the printer. Ask if your printer needs a paper feeder. How much extra room does that take? How easy is it to load? Even with a feeder, some systems foul up on cut paper, sending it through at an angle or failing to print the last few lines correctly at the bottom of the page. You'll have to demand a dozen test runs to make sure your printer doesn't do this.

Some helpful extras: a warning light that you've left the cover open (in case someone dropped a hairpin into the mechanism), a signal that you have run out of paper, an alarm showing that the tractor mechanism is not locked in tightly enough, a light showing that the feeder is working properly, and a mechanism for telling the machine where to start printing on every sheet of fanfold paper (otherwise, it might print right over the creases).

If you're planning to fill in forms with your printer, make sure that the machine will accept that size of paper, whether in cut sheets, continuous rolls, or pasted onto the regular computer paper. You'll definitely need a mechanism for telling the printer where the top of the form is. You may also need a control knob for paper thickness if your forms have several layers. And you'll want to make sure that the feeder, too, can handle the forms.

Ease of Control and Reliability. Some companies boast that you can add hundreds of different character sets to their system. However, they don't provide you with the program: you have to make it up. Is that easy? Or is it so difficult that it effectively prevents you from adding anything? Lots of systems claim to perform fancy functions, but how easily?

If you're not interested in learning to disassemble your printer, and put it back together again, you'll want to find out how easy it is to:

- Tell the system where you want the top of your pages (on continuous paper).
- Fill the feeder.
- Insert a new daisy wheel, or a new character set.
- See what you've done wrong. (Does an error message show up on-screen?)
- Install and troubleshoot. (Does the manual really tell you what to do?)

One good sign is a readable manual. If it's got an index, and large pictures with labels that you can understand, and step-by-step directions, you'll find it a lot easier to diagnose and repair any problems.

Another good omen is reliability. Some vendors run their printers for long hours, to find out when they break down. You can use these studies to see if a machine is out of order frequently. A printhead should run for at least a hundred million characters, and a drive mechanism for ten million; there should be at least 1000 hours between trips to the shop. Ask your dealer what the life expectancy of the system is. In general, a dot matrix system outlasts letter-quality, simply because it has fewer moving parts to break down; a metal daisy wheel outlasts a plastic one.

If possible, ask someone who uses the printer how often they have to call for service and how fast the service comes.

Sound. It may seem like a small thing, but the sound a printer makes can set your teeth on edge; some printers make such a racket that no one in the office can think. Don't overlook such a seemingly minor problem. Once you're actually using the system, the noise may seem gigantic—slapping and clacking and flipping paper, whirring and beeping. The quietest printers are the thermal and electrostatic systems—not much use for correspondence—or ink jet and laser, which are well beyond the budgets of most offices. Both dot matrix and letter-quality printers can drive you deaf in a small space.

If the printer sounds loud, ask your salesperson about hoods. These are insulated cases that surround the whole printer and enclose much of the sharp ping and clatter. Most companies do rate the sound levels of their printers; anything above 60 decibels is loud, and you'll want to buy some kind of cushion to put around the machine—or lock it in your attic.

Cost. The cheapest printers for general correspondence and graphics remain the pin-punching dot matrix ones. Slightly more expensive—often as costly as the word processor itself—are daisy wheels, known as letter-quality impact printers. Beginning at $5000 and soaring well over $400,000, the ink jet and laser printers outprice even the biggest and heaviest versions of the other printers. Plotters range from a few thousand to more than $20,000. Thermal and electrostatic printers cost a few hundred dollars at most, but you usually can't buy them apart from a calculator.

PHOTOCOMPOSERS

If you spend more than $20,000 a year having text typeset for publications, brochures, or ads, you may want to consider buying a photocomposer. This machine will take text you've written on your word processor, then set it in sharp images ready for an offset printer to photograph and print. The advantages of the photocomposer over most printers, including some laser and ink jet ones, are:

- Cleaner image, with results that resemble *National Geographic* or *Time* magazine—not just fancy typing.
- More sophisticated control over spacing. You can make every line justified, ending at the right margin without looking somehow stretched out or shrunk. You can pull together letters that might otherwise look odd far apart, like "AY."
- More type fonts per page. Without having to switch daisy wheels or typewriter elements, you can change type sizes and styles—boldface, italics, etc.—within the same line or page.
- Reduced size; two typed pages can be condensed into one photocomposed page. You can use less paper—and that means lower costs for printing, mailing, and distribution.

Photocomposers compose pages with light. They flash each character onto photographic paper or film, then expose and develop that, so what you get is ready to be photographed by an offset printer, made into plates, and put on the press.

Originally designed for newspapers and magazines, photocomposing machines allow you to do anything that the old typesetting machines did in molten lead. While those produced hot type, photocomposers roll out strips of cold type—more convenient to cut and paste and rearrange, if you want to, and easier for offset printers to make into plates.

As on a Linotype machine, you can change fonts—but much faster—you just press a few buttons. You can set general patterns for spacing between letters, justifying lines, hyphenating, tabulating, making room between one line and the next. You can also modify these on the spot if you don't like the results.

But if you're not used to the terms and measurements used in the printing trade, you'll encounter a lot of mysterious new commands, such as "kerning" and "quadding." (Kerning means adjusting space between letters so the combination of two letters looks better; quadding means making sure that the short last line of a paragraph doesn't get moved all the way over to the right.)

You may want to do word processing on your own equipment, then take the completed disks to a phototypesetting company, to have an expert typesetter insert the proper codes. If so, you'll want to make sure that the typesetter's photocomposing system can read your disks.

Perhaps there is a photocomposing system that already has a program that can translate your word processor's disks. Perhaps the typesetting company will write one for you. Another method of translation is called an "interface," or "black box," which will take your word-processing disk, read it, and transmit the text to a photocomposing system in terms it understands. As you can imagine, these jobs of translation sometimes get ticklish. If you're going this route, you'll want to make sure that all the letters in your text, and all your commands, get across successfully. (For a taste of the complexities involved in this kind of communication, see Chapter 8, "The Office of the Future.")

Another possibility is that you can do word processing on a photocomposer. This may be a bit crude, and it does involve learning printing terms along with word processing, but at least you will have direct access to the photocomposer, which is recommended if almost all your text gets printed. Or your word-processing manufacturer may have prepared a translation program; if so, you can enter some strange new commands on your word processor, and these will be immediately recognized by the photocomposer.

Communication with your word-processing system, then, is the biggest problem you face when thinking about purchase of a photocomposer. You may want to have the photocomposer online all the time, so that your word processor can be directly linked to the photocomposing system by cable or phone lines. But if you don't have a steady high volume of work to transmit, you could probably manage with delivering disks by hand or by mail.

Speed of output is another factor to consider. If someone is going to key in your text a second time, you need a system that can turn out at least 20 lines a minute, to keep up with a fast typist. But if you're going to have your word processor transmit the text by cable or by disk, then you can expect the photocomposer to move faster; it should be able to turn out 50 to 75 lines per minute this way. (Some produce more than twice that many.)

Other things to consider are: How many different typefaces and sizes do you want to use at the same time? Most systems offer you only ten or fifteen typefaces at one time, in more than a hundred sizes; you can also make a manual switch, putting in a new set of typefaces. If you need to use certain typefaces together, make sure they're all on the same set.

Some photocomposers can only handle lines about 7½ inches long; others go as long as 15 inches. If you want to set an entire page on the photocomposer rather than have a graphics artist paste up the page later, you must make sure that the system can set type in every corner of the page. For instance, if you normally have 7-inch lines of text next to 1½-inch marginal glosses on a 10-inch-wide page, a smaller photocomposer, able to handle only 7½-inch lines, won't be right for you.

Some people like to vary the vertical distances between lines. If you're not content with standard settings, find out how much play you'll have in this area. Also, if you like to set text so that the line endings follow the contour of a drawing, then you should make sure that your system has that capability. At minimum, you should be able to set your copy so that it is either ragged right (that is, irregular on the right, as in copy typed on a typewriter) ragged left, left or right justified, or centered.

You'll probably want a system that can show you what a fully made-up page looks like onscreen, unless you want to hire a graphics artist to paste up type. It's best to have a photocomposer that lets you see everything the way it will look in type—a display option. (You need to be able to look at the codes you've entered, too, so you can change these, if necessary.)

Consider the sharpness of screen image. Some photocomposing systems offer spectacular clarity—far beyond that of most word processors on the market today.

How flexible is the screen image? Most photocomposer screens will show you italics, boldface, sub- and superscripting, proportional spacing—things that only a few word processors can manage onscreen.

Another thing to find out is if the system can process an entire document at one time. Even if you've done a perfect job of word processing, there are some typesetting commands that need to be put in throughout a document, and it's a lot faster if the computer can reach the whole text at one time. For instance, you might want the photocomposer to search for every instance of a book title, to make it italic throughout.

Since many photocomposers are built around much larger computers than those used by stand-alone word processors, they can often do more jobs at once. For instance, some systems can search throughout a document for as many as a hundred items, replacing each one with a new version while you go on to insert other typesetting commands on the first few pages.

Photocomposers are not cheap, though. Depending on how many people send material to the photocomposer, and how many refinements you want, you could be looking at a bill for $20,000 for one small machine, a lease running to $100,000 a year, or a million-dollar purchase.

MODEMS

Using your word processor and the telephone lines, you can dial up information onscreen from hundreds of libraries that have been stored on computers around the world. You can read the information on your video display screen, then print out whatever you want on paper, or have the system store the information on disk for future reference.

What kinds of information? You'd be amazed at the enormous range of material that has been put onto data bases in large computers. Just for example: today's *New York Times;* current government statistics on the economy, the census, and the weather; where to buy coal; every patent in the U.S. (you can get a diagram and complete text); a list of every piece of junk orbiting the earth—and where it is; every law passed in Italy, or New York, over the last ten years; every legal trademark. There are now so many electronic libraries that their staff members have formed national and international associations, which hold conferences (at least half a dozen a month), publish magazines, and prepare data bases that just list other data bases.

In one popular information service, you can get current quotes on stocks and bonds, mutual funds, treasury notes on four major exchanges, plus files of recent stories in *Barron's* and *The Wall Street Journal,* which are called up when you press a symbol shown next to a key word on the menu for this package. To get the menu, you first load a communications program into your word processor or microcomputer (the program's on a disk, just like the one that holds your text), and use your modem.

With modems, you can use the telephone lines to send a memo from your video display screen to someone else's—even if she's three states away. If she's not in, her word processor will store the memo and blink, so when she returns, she'll see you've left her a message, and she can call it up on her screen immediately. That's called electronic mail. But what is a modem?

WHAT MAKES UP A WORD PROCESSOR? ‖ 97

A modem is a small box that looks like an answering machine, but acts like a matchmaker. It lets one computer talk to another computer—even over the phone lines, which don't really speak computerese. The computer inside your word processor thinks in terms of ons and offs, yes and no. Since these can be represented as the numbers 1 and 0, and since some people call numbers "digits," this way of storing and sending information has been called "digital." But telephone transmission is called "analog." When you speak on the phone, your voice sets off a whole range of sound waves, all vibrating at frequencies that range from 300 cycles per second to around 20,000. Your phone takes some of these sound waves and turns them into analogous electrical waves. Hence, a message sent along the phone lines is called an "analog" transmission.

A Hayes "smart" modem, with signal lights to tell you what it's doing. A modem lets your word processor talk to other computers. (Below) Here's what you may need: an extra card to fit into your word processor, a disk with the communications program on it, some cables to plug into your phone jack, and the actual box. Shown here is the Micromodem II from Hayes. (Photo courtesy of Hayes)

What a modem does is translate your word processor's digital information (ons and offs) into analog information (continually shifting waves). Then, at the other end, it converts those waves back into digital code, so the other computer can understand. Usually a modem sets up a basic wave, then deliberately disturbs its height, width, or frequency to indicate a 1 or 0.

The crudest modems work as follows: you dial the number of another computer, and when you hear a high-pitched whine at the other end, you place your phone into two rubber-circled holes in a small plastic box, and turn the modem on. From then on, one computer communicates to the other, through their respective modems. (This is known as an acoustic coupler, because it makes sounds; it also risks a lot of static, so if you care about precision, you need a modem that has a jack just like the one attached to your phone, so it can plug directly into the phone outlet on your floorboard. Essentially, the phone lines link us as if your modem were a phone.)

But which modem is best for you? You can distinguish between modems in a number of ways. First, by speed and volume: some can send a lot of text very fast, some not so much text and more slowly. Next, compatibility: does a particular modem really fit your word processor and phone lines? Then, features: can the modem do the type of basic sending and receiving you need, plus provide extra options? Here are some issues to consider:

Speed

How fast can the modem send and receive? Your word processor can probably transmit at a rate of somewhere between 300 baud and 9600 baud. (One baud is one signal per second. You'll also see speed listed in bits per second, or bps. A bit is one on/off pulse, and you can figure there are 5 to 8 of those per character. So in most cases 8 baud can carry one character per second.) Your modem should be able to handle at least as much as your word processor can send and receive.

Interface

An interface is a connection and here we're basically talking about a simple plug or jack. Your word processor should have some "ports" through which it can communicate with printers, other word processors, and a modem. These interfaces have standards, with names like "RS 232C." On the specification sheets for your word processor and the modem, then, look for the word "Interface" and hope you find at least one name in common. (Some modems can handle several different interfaces.)

Mode of Transmission

Your word processor probably sends out information at irregular intervals—an "asynchronous" transmission. This means that your word processor inserts a code before and after each character, warning the receiver that another character is being transmitted. That takes up a lot of time, but if you're not sending much information, the time lost is milliseconds.

On the other hand, if you need to send a lot of information very fast, you should send it synchronously. This means that there is a clock establishing a beat at the beginning of each message to establish "sync" with the other computer. From that beat on, it's clear what is a character and what isn't—so the message isn't garbled.

You'll probably want a modem that sends out one bit after another, serially, over one channel. (If you have a very slow word processor and you're not sending signals too far, you could use parallel transmission, in which the modem sends consecutive pulses down 8 or 16 wires, all at once; all this does is to add a little speed to a slow system.)

Compatibility

Can a modem actually use phone lines? Some talk only to Western Union, while others send only Telexes. If a particular modem can talk over the phone, it will be labeled something like "Bell 103 compatible," which means it can deal with Ma Bell.

Connections

For accuracy and reliability, your modem should be able to plug into your phone lines with a jack much like the one attached to your phone. If it can, the specifications will say something like "FCC Registered for direct-connect," since the modem manufacturer is supposed to file its equipment with the Federal Communications Commission, which looks on a modem as a telephone.

Multiple Channels

Some modems include a device known as a multiplexer, which lets you turn one phone line into several channels, so that you can send or receive half a dozen messages at one time. You might want this feature if you're thinking of connecting up more than one terminal to the modem. In this way, six different people could be communicating with six off-site data bases, all through one shared modem.

Audio Monitor

When you are transmitting, it's helpful to hear what is happening at the other end of the line. For instance, you may enter an old telephone number, and if your modem doesn't have a speaker to monitor the call, you'll never hear the operator saying, "I'm sorry, that number has been changed."

Status Indicators

These are special lights to answer questions you may have, such as: Is the modem on? Is it ready to answer the phone if someone else calls? Is another computer sending information to us now? Is my modem ready to send or receive? (This is often termed "off hook," as if you had a phone receiver off the hook, next to your ear, ready to start the call.) The terms used to answer these questions are often obscure, since the designers still think the equipment is used only by engineers, who prefer the initials MR to the phrase "Modem Ready."

Send/Receive

Some modems can only send, some can only receive, some have to be switched back and forth, and others can do both at once. You'll probably need both to send and receive, even if all you want to do is establish a connection with a distant computer and retrieve some information, but you may not need to send and receive at the same time, unless you have a great deal of traffic. Transmitting both ways at once is called "full duplex." Transmitting both ways, but one at a time, is called "half duplex."

Automatic Dial

If you want to take advantage of low night rates, you need to be able to tell your modem, "Make this call at midnight." Automatic dialing will do this for you. And if you think someone else might be sending to you at that hour, you need automatic answering.

Commands and Features

How do you tell the modem to do something complicated, such as calling someone later in the day? First you have to load a communications program, on a disk, into your word processor. That may or may not work. Be sure to ask the salesperson if you need a new program to make the modem work—and if so, make sure that it really works on your machine. Once it does work, though, you'll have a lot of flexibility; you can use any modem that has a built-in microprocessor. These modems are called "smart" because they can almost think. They offer a range of features that you can select, using the software:

- Automatic time stamp: marks the time and date of every message sent and received.
- Dial—and dial again: automatically calls back up to a dozen times, say, if it gets a busy signal.
- Phone directory: you can type in "Sam," and the modem will remember his number.
- Diagnostics: this way the machine can test itself and tell you what's gone wrong.

Buffer

This is essentially a storage bin, so that the modem can collect a lot of information from slow-sending terminals, then zip it out fast; or receive a lot of information very fast over the phone, then dole it out in short, slow packages so your terminals can digest them.

OPTICAL CHARACTER READERS

Perhaps you have a lot of old office manuals that you'd like to bring up to date, if this didn't involve retyping them. Or maybe you have a mass of forms pouring into your office that need to be stored on disk. You might also want to put a certain book on disk, so that you could quote passages from it in various letters, without retyping each time.

A machine that recognizes characters optically can be of great use in performing any of these tasks. Called an Optical Character Reader or OCR, it can "read" certain typed or printed copy directly onto a disk, without typing. It works by flashing a bright light onto the typed or printed page, then measuring the reflection very carefully with light-sensitive cells. If light bounces back unabsorbed, the cells assume that part of the paper is blank. If light gets absorbed, there must be type there. The machine breaks down the type image into hundreds of dots, then pieces them together until a rough image of the letter emerges. Then the computer inside the OCR compares the rough image with the alphabet, to confirm which letter the rough image seems to be. Sometimes the OCR guesses wrong, confusing a capital "B" with a number "8," or a "5" and an "S." But usually it is correct. Then it sends the computer code for that letter to a disk, so that you can display the copy on your word processor later.

The average typist produces 60 words per minute, but the OCR can manage anywhere from 500 to 1000 words per minute. A fast typist

This Optical Character Reader is manufactured by Hendrix, Inc. They call it a Teletypereader. (Photo courtesy of Hendrix, Inc.)

can turn out a page every five minutes, or ten or twelve an hour; some OCRs spew out 300 pages an hour. If you have enough material to use it steadily, an OCR can do the work of ten typists, freeing people to do the harder work—editing, revising, correcting formats.

Insurance companies use OCRs to enter filled-in forms on their word-processing system; banks use OCRs to sort checks; credit card companies funnel all those flimsy slips through an OCR, to get data onto their computers. Some companies publishing the collected works of an author put the single volumes through an OCR, instead of having them all typeset again.

OCRs have advanced a lot in twenty years. In the early sixties, the first OCRs only read capital letters. Evidently the engineers figured that computer printout would be the only "input." By the late sixties, a less limited OCR had been developed: it could read upper- and lowercase letters, but only if they were typed in the one or two fonts the machine recognized. In fact, some companies designed type fonts especially for the OCR, so there would be no mistaking the number one for a capital "I," or a lowercase "l." Of course, if your document hadn't been typed in one of those fonts, you were stuck. And there was only one code the computer knew. If your word processor didn't understand that code, you couldn't use the disk.

Now there are multipurpose OCRs, costing between $20,000 and $150,000. These let you edit onscreen as you watch the text materialize; you can also reformat the text as it goes in, according to your specifications, and translate text into several different codes, in case you have more than one word-processing system. But these machines may still not be able to read more than a half dozen type fonts. Essentially, the manufacturers expect you to retype everything, fast and sloppy, on an electric typewriter, using an OCR-readable font, then feed in the typed sheets. This is not exactly a labor-saving technique.

This problem is why a man named Raymond Kurzweil has become so famous in OCR circles. He invented the Kurzweil Reading Machine, which is an OCR connected to a speech synthesizer; in this way, a blind person can have a book read by the OCR and then hear the words spoken out loud. But his invention showed Kurzweil the need to be able to "train" the OCR to read almost any typeface—not just a few. So he wrote a computer program that looks at an unfamiliar letter, makes a guess, and displays it onscreen with an enlargement of the dot pattern perceived. Then the OCR asks you if it has guessed right. You type in the correct letter. From then on, the computer knows that a particular shape equals a particular character. You can train the machine on as many as seven typefaces at the same time, so it can handle a book that has italic and regular text, boldface headings, large titles, and an entirely different typeface for picture captions. Because this OCR can read any type font once you've trained it, the Kurzweil Data Entry Machine is called an omni-font OCR.

The earlier models of the OCR had problems: they misread specks of dust, ripples on the paper, smudges. Grays confused them—they couldn't read type prepared with a nylon ribbon. A broken character—one typed over white-out, say—frequently came out as another letter. If the typewriter paper had been entered in the roller at a slight angle, the skew of the lines would baffle the OCR. Characters typed too close together could also nonplus the computer. Many of the multipurpose and omni-font machines can sidestep these difficulties, but before you buy an OCR, you should put various kinds of copy to the test. (Every salesperson quotes you a very low error rate, but these assume you're always working from perfect copy.)

Given all these difficulties, when would you want to spend $15,000 to $150,000 for one of these machines?

- If you have a steady flow of material coming in, and it would take at least four or five full-time typists to enter it.
- If you have a backlog of material that you need to change, but you've been putting off working on it because of the time it will take to reenter the material in your word-processing system.
- If you have a lot of material produced on someone else's word-processing system, and you have no way to translate from their disks to ones that your own word processor understands. In this way, the OCR acts as a disk converter.
- If you need fast turnaround time on long documents—even if this happens only once or twice a month—and you can't wait a week while a typist grinds out the thousand pages.

- If you have an office that has resisted forming a word-processing center so that every executive can continue to have his own secretary, but the secretaries want to use the word-processing system for revisions. The secretaries can type rough drafts on their electric typewriters, zip those through the OCR, use the word processor to make revisions, and produce a clean final copy.

If you're thinking about buying an OCR, you need to analyze the kind of material you'll be feeding into it, so you can make sure that the model you're considering can handle it. Consider each of the following, and then bring samples to the vendor, to make sure the machine doesn't conk out when confronted with your particular input.

- What size paper will you be feeding in?
- Will you be putting books through, too? What else?
- Does some of the material come single-spaced, some double-spaced, some triple-spaced, some with sub- and superscripts?
- Do your typists occasionally put a piece of paper in the typewriter at an angle, so the text comes out skewed?
- Do you want to feed the OCR cut-and-paste material?
- How many different typefaces will you be sending in?
- Is some of your typed material a little gray? Do you use nylon ribbons? Bad copies?
- How many characters wide is the widest line of type you'll be putting in?
- Do you need the machine to read complex math formulas, or foreign languages with umlauts or other accents?

And then, thinking about the output of the OCR, you might ask:

- How does the machine show it can't figure out a letter?
- Can the OCR be trained to read new fonts?
- How many characters per second, or words per minute, can it handle?
- What code does the OCR translate the text and commands into? And is that exactly the one my word processor uses?
- How many errors can I expect with perfect copy?
- Can I specify a new format, so that what goes in with one set of margins comes out with a different set?
- Can I intervene and edit as I watch the text being processed?

COMPONENTS CHECKLIST

Use this list to check off the components you need and what features you want them to have. Put a check next to each item that you'd *like* to have and an asterisk (*) next to the items that are most important for your word processor. After the listing of each component you'll find a page reference back to the text, for more detail.

DO I NEED THIS?	FUNCTION	SEE PAGE
	VIDEO DISPLAY SCREENS	
	ADJUSTABLE SCREEN	56
☐	I want the screen to be able to tilt and swivel	
	BACKGROUND COLOR	57
	I have a preferred background color:	
☐	Black	
☐	White	
☐	Green	
☐	Other: ———	
	CHARACTER COLOR	57
	I have a preferred character color:	
☐	Black	
☐	White	
☐	Green	
☐	Other: ———	
	SCREEN SIZE	57
	I prefer a screen which can display:	
☐	A full page of text (66–68 lines)	
☐	A partial or half-page of text (20–30 lines)	
	WIDTH	57
	The number of characters I need to see on each line is:	
☐	80	
☐	132	
☐	Other: ———	
	SPECIAL EFFECTS ON THE SCREEN	
	HIGHLIGHTING TEXT	58
	I want highlighted text to display using:	

DO I NEED THIS?	FUNCTION	SEE PAGE
☐	Reverse video	
☐	High/low intensity	
☐	Other: ―――	
☐	Underlining should display on my screen	
☐	Boldface should display on my screen	
☐	Special spacing should display on my screen	
☐	Sub- and superscripts should display on my screen	

CHARACTER IMAGE

☐	Descenders should display on my screen	59
	ALTERNATE CHARACTER SETS	60
	I need alternate character sets to display on my screen:	
☐	Scientific and mathematical symbols	
☐	Legal notation symbols	
☐	Another language ―――	
☐	Other: ―――	
	GRAPHICS	60
	I need to display graphics:	
☐	To draw boxes	
☐	To show bar and pipe graphs	
	CHARACTER RESOLUTION	59
☐	I can live with fuzzy characters	
☐	I want characters to be sharp and clear on the screen	
☐	I want characters on the screen to look as good as typewritten text	

KEYBOARD

	ATTACHED OR DETACHED FROM THE SCREEN	56
☐	I want a detached keyboard which can be moved separately from the screen	
☐	I want the keyboard and screen to be in the same unit	
	FUNCTION KEYS	62
☐	My keyboard should have separate, labeled function keys	

DO I NEED THIS?	FUNCTION	SEE PAGE
☐	My keyboard should have separate function keys; I don't care if they're labeled	
☐	If there are no special function keys, I'm willing to use "control keys"	
☐	Control keys should be "mnemonic"	
☐	Control keys should have function names engraved on them	
☐	Control keys should come with labels to attach	
	KEYBOARD TOUCH	61
☐	I need the touch of the keyboard to be at least as good as that of a Selectric typewriter	
	NUMBER KEYPAD	64
☐	I need a number keypad to be used as a 10-key	
☐	Repeating keys should work on my keyboard	
	CAPS LOCK	65
☐	I want the Caps Lock key to act as it does on a typewriter	
☐	I want the Caps Lock key to lock letter only	
	KEYBOARD BUFFER	65
☐	I type fast, so I need a keyboard buffer	

COMPUTERS AND PROCESSORS

	PROCESSOR	65
☐	I have a particular processor in mind:	
	OPERATING SYSTEM	
☐	I need a particular operating system: ———	
	NUMBER OF TERMINALS TO BE ATTACHED	
☐	I need only one terminal	
☐	I need two terminals	
☐	I need three to five terminals	
☐	I need six to twelve terminals	
☐	Other: ———	
☐	I need to be able to add more terminals later	

108 || THE DEFINITIVE WORD-PROCESSING BOOK

DO I NEED THIS?	FUNCTION	SEE PAGE
	NUMBER OF DISKS TO BE ATTACHED	69
☐	I need individual disks for each terminal	
☐	I want share disk storage among the terminals	
	NUMBER OF PRINTERS TO BE ATTACHED	
☐	I need to have one printer attached	
☐	I need to have two printers attached	
☐	Other: ———	
	MEMORY	68
☐	I want to to add additional memory	
	DISK STORAGE	
	FLOPPY DISKS	70
☐	I want to use floppy disks.	
	They should be:	
☐	Mini floppy disks (5¼″)	
☐	8″ floppy disks	
☐	Single-density	
☐	Double-density	
☐	Single-sided	
☐	Double-sided	
	Number of floppy disks I need:———	
	HARD DISKS	72
☐	I want a hard disk on my system	
	TAPE	73
☐	I want a tape drive so I can back up my documents on tape	
☐	I want to add more disks later	
	DISK COMPATIBILITY	71
☐	I need to be able to use the same disks on more than one model of word processor	
	SOFTWARE	
	ORIENTATION	75
☐	I want a page-oriented word processor	
☐	I want a document-oriented word processor	
	SIZE OF EACH DOCUMENT	75
☐	My longest standard document is about ——— pages long; I want to be able to work with it as one document	

WHAT MAKES UP A WORD PROCESSOR?

DO I NEED THIS?	FUNCTION	SEE PAGE
	ENTRY LINE	76
☐	I want always to enter text on the bottom line of the screen, simulating a typewriter	
☐	I want a floating cursor so that I can enter text anywhere on the screen	
	WHAT YOU SEE IS WHAT YOU GET—OR IS IT?	76
☐	I want special formatting displayed on the screen at all times	
☐	I can work with control characters inserted in the middle of my text	
☐	I want a separate view mode for the display of formatting	
☐	I want to use dot commands for formatting	
	SPECIAL CAPABILITIES	79
☐	Merge list capabilities	
☐	Sort capabilities	
☐	Math capabilities	
	COMMUNICATIONS SOFTWARE	79
☐	To work with other word processors	
☐	To work with other computers	
☐	Spelling check	
☐	Index generation	
☐	Table of contents generation	
☐	Electronic worksheets	
☐	Data base management systems	
☐	Calendars	
☐	Accounting packages	
☐	Other: _____	

	PRINTERS	
	QUALITY	83
☐	Dot matrix?	
☐	Letter quality?	
	CHARACTER SETS	87
☐	Limited number of fonts OK?	

DO I NEED THIS?	FUNCTION	SEE PAGE
☐	Need special character sets?	
☐	Need to create my own character sets? (programmable)	
☐	Need to expand, condense text?	
☐	Slant?	
☐	Descenders?	
☐	Serifs available?	
☐	Underlining, without slicing through letters?	
☐	Proportional spacing?	
	SPEED	87
	Do I face big volumes, with little time? If so, I want:	
☐	Big buffer	
☐	Bidirectional printing	
☐	Short-line seeking	
☐	Parallel interface	
	If quality is more important than speed, and I am going with a daisy wheel or typewriter system, then I could speed even that up with:	
☐	Buffer	
☐	Bidirectional printing	
☐	Short-line seeking	
☐	Parallel interface, not serial	
	GRAPHICS	89
	Exactly what graphics do I want?	
☐	Charts and graphs	
☐	Drawings	
☐	Pictures	
☐	Do I need to add another program, to get the graphics?	
☐	Do I need to add hardware, to get the graphics package to work?	
☐	Can I see the pictures on my screen?	
☐	How many colors do I want?	
☐	How fast do the graphics actually print?	
	PAPER	91
☐	Continuous computer paper OK?	
☐	Roll paper OK?	
☐	Cut sheets required?	

DO I NEED THIS?	FUNCTION	SEE PAGE
☐	Will this printer need a feeder?	
☐	Does it have a top-of-page control?	
☐	Warning lights for out-of-paper?	
☐	Misalignment warning?	
☐	Control knob for paper thickness?	
	EASE OF CONTROL AND RELIABILITY	91
	How easy is it to:	
☐	Change ribbon	
☐	Set top of page	
☐	Fill the feeder	
☐	Insert a new type element or character set	
☐	See what went wrong	
☐	Install and troubleshoot	
☐	How clear is the manual?	
☐	How long does the equipment last?	
	SOUND	92
☐	How loud is it?	
☐	How much does a hood to quiet it cost?	
	COST	92
	I can afford:	
☐	Under $500	
☐	Under $1000	
☐	Under $2000	
☐	$2000–$10,000	
☐	$10,000–$30,000	
	PHOTOCOMPOSERS	93
☐	Could a photocomposer save me money by reducing costs of outside typesetting, paper purchases, mailing expenses, and distribution outlays?	
☐	Can it read files from my word processor? or does it provide adequate word processing on its own?	
☐	How many people will be sending material to it?	
☐	Do I want it online? or is offline OK?	
☐	How fast do I need it to work (how many lines per minute or hour)?	
☐	How long lines do I need?	
	Besides regular typesetting features, what else do I need:	
☐	More precise control over space between lines?	

DO I NEED THIS?	FUNCTION	SEE PAGE
☐	More precise control over copy position?	
☐	Do I want to see what my page will look like before I put it on film or paper?	
☐	Can it work on my whole document at once?	
	MODEMS	96
	Speed (should be at least as fast as your word processor, and any other computer you'll be talking to)	98
	Interface (should match your word processor and any other equipment you want to put online)	98
	Mode of transmission:	99
☐	Asynchronous	
☐	Synchronous	
☐	Parallel	
☐	Serial	
	Compatible with:	99
☐	Phone lines	
☐	Western Union	
☐	Telex	
☐	TWX	
	Connection:	99
☐	Jack	
☐	Acoustic coupler	
☐	Multiple channels: how many?	99
☐	Audio monitor	100
	Status indicators:	100
☐	On	
☐	Automatic answer, dial	
☐	Receiving	
☐	Ready to send or receive	
☐	Sending	
	Send/receive:	100
☐	Send only	
☐	Receive only	
☐	Both at once	
☐	First one, then the other	
☐	Programmable commands	100
☐	Automatic time stamp	101
☐	Redial automatically	101

WHAT MAKES UP A WORD PROCESSOR? | 113

DO I NEED THIS?	FUNCTION	SEE PAGE
☐	Phone directory	101
☐	Diagnostic program	101
☐	Buffer	101
	OPTICAL CHARACTER READERS	101
☐	Paper size it must handle	
☐	Types of documents I will put in	
☐	Ability to handle lines at an angle	
☐	Ability to read cut-and-paste material	
☐	Ability to read many typefaces	
☐	Reads only one or two typefaces (which?)	
☐	How wide a line of type must it read?	
☐	Must it read formulas, foreign languages?	
☐	Will it learn new fonts?	
☐	How many characters per second, or words per minute do I want?	
☐	What codes will my word processor accept?	
☐	How many errors are OK?	
☐	Does the OCR reformat?	
☐	Do I want to be able to edit on the OCR?	

4

Narrowing the Field

Once you've decided that you want and need a word processor, how do you choose one from all the equipment available on the market? Word processors come in a variety of shapes and sizes, and offer a wide range of capabilities. Which vendors should you talk to? Which products should you examine? Should you go to a computer store?

You may find it helpful at this point to think first about the *type* of word-processing system that you want. Although the boundaries between them are starting to blur, you'll find five different types of, or approaches to, word-processing systems. You'll find:

- *Electronic and Memory Typewriters.* These look like typewriters, but can store some of your text for revision and automatic retyping. Some have very small internal memories, while others have removable cards, cassettes, or diskettes. Some can even be upgraded later with video displays.
- *Dedicated Word Processors.* A computer system specifically designed for word-processing tasks. Other programs may be available for purchase, but the hardware and software have been designed together first and foremost as a word-processing system. Such dedicated systems may be single-user (stand-alone) or multi-user.
- *Hybrid Systems.* Word processing combined with data processing. Not long ago these systems were described as "integrated word- and data-processing systems." Today you'll also hear them called Information Systems, or Office Systems.
- *Microcomputers as Word Processors.* Often called personal computers, microcomputers are being bought for offices and homes

at an amazing rate. Word processing is only one of many jobs you can do on them. You can choose word-processing programs from many different "off the shelf" software packages and match them to quite a few different microcomputers.
- *Word-Processing Software for an Existing Computer.* If you already have a computer, you may discover that it has an "editor" which can be used for word processing, or that you can buy an additional software package that allows you to do word processing on your computer.
- *Total Office Systems.* You may want to consider automating other functions in your office, in addition to word processing. The "integrated office" or the "office of the future" promises to link your word processor with data processing and communications, hooking your system into phone lines so that you can send messages back and forth electronically. Many computer companies now offer complete office systems that purport to solve all your computing and communications needs.

While evaluating the type of word-processing system best suited for your needs, you should keep certain questions in mind. You should consider:

- *Cost.* Can you afford the system? Is it within your budget? The cost of a word-processing system can vary from as low as $2000 or $3000 for a simple software package and a microcomputer to $100,000 and up.
- *Capabilities and Functions.* Does the system do what you need it to do? It may not have lots of bells and whistles, but does it do what *you* need?
- *Ease of Use.* Is the system easy to learn? Does it do the tasks you want easily? "Ease-of-use" is a tricky term, since almost all vendors or software writers think their word processor is easy to use—and most of them are, given a particular audience. Your own experience with both word processing and computers may determine what's easy for you to use. We figure that a system is easy to use only if an inexperienced, nontechnical person can use the system to accomplish useful work.
- *Flexibility.* Will the system meet your needs a year from now? To answer this question, you must consider your own expanding needs and the potential of the system. Does the vendor plan to add new features to those currently active in the system? Can you add more memory, disk storage, video terminals, or printers? Can you use programs for other tasks with it?

We've posed a lot of questions here. In the following sections, we will discuss these questions in more detail, and will help you answer them for yourself, as we discuss the various types of word-processing systems.

ELECTRONIC AND MEMORY TYPEWRITERS

Most of the material in this book refers directly to word processing on computers, whether they have been designed specifically with word processing in mind, or not. We have assumed that a system will have the main components discussed in Chapter 3, "What Makes Up a Word Processor?": computer, video display screen, keyboard, disk drives, and a printer. Typewriters are word processors of a sort, however, and much has been done to improve them in the last decade. Since they are truly the "low end" of word processing, we'll talk briefly about electronic and memory typewriters as a step between the standard electric typewriter and the fully computer-based word processor of today.

Electronic typewriters look and sound different from the old standbys. They often have a "daisy wheel" print element, which looks something like a many-legged spider. Fitted with sound covers, they can operate much more quietly today. Making corrections is easy. Often an entire line of text can be "lifted off" by holding down one key, much as the IBM Correcting Selectric treats one character. Centering, indenting of paragraphs, decimal tabs, and other special formatting can be done automatically. The electronic models do not cost much more than a regular typewriter; we've seen some for as low as $1300. Some word processors can now be wired to use them as printers. However, the electronic typewriter is still a typewriter. You insert a sheet of paper, type on it, and remove it.

Memory typewriters contain some kind of storage medium. This may consist of magnetic tape inside the machine (you never see it), removable cartridge tapes, or disk drives. Magnetic cards were common in early memory typewriters, such as IBM's MagCard, but are seldom used nowadays. You can use this kind of system just as you would a typewriter, or you can store your text, then change and reprint it later.

Memory typewriters with nonremovable storage media are the most primitive. You are limited in the amount of text you can save, usually from a few dozen words to about 50 pages of copy. Although they can be timesavers on the desks of secretaries who retype the same paragraphs with minor changes over and over again, there are, nonetheless, problems presented by the internal tape mechanism. For one thing, there is no way to make a backup copy of your text. If something happens to the tape on inside the machine, that's it. The repairman may replace the tape, but your text is gone. And the tapes do eventually wear out, a fact that may not be mentioned at the time you buy one.

More sophisticated memory typewriters use removable text storage, in the form of cassette tapes or disks. These are actually low-end dedicated word processors, which can still be used as typewriters. They provide many of the capabilities found in screen-based word processors and may even have a one-line display. Some even allow you to add a display terminal to the system later on.

An electronic—not just electric—typewriter from Olivetti. (Photo courtesy Olivetti)

Capabilities and Functions

Electronic and memory typewriters are limited in their capabilities. Electronic typewriters make typing easier but don't allow you to store and reprint your documents. Memory typewriters let you store and reprint, but since they don't provide you with a screen to view the text, you can't tell how your document will look before printing it. Although on some memory typewriters you may be able to add additional features, most of these machines were not designed with much expansion in mind.

Ease of Use

Since these systems are similar to typewriters, they're often easy for a typist to learn. But they are often "code-intensive," requiring the user to press a code key and then another key to indicate special formatting. These codes must be memorized.

Advantages

- Electronic and memory typewriters are usually less expensive than other types of word processing.
- The typist who's afraid of computers may feel right at home with a system that seems more like his/her typewriter.
- The machine doubles as a typewriter.

Limitations

- You can't easily add other features when you need them.
- Storage of text is limited.

Some Questions to Ask

- Does it do what you need?
- Can you upgrade it? Can more storage be added as you need it? Can a video screen be added to turn it into a word processor? Can communications capabilities be added?
- How often does the print mechanism break down? Since the printer is often the weak line in a word-processing system, it is more likely to break or need adjustments than any other part. On electronic and memory typewriters, the print mechanism is at the heart of your system and will get a lot of wear and tear.

Cost

Electronic typewriters start at about $1300 as of this writing, and the price is dropping. Memory typewriters can cost from $2500 to $6000—almost as much as you'd pay for some stand-alone word processors with screens and removable disks.

DEDICATED WORD PROCESSORS

Dedicated word processors, from stand-alone systems to multi-user versions that allow eight or more operators to share the same document files, were built to make writing, typing, and reproducing words easier. At core they're built around a computer, but they are different from other computers that offer word processing as one of a number of capabilities. We asked some vendors who specialize in word processing to explain the differences.

Gerald Schacter, vice-president of marketing at Lexor Corporation, said that although their Lexoriter systems are built around a microcomputer, they are built from the ground up to be word processors. Since most word-processing operators are typists, he said, Lexor has kept their keyboard as close to that of the Selectric typewriter as possible—most typists are used to it. Special word-processing functions are activated by pressing one of twenty labeled keys located on either side of the keyboard. No complicated sequences of keystrokes (pressing a control key and then a letter key) are required. In addition, Schacter emphasized that their screen has the ability to display black characters on a white background, keeping the visual effect as similar to typing on paper as possible.

The Lexoriter system displays dark characters on a white background, keeping the visual effect as similar to typing on paper as possible. (Photo courtesy of Lexor Corporation)

The basic design reflects consideration for the individual who writes, types, and edits; both the video display screen and keyboard have been set up to make those tasks easy.

Sometimes the term "dedicated word processor" implies that the system is limited to word processing. This is less true than it was a few years ago. Increasingly, companies are offering products that allow you to automate more than text. As this happens, the distinction blurs between a dedicated system and a general business computer system that includes word processing. Some vendors seem to be avoiding the term "word processor" now. Terms such as "office automation," "information processing," and "*work* processors" are in vogue. Sometimes these are used merely as more glamourous names for word processors, but more often they imply the addition of other office and business capabilities.

Some long-time dedicated systems now provide the means to add other software packages. Lexor, which considers itself first and foremost a word-processing company, nevertheless has developed the capability of adding an operating system called CP/M (used in many microcomputers) to their Lexoriter, opening the door to a wide variety of other programs that you can buy and use on their machine. Lexor is not alone; Lanier, CPT, and others also provide this capability.

In addition to letting you use other software packages, many dedicated word-processing systems now offer features that once would have been considered data processing. You'll find systems that let you add rows of numbers within your documents, while others let you pull information into your documents from computerized accounting files. You can even set up an automated calendar on some systems.

NBI Corporation is a word-processing company that doesn't seem to be trying to switch its image to "information processing," yet Paul Harris of NBI says that they plan to continue the addition of computing capabilities to their word processors. As they add more applications, such as personal computing, data-base management, and communications programs, however, NBI will maintain its position as a word-processing company, with a "document bias." (They've even introduced a word-processing package for personal computers.)

Different Shapes and Sizes

Stand-Alone Systems. The term "stand-alone" indicates a single-user system that is complete in itself. Stand-alone dedicated word processors have a keyboard and video screen, disk drives, a processor (or computer), and a printer. Sometimes these will be housed in the same physical unit; sometimes they will be separate components.

These systems are designed for use by one operator, or in an office where several people need a word processor for a few hours a day, but not full-time.

The Wang Writer shown here in a stand-alone system. It comes with everything an individual user needs: keyboard, video screen, disk drive, processor, printer, and software. (Photo courtesy of Wang Laboratories, Inc.)

Multi-User Systems. Multi-user word processors have one central processing and storage unit, several keyboard and video screen units, and one or more printers. Each screen and keyboard is its own "workstation," connected to the processor and storage unit by cable. The term "shared logic" is used to indicate a multi-user system in which multiple terminals share the same "logic" of the computer.

These systems are designed for organized word-processing "centers," or for situations in which anywhere from two to sixteen (and sometimes even more) operators want to use word processing on a regular basis. When several workers in a company or department need word-processing equipment, a multiterminal system may be less expensive than buying multiple stand-alone units. The disadvantage to a multiterminal system is that all your eggs are in one basket. If the system goes down, all of your word-processing ability comes to a halt.

Clustered Systems. Clustered word-processing systems are more an *arrangement* of dedicated systems than a separate type. A cluster is made up of more than one word processor (stand-alone or multiterminal), connected by cable to allow the sharing of printers or document files. Each word processor can work by itself, yet it can share some resources with other systems.

Clustering word processors instead of buying one multi-user system ensures that if one machine breaks, all word-processing capability is not lost.

The XMark system can be used as a stand-alone word processor, but may also have other work stations attached. Here three display terminals are attached to the same disk drives and printer. (Photo courtesy of XMark Corporation)

Capabilities and Functions

Since dedicated word processors are designed to make writing and typing tasks easier, they offer a pretty comprehensive set of functions. Different systems have been designed for different types of users, however. Some systems are tailored for the secretary whose main typing task is letters. Others are designed for use in lawyers' offices; they include special features for footnoting and overstriking, and special characters for legal notation. Other systems make writing long projects, such as manuals and books, easier; they provide direct "go-to-page" facilities, ways to link chapters entered as different documents together for fast printing, and even functions to help you create a table of contents or index.

Ease of Use

As we said before, ease of use is relative—it depends on the user's level of expertise. It also depends on what the system was designed to do, and what you want to do with it. The basic idea behind a dedicated word processor is that it makes text entry, editing, and printing easy. Whether it makes *your* text entry easy depends on what you need to do. A system designed to make letter-writing easy may be a breeze to learn. However, if you need to include multilevel formulas for scientific reports, it may be very difficult to use. If a system lets you work with only one page at a time, and you frequently produce 30-page reports, moving information around within the document may be very clumsy. If you write mainly one-page documents, however, a page-oriented system may be just what you need. Again, we stress, *know what you need the system to do.*

Advantages

- Dedicated word processors are designed for processing text. Their combinations of hardware and software have been designed to work together for word processing. The keyboards usually have a good "touch," much like a Selectric typewriter, with separate, clearly marked function keys, to make changes easy.
- They are easy to use. The person using a dedicated word processor doesn't need to think of the machine as a computer; when it is started, word processing is available immediately, without having to know that there is a computer operating system present.
- Levels of support, training, and commitment to future enhancements by the manufacturer are usually good. Since the purpose of the equipment is word processing, the vendor's resources are aimed at maintaining a satisfied customer base of word-processing users.

We should mention that the companies that make dedicated word processors are not necessarily limited to the manufacture of word-processing systems. Some are; some aren't. Many large computer companies have divisions specializing in word processing. These companies, such as IBM, Nixdorf, and Wang Laboratories, manufacture computers, but they have also custom-tailored some of their hardware to work with software developed for word processing.

Limitations

Dedicated word processors may not do other tasks. This is changing rapidly, though, so by all means, *ask* if they do. Sometimes "dedicated" means that the equipment is limited to word processing. At other times the phrase just emphasizes that the system was designed with word processing in mind, *not* that word processing is its only capability.

When Do You Want a Dedicated Word Processor?

You'll want a dedicated word processor when the majority of the work you need the equipment to do is writing, typing, storing, and updating text. Although many dedicated word processors are adding other capabilities, *they were designed to manipulate text.* You may find a dedicated word processor that also allows you to do other office tasks, but if your need for accounting, records management, sorting, or other nontext tasks is greater than for word processing, and you're buying the same equipment to do both tasks, you need a hybrid system dedicated to both word *and* data processing, or a computer designed for data processing with word processing available on it. You may also find that your data-processing needs may be best handled by one system, and word processing by another.

Some Questions to Ask

- Does it do what you need? We keep repeating this question, because it really is the most important one. It's all too easy to be dazzled by a demonstration and find yourself with a $15,000 purchase that just doesn't fill the bill.
- What upgrades are planned? "Upgrades" are new versions of software or hardware that will change the way existing features work, or add new features. Will they work on the same piece of equipment you're buying, or is the company planning a new model that won't be compatible with yours, requiring you to purchase another system when you need to expand capabilities? Is there a standard fee for upgrades or new versions, or are they free to current users? Are new versions of software considered new products that you will have to buy? It's good to get these answers before you invest in a system, because they represent hidden long-range costs.
- What can you add to the system later? If in the future you need more disk space, can you add another drive? How about hooking up another terminal? What about sending text over phone lines to another word processor?

A host of new questions arise when you consider multi-user systems. The following questions apply if you are considering either a dedicated multi-user system or a multi-user computer with word processing as one option available on it.

- How many users can the system support? How many terminals can be attached to the computer *and used at the same time?*
- How much does the system slow down when more than one operator uses it at the same time? What is the optimum number of users at any one time before the system noticeably slows down?
- Does the system have print queues, i.e., can each terminal send documents to the same printer and have them "queue up" to print when the previous one stops?
- Can the terminals share documents on the same disk? Can disk drives be "assigned" to some of the terminals and not to others?
- What about security issues? Can documents created on one terminal be protected so that users at other terminals can't have access to them?
- What happens when the computer breaks down? If the entire system is connected to one processor, when the processor is down, each terminal is down. If you buy a multiterminal system, you may want to consider buying one of the terminals as an additional, *compatible* stand-alone, so that your business won't come to a standstill if the larger system breaks down.

Cost

Some stand-alone word processors can now be had for $5000 to $6500, including the printer. With more disk capacity, extra features, and the ability to add more terminals and printers, that price can go as high as $150,000, or even more. On a multiterminal system, as you add more terminals, the price per workstation should average out to $10,000 to $15,000, or less.

HYBRID SYSTEMS: WORD PROCESSING COMBINED WITH DATA PROCESSING

Hybrid word processors are computers designed to do word processing, data processing, or a combination of the two. The number of available systems is increasing continually, as more and more computer manufacturers add word processing to their line of products, and as word-processing companies add data-processing capabilities. Sometimes the term "integrated word and data processing" is used to describe what we're calling hybrid systems. More recently, similar systems, called "information-processing systems," have arrived on the market.

You might buy a hybrid system for data processing, then add word-processing software and a letter-quality printer to it later. Or you might buy a hybrid to fill your word-processing needs, then add business software later. Or you might buy it to fill both needs at the same time.

The line between dedicated systems and hybrid systems, and between hybrid systems and computers with word-processing packages, is not always apparent. As we talked to manufacturers, however, they seemed to see it clearly. Some companies stated, "We don't have a dedicated word processor. There are word-processing packages that can be used by our customers, however." Others said, "We've developed very fine word processing for our systems, but that's only a part of what we have to offer." It's these latter systems that we consider "hybrid."

Comptek, for example, offers word processing designed to fill the writing, typing, and editing needs of lawyers as part of their Barrister system. Their specialties include features such as ability to generate a table of contents for a document, and some special legal features, such as generation of tables of authorities. From what we've seen, Comptek offers a very fine word processor, but they don't consider their system a word processor. They consider it first and foremost a special system for attorneys, with word processing only one part of the software they provide.

The same care and consideration for the word-processing user that you find in dedicated systems also is present in truly hybrid systems.

The 800 XR Business Computer from Durango Systems Inc. is a stand-alone hybrid system. The unit may be used with Durango's Startext word-processing software and with other software packages. (Photo courtesy of Durango Systems Inc.)

A system with many terminals tied to one computer. (Photo courtesy of Wang Laboratories, Inc.)

Digital Equipment Corporation, for example, has a product called the DECMATE. It's a small stand-alone hybrid system for word and data processing. The keyboard features clearly labeled word-processing function keys, and it provides good, all-purpose word processing. It could be considered a dedicated system, and certainly could be purchased as one, but accounting packages are also available for it.

Types of Hybrids

You'll find that hybrid systems come in stand-alone or multiterminal styles. In addition to size, there are two approaches to word- and data-processing systems.

A Computer That Can Do Word and/or Data Processing. This system does basically what the title implies, and may not imply any more. You can do word processing on it. You can do data processing on it. That doesn't necessarily mean that you can do them both at the same time, or that you can incorporate the figures your accounting software produces into your word-processing reports without retyping.

In part, the size of your system dictates what you can and can't do. If you buy a single-user stand-alone system that can do both word and data processing, chances are that they will be treated as separate tasks. If the system uses floppy diskettes, the chances are even greater that this will be so. You'll probably insert one disk to do word processing, remove it, and then insert another disk to do data processing. If the system has a hard disk, you may be able to store multiple programs on it and switch from word processing to data processing with a few keystrokes.

Most multiterminal systems have hard disks, enabling both word and data processing to be online, or at the fingertips of the computer, at the same time. That doesn't always mean you can have one operator doing word processing and another updating inventory. The amount of memory in the computer and the way the software is written will decide that. When you use some programs, they must be completely resident in the memory of the computer. If the memory is only large enough for one program, then you're limited to running one program at a time. Other programs make use of "overlays." Part of the program must be resident in the computer's memory, but other parts remain on disk until you activate a function that requires them. At that time, the computer goes to the disk, fetches the information it needs, and lays it over what it previously contained in its memory—thus the term "overlay." Theoretically, the fact that software uses overlays might seem to indicate that word and data processing could be active at the same time, but this is not necessarily so. One reason overlays are used is because some programs can't fit into the computer's memory at one time by themselves, let alone when competing with another program.

There are a great many systems on which you will have no problem using word and data processing concurrently. We stress the possibility that you may *not* be able to in order to emphasize that you shouldn't necessarily expect it. *If you need concurrent word and data processing, be sure to ask, and to see it in operation.*

A Computer That Integrates Word and Data Processing. Webster's New Collegiate Dictionary defines "integrate" as "**1:** to form or blend into a whole: UNITE **2a:** to unite with something else **b:** to incorporate into a larger unit. . . ." That's the definition we have in mind when we think of integrated word and data processing, i.e., word and data processing that can unite, not just within the same machine, but within the same usage. If your computer system already contains a mailing list, an integrated system should let you have access to that information to use with word processing. If you have to retype names and addresses into a separate word-processing file, then you have a computer that lets you do word processing and/or data processing—not a truly integrated system.

Unfortunately, the number of hybrid systems that allow the kind of integration we're talking about form a small percentage of the hybrid systems available. Some systems can go halfway toward integration, allowing you to run a conversion program that will make data-processing files accessible to word processing.

Size will also decide whether multiple programs can share files and data. An integrated stand-alone system, if it uses floppy diskettes for storage, will still require that you remove one diskette and insert a new one to run different programs. You should be able to use the data generated from accounting or financial modeling programs directly with your word-processing documents, however. On a larger system, with more memory and disk space, where multiple programs can be resident at the same time, you can have one operator doing word processing and another doing accounts payable, and be able to merge the information they use.

Word-Processing Capabilities and Functions

Hybrid systems by definition provide you with data-processing as well as word-processing capabilities. But what about the word-processing capabilities they offer? How do they match up to dedicated systems? Just as different dedicated systems offer you different capabilities, so do hybrids.

Although many hybrid systems are very fine word processors, they can suffer when it comes to word-processing capabilities. If initially designed for data processing, with word processing "tacked on" to please customers, word processing may not have been given the care and thought in design, and therefore in features, that you will find in dedicated systems. On the other hand, the hybrids may offer greater capabilities because they can make use of their data-processing functions in word processing. A system that excels in another application, such as data-base management, and lets you insert information from it into your word-processing documents, gives you capabilities most dedicated systems can't offer.

Ease of Use

A good hybrid system will be as easy to learn as any dedicated word-processing system. If a terminal designed for data processing is used for word processing, learning word processing may be a bit more difficult. On the other hand, it can cause the manufacturer to rethink how word-processing features are implemented typically, which can lead to more original, and sometimes better, approaches to word-processing functions.

Advantages

- You can often add more disks and hardware to hybrid systems.

- If data-processing documents can be integrated with word-processing documents, you will have much less rekeying of text.
- It may be more cost-effective to buy a hybrid system that can fill a number of processing needs than to buy two separate computers. Even if you're just beginning to automate your office, with word processing as the first step, you may want to add an accounting system a year from now.

Limitations

- All the work is on one computer. If the system malfunctions, word and data processing both come to a halt.
- If it's a stand-alone system, will your word- and data-processing operations conflict? You will need to decide who has priority on the machine.
- If it's a multi-user system, will there be a printer near the word-processing workstations? If not, where will your operator have to go to retrieve printed copy?

When Do You Want a Hybrid System?

- When you want computer equipment to fill both word- and data-processing needs.
- When you want to start out with one application and be able to add others later.

Questions to Ask

- Does it do what you need?
- Can word processing be done at the same time you're using the computer for other tasks?
- How much does the word-processing capability slow down when other tasks are in progress? If possible, talk to a customer who uses the system for more than word processing. Seeing a demonstration at the vendor's office may not give you the same results as you will get in a live office with people hard at work.
- Can the different programs use the same disks? Can you store word-processing documents on the same disk you store other data? If not, how are the files to be managed? On most floppy-diskette-based systems, you'll need to keep the programs and the files separate. On hard-disk systems, with more storage space available, you'll have a better chance of being able to use programs and files simultaneously.

- Can word processing use the printer at the same time another program is in use? Will your document automatically get into "queue" to print after Accounting's profit-and-loss statement, or must you "take over" the printer after Accounting is through with it? Do you need two different printers?
- If it's a multiterminal system, how many terminals can run word processing, and how many data processing, at the same time?
- Do different programs work together? Can the output from an accounting file be incorporated into a word-processing document, to make producing reports easier?

Cost

A stand-alone hybrid system can cost as little as $7000 or $8000. Multiterminal systems can go from $15,000 into the hundreds of thousands.

MICROCOMPUTERS AS WORD PROCESSORS

Microcomputers are now being called either personal computers or small-business systems, depending on whom you talk to, who is selling them, how big they are, and what they can do. You may see a micro advertised as a personal or home computer, and then see it at work in a small business office.

We think of microcomputers as being "modular," because you can, to some extent, mix and match pieces. With the microcomputer, you find the word-processing software that does what you need it to do. Then you find out what equipment the software will work on. You'll probably have your choice of several processors (the computer), a dozen or more video display terminals to use with it, and a wide range of disk drives, from mini-floppies to hard disks.

Some micro manufacturers, such as Vector Graphics, have developed a word-processing program especially for their own equipment. In that sense, their product is similar to a dedicated or hybrid system. The difference is that the Vector computer uses CP/M, an operating system common to many microcomputers and for which many programs have been written. If you wanted to, you could purchase different CP/M-based word-processing software to run on the Vector computer, and not be dependent on the manufacturer's software.

In fact, most word-processing software for micros is written with the idea that it can be used on a wide range of hardware. WordStar, by MicroPro, is one such example. Spellbinder, from Lexisoft, is

The Apple II Plus personal computer system equipped with a Monitor ///, a Disk II floppy disk drive, and Apple Writer software provides a powerful text-editing capability that enables users to write, revise, edit, and print a wide range of documents quickly and easily. (Photo courtesy of Apple Computer Inc.)

Here the Apple II is shown with one disk drive and without a monitor attached. Some of the many software packages available are shown. (Photo courtesy of Apple Computer Inc.)

another. Another is Select, from Select Information Systems. Each of these will work on microcomputers that use the CP/M operating system. If you like one of these software programs, you can try it out on any hardware that uses CP/M—you've got quite a choice: TeleVideo, Micromation, the Xerox 820, Archives, North Star, to name only a few. And if you want a terminal with a detachable keyboard, or a system with a hard-disk drive, you can find one of these too.

CP/M-based micros aren't the only ones around, although you'll hear about this operating system often, because it is common to so many kinds of hardware. There are other word-processing packages written specifically to run on one company's machines, such as Apple's Apple IIe or IBM's Personal Computer. However, Information Unlimited Software's EasyWriter is available for both the Apple and the IBM PC, despite the fact that these computers use different operating systems. Apple also has its own word-processing package, Apple Writer. Radio Shack offers SCRIPSIT for its TRS-80 microcomputer; other word-processing programs, such as LazyWriter, are available for the same computer.

Looking at microcomputers with word processing in mind can be exciting, but it can also be confusing. We'll talk about buying microcomputers in Chapter 6, "Shopping for a Word Processor."

The first word-processing packages on micros started out as line editors—software used by programmers to make writing and changing the lines in their programs easier. Then the software was adapted for general text entry, editing, and printing. Features and capabilities were added to meet the needs of office workers. Because the initial structure was for programmers, the software assumed a certain amount of knowledge of and experience with computers on the part of the user. Often they were rich in capabilities, but difficult to learn, forcing you to memorize different series of keystrokes to perform different functions.

As microcomputer vendors go after business accounts, they are making their word-processing packages more "user-friendly"—easier to use and less technical. They are adding special keys to be used as function keys, and simplifying the dialogue (what you have to key in, and what the computer displays in response on the screen).

Capabilities and Functions

The range of functions available on microcomputer word processors is much the same as it is on dedicated systems. Some packages have basic all-purpose text entry and editing features, while others provide extensive footnoting and other special features. One big difference is that you're not dependent on one vendor to provide all your features. This has pluses and minuses. Let's say you buy a CP/M-based microcomputer and the WordStar package for it. You can now purchase additional packages to provide other features, such as:

A grammar checker	One of several spelling checkers
An index and table of contents generator	A footnoting package

If you have a dedicated system and want some of these features, you are dependent on the manufacturer of your system to provide them. In the micro world, it's more common for someone else to see that your computer and software could use a new feature, write a program to do it, and sell it.

That seems wonderful! But is it? The new features may work simply, easily, and accurately with your system. On the other hand, they may or may not have been well tested, and can be clumsy to use. And you are spreading yourself among vendors—when you have a problem, where do you go for help? To the company who sold you your basic word-processing package, or to the company who wrote the spelling package, or to the stores where you bought them? (We'll talk more about support in a later chapter.)

Ease of Use

With micros, you invariably must learn some "computer-eze" in order to use them. You'll probably learn some of it in the process of buying one, but you'll learn more once you own one.

Unless you buy a micro with word processing designed just for it, you'll be dealing with at least two companies' products, and so there are at least two factors in the ease of use: the hardware and the software. Although this is also true for dedicated and hybrid systems, at least you know that the designs have been worked out by the same company.

Many microcomputer terminals don't have any function keys, which means that it's more than likely you'll be using control-key sequences to activate functions. If you're lucky, the codes will be mnemonic (the letter used will be the first letter of the function name, such as "I" for "insert"); if you're not, it means more memorization. Some terminals do have special "programmable" function keys that can be used with word processing—if the software is programmed to use them. Some software companies make the effort to customize their programs for particular terminals and make use of any special keys; other hardware manufacturers buy the rights to a software package so that they can tailor it to their keyboard and offer users a simpler system. Often you'll find companies, both hardware and software, who think it's the other guy's responsibility to implement ease-of-use. Shop around. The software package that has all the functions you need but seems clumsy to use may be easier to use with other hardware. Archives, for example, has programmable function keys that they've integrated for use with the WordStar program, so that you have specially labeled keys as you would with a dedicated word processor.

One of the factors that determines how easy a system is to *learn* is the quality of the operations manual. Unfortunately, this is one area in which micro software lags way behind dedicated and hybrid systems. Many designers of micro software don't seem to understand that word-processing users need simple, clear, step-by-step instructions. As more systems are sold to business people who can't afford to spend days paging through reference manuals, consumer pressure will change this.

Advantages

- Micro systems are definitely some of the least expensive word processors available. The initial draft of this book was written on a micro that cost $4800 (hardware and software, but no printer—we borrowed a friend's). A letter-quality printer can be added in the future for about $2000, and a hard-disk drive (for increased document storage and faster response) for about $2000.
- You have a great many choices and a lot of flexibility with a micro. You're not necessarily stuck with wonderful software but a screen you can't abide. And the range of software available for microcomputers is extensive.

Limitations

- You have so many choices that it can really be mind-boggling to select a microcomputer if you don't know what you're doing. You need salespeople you can trust to steer you between all the options. We'll talk about that more in Chapter 6, "Shopping for a Word Processor."
- The micro wasn't designed first and foremost for word processing, so some of the little niceties of dedicated word processors just don't show up.
- You'll probably be dealing with products from more than one vendor. If you don't know what's causing a problem, you may have trouble getting help.
- If your system malfunctions, you may have to send it somewhere to be fixed. Unlike vendors who sell whole systems (hardware and software), microcomputer companies may not have local branches to fix their products.

When Do You Want a Microcomputer with Word-Processing Software?

- When low cost is critical.
- When you want to use the system for other tasks besides word processing.
- When you want to be able to purchase a wide range of "off-the-shelf" software packages.

Questions to Ask

- Does the combination of hardware and software do what you need?
- How clear is the documentation provided with the hardware and the word-processing software?
- Does the software you like work on other microcomputers? Have you tried it out on two or three different machines?
- Are there known "bugs" (things that don't work quite right) in the software?
- Where will the hardware be serviced locally if there's a problem? (Sometimes you may have to send your machine away to be fixed.)
- Does the word-processing program have to be specially "installed" for your machine? Will the store help you install it? (An "installation program" may have to be run, which tells the software what kind of video tube, keyboard, disk drives, and printer the hardware has. These programs are notoriously complicated. We are both experienced micro users, and the installation programs still throw us sometimes.)
- Will there be new options for the hardware available? Can you add more disk drives or memory?
- Will someone in the store help you learn to use the computer and the word-processing software?

Cost

Microcomputers with word-processing software can cost anywhere from $1000 to $20,000, depending on which hardware and software you select.

WORD-PROCESSING SOFTWARE FOR EXISTING COMPUTERS

If you already have a computer, you may already have your ticket to word processing. Do you want to add a software package to it that allows word processing, or would you be better off getting a different system? What are the trade-offs?

Before you add any additional tasks to an existing computer, be sure to ask yourself (or your computer manager) some questions. Is the system heavily in use all the time now? If so, can additional hardware (memory, terminals, printers) be added to it, along with word-processing software, in such a way that the current jobs it performs can be run without interference? Running concurrent word and data processing can slow down the response of a computer considerably. And if word and data processing must be run at separate times, how much time in a day can be allowed for word processing?

If adding word processing won't interfere with performance of current jobs, the next question is, what software is available? Talk to the company from which you bought your system. It's possible that you purchased a hybrid system—one designed for word and/or data processing—without knowing it. If so, read the preceding section on hybrid word- and data-processing systems. If you already have a microcomputer, there may be a variety of "off-the-shelf" software packages available (see the preceding section on microcomputers as word processors).

If the company that sold you your computer doesn't have word-processing software for it, they may know of another that does. Many companies thrive on developing software packages for computers. These firms are called software companies, systems houses, distributors, OEMs, or third-party vendors. Often they combine the software they've developed with a computer and sell the entire system (thus the term "systems house"). Even if they wish you'd purchased your entire system from them, they may be willing to sell the software on its own.

It is third-party software that we're really discussing in this section—"third-party" because it involves another company besides yourself and the company you first bought the computer from.

Why do some companies write word-processing software for other companies' computers? Because people want it and the manufacturer hasn't provided it. How good is it as a word-processing tool? As you'll find in any word-processing system, it varies. There are some excellent third-party packages and some clumsy ones. We'll discuss what you should watch out for and questions to ask in just a minute. First we want to touch on word processing that you may already have.

If you have a computer, you may already have a word-processing tool, in the form of an "editor." Editors are programs designed to help programmers write their programs. They often come as part of the operating system on a computer. Earlier we said that an operating system provides the backbone programs, or software, of a computer, allowing it to talk to the different pieces attached to it (such as the disk drives). Well, an operating system often comes with what are called "utilities"—programs that help the computer (and the person using the computer) perform basic tasks, such as write programs.

Programmers write programs in words, numbers, and symbols, much as you might write a letter or paper. The information entered must be in a particular order, one that is logical to the computer. Consistent terms must be used. Programs are sometimes thought of as "code," and are written in lines. Sometimes they are very long (thousands of lines). To make changes, programmers need to find specific places in their text, quickly. They may need to change all occurrences of one word to another. If this sounds familiar, it's because they are using many of the features you use when writing text. In fact, many word processors started out as editors written for programmers.

The main difference between editors and word processors is that editors were designed for programmers. They may have many of the capabilities you need in a word processor, but they assume you already know quite a bit about computers, such as how to talk to them in their language. They are designed to be efficient, but they are not necessarily easy to use (by our standards).

Editors are designed to create and change text—that's one need of a word processor. But when you create a document, you also want to format it, so that you can print it out in the way you want it to appear. Editors don't necessarily have the ability to format text into paragraphs and pages. You may need a separate program, called a "formatter." After using the editor to create text, you would use the format program to make the text look right when you print it out. Most likely you'll tell the formatter how you want your text to look by including instructions in your text. For example, you might enter the beginning of a letter like this:

```
Mr. Bob Jones
ABC Company
1345 Saratoga Drive
Ann Arbor, Michigan
.sp
Dear Mr. Jones:
.sp
.in 5
```

Each line that begins with a period (.) is seen by the formatter as an instruction instead of part of your text. The ".sp" tells the formatter to leave a blank space, or line. The ".in 5" tells it to indent the line that follows 5 characters.

"Dot commands," as these instructions are called, are still used in some word processors which started out as editors, particularly those available for microcomputers.

If there's an editor program that comes with your computer, try it out. See how you like working with it. If you're a professional and don't mind learning what you need to make the editor work, you may be quite pleased with it. If you just want a tool to cut down on repetitive typing, however, an editor is probably not your best bet.

Third-Party Word-Processing Capabilities and Functions

You'll find the same kind of variance in word-processing functions in third-party software as you will in word processing provided by the manufacturer of a dedicated or hybrid system. Some will be very powerful; some will be more limited. Some are so good that the manufacturer buys the rights to the software and sells it directly.

Ease of Use

We're going to talk here about what may make "add-on" word processing *not* easy to use. For instance, how easy it is to tell the system you want to use a special function? The keyboard plays a very important part in this, as we've seen before when discussing special keys and keycap labels. If you add word-processing software to your computer, there's a very good chance that you're going to be using the display screen and keyboard that you already have. And chances are even better that that keyboard was designed for data processing. What will you be missing? The keyboard touch may be clumsy, because it wasn't designed for speed typists. And any function keys that are present are probably set up for data processing.

Another factor influencing ease of use is the intent of the software developer. Was their intent to provide really good word processing, or to pacify their customers by providing *some* word processing at a low cost? There's a big difference.

Advantages

If you already have a computer, the biggest advantage in buying a word-processing package for it instead of acquiring a special system will be cost. You'll be paying only for the software, and perhaps an additional terminal and printer. If the software package costs you $5000 to $10,000 and it will be used by only one person, this is a questionable advantage, for today you can buy a stand-alone system for the same price. If it provides many people on the system with additional capabilities, however, it will keep your costs down.

Limitations

You may give up some creature comforts, such as special word-processing keyboards. And you're tying your word- and data-processing needs to the same system. What happens if the computer breaks down? The computer may slow down, too, with more users on it. For some reason word-processing programs seem to be hogs when it comes to computing speed.

Some Questions to Ask

- How will the use of word processing affect the other tasks being handled by the computer? Will it slow down?
- Can word processing be used while the computer is handling other tasks?
- How many customers are already using the software? (It is a good idea to talk to some!)
- Is a special word-processing terminal available to use with the software?

Cost

Add-on word-processing software can cost from $500 to $20,000, depending on your computer and the sophistication of the package. The cost of hardware is not included here; you already have it.

TOTAL OFFICE SYSTEMS

The need is growing to tie together word processing, data processing, scheduling, phone systems, and other equipment. Companies who have word processors and other computers want to share the information each one contains, to be more productive and cost-effective. And computer manufacturers are doing their best to provide products that fill this need.

If you're considering a computer system or network that will solve all your communications needs, you probably already have a mishmash of equipment from different vendors. Or you may have a stand-

NARROWING THE FIELD || 141

alone word processor and a small computer or two, and realize that your company is growing so fast that you need to do some long-range planning now.

"Integrated office automation" is but one term used to describe these total office systems. If you think this book raises more questions than you knew there were about word processing, you've just scratched the surface of office automation. Because technology is changing so fast and new terms and products appear every day, we have devoted Chapter 8 to "The Office of the Future." You'll find a good introduction there to what you can expect when you want word processing to be just one part of a total office system.

YOUR NEEDS CHECKLIST

This checklist will help you decide what type of word processor you need. Check the statements that apply to your word-processing needs. Below the statements you'll find the different kinds of equipment that you should look at. Remember that your needs may change and expand in the next few years. The equipment you select should meet your needs today and leave room for changes in your business.

WHAT DO I NEED?	QUESTIONS	SEE PAGE
☐	I'm not ready for a word-processing system, but I want more than a typewriter	
	• Look at electronic and memory typewriters	116
☐	I want a system to be used primarily for word processing	
	• Look at dedicated word processors	118
☐	I want a system to be used mostly for word processing, but I want some data-processing capabilities	
	• Look at dedicated word processors and ask what other capabilities they have	118
	• Look at microcomputers with word-processing software packages	131
	• Look at hybrid word- and data-processing systems designed with the word-processing user in mind	125

WHAT DO I NEED?	QUESTIONS	SEE PAGE
☐	I want a system that can be used equally for word and data processing	
	• Look at hybrid word- and data-processing systems	125
	• Look at microcomputers and the software available for them	131
☐	I want a computer primarily for data processing, but I want word processing available on it	
	• Look for the computer and software you need for data processing first; then find out what word-processing software is available for it	125
	• Look at hybrid word- and data-processing systems	125
☐	I have a computer and I'm debating whether to add word processing to it, or get a separate word-processing system	
	• Look at software packages available for your computer	136
	• Look at dedicated word-processing equipment. Compare the functionality of word processing available on your existing computer with the capabilities of word processors that would do what you need. Compare the cost of a separate word processor to the cost of adding word-processing software, a special terminal, and a letter-quality printer to your computer. Find out if a separate word processor can communicate with your computer	118
☐	Only one person will use the equipment, and will use it most of the time	
	• Look at stand-alone word processors	120
	• Look at stand-alone hybrid systems	127
	• Look at microcomputers and software packages	131

NARROWING THE FIELD | 143

WHAT DO I NEED?	QUESTIONS	SEE PAGE
☐	A few people will use the equipment, but will share it, using it two to three hours a day	
	• Look at stand-alone word processors	120
	• Look at stand-alone hybrid systems	127
	• Look at microcomputers and software packages	131
	• Look at small multiterminal systems, dedicated, hybrid, and microcomputer	121
☐	Two to four people will use the system regularly	
	• Look at multiterminal, dedicated word processors	121
	• Look at multiterminal hybrid systems	125
	• Look at individual (stand-alone) systems that can be clustered together to share printers or disks	121
☐	More than four people will use the system regularly	
	• Look at multiterminal dedicated and hybrid systems	121
	• Look at systems that can be clustered together	121
☐	I want to automate as much of my office as I can in the coming years, and I want equipment which can work together	
	• Look at networks and systems with communications	140
	• Look at dedicated word processors with communication capabilities	118
	• Look at hybrid word- and data-processing systems with communications	125
	• Look at microcomputers with software packages and communications	131
	• Make sure the communication protocols are the same on all equipment	

5

Making the Change Easier

Switching from typewriters to word processing isn't easy. Even the right machine—one that can handle all the functions you want—can cause problems, if you don't consider its impact on your health, your office society, and your company as a whole. Of three "perfect" machines, one may give you headaches, another may drive half the staff to quit, and a third may turn out to be a financial disaster for the company. You can sidestep many of these difficulties if you anticipate these problems before you buy.

Remember that the people who want to sell you a word processor describe you as "the user." They often consider you naïve, because you do not know how to program a computer. They claim that their system is "user-friendly," because it's not actively hostile. Their advertising copy describes the equipment as "ergonomic," by which they mean that it shouldn't really hurt you. But if you don't carefully think through your decision about a new word processor, you can end up being used by the vendor—and even abused.

You've now had a chance to think about the various functions you might want in a word processor, and you probably already have an idea of what kind of hardware might help you. But there's more to installing a word-processing system than buying new machines. The way you plan, choose, and install your equipment can have a startling impact on morale, productivity, and even health.

THE EFFECTS ON HEALTH

It's true: if you don't plan well, your word processor could make you sick. Your eyes might start getting red and itchy, from having to focus too hard. Your ears and head might begin to ache from the unrestrained noise of a printer in constant operation. Your skin could dry up because of the extra air-conditioning needed to cool down a small room jammed with terminals. Feelings of frustration, confusion, and fatigue could be stressful enough to give you high blood pressure, chronic heart disease, cataracts, and a blitzkrieg headache.

The National Institute for Occupational Safety and Health (NIOSH) has studied the people who have to sit in front of video display screens all day, entering data and pulling out facts, typing in new material, squinting at numbers, moving text around. NIOSH found that these people—not all of whom are word-processing operators, since some are using display screens to type in airline reservations or credit information—suffer from more stress than any other group of workers, including air traffic controllers. Their biggest complaints are that it gets too hot, there's too much glare, and they can't hear over the noise of the printer. But behind these physical stresses lurks a serious problem: poor management.

Some managers crowd people together, so that one person has to hunch a chair before another one can get up. Crowding heats up the room even more than the terminal, and irritates everyone. Studies suggest that each person needs at least a hundred square feet for an office workspace—and permission to make that space personal, by adding pictures, plants, mementos.

Coping with glare on the screen is a big problem. Our eyes automatically adjust to the light from a bright window, making it hard to read letters on a dim screen. And although we can read the video display screen all right when there are no reflections, we wince when we hit a blazing white spot caused by direct sunlight. To avoid such sudden changes in brightness, plan to put your word processor in an area without white walls, without direct sun, without too many shiny objects lying around—no high-gloss tables, no fluorescent light fixtures overhead. Venetian blinds or thick drapes on every window are a big help. In general, you want to reduce overall lighting and let every operator have an individual lamp. Sunglasses won't work—but taking a break will. If possible, you should take fifteen minutes off for every hour you work on the machine—and in most circumstances, you should never work more than four hours straight. You can also buy a glare shield for the screen. (Don't get a plastic one: it smears.) Some managers refuse to allow any of these changes, so workers put up crude cardboard visors, and get sick.

Another problem is noise. Normal conversation usually registers at about 60 decibels, but you'll find that many printers make ten times, even a hundred times as much noise as that. Any constant noise above 80 decibels can be considered an occupational hazard, according to Marvin Dainoff, a researcher at NIOSH. If you have to work in the same room with a printer, then get a hood for it—a contraption of sponge rubber and padding that fits over the printer to baffle the clatter. Acoustic ceiling tiles, cork or heavy drapes on the walls, thick carpeting—all these can help. But the best solution is to move the printer into its own soundproofed room.

If you have too many people and too many terminals together in too little space, regular air-conditioning is not going to clear out the air fast enough. If you raise it, you will dry the air out enough so that people get skin rashes, but not enough so that they're cool. It is best to spread people out, into their own offices or cubicles. If management disapproves of that, then push for extra air-conditioning that you can adjust—or bring a fan from home.

It is also a good idea to test out your furniture. It may have been designed for a six-foot man doing occasional paperwork, not a five-foot-three woman hunched over a terminal all morning. At minimum, you need a chair with a five-point base (so it doesn't wobble or tilt), adjustable height, and a really firm back support. At the desk, you should be able to put both feet flat on the floor and not bump your thighs. You shouldn't have to lean down onto the keyboard, or reach up. Basically, according to Dainoff, the home row of keys should be at about the level of your elbow.

You can see that from the beginning, buying a word processor may involve a lot of expense to redo the office. Since these changes cost money, many managers ignore them, figuring that making workers comfortable is just a luxury. But we're not talking about luxury; we're talking about health—absenteeism, high turnover, poor employee morale, resentment, backbiting—and, ultimately, productivity. Unhappy workers just don't turn out as much work as they could.

Of course, picking the right word processor can help a lot. For instance, take a long look at the letters onscreen. How steady and clear is the image? Every fraction of a second a cathode ray gun inside the terminal shoots an electron at the dots of phosphor on the screen, lighting up a pattern we recognize as a letter of the alphabet. If the pace slows down, the image jumps and jiggles. To preserve a steady image you need a "refresh rate" of at least 60 cycles per second. To see if a screen is shaky, turn the brightness control up full—that usually makes flicker worse. Small screens mean trouble, too, since they often come with tiny letters. You should be able to read the screen from arm's length.

You should also take the time to see how well the programmers have designed the software. Is the average page cluttered with commands and reminders? How often do you make mistakes when you're just trying out a new feature? When you make an error, does the system help you correct it—or does it just say something enigmatic and hostile, such as "illegal entry," or "your entry has failed: abort program"? Once you've set up a page, is it hard to make changes? Are similar tasks done in the same general way? Do the commands make sense to you? If you run into a cluttered, inconsistent, uncommunicative, and rigid system, scratch it from your shopping list—why let the computer add to your headaches?

For years now, engineers have built terminals any which way, then turned them over to industrial designers to pretty them up. And programmers have operated on the idea that if a computer pro can use a system, anyone can. Furthermore, the people in charge of buying word processors for large corporations have tended to scorn any features that might make machines easier on the ear, eye, hand, or mind.

These features cost more, and what do you get for the money? Just an employee who's comfortable. That's the way many managers thought, and they told the vendors that, so most engineers were encouraged to ignore what they called "the human factor."

Recently, thanks to pressure from some buyers, many unions, and even a few governments, vendors are taking another look at what is known as ergonomics. *Erg* is Greek for work. And ergonomics, in this situation, means designing a word processor that does the work without giving the operator so many aches and pains.

Unions in Europe have forced national governments to limit the number of hours a day a worker can be forced to sit in front of the tube (usually four hours), and to set health standards for a wide range of features. You can get an idea of the detail the unions go into from this health checklist:

ONSCREEN
- How much contrast is there between the character and the background?
- How bright is the character?
- Can the brightness be changed?
- Are the colors acceptable?
- Does the image remain steady?
- Does the screen have glare control?
- At arm's length, can you read the message?
- Has the designer left at least a little blank space on the outside edges of the screen, so it is not completely jammed with text?
- Are the characters clear? Large enough?

THE SCREEN AND YOU
- Can you move the screen around easily, to avoid glare and to change your own position?
- Do you have to tilt toward it or away from it to read a message?
- Is the display at eye level?
- How much heat does it give off?
- Does the cabinet reflect light into someone else's screen?

THE KEYBOARD
- Do the keys require too much effort to press? Are they too stiff?
- Do the keys bounce back nicely, so you can type the same letter twice in a row without waiting for the key to ooze back into place?
- Are the keys big enough for your fingers?
- Are the keys far enough apart—but not too far?
- Is the slope of the keyboard convenient?
- Do the keys have a matte finish, so they do not reflect into the screen?
- Is the keyboard detached, so you can move it around to suit your posture?

THE ENVIRONMENT
- Is there too much light in the space you will be using for the word processor? Too little?
- Do you have indirect lighting (no overheads)?
- Is there too much reflective material around the room?
- Is air-conditioning adjustable, so that the air remains crisp?

The United States lags far behind Europe, Canada, and Japan in insisting on humane standards for the equipment and the office it's used in. But because American vendors want to sell in Europe, they are gradually incorporating these standards into their equipment—but not too fast. You'll still find wild variations from one brand to another in readability, reflectivity, comfort, and convenience.

THE EFFECTS ON YOUR OFFICE SOCIETY

Introducing word processing into your office may affect more than your health. Social relationships may be disrupted if you're not careful. For instance, in response to thousands of complaints, NIOSH, the National Institute of Occupational Safety and Health, has undertaken half a dozen studies of the video display screens used by almost ten million workers in the United States, measuring radiation (after all, they shoot electrons at you), airborne pollution, glare problems, stress and strain, and workstation design and its effect on posture and health. One thing the studies have found already: when a clerk uses a video display terminal, he's likely to feel a lot more stress than a professional does in front of the same tube. How come? Because management has had a tendency to use word processors to turn the clerk's office into what NIOSH calls "a clerical assembly line." Unlike professionals, the clerical "users" have almost no control over their jobs; little feeling that they form a group; a heavy work load, but little sense of what it means; low self-esteem; and great fear about getting fired.

One worker, reflecting on the change that took place when her office brought in word processing, said:

> I used to be an administrative assistant. Now I'm in the pool. We make jokes about it, but we're like fish in a tank here—nobody can tell us apart.
>
> I don't even have my own desk—just whatever terminal's free when I walk in. I keep all my paraphernalia in a paper bag.
>
> We don't get to make any real decisions any more. I can't even turn down the air-conditioning—our boss keeps it freezing in there, so the machines don't break down. But what about us?
>
> From the time I walk in until the time I get up to go home, I never see the sun. I don't know what the weather is like outside. And see this chair? I've asked and asked for another one, but they're too cheap to get one that doesn't have these arms. See how they keep my elbows up? But the screen's low. So I have to sort of scrunch up and over. I'll probably be a hunchback by the time I get out of here. And all the time worrying, have I done enough lines? She monitors us every hour, and when I get behind, she has to know why. Guess that's why most everyone in here gets headaches, backaches, what not. I'm going to get out, too, soon as I see a good ad in the paper. I've been here longer than anyone else and I've only been here a year. All my other friends from before—they've all left.

In the seventies, many large companies thought that they could increase productivity in the office by turning it into an assembly line. Bright computer people known as systems analysts went out into the offices, and discovered that most secretaries got interrupted a lot, that they couldn't just start a job of typing and carry it out without a break, that they had to establish certain priorities, then keep reestablishing them as the work changed—and that all this thinking took time. The systems analysts saw that the work load rose and fell as the boss came and went, or as reporting periods loomed closer. They saw secretaries waiting around, when the boss had nothing special for them to do. They saw a lot of trips to file cabinets and to the copier—

trips that might be made via a video screen, if the files were on a word processor or computer. In a word, the systems analysts saw inefficiency.

The analysts had a two-part solution: bring in word processors and then, because word processors can handle so much more typing than an old-fashioned secretary—as long as you use the word processor all day—fire the old-fashioned secretaries. Replace them with word-processing operators who just sit and enter text all day. Keep a few of the old secretaries around to do "administrative tasks"—everything they used to do, except typing, filing, and copying. This logic led directly to layoffs, cutbacks, reassignments—and a new entity, the word-processing center.

Modeled on the operation of a factory, this division of labor into a series of specialty tasks meant that most managers could no longer have a personal secretary who did "everything"—a generalist. The generalists had done a little typing, a little phone calling, a little reception, a little filing, a little copying, and that was all the systems analysts noticed. What went unnoticed was the fact that these generalists also came to know the boss's work so well that they could often do the job without the boss—they understood it. Furthermore, they developed close personal ties to the boss. They worked as a team, and, since they understood the boss's aims and endeavors, they felt part of that drama known as office politics. They had status, they had meaningful positions, they made a difference.

Now these generalists were being asked to go back to the typing pool. To become a specialist in one thing—even a high-technology trade such as word processing—meant that these secretaries lost a lot of what gave meaning to their work. Sure, the systems analysts could point out that the quality of output did go up. And the volume went up too. But, oddly, morale went down. And, after half a year or so, productivity began to dip.

People started quitting. The word-processing supervisor had to hire new people constantly and train them. Then they quit. None of the operators had much stake in using the system to do a job—they were just putting in time. True, there were fewer interruptions, fewer decisions to make, less contact with other people—nothing but typing. And as long as the supervisor could hire enough replacements, the paperwork kept pouring out, and the systems analyst could boast that the company was paying fewer people to churn out more pages than ever before.

But what is it like to work in one of these centers? Hot and loud, most say. "I begin to wonder what sunlight looks like," says one operator. "And I miss fresh air." Too many operators get crammed into too little space. They do the same job over and over. And the systems analysts, in cahoots with the word-processing supervisor, devise ways in which the machine itself keeps the worker moving, with prompts ("Are you ready for the next page?") and constant measurements ("How many lines have you typed today?"). Studies have shown that these computerized work monitors cause much stress and lead to even more errors. But management often feels that production counts are the only way to justify the cost of the equipment, so until a union speaks up, or a manager wakes up, this constant threatening will go on.

Word-processing centers become clerical ghettos. More than 90 percent of the operators are women. A recent survey by the International Information/Word Processing Association of a thousand such centers showed only 15 percent reporting any men at all. Usually there are about a dozen operators serving eight times that many executives. In two-fifths of these companies the secretarial staff decreased when they put in the center; in two-fifths the numbers remained the same; in the rest, the numbers went up because the business, as a whole, was expanding so fast. Yes, efficiency went up—sometimes as much as 40 and 50 percent. But the operators began to complain that typing all day was too boring, impersonal, confining, difficult. Half of the companies, though, reported that less than 10 percent of their staff left during the last year. Another 13 percent reported that 11 to 20 percent left. The bosses' explanation for this high turnover rate suggested the problems:

- Former secretaries who could not accept the word-processing concept.
- Dissatisfaction with central environment.
- Did not like typing eight hours a day.
- Job burnout.
- Did not like constant typing.
- Inability to use the equipment to full potential.

Almost a third of these companies reported that they had a very hard time finding qualified people to work in these centers, and no wonder.

Of course, you can expect that there will be resistance to any change. Whether you intend to set up a word-processing center or just to hand out word processors to people whose jobs will stay the same in other ways, you're likely to arouse a lot of fears:

- Maybe I'll lose my job.
- Maybe I won't be able to use this new equipment.

- Maybe I won't have any say in what gets bought.
- Maybe the boss will buy the wrong equipment.
- All my routines are going to get disrupted.
- I won't see so much of the people I've been working with.

Harder for people to express are feelings of genuine loss. As Carol Gaffney, an office automation expert, points out, moving a secretary into the word-processing center may mean the breakup of an office marriage. "We have mandated that two people who joked together, who brought coffee and lunch for each other, who shared opinions of other people that helped to screen calls or appointments, now don't get to do that anymore. The secretary made office life more comfortable; the boss advised on personal matters. . . . They are grieving for a lost friendship."

Ms. Gaffney sees change as a challenge to the social fabric of the office, upsetting relationships, threatening opportunities for growth, making people feel helpless, incompetent, and useless. Top executives worry about spending too much, fouling up the flow of work, shaking up the employees. Middle managers worry that they'll be expected to turn out the usual amount of work—plus install a new system, and coax the employees to use it. The staff senses that their jobs are on the line—and even if they figure they'll survive the firings, they worry that they will lose competence, power, and meaning; that they'll be measured by people who don't understand their work; that they won't be able to learn the new system fast enough; that they'll be stuck in a typing pool.

This is not irrational anxiety. Most of what the staff fears comes true when management decrees a word-processing center, particularly if the boss never consults with the workers along the way. A study of one Canadian word-processing center showed that the employees "no longer felt that they were an integral part of an interesting human system, but rather members of a segregated, low-status unit," according to Professor David Conrath, of the University of Waterloo. "You don't get to talk to many people when you're stuck in the center all day."

Another professor, Arnold Picot of the University of Hanover, compiled statistics showing that in most German companies, four-fifths of all communication took place out loud. "Oral communication is the glue that holds the organization together," he says. If that's true, then people who are cut off from conversation may be forgiven for not feeling that they're part of the larger organization—the company. The net result is absenteeism, low morale, indifference to errors, increasing isolation, interdepartmental wars, a disruptive amount of employee turnover, and illness.

In any change you make, then, you're doing more than putting in new equipment. Your decisions may lead to more or less:

- Cohesion between units in the company.
- Social harmony.
- Meaningful work.
- Cooperation between labor and management.
- Productivity.
- Well-being for the people involved.

What can you do to make the transition to word processing easier? Here are some general policies that seem to keep workers interested and healthy, while increasing their productivity:

- Start the whole decision-making process by defining the long-range objectives of your unit. How do you measure your own success? What are the critical factors for that success? (Later, you can gauge each potential word processor against these benchmarks. How much will each word processor help you to succeed?) Take time to think before you buy. Chances are that whatever you do buy will be what you have to live with for another five years, minimum. Take at least a few months to narrow the field, then pick the right system for you.
- Look at more than typing. Study the way the whole office works, to see all the areas in which automation could help—or hurt.
- Don't prejudge your "solution" until you've really pinpointed some problems. That is, don't assume you're going to get word processing, or a word-processing center, no matter what.
- Make sure that the people who will have to use the equipment—or those who will rely on someone else using it—are all involved in the study and decisions. This lessens anxiety, because people then know what is going on and feel they can take some control over their own destinies. Plus, they often know what's going to work best.
- If possible, don't fracture anyone's job. Avoid turning a generalist into a specialist.
- Invest in the necessary extras—soundproofing, air-conditioning, desks, chairs, lights.
- Leave plenty of time for training. Don't expect everyone to get up to speed after the measly two days of training most vendors offer. Figure that it will take six weeks for most people to get up to top speed on basic, ordinary functions, and even longer for functions that are more complicated and not used so often. Let the people using the equipment figure out how to train each other. And give them time to play around.

How, then, can you start nudging your office toward a collective decision on word processing? How can you be sure that you are picking the right machine—and the right social arrangements—for your office? How can you sidestep disaster?

You might start by taking an informal poll, asking everyone what they see as the biggest obstacles to getting their work out on time. Where is work being needlessly duplicated? Where does the production of paperwork slow down? Where do file trays overflow? Which problems seem to stem from the way the department is set up? From one person's habits? From poor management? Weed out the problems that you think *can* be corrected, then sketch out some hypothetical solutions for the boss to look over. Make it clear you aren't committing yourself to a particular word processor or office arrangement. But suggest that you might be able to save X dollars a year by restructuring jobs, and bringing in some form of automation.

In a small office that isn't likely to grow much in the next few years, that may be all you need to study. If you're the only one who's going to use the gear, you can probably just go out and start shopping.

But if you have a boss who demands justification, or if the change is likely to affect more than a few people, then you may need to do a feasibility study. Is it feasible to improve your office's productivity? Some feasibility studies take three people six months to complete; some take one person a week. Some result in hundreds of pages of notes and stacks of reports. Others end up as two-page memos.

We'll outline how a giant feasibility study works. It's probably more work than you want to do by yourself, and because it's a composite model, few companies will need to carry out every step. If you don't feel you need to get into a lot of detail, you might as well skip the rest of this chapter. And if you're curious, don't get overwhelmed. You don't have to do it all!

THE EFFECTS ON YOUR COMPANY

Without a thorough study, the change to word processing may foul up a whole department's work, causing a crisis throughout an entire company. Fearing this disruption, big corporations often demand extensive feasibility studies.

Too often, though, companies leave studies like this to systems analysts from the computer department or outside consultants, who usually ruffle people's feelings. Remember that even an "objective" study can raise anxiety, since people see it as a forerunner of change over which they will have no control. Anticipating threats to their jobs or their way of working, they refuse, in many subtle ways, to be helpful. They may even develop a stake in seeing the study foul up. Some people pretend everything's fine when it isn't. Others distort figures, or clam up when they're asked what they think. Then, when an inappropriate system is installed, they jam it up—to prove the consultants were wrong.

Because of this, we think that feasibility studies should be carried out by the people whose jobs may be transformed by the results. When all the workers get a chance to collect and analyze data, they know that they are being listened to, and they tend to have less resistance to the study—and the changes that follow. Anyway, they're the ones who really know what's going on now—and they probably have some great ideas for speeding up information as it flows through their hands.

The most successful feasibility studies—those that lead to real improvements—go through six major phases:

- *Phase One:* Defining the goals of the company and a particular department.
- *Phase Two:* Analyzing the major tasks performed in this department.
- *Phase Three:* Defining exactly how each of those tasks gets done now—and pinpointing areas that might be speeded up, coordinated better, smoothed out, or otherwise improved.
- *Phase Four:* Writing up the results of the study, and reaching department-wide agreement on what you think could be changed.
- *Phase Five:* Designing a new way of working—in which word processing may or may not play a part—and demonstrating how this will help your department do its major jobs more efficiently.
- *Phase Six:* Creating a budget and justifying the expense.

In this way you will diagnose problems and offer solutions that do not simply promise to improve one person's typing speed. You can show how your overall plan will help your office do the work that the company really needs—faster, smarter, better.

Phase One

Before looking at what you type, ponder your company. Where is it going? What are its strategic advantages in the marketplace? What problems does it face, and how are you going to solve them?

We call this thinking like a boss. And when you take that perspective, how would you measure the success or failure of your particular department? What is there that you do that, if done well, contributes to the success of the company, and if done badly prevents the company from achieving its objectives? That's the critical factor. Professor Michael Hammer of M.I.T. suggests that benchmark might be dollars (saved, returned on investment, flowing through); quality (speed, look, accuracy); competitive position (market share, growth rate, rate of product introductions, public image); or organizational health (morale, absenteeism, turnover). "In some circles, all measures other than direct financial ones are classified as 'soft' or 'intangible,'" says Hammer. "We reject this viewpoint."

So do we. The costs and the benefits of any word processor go way beyond the purchase price and the number of lines being turned out. Too often people assume that if you automate everything, you'll get some kind of magic benefits. But what often happens is that you get more paper, more reports, and no particular change in the factors critical to the success of the department and the company. That's why you need something more than piles of paper by which to measure your department's success.

Once you have some rough ideas of what those critical success factors are, you can start asking people what changes might help you achieve them—lesser goals, perhaps, but more tangible. Here are some that might apply to your office:

- Automating some repetitive manual tasks.
- Cutting back on expensive temporary help and outside contractors.
- Speeding up customer service.
- Cleaning up the look of proposals.
- Making letters to customers more accurate.
- Increasing the volume of form letters sent out.
- Distributing the work load more evenly.
- Reducing turnaround time.
- Lowering the cost of mailing and distributing information.
- Giving everyone instant access to computerized files.
- Wiping out a backlog.
- Improving employee morale.
- Using space more efficiently.

Phase Two

Now that you have a list of goals culled from the suggestions of everyone in your department, your team can analyze the work you actually do today, to see how you are meeting those objectives. But how? Just counting the number of phone calls made and pages typed doesn't help you understand how those activities help achieve the goals of the department. So perhaps your team ought to define the exact tasks you perform there—meaningful tasks, not just outward actions. Collecting or paying out money, hiring people, selecting real estate sites—these might be the main functions of your office.

At M.I.T.'s Laboratory for Computer Sciences, a team of professors and graduate students has been developing a method for analyzing office procedures in terms of these major functions. They point out that a function usually has three stages: when it starts, when you manage it, and when you stop doing it. Each procedure you do helps carry out one or another stage of that function. And each procedure tends to focus on one or more objects—something tangible, or an idea, such as an application for employment, which involves several different forms and bits of information. An "object" is not a form—that's just one way to collect the information.

The M.I.T. team suggests you talk with everyone in the office about the main lines of each function, its major procedures and objects, before getting into details. The reason is that this way you can see the way each procedure relates to the function it is supposed to serve. And it keeps you clear of the particular forms you are using today, since those might easily be changed. At this point you are looking, in a way, for the ideal procedure.

For each procedure, your interviews will help you figure out the main steps. And about each step, you might ask:

- What sets this step in motion?
- What do you do here?
- How can you tell that this step has ended?
- How long does that usually take? How long should it take?
- Where do you get input from? And where do the results go?
- What files, data bases, or mental lists do you consult?
- What problems give you trouble in this step?

The M.I.T. team, then, suggests analyzing procedures in two passes—and the first time at a fairly abstract level, to get the general idea. Then you might write up a general report and show it to the people who actually do the procedures, to make sure you've got it right. And only then would you go into all the details.

Phase Three

Having worked out a general description of the functions, procedures, steps, and objects as they currently exist in your office, you can go back to your staff with your description of their work, to see if they find it accurate. In each stage of each major function, then, you can begin to find out exactly what goes on in the procedures. Your aim, in this phase, is to figure out the volume of work being done, whether typing, filing, copying, opening and sending mail, bookkeeping, arranging meetings, proofreading, retrieving information from the files, or greeting visitors.

And, looking at all the procedures, you can start adding up the time it takes to do a certain volume of work, and the costs involved, so that you can begin to decide whether it makes sense to turn to automation for help in that particular area. For instance, if you don't use the files more than two or three times a day, you probably don't need to put them on your computer. But if you go to them a hundred times a day, you'll probably speed up access if you do.

For example, concerning typing, you might end up with figures like these:

- Number of minutes it takes to produce a final page.
- Number of revisions on an average page.
- Number of keystrokes performed each hour.
- Number of hours the equipment didn't work in a week.
- Number of hours, on average, a person spends typing.
- Number of lines typed, on average, each hour.
- Number of "objects" being handled at any time.
- Total time to complete each procedure.
- Number of times you repeat a procedure.
- Frequency at which exceptions seem to occur.
- Number of people involved in each step or procedure.
- Size of the relevant files.

How in the world are you going to find out all that, about everything from bookkeeping to photocopying? There are five main techniques:

1. Questionnaires
2. Work Sampling
3. Document Analysis
4. Interviews
5. Background Research

You don't need to use all these techniques. You can pick and choose parts of each—whatever seems right for your office.

1. Questionnaires. Don't just send around a questionnaire—take it to your staff in person. Explain what your team is up to, why you want the information, what you're going to make out of it. Assure people that they'll get a chance to look over the results before you send them on. Show them a "completed" questionnaire, as an example. You might even set up a form so that they can record their time over a week, or a form to describe each document worked on. Some typical questions follow, but you'll think of more that apply to your own situation:

- What are the main procedures you carry out, and what do you see as the major steps in each one?
- Keeping a record of your work, what percentage of your time do you spend in one week typing, filing, copying, talking on the phone, calculating, handling mail, arranging meetings, receiving visitors, or something else?
- In this week, how many different types of documents did you handle? Were they letters, form letters, straight text, boilerplate text, statistics, forms, or something else?
- For each type of document you've handled this week, could you tell us: How many of these did you do this week? In all, how much time did you devote to this type of document? How long does it take to produce one from start to finish? How many lines, on average? How many times did you revise it—either because the original author requested changes or because you made a mistake and had to retype a page?
- How many copies did you make of each type of document? What kind of input do you receive—handwritten, steno notes, typed copy, or machine dictation? How many errors does it take to force you to retype a page in this type of document? Do you have clear standards about format? Do you use any symbols not on the ordinary typewriter? How wide is the paper? Do you enter this on special paper, such as carbon forms? Could this be printed in cheap but fuzzy dots? Or does it have to be letter-quality? What percentage of your typing ends up being photo-typeset for printing?
- On copying: What percentage of the material you copy comes out of your own typewriter? What percentage is from someone else within your own office? How much from another department? How much from outside the company?
- On calculating: How many of the figures you are manipulating come from documents already in your files? Do you do anything beyond adding, subtracting, multiplying, and dividing? Do you use a spreadsheet? Do you need to type up the results?
- On mail: How much comes from within your own department? How much comes from within the rest of your company? How much from outside? When you send mail, what percentage circu-

lates within your office? Within the company? Outside of the company?
- On phone calls: How many phone calls do you make each day? How long do they last, on average? How many of the people you talk to are within your own office? The company? If you had a system by which you could record a message whenever you couldn't reach someone, how many calls could you use that on?
- On filing: What percentage of your day goes to sorting material to go into the files, filing, and retrieving? What percentage of the material you add to the files originated from within your own office? Within the company? From outside?
- On general matters: What are the top priority procedures for you? What are the biggest problems you face? What do you like most about your job, and least? What career path do you see ahead of you?
- On job situation: Do you prefer working for one boss only? Working with a team? Answering to several bosses? Being part of a pool?
- What changes do you suggest to help our operation achieve the objectives we agreed to before?

Obviously, one of the things you're trying to figure out in this way is how much of the information you process starts within your office, spins around it, and settles down there. If a lot does, you might be able to cut out paper and put the information on the computer—electronic mail, computerized files, direct transfer to phototypesetting and printing.

You're looking for patterns of reduplicated efforts—one person writing a report, copying it, sending it to someone else in the office, only to have that person retype parts of the report and add statistics that are already on file, then copy that and walk around distributing copies. What takes four hours that way might take less than an hour if the second person could just call up the report on the word processor, copy parts electronically, call up the other files, copy those, and then send the new letter around to everybody's terminal electronically.

You're also looking for problems—slowdowns, obstacles, antiquated routines that don't make any sense any more, two people doing the same work twice, expensive shortcuts used in "rush" situations, and almost anything else that disturbs or distracts the employees. And suggestions—in fact, these may be so helpful that you have to consider new topics in another questionnaire.

2. Work Sampling. You can also wander around the office, observing. By using a random numbers table, you can set up a truly unpredictable schedule for popping in on each person. Or you can just swing around every twenty minutes for a few days. In this way you uncover activities that neither you nor the other employee thought of, and you can confirm that an employee is, in fact, spending about the time you estimated on each activity.

What you need is a checklist, showing major functions and procedures, then activities like typing, filing, bookkeeping, and so on. You walk in, see what an employee is doing, and check off a box. That's all. After you've done that 40 or 50 times, you can begin to work out some rough percentages. For instance, if you dart in 50 times, and find someone typing 25 of those times, you can figure that person types 50 percent of the time.

The longer you do this, of course, the more of a nuisance you are. So be sociable. Chat when people look like they want to be interrupted. Leave people alone. And make sure they understand *why* you are doing this, and that you're not going to turn them in if they're sound asleep. (Mark that "personal time.")

3. Document Analysis. This is another way to total up the amount of work that passes through your typewriters, to see how much typing—and what kind—went into a given page of the final report. You distribute "action paper," to be put behind every sheet of paper that goes into the typewriter; it makes a carbon of everything typed, including all mistakes, half-done pages, forms, rough notes. Or you can ask everyone to save whatever they do and make an extra copy of the final versions for you.

In this way, you end up looking at exactly what got typed. You can then analyze the material to see what word-processing functions might be helpful—and to confirm your measurements of volume. For instance, you can tell:

- Total number of lines typed in a day.
- Average number of lines in each document.
- Total number of lines in final versions.
- Total number of lines retyped because of errors or revisions.
- Total number of lines of standard material that gets retyped and retyped.
- Total number of lines that use special functions available on word processors, such as boldface, centering, columns, complex calculations, different spacings, double strike, extra-wide paper, footnotings, foreign language, formulas with sub- and superscripts, forms, global search and replace, headers and footers, indexing, mailing lists, multiple type fonts, multiple indentations, right justification, repagination, underlining.

4. Interviewing. You've interviewed people during your preliminary survey, and then again when you were defining the main objectives, functions, and procedures of the department. You've handed out your writeup of that information, so that people can tell you their reactions and suggestions. And now, with completed questionnaire in hand and document analysis done, you can go back for a detailed runthrough of each person's work, answering the questions that have occurred to you and confirming that patterns you see are really there.

Show the results of your analysis to your staff and find out if they feel the analysis seems reasonable. Discuss what people fear in any changeover—whether it's losing contact with others in their area, getting sent to a typing pool, or facing a computer. Ask, too, about exceptions to the general rule: what do people do about misplaced letters, mistakes, people who haven't conformed to the rules or to a switch in policy. And what about bottlenecks, delays, backlogs, problems, duplication of effort, stupid rules, clumsy equipment? What could be changed, besides the typewriter?

Speak, too, with the people who originate the work:

- Do they feel they are getting enough secretarial support now?
- Is turnaround fast enough?
- Do certain types of documents seem to cause more hassles than others? How come?
- How often do they have to send out for temporary help?
- Are there times when the work seems to jam up?
- Are they satisfied with rough drafts on some material?
- Would they be willing to use word processors themselves?
- What would they think about turning all their typing over to a pool?
- What if their own secretaries could do filing, typing, printing, and distributing—all from the desk?

Sketch out various suggestions you've picked up from people in the office and find out how various managers feel about the ideas.

Remember that the point is not just information. Only if you really listen will people feel they're part of the decision-making process.

5. Background Research. To find out how much money it costs to produce each page or each line of paperwork now, you need to get some figures from management concerning salaries, fringe benefits, overhead, equipment's depreciated value, outside expenses. Ask around, too, to find out if any other departments or offices have tried automation. If their experience went sour, you need to find out why, so you can avoid the pitfalls.

And keep listening for news of any other changes being planned. They may limit your options, or offer solutions you hadn't thought of.

Phase Four

Now you have to write up your results and present them in a way that anyone—even a boss—can see what the problems are today. A lot of this involves calculating averages and totals. You'll want to show conclusions such as:

PROCEDURES
- Average time needed to complete each procedure.
- Average number of objects (such as forms, reports, letters, application packages) being handled at any one time in each procedure. Remember, you can define a procedure any way you want—basically, it's any major job you undertake in carrying out one of the functions of your office.
- Average number of times each procedure is performed in a day or week—and average number of exceptions to the standard procedure.
- Average number of people involved in each procedure.
- A flow chart showing how paper travels from person to person, step by step.
- Average amount of time it takes to respond to a customer.

OVERVIEW OF ACTIVITIES
- Average number of lines per hour, using various functions that could be done on word processor, including filing, copying, distributing, calculating, and printing. Use of special features like centering, compared to the average number of lines per hour.
- Costs of the current system. How much does it cost per page, per line, per type of document, to enter it, copy it, file it, distribute it?
- Current turnaround time for each type of document.
- Average amount of time spent by each person filing, copying, typing, retyping, distributing each final page, of each document type.

COMMUNICATION
- Percentage of mail that comes from within the department, within the company, outside. Percentage that goes to the department, company, or outside.
- Percentage of material filed or retrieved from files that originated from this department, from the company, or outside.
- Percentage of typed input that comes from within the same office, within the company, or outside. Percentage of typed output that goes to same office, company, or outside.
- Percentage of material you copy that comes from your department's typewriters. From the rest of the company. From outside.

- Percentage of figures you use in calculations that come from documents already in office files.
- Total number of pages in each major file, and the number of people who use that file regularly.
- Average number of pages distributed to each person, or by each person, each day.
- Percentage of phone calls within the department, within the company, or outside. Average length of call. Number of office or company calls that could be handled by a system allowing you to leave a real message.

TYPING
- Average volume of work turned out in an hour, in lines and pages per document, sorted by type of document.
- Average number of lines entered by each person in an hour.
- Average number of minutes it takes to produce a final page, by document type.
- Percentage of input that is handwritten, typed, on machine dictation, or in steno notes.
- Average number of revisions per average final page, by document type.
- Percentage of final pages that can be rough draft, as opposed to percentage that must be letter-quality.
- Specific math functions used, shown as percentages of all calculations performed. Percentage of these calculations that must be typed.
- Average lines per hour using special functions such as underlining and centering, compared to average lines per hour.

PRINTERS AND OTHER PERIPHERALS
- Percentage of final pages using extra-wide paper, special forms, envelopes, or other unique paper.
- Percentage of all typing that ends up being phototypeset.
- Average number of pages turned out per hour, at peak periods.
- Average number of lines using features that some printers can't handle, such as underlining, bolding, sub- and superscript, half lines, wide paper.

PROBLEMS
- Brief descriptions of each major problem, with indications of different ways it could be solved, either through word processing or some other way.
- List of all major suggestions for improvement.

JOB SITUATION
- Average work load by employee (to show uneven distribution).
- Dollars spent on temporary help, or outside contractors, total, and by page.
- Percentage of current employees preferring various job situations (one boss, several bosses, working as a team, being in a pool).
- Major sources of job satisfaction and dissatisfaction at present.

Facts like these provide the "before" picture, and suggest what kind of system might help. For instance, if you have huge files and your staff spends a third of every day putting things in and taking them out, you certainly should consider a system that allows you to create a data base and get instant access to each document that way. But if most people use the files only once or twice a day, and it takes them only a few minutes to find each memo, then you probably couldn't justify the expense.

But these are the decisions you make in the next phase.

Phase Five

Now you figure out what you can do—or buy—to improve your office's efficiency. You may be able to make some changes right away, just by reassessing jobs, moving files around, reconstructing procedures. That's a likely outcome of your study. But there may be some changes that only a word processor can help you with.

In this phase, you figure out exactly what you need, based on your study, and then design a new office—new jobs, perhaps, new reporting relationships, new equipment, perhaps even new furniture, and lights. In this phase, you go back through your results, looking at them with one question in mind: how could we do better?

Job Situation. What arrangement do most people say they want? Probably not a word-processing center, or pool. Most people would like the current social relationships to stay the same—with maybe a firing here or there. But if you have worked closely with your staff in doing the study, they may be willing to shift the work around, or work on some activities or procedures as a team.

Even though a word-processing center appears to be a more efficient way of using expensive machinery, you're so likely to encounter resistance with this approach that any paper productivity gains may slacken off after a few months. We don't recommend it. But many vendors urge it on you, because it makes their machinery look so efficient, and some managers like the idea for the same reason. Resist, if you can. Unless, of course, you find real support for the idea among your fellow workers.

Another solution is to set up a center and hire all new people to staff it—specialists.

If you want to add word processing but keep your office pretty much as is, you need to decide whether everyone's going to work on his or her own machine without sharing any files, or sending messages back and forth. Probably not. But that depends on the way you assign people to various procedures and the amount of information that's shared, or passed along. In this way you can decide between a bunch of stand-alones and a multi-user system.

But don't expect several employees to share one keyboard. This leads to bickering, and, after a while, most people stop using the equipment, going back to their typewriters. Think of the telephone as an analogy. Professor Louis Gauges, of the University of Paris, says, "Let's take the actual percentage of time spent using a telephone. All studies of a manager's time show that it is in the range of six percent. This is not a reason to share one telephone between fourteen managers. The same will be true with the new office tools."

Perhaps you can think of a way to clear up some of the dissatisfactions people have expressed, some of the bottlenecks and breakdowns. But pay particular attention to what people say pleases them about their current job. For instance, if they like meeting the public, make sure you're not blithely assigning them to some backroom. If they value the chance to do their own research, try not to make them more "productive" by relieving them of this task. Where possible, check back with everyone with your idea of the new social and reporting relationships, to make sure people endorse the general idea, even though each will have a few qualifications. Without such support, no plan will succeed for long.

Whether or not you're going to move toward a word-processing center, you'll need someone to control the flow of work in and out of a shared system, to set standards (how are new files named?), to assign priorities (Al gets to print his report before Susan does hers), to call the vendor for repairs. It's hard to tell how much of someone's time this will take, but as you approach a half a dozen terminals working full-time, this person will begin putting in forty hours a week on word processing.

And since everyone will have to learn the new system, budget a realistic six weeks to two months for *lower* production while people feel free to take risks, play games, trade what they've learned. If you expect everyone to get up to speed after the vendor's quickie seminar (usually a few days, just enough to teach basics), you'll find that most people resent the increased pressure, and, in resistance, refuse to use any of the advanced functions—the ones you bought specially for this system.

Typing. Are most of your documents just one or two pages long? Then you could settle for a page-oriented system, in which you have to work on a page at a time. But this is clumsy if you have a substantial amount of work involving long documents. If you fill out a lot of forms, you may have to look for a system that lets you create those forms on the computer, then call them up onscreen, so your printer can create a new one every time; or you might get a system that allows you to enter material in half lines, so you can fit text into the odd shapes of a preprinted form. (And you'll need a printer that will accept those forms.)

If you've found that your people use a lot of boilerplate-type material, then you'll need some kind of merging capability—bringing together an address and a letter, pulling in one-line definitions of key ideas, or blending together whole paragraphs and pages.

In just this way you can go through every function we've listed in this book marking some as essential, others as attractive, and some as pleasant to have but unnecessary. Statistics? Graphics? Complex calculations? Automatic repaginating? Gradually, you get a picture of your ideal system—and, perhaps, your second choice.

Now's the time to go out and look at some actual word processors. Take along the list of questions that we raised earlier in this chapter. That should eliminate quite a few systems. And you'll find that several others just don't have the functions you need—even though the salesperson, with about twenty keystrokes and a lot of palaver, tells you the machine can do "almost the same thing."

Communication. In addition to word processing, you may be able to increase productivity by adding the ability to communicate electronically within the department, using central files. Of course, as you move in this direction you will have to discard more systems, since few offer *all* these possibilities.

For instance, if your staff spends a large portion of their time putting paper into files and taking other paper out, you might consider creating a computer data base or buying a sophisticated filing program, for faster access and fewer losses. But you'll need a special computer program for that and a very large amount of storage. (You can figure that you'll need at least as many pages as you already have in all those cabinets.)

If you distribute a lot of material within your department, you may want to look into electronic mail, so that you can just send a memo from your terminal to someone else's, never bothering to put it on paper.

Or perhaps you could use a system of voice storage, so that when you call someone who's out, you can still leave a detailed message that can be played back when the person returns. You can do this on some networks now.

The more you tend toward an interconnected network, sending messages back and forth along the cables, the more you're going to have to study office automation. And that may make sense only if you look at the whole company—main computers, phones, information circulating throughout. You'd best postpone buying anything until you perform that wider survey—otherwise you may find you've got a word processor that can't talk to any other department.

Printers and Other Peripheral Devices. If only a small percentage of your documents require letter-quality printing, you'll still need a daisy wheel printer, but you can buy one that doesn't print very fast. On the other hand, if you have a large volume of work that demands that kind of quality, you will have to look at faster, and more expensive, "impact," laser, or ink jet printers. On the other hand, if you have a lot of forms that don't have to look fancy, a dot matrix printer can do those quickly.

From your analysis of document types, you know which kinds of paper your printer must handle. You now have a list of those functions that require special features in the printer, such as underlining, sub- and superscript, half lines, extra-wide paper, special forms. Having this list of requirements should help you rule out a lot of printers.

Your average of the number of pages being turned out every hour at peak periods will give you a crude measure of the minimum speed you expect in a printer. But don't buy a printer that can just barely meet that requirement, because you'll probably wear it out.

If a lot of your material gets typeset and printed you may want to get a photocomposition machine that will accept text from your word processors. And if much of your input is from printed or typed material, consider buying an Optical Character Reader, which will enter the material automatically.

If possible, put your printers in their own soundproof room. If they're going to be around people, you need to budget for hoods, thick carpets, cork on the walls, acoustic tiles, maybe even drapes.

Office Setting. If you intend to put a lot of terminals in one room, remember that you're probably going to have to strengthen the air-conditioning—and make it adjustable. And try not to cram people too closely together.

Wherever you put the terminals, you'll need to adjust desk levels—or buy new desks and chairs. And to avoid glare, plan to repaint any bright walls, replace any shiny surfaces, and put blinds or drapes over any large windows.

And don't forget to consult with the vendor and your engineer to find out if you have enough power, enough outlets, protection against power surges, and brownouts. You may have to rewire.

Larger Objectives. As your ideal system emerges, you can begin to see how it will help you achieve the goals you spelled out way back at the start of your study—eliminating repetitive manual tasks, for instance, or speeding up customer service. As part of your report, it's important to spell out exactly what you expect these changes to accomplish. Don't go as far as a vendor suggests, or your people will be disappointed. But do relate the system to the larger objectives of the office, and the company.

For instance, if you aim to make your letters look better, you can point to the letter-quality printer as a way of achieving that. If you're planning to cut down on filing and copying time, show that the new system can hold all the files and print out plenty of copies in a fraction of the time your people spend now.

Phase Six

Having designed your ideal system, and perhaps a fallback, smaller version without so many functions, you can get some rough estimates of the cost from vendors of word processors, desks, air-conditioners, and drapes. In this way, you can generate one budget for renting the equipment, and another for buying it outright. And you can create a rough schedule of expenses, so that management can see when the funds will actually flow and when each part of the installation will be ready. But how can you justify the expense?

You can start by comparing the amount of work turned out before and after word processing. With word processing, most people can double their output per hour. In a full four hours of word processing—the maximum we recommend in an average day—you can usually turn out about 300 lines of new copy, 400 lines of revised material, or about 500 lines of standard materials. Another way to think of these figures is that with word processing, you can usually figure that, in that same half day, you can turn out about 40 pages of new or revised material (you can at least double that with stored material). These new speeds let you cut down the hours your staff spends producing.

Now that should let you clear up the backlog you face, or shift some people to new jobs, or simply have everyone do a bit more than before.

Whichever goal you're aiming at, you can now show that this equipment lets you cut down the time required, steps up the quality of the output, and reduces the number of people needed to do the old amount of work. You can now compare the cost per page before and after—and usually you'll find that there's a dramatic savings when you move to word processing.

Harvey Poppel, a senior vice-president with the consulting firm of Booz Allen and Hamilton, led a study of 300 managers which concluded that automating their work could save an average company 15 percent of their pretax operating income. But he warned, "No cookbook exists for taking or measuring the benefits of automation."

Certainly you—and an eager vendor—can work up some suggestive statistics:

- How many pages you will be able to distribute how fast within your office if you have electronic mail, and how much of your time that will save.
- How much faster people will be able to turn out a page of each type of document—and therefore, how much time you'll save.
- How much faster each person will be able to enter, calculate, copy, file, print, and distribute each type of document.
- How much money you'll save per final page of each type of document, on entering, calculating, copying, filing, printing, and distributing.
- How quickly, and how much more efficiently, you can handle each procedure, thanks to automating some of the steps involved.
- Approximately how much extra work you'll be able to process, once the system gets going.

But don't forget the "soft" benefits. These are the ones you can't easily measure in dollars—improved morale, quality, expandability, accessibility of stored information. There's no quick way to measure how much a backlog of orders "costs" you—or how much money you'll make by getting in touch with customers the day after they write you. But surely such changes will help you in the long run.

Probably the most important thing you can do in this section of your report is to show how the new system will help you perform the procedures your office was set up to carry out. How will your new design help you achieve those goals you've already found were critical to your office's success? By spelling out this contribution, you can help management understand that what you have in mind is more than a glorified typewriter—it's a new way of doing the real work your office was set up to do.

Perhaps all this studying, planning, and figuring is enough to make you give up the idea of automation altogether. Of course, if you have a very small office, or a very big budget, you can probably finesse a lot of these phases. But if you have a medium-sized office and budget, a few months of careful research can help you avoid investing in future headaches, backbiting, and equipment breakdowns. You'll be able to ask vendors intelligent questions. You'll feel more certain of your own recommendations. And because you've consulted with everyone who will be affected, they may even help make the system a success—rather than blaming you and sabotaging the installation.

You and your staff are not just "users." You're people. You don't need to be a human factors engineer to understand what your office-mates want. Their help can make the difference between an idea and a system that actually works. More important than your proposal, then, is the activity you've gone through, drawing everyone together, encouraging consensus, creating a new team. That's healthy.

6

Shopping for a Word Processor

You probably have an idea by now of what you want your word processor to do, what extra comforts you'd like, and which attachments. You probably have a type of system in mind—dedicated, multifunctional hybrid, or microcomputer—and how many workstations and printers you need. You may be starting to see that many products could fit your needs.

Before you buy something special, like a new car, washing machine, or video recorder, you do some research: read magazines, ask your friends for recommendations, window shop, watch some different brands at work, and check out warranties and service contracts. Acquiring a word processor requires the same kind of preliminary study.

Step One: Research

Since you're reading this book, your research has already started. You need to understand what word processing is, what it can and can't do, and what your word-processing needs are.

Deciding what you need is really your biggest task. Knowing your word-processing needs will help you ask the right questions and select the best equipment. Of course, to define your needs, you have to know what you can expect word processing to do for you.

Deciding what you want is also important. What you need and what you want aren't always the same thing. What you need may be a Volkswagen Bug; what you'd like might be a Cadillac. And what you can afford may be somewhere in between—a Buick, say.

As you think about what you want your word processor to do, set priorities and grade the features and capabilities. What's critical, what would be nice to have, what would really be luxurious? Keep them all in mind. Chances are you won't find a system that's 100 percent of what you want, but you may be able to come pretty close.

How do you find out about specific word processors and whether they fit your needs?

Read. In the back of this book, in Appendix A, you'll find a long list of word-processing software and equipment, suggesting what each can do. We've covered a wide range of systems available on the market today. Yet almost every month we see announcements of new products or enhancements to existing products. Word processing isn't a static field. It's a good idea to subscribe to (or borrow a friend's copies of) some computer and information magazines. Read the articles, look at the ads, look for the "new products" section. At the back of this book you'll find a list of some of the periodicals and books we've found useful. Many business, trade, and news magazines have articles on selecting word-processing and computer systems, too.

Talk to Your Friends. Start mentioning your interest in word processing to your friends. You'll no doubt find some word-processing "buffs" in the woodwork. Friends, colleagues, even competitors can help you a great deal. Some may have found the perfect system. Others will have horror stories to tell. Both will help you. You'll get an idea what it's like to acquire word processing and may learn from other people's mistakes. You'll find out which companies or salespeople are like used-car salesmen at their worst, and which ones honestly want to help you find the system you need.

Look at Ads. Taking a plane trip? Read the airline magazine for word-processing ads. Flip through *Inc., Business Week, Fortune, Forbes, Newsweek, Time,* and other upscale magazines. You'll find plenty of computer ads. Often the same companies have word processing. Keep your perspective, though. Beautiful ads mean a large advertising budget; they don't always mean the best product.

Use the Yellow Pages. Find out which word-processing companies have offices in your area. Word processing now has its own category in many Yellow Pages directories. You might also look under Data Processing or Office Equipment.

Attend Word-Processing Shows. If you live in a big city, a word-processing or computer show may come to town. If not, it might be worth a trip to see one. You'll get mass exposure to products and sales pitches, and you'll learn a lot. Many shows have seminars on issues relating to word processing and the office. You'll get a chance to hear the experts talk and meet people like yourself who are trying to decide which word processor to use.

Associations. There are many computer and word-processing associations throughout the world. Some are local groups, some national or international organizations with local branches. Often they've done research on equipment, which they make available to their members, and again, you'll meet other people only too happy to tell you their word-processing stories.

If you haven't the time or inclination to analyze your word-processing needs and select the equipment as suggested in Chapter 4, or if the amount of information and products available overwhelms you, you can get some help.

Paid Help. Many consulting companies or individual consultants will come in, ask you questions, watch the work flow in your office, examine your procedures, analyze how the work is done, and recommend word-processing equipment that will fill your needs. This can save you lots of time and legwork, because most consultants are already familiar with much of the equipment on the market and what it can and can't do. And they know from experience what to look for in your office and what questions to ask. Their services can cost anywhere from $25 to $75 per hour, and possibly more. Selecting the right consultant to help you takes some work, however. You should talk to several, and you'll need to ask some questions and consider some issues:

- How experienced is the consultant? Has this person recommended equipment for other companies in your line of work? How many other companies? Get some references and talk to them.
- How long has the person been a consultant?
- How long has the person been in the word-processing and computer field?
- If the person is a computer consultant, has he or she helped select word-processing equipment before?
- Is the person familiar with your industry and the type of work done in your office?
- How does the consultant plan to analyze your needs? Will it require talking to everyone in the office, doing a study of existing work flow, or both?
- How does the consultant plan to evaluate equipment for you?
- Does the consultant specialize in one or a few types of word-processing equipment?
- Is this person or company affiliated with a word-processing company?
- Does the consultant get a kickback for recommending certain types of equipment?

- How much of your time and other company employees' time will the consultant need?
- Will the consultant write up the findings of what word-processing needs exist in your office, and how available equipment matches up?
- How long will it take to analyze your needs and to recommend a system? It's a good idea to get an estimate.
- What is the ballpark fee for all the consultant's services? You must get an estimate up front!
- Who pays for what? Are materials included in the consultant's fee, or will you be billed for parking, making copies of reports, long distance phone calls, etc.?
- How does the consultant get along with the people in your company? If the person is going to be around a lot, be sure he or she has a good rapport with your staff.
- Who in your company will the consultant work with and/or report to?

Consultants can help. But remember, you're looking for someone to take over a task that you either haven't time for, want experienced advice on, or are overwhelmed by. Make sure you're getting good help.

A consultant doesn't have to do the whole task, either. If you've already evaluated your internal needs and want to make sure you've covered the bases, a consultant could review your findings. Or if you want someone to take over at that point and look at equipment, a consultant could do the legwork for you. Or you might ask a specialist to do a feasibility study for you and use the results yourself to select equipment.

Help Without Charge (But Not Without Time). Word-processing vendors can help you decide what you need, and you don't have to do all the work on your own before you approach them. Good salespeople want to sell you the right word-processing system, not just any word processor. Ethical and business-wise companies don't want to sell you equipment that won't meet your needs—it's bad for their reputation, and gives them headaches they can live without. Besides, they want your business the next time you need equipment.

Many salespeople actually have skills similar to those of a consultant. They should find out what you need before trying to sell you anything. If you're uncertain what features and functions are important, they can help you find out. They may even have a questionnaire to find out exactly what you do and don't do. Be wary, however. It's only natural that sales representatives will think of matching your needs to their solutions, so you may get a biased view of what you need. When you get help from word-processing salespeople, talk to several of them.

Before you approach a salesperson, you'll want to do some window-shopping, to see what these funny machines look like up close. Computer shows are a great place to do this, but they don't always happen close to home, or when you need them.

Stores. You can see some kinds of word processors in retail stores. For the most part, these are small systems, but they can introduce you to word processors even if you need a larger system. Try your local computer store. Browse, and then ask to see word processing run on one or two of the computers. You may find some stand-alone word processors among the microcomputers. Some big-name brands have their own stores across the country. IBM, Digital Equipment Corporation (DEC), and Xerox have all opened retail stores. Even some department stores now carry personal computers, and they may have word-processing programs for them. Sears and Macy's have both added departments for this purpose.

Word Processors in Use. If you know people using word processors, go see them, preferably during working hours. That way you'll get to see how the systems fit into offices. Display floors and demonstration rooms don't convey what it's like to have a word processor in an office. You'll get to see how much special furniture was required, how noisy the system is, and how it's been put to work in some other offices.

Step Two: Selecting Equipment to See

While researching and window-shopping, you will acquire quite an extensive list of word-processing companies and products. Some you can tell right away aren't for you. Some sound perfect, and some you can't tell. The next step is to get details. Take your list of "sound perfect" and "can't tells" and call or write them, asking for information. Some magazines have a "service card" in back for their advertisers. You can circle the companies or products you want information from, send the card in, and they'll notify the vendors for you. It may take four to six weeks, and then you'll start getting calls and letters.

When you want to contact companies directly, you won't find listings for all of them locally. Your phone book listings may give you the impression that there are only about 25 systems on the market. Don't give up hope if the companies who make the systems you're interested in don't have local offices. They may have a local dealer or distributor.

Companies Who Sell Their Own Word-Processing Products Through a Direct Sales Force. These are some of the best-known word-processing and computer names. IBM, DEC, Wang, CPT, NBI, Lanier, and Lexitron are a few of the companies who sell direct to you, the user. These companies have branch offices, with salespeople dedicated to finding and selling to people like you. If you want to start with information and don't want a sales pitch yet, try asking the receptionist when you call. She may be able to send information to you. But chances are you'll be referred to a salesperson as soon as you say, "I want some information on your word processor." Tell the person exactly what stage you're at. If you're doing research and checking out word-processing capabilities, ask for brochures and literature on the system you're interested in. If you're looking for specific functions or a certain style of word processing, ask whether the company's products include what you're looking for. There's no point gathering brochures on every word processor available if they won't meet your needs.

Companies Who Sell Other Companies' Products. These companies may be called dealers, distributors, systems houses, or OEMs (for "Original Equipment Manufacturer"—an odd term, since OEM denotes a company that buys a machine from one firm and makes hardware or software changes before reselling it). Retail stores are not included in this grouping; we'll talk about them separately.

Among this group of sellers, you'll find a few different approaches. Some sell and support the product without changing or adding anything to it. Others "add value" to the product by offering additional software programs, "customizing" the software that comes with the machine (changing it to fit your needs), or changing the hardware itself. Some sell only one kind of word processor or computer; others have a variety for you to choose from.

These kinds of companies are sometimes the hardest to find. Their company name may hold no indication of the type of products they sell. Often they're local companies, with only one or two offices. They don't do much advertising. You may get their name by word of mouth from friends and associates, or as a referral from the company whose product they sell.

If you're a small company, you may find that buying through a small company has advantages. Salespeople are often paid on commission, and when you contact some of the big-name companies, you may find that the salespeople are more interested in selling to large companies who want larger machines or more units than in selling you a single stand-alone system. Small local companies are geared to selling to small companies. And they may understand and care about your needs more than some of the larger companies. On the negative side, if they should go out of business or fail to provide the support you need, the original manufacturer may not want to help you because you didn't "buy direct."

Retail Stores. You can now find word processors in a variety of retail stores. First, there are the ones called computer stores. These stores, with names like ComputerLand, the Byte Stop, and Computer Connection, are largely known for selling microcomputers. They often have word-processing software packages available for the micros, and may also have some dedicated word processors that can also be used with other software packages. The WangWriter, for instance, Wang Laboratory's smallest word processor, can now be purchased in some computer stores. So can the Xerox 820, the Apple IIe and Macintosh, and the IBM PC, all microcomputers that can be used for word processing.

Brand-name retail stores are retail outlets for some large computer companies, such as the DEC Store (Digital Equipment Corporation), the Xerox Store, and the IBM Store. Most of the time these stores stock only their brand-name equipment, although some, such as Xerox, plan to sell other computers as well. You'll often find the company's low-end word processors in these stores. IBM sells their DisplayWriter in their store; DEC sells their DECMATE.

In the department stores, companies like Sears and Macy's have already added personal computer departments, and more department stores will probably follow. These stores sell microcomputers, and word-processing software should be available.

Your local office equipment and typewriter stores may be getting into the word-processing business too. So far they seem to be moving from electric typewriters to electronic typewriters, and then memory typewriters or one-line display word processors. Some are already carrying screen-display word processors. Before too long these stores should be a common source of word-processing equipment.

Requests for Proposals. Requests for Proposals, or RFPs, are commonly used by the government and by some other large companies when selecting equipment. An RFP is a written report specifying your needs and requesting a proposed solution from vendors. You might want to consider this as a means to finding which companies have products that fill your needs. There's plenty of work in preparing an RFP, however. Essentially, after studying your needs for equipment, you write a report about your findings. For each problem or task you want to solve in your office, you ask how the vendor can solve it. These questions may be general or specific, and usually a mixture of the two is necessary: what kind of writing, typing, editing, proofing, filing, etc., you do; how long your documents are; your special formatting needs; nonstandard symbols; mass mailings; everything you do should be included. And ask how much the vendor's proposed solution will cost.

Then send the RFP out to the companies you think have products that you should consider. Give them a date to respond by, let them know you're sending it to a number of companies, and see what happens. Their replies should help you identify the word processors you should look at.

Step Three: The Sales Cycle

When you're familiar with what you need and want a word processor to do, and have come up with a few products that look like they might fit the bill, it's time to talk to salespeople, see demonstrations, and test equipment.

Your first contact with a company will probably be by phone, followed by a sales representative's visit to your office or your visit to his. Be prepared. Be ready to discuss what your company does, how you see a word processor being used in your office, what your budget for word processing is, what level of support you require, and any special questions or concerns you have. Have some sample documents ready, too. You'll want to show your work to the salesperson and, later, test it out on the equipment.

Setting Up a Demonstration. Some companies won't demonstrate their equipment until they've "qualified" you. They want to be sure you're really interested before they take the time to show you their product. This makes sense from your standpoint, too. A demonstration can take most of a morning or afternoon. Qualify your vendors. If you know upfront that their word processor only works with 5-page documents, and you produce 35-page reports regularly, is it worth your time?

By the time you get to the demo room, you should know your sales representative fairly well, and he or she should know whether their product meets your needs. The salesperson may demonstrate the equipment for you, but often you'll find yourself turned over to someone else with a title such as MSR (marketing support representative), WPS (word-processing specialist), or software support specialist. This person probably knows the system inside out and backwards. Your salesperson may know what the word processor can do conceptually, but may not actually use the system. (Some vendors require their sales representatives to have hands-on experience; others don't.)

Often the person in the office who does demos is also responsible for ongoing customer support and training. This person probably knows better than the sales representative whether the word processor you're about to see does what you need quickly and easily. She (most often it will be a woman) also knows "ways around" features that the product lacks, and can make difficult procedures seem trivial.

The "Canned" Demo. Many companies have what are called "canned" demonstrations. This is a standard demo, which steps the machine through some basic functions, shows off what it does best, and leaves out what is difficult to do. You'll be introduced to the company's jargon, too. Word-processing vendors love to come up with new names for old features.

Before the demonstration begins, make it clear that before you leave you will want to see some of your work done on the system, and that you want to try the equipment yourself. Then sit back and enjoy the standard demo. It will give a good introduction to the product.

Watching Canned Demos. Some demonstrations seem designed to keep your eyes on the screen as formatting rearranges text in miraculous formations. Other demos seem to keep you looking at the keyboard, focusing on colored keys or actions executed at the press of a key. When you find your focus being drawn to one part of the system, make a point of looking at the rest of it. If great things are happening on the screen, watch the MSR's hands for a while. Are her fingers darting around quickly to unlabeled keys and rapidly executing contorted gymnastics? On the other hand, if you keep being directed to the clearly labeled keyboard, be sure to take an extra look at the screen, too. Are the characters clear? Are you being steered away from formats that can't be displayed accurately on the screen?

Whoever demonstrates the system will be talking while demonstrating, and it will probably be interesting and relevant to what's being shown. It also holds your attention while the computer does its work. This can be a pleasant way to keep you from noticing how long it takes for the computer to respond to some commands. For example, the computer may have to fetch information from disks periodically. This procedure may take, say, three sentences' worth of time. This doesn't seem like very long while you're talking and watching. It may seem a lot longer when you're working on it in your office. So be aware.

If at all possible, ask questions as they come up during the demo. Sometimes you'll be asked to wait until the end. If you are, *take notes*, and be sure to ask your questions later. It's very easy to skip over limitations when demonstrating word processing.

Let's say your documents contain lots of columns of numbers, and you've let the sales rep know that statistical typing must be easy on the word processor you acquire. So part of the demo includes numbers being entered in columns. The demonstration shows you how easy this is and how you can even have the system total the columns for you. And then how you can go directly from columns of numbers to entering a paragraph of explanatory text beneath them. But you're still back on the columns of numbers, and you ask if they can be moved around or swapped. The MSR says, "Uh, yes, you can do that," and continues on about the paragraph following the numbers. *Alert!* Why isn't she showing you how easy it is to swap columns? Pursue this now, or make a note to be sure you see it later. She may know a way to do it, but if she's not volunteering, it may take 15 keystrokes and 5 minutes.

Let's say your documents are anywhere from 3 to 25 pages in length. You're watching a demonstration of a word processor that works with one page at a time and stores each in its own document. The sales rep has assured you that the way their system handles pages, this won't be a problem for your work at all. See it. Don't worry about hurting anyone's feelings. Find out how difficult it will be. Have them create a multipage document, and then take page three, insert it in the middle of page one, and repaginate the document. Whatever equipment you select, you or someone in your office will have to use it regularly. Don't stint when it comes to pushing equipment to its limits at demo time.

Get Your Hands on the Keyboard. When the standard demo is finished, make sure you get some testing time on the system. Ask the MSR to show you how to create a document, enter text, change it, file the document away, and print it. Get a feel for the keyboard and what it takes to create and edit text.

See Your Work in Action on the Word Processor. Always take along samples of your work when you go to a word-processing demo. Pick a few documents that show a good cross-section of what you want a word processor to do. Include documents that are difficult typing tasks, such as tables, reports including scientific equations, paragraphs that need to be assembled into a proposal, or whatever your work requires. Plan to try the same documents on each word processor you look at. This will give you a good comparison of features, ease of use, and quality of printed reports from one system to another.

Take the checklists in this book along too, filled out with the functions and components you need. After seeing a few demonstrations, go over your answers again. You may find that features you thought would be very important before seeing word processing in action aren't critical, and that others that didn't make sense to you are more relevant to the work done in your office than you'd thought. With some demonstrations under your belt to contribute to your understanding of what you need a word processor to do, your checklists should provide a good tool to help you evaluate systems as you see them.

If possible, try entering some of your documents yourself during the demonstration. A second choice is to watch the sales representative or MSR do it. Have one of them enter your text, make the type of changes that occur in your office to it, and print it out. If you work with really long documents and want to see how changes are made to them, provide your sales rep with a copy of the document in advance, ask him to have it entered on the word processor, and you can see changes made to it when you see the demonstration.

After the Demonstration. At the end of a demonstration, you may find yourself confronted by the salesperson with contract in hand, made out in your name, just waiting for your signature. Or the salesperson may ask you, "Where do we go from here?" Don't let yourself be harassed or hurried. Be honest. Say what you liked and didn't like about the demonstration, and what reservations you have, if any. Make it clear that you're looking at other equipment and will keep in touch with him. (And you should be looking at other equipment—three to six systems is about right.) If someone else in your office must review your findings, make that known, too.

A Word About "Feature Wars," Bells, and Whistles. Feature wars are the competitive battles between vendors to have more and better features than the other guy. Don't get suckered into them. Keep in mind what you need a word processor to do. If a system meets your needs, has built-in extras, and is in your price range, terrific! But don't sacrifice the features that will be crucial to your productivity because you were wowed by the demonstration of a feature you'll only use once every four months. Also watch out for the anti–feature war salesperson. Is he honestly concerned about your getting the equipment you need, or is he denouncing competition because the equipment he sells lacks the extra "bells and whistles"?

When You Love the Product and Hate the Salesperson, or Vice Versa. Salespeople are the butt of many jokes and snide comments. Some of them certainly deserve it, but others don't. Some companies don't even call their sales force "salespeople" because of the associations people have with the word. They may be called "marketing specialists" or some other name. Whatever their titles, they are going to influence your buying decisions. If you can't abide the sales rep, you'll be disinclined to buy the product. On the other hand, if you've formed a fast friendship with one, you may find yourself willing to overlook limitations in the word processor they're selling.

Salespeople come and go, and in the computer industry, they move around very quickly. However, the equipment you're going to buy will be in your office for several years. If you find yourself thinking "I'd never buy anything from this person," but the equipment seems right for you, ask to have another representative work with you. If the equipment isn't right at all, but you want to do your new friend a favor, bow out gracefully and compensate yourself with the thought that a year from now that person may be selling for another company.

The Sales Cycle at Retail Stores. If you're looking at microcomputers with word-processing software packages, you'll probably be shopping in retail stores of one type or another. You'll find a very different approach in most of them—one more akin to buying an appliance or other large purchase in a retail store. Someone may ask if they can help you, but if you say you're just browsing, you'll probably be left alone to push buttons and try out the computers. Or a salesperson may load a program for you on one or more of the computers and let you try it out yourself.

Of course, there's more help if you want it, and unless you're very familiar with personal computers, take it! As any good word-processing salesperson should, those selling equipment in computer stores should be able to guide you. Let them know what you're looking for, and they can steer you in the right direction.

We've found shopping in computer stores to be very different from looking at equipment in manufacturers' offices, or the offices of their dealers or distributors. There just doesn't seem to be the same push to get you to make up your mind. Maybe that's because they understand that you've got a lot to learn, and it will take some time.

On the other hand, we've heard stories of people being sold the first microcomputer they looked at, even though it was completely inappropriate for their needs, just because they didn't understand what their options were, and a salesperson took advantage of them. It's also possible that the salesperson won't know what options are available to you. If he's familiar with micros but has never used dedicated word processing, his view will be narrower than otherwise. You need to know what questions to ask.

One thing you may find when shopping in computer stores is that you need more technical education. The initial microcomputer buyers were hobbyists, people with a background in computers or electronics who wanted their own system. Although today microcomputers are frequently sold as small-business computers or word processors, some salespeople still have hangovers from the old days, and may expect you to know what you need and what to ask for in bits and bytes. Their conversation may be full of technical terms.

If you're looking at microcomputers to do word processing as your primary computer application, we recommend that you also look at some dedicated systems, so that you can see the differences. The world of traditional computers and word processors is very different from the world of microcomputers, and inhabitants of the two sometimes act as though other types of equipment don't exist, or don't count.

Buying Hardware and Software: Two Purchases, Not One. When you talk to companies who sell dedicated word processors, you may be shown two or three different systems, based upon the number of operators you plan to have and the size of your word-processing work load. But the systems come as whole units—hardware and software that work together. If you'll be adding more hardware later, you'll add what the company has available. With micro or personal computers you usually have a choice of at least three or four word-processing software packages for any given equipment, and you can mix and match the equipment pieces themselves from different companies.

Select the word-processing software you want first. Try out several packages on different microcomputers. If the software you like works with different types of equipment, see it in action on different models, too. When it comes to selecting hardware, be sure you see the system connected together and working with the software before you take it home. Nothing can be more frustrating than discovering that the printer you bought requires cables you don't have and needs changes in your program that require a specialist.

SUPPORT

So far we've talked mostly about shopping for word-processing equipment and software. But there are other considerations. You're also shopping for a company to do business with. Your transactions don't end by signing a purchase agreement, handing over your money, taking your machine home, and plugging it in. You're going to need help once the boxes arrive in your office, and what kind of help you'll get should be discussed and included in your contract. Think about:

- When the equipment arrives in your office, who connects it up and makes it work?
- When you discover that you need a special cable to connect your printer, where do you get it?
- When you've never used anything more complicated than an electric typewriter, how do you learn to use a word processor?

- Later, when you know the basics but don't know how to use a special "advanced" feature, who will help you to learn it?
- When you try to recall a document from the disk you stored it on and your screen displays "Disk Error" and freezes, what do you do?
- When you're ready to add a modem to your system so you can send information to the computer in the home office, who makes sure you have the hardware and software you need, and shows you how to do it?

The answers to all of these questions depend on the quality and quantity of support that comes with your word processor. "Support" is a nebulous term; it can imply anything from vague encouragement to direct assistance. You can and should pin it down to a concrete definition (agreed on by you and the vendor, in writing) before you purchase equipment. The level of support you receive can mean the difference between the success and failure of word processing in your office.

How do you know how much and what kind of support you'll need? Some types of support will be obvious. For example, you can look at the documentation and manuals that are provided with the system, to see if they're clear and easy to read. You can find out if personal training sessions are available for your staff as part of the "package," or at additional cost. You can take out a maintenance contract for the servicing of the hardware. But there are other support issues that may not occur to you until you need them. And you may find yourself relying on the level of support provided by your vendor. Does the company have a large enough staff to help their customers with problems down the road? Are they interested in helping you solve obscure problems that you didn't expect? Is the staff experienced? If your problem is beyond their technical knowhow, will they find someone who can help you?

These are important questions to ask. The lack of expected support can be very frustrating, as we found out ourselves. Interestingly, our problems arose as we were starting to write about support. As a result, this section took much longer than we expected. As you'll see, our experience brought home clearly why we should all check out track records, support levels, and compatibility of equipment before we buy. We purchased our equipment from a reliable computer store. The company owner was honest and well-intentioned. The staff was courteous and friendly. And we thought we knew word processors and computers well enough so we would not need much support. We were wrong.

The manuscript of this book was originally produced on a personal computer with a word-processing software package. At the time we purchased the system, we didn't have the funds for a printer, but the computer and software seemed to be just what we needed. Our friend Alan had a different kind of microcomputer with compatible disks and software, and kindly let us cart our disks down to his nearby office and use the printer. For the first few months of writing, everything went perfectly. Then, on short notice, Alan decided to move out of town. He offered to let us store and use the printer with our personal computer. Happily we loaded the printer into our car and brought it home—local printout at last!

Unfortunately, Alan's printer had come without any manual, he said. But we figured out which cables to plug into which "ports," or outlets, turned on the computer, sent a document to the printer, and the first sheet of paper form-fed its way up and through the printer, blank.

Obviously there had to be something a little more to this business. The manual that came with the computer had this to say about interfacing with printers other than their standard letter-quality printer: "This single-board computer has provisions for two completely independent RS-232 serial ports that can be used to interface to printers, CRT terminals and data communications equipment." This didn't tell us much, so we called up Mark, a friend and programmer who had lots of experience with hooking devices together on similar computers and getting them to work.

Scrutinizing the operations manual that came with our computer and the switches on the back of the printer, Mark decided that they were set for different baud rates (the speed at which characters are sent and received). So he took the cover off the computer, looking for a baud rate switch where one would normally be found. No such luck. It turned out that baud rates got changed through the software. A lengthy search through the operations manual (for which there is no index) finally yielded the commands to change the baud rate. A simple, seven-character command changed the rate. And now, lo and behold, the first line of our document printed out. But it was followed by a form-feed pushing another piece of paper up and through the printer, and "hanging" the program. (A program is "hung" when it freezes, accepting no input from the screen and requiring you to start the computer over again.) Somehow the printer interpreted our document's "end of line return" signal as an "end of page" signal.

Lacking a manual for the printer, we called the local computer store where we purchased the computer. What we needed to know was how to make this computer work properly with a TTY (Teletype-like) printer. This is a fairly common need, and when we purchased the system, they'd informed us that they could get the system to work with a variety of printers. Our primary contact was out sick, so we asked for a technical person. The technical person knew next to nothing about the computer model we'd purchased from the store he worked in, and nothing about how to interface to a TTY printer. Furthermore, he insisted it would be very hard to help us without a manual for the printer. Finally a salesperson told us that the owner, who was sick, might have the instructions for how to patch (make changes to) the word-processing program we had so that it would work with the printer. She'd be out for at least three days. We tried telling the salesperson that it was a problem with the computer, not the word-processing software (we have other programs, and wanted the printer to work with all of them), to no avail. We asked for contacts at the company that manufactures the equipment, but she discouraged us from calling them.

Calls to three other computer stores rendered no help. Calls to several of Mark's programming friends led him to believe that "the number of the data bits and 'start-and-stop bits' must be set differently in the computer and in the printer." (A set of eight bits is sent through the cable to the printer to specify each character. Some of those bits are "data bits." Others are "start-and-stop bits," indicating the beginning and ending of the data bits, so that the printer can tell the characters apart.)

Three hours into our session we thought we had a clue: we needed to know the number of data bits and stop bits sent by the computer to the printer. Naturally (as it began to seem), this information was not provided in the operations manual. Nor did our friendly but ignorant computer store have this information.

Now as things go, three hours isn't bad to figure out a computer-printer interface. Except that after three hours all we had was a clue, not a solution. And all of us had lots of work to do. We didn't have much more time to devote to phone calls. We didn't know how much it would cost to hire a specialized programming consultant to fix our problem. Fortunately, one of our calls turned up a friend at a company who offered to rent us a different printer they thought would work with our computer model (they knew both the computer and the printer). Our friendly computer store had not helped us and had offered no suggestions (whether they would have rented us a printer remained unknown). The most we understood after talking to them was that we might have to "write a special printer driver" (program). And the operations manual provided by the manufacturer had proved lacking when it came to technical information about how the computer worked.

The following week we took our disks containing the operating system and word-processing software and our manuals to our friend's office, where he had the rentable printer and a computer just like ours. (We wanted to be sure the printer would work with our disks before carrying it home.) When we arrived, the systems consultant, John, had the printer and cables in pieces on the floor, swapping "cable pins" to get the computer and the printer to work together. He'd done this with other computers and never had any problems. But for some reason nothing seemed to work this time. The problem was very similar to the one we had with the first printer: one line would print, and then the system would hang. The standard printer suggested for use with the computer worked fine, but other (dot matrix) printers didn't. Unfortunately, our friends could not rent us one of the standard printers.

After three more hours of bafflement we were discussing how the connection between the two should work, and why it might not. Trying to understand from our stance of well-experienced but not technical users, we kept asking questions about what the computer and printer were trying to do. By examining the manual for the printer that did work, we discovered that the communications protocol between the operating system and the printer used something called "ETX/ACK," meaning that the computer sent a message saying "ETX" to the printer and expected an "ACK" (for acknowledgment) in return. The dot matrix printer was set to use messages which ran "XON and XOFF."

So, our first clue (suspecting the number of data bits and start-and-stop bits) had been wrong. Now we knew the real problem. But how to solve it? Examining something called the "BIOS" in the operating system, John could see that the protocol was set in the software. To use XON/XOFF, the assembly language program would have to be changed and "compiled." John had never done that before, and told me it would take about a day's work to figure it out, which he couldn't afford.

What options did we now have?

- Buy one of the standard printers.
- Rent time on a compatible computer with a printer attached. Our contact for this said the system we needed to use was out of the office, but would be available in a few days.
- Go to our friend's office with our disks and borrow their printer. Although inconvenient, because the office was not close at hand, and our friend's business is busy, this would at least get us printed copy and let us go on writing. It's very nerve-wracking

to enter text into a word processor and not know if you'll be able to print it out.

In frustration, we drove to the computer store to ask for help—anything. A programmer who could "patch" the BIOS, a rentable printer that would work, a local contact who had a similar system and might be willing to rent time on it. Here's what happened:

Our friend the owner, who had sold us the system, was surprised to see us. She took one look at our faces and asked what was the matter. 'We need *help*," we said, somewhat frazzled. "Didn't anyone tell you we called here several times last week?" No one had. She took us under her wing and asked what help we would like. So we told her the whole story. "Well, you need the least expensive solution, right?" she said. We nodded. Pulling out her little options list, she found a part we could order from the manufacturer that would "adapt" our computer to work with other printers, hopefully the one sitting in our office. This "interface" would supposedly translate the ETX/ACK to XON/XOFF. "What if it doesn't work?" we growled suspiciously. "You won't have to buy it," she assured us. "We'll take care of getting it and getting you back in business." It was a relief to have someone say that. But lots of people had been trying to help, so holding our disbelief in check, we left to await her call.

In the interim, we needed a printout of our rough draft chapters. Proofing text on the screen never satisfies us—we want hard copy. So we decided to take old John up on his offer to print at his office occasionally. Although somewhat inconvenient, at least we'd get copy fast.

This experience is fairly common, and it shows how much trouble you can get into, even with the most careful planning, and expert advice from friends. As it turned out, our story had a happy ending. But at this point our experiences seemed to confirm Murphy's Law. We figured we'd fallen into every conceivable trap, because we had made certain assumptions that some computer experts and vendors would laugh at.

- We assumed that since the printer worked with a computer that could read our disks and which used the same kind of computer processor, it would work with our computer. (The voice of experience says: Never assume two products are compatible until you've seen them work together.)
- We thought that whatever effort was required to hook the two up should be fairly easy for an experienced programmer who had worked with similar products. (Each product is unique in its own way, so that you need a specialist to work with it.)

- We expected to find the information we needed in the manuals quickly and easily. (Technicians figure the user doesn't need technical information in manuals in the first place, and in the second, she shouldn't try to read it if she's not technically conversant, and besides, who can take the time to write an index?)
- We expected the staff at the computer store to have more knowledge than they did, or at least to try to find the information for us, or refer us to people who might be of help. (Actually the staff was only half-experienced, and somewhat knowledgeable. In our case, the one person who knew how to solve our problem was out. The other staff were not very forthcoming; they didn't even offer help for a price, which we might have taken.)
- We tried to make it work on our own, to save time and money.
- We tried to make two products from different sources work together. (From a vendor standpoint, you should purchase all parts of your word-processing system from the same company, and better yet, they should have the same brand names. Then you don't need all this extra information we were looking for.)
- We were in a hurry, and didn't allow the necessary weeks or months to accomplish such a monumental task as this. (Changes to your word-processing hardware or software require planning and time.)

Now we did get a happy ending for our story. Our dealer's promised "interface" worked. Although it sounded like some mysterious box, it turned out to be a fast and simple program, which modified the BIOS for us in less than one minute. So some of our expectations hadn't been out of line. But some questions remain:

- Why was this interface mentioned nowhere in the operations manual? We can draw our own conclusions, but after all, this system is being billed as a personal computer. Don't they think their small-business and personal-use customers might want to hook up other printers?
- Why did only one person (the owner) at the computer store know about this interface? This question we raise both for the computer stores (why isn't information passed around better in a small company?) and for the vendors (don't they provide training for their dealers?)

We made some mistakes, and learned some things from this experience. Our biggest mistake was in not repeatedly calling back the computer store where we purchased our equipment and insisting on their help. When we eventually did, we got the support we needed. We should not have given up in the face of their lack of information and seeming misunderstanding of our problem. Despite their insistence that we needed the missing manual for our borrowed printer, in the end we did not. The interface program talked to the printer without a bleep. What we needed was to find the person who had the answers.

Our support problems were "down the road"—they happened months after we acquired the system. Our system was a microcomputer with a word-processing software package, but you may encounter similar problems and frustrations no matter what type of word processor you select. As you can see, you'll want to discuss and evaluate long-term as well as initial support when you select equipment.

Initial, "Upfront" Support

Pre-Sales Education. The first support issues actually come up when you're looking at equipment. Salespeople should be asking you questions about your business and word-processing needs and telling you what solutions their products can offer. When you have questions that the salesperson can't answer, they should find the answers for you, or refer you to someone in their company who can. If you get shuffled through four or five people over a period of several days or a week before you can get the information you need, ask specifically about support. If you buy their equipment, will you be assigned one main contact to help you? Try to meet the person and assess their level of experience and knowledge. If it takes a week for you to get information while you're a potential customer, how long will it take when you're an established customer and have day-to-day problems?

Documentation. "Documentation" is a general name for all the written materials provided with your word processor: training guides, reference manuals, and technical specifications on how the hardware and software of the word processor, printer, disks, and other devices work. Ask to see what documentation comes with the word processors you're testing. Some word processors come with stacks of manuals; others with only one binder. The quantity of paper doesn't in itself tell you how well documented the system is. Open up the manuals and binders and take a look.

- Is the text clearly laid out on each page?
- Are topics clearly marked?
- Do pictures illustrate steps such as working with the screen and keyboard, or hooking the different pieces together? Where do

you plug in the printer cable? How do you feed the paper into the printer, or change printwheels and ribbons?
- Does the language look like the English you're used to, or is it full of new jargon and terms you've never heard before?
- Is there a detailed table of contents and index?
- Is there a "troubleshooting" section?
- How about a quick reference card or command summary?
- Are there step-by-step instructions showing you how to use the word-processing functions to create documents, or only brief explanations of how to execute the functions?
- Are there separate manuals or sections for learning the system, using it, and looking up more obscure reference material?
- Do you think you could locate information you need in these manuals, quickly and easily?

Most often when you ask about documentation, you'll be shown training and reference manuals on how to use the word-processing software. You may not be shown the more technical manuals, which provide detailed information on the computer, printer, disk drives, operating system, or languages that come with your system. Ideally you, as an "end user," shouldn't need to worry about the technicalities. If you have problems, a service representative will come to your office and help you, and they'll use these more technical manuals. And, ideally, you'll have help getting the software to work initially on the equipment. Unfortunately, circumstances are not always ideal, and you may find that you have to run an "installation program" to get started, hook some of the cables together, or provide technical information over the phone to the company when you have problems. All manuals should be clearly written and well organized.

Training. How will you or your staff learn to use the equipment? Often word processors come with self-paced training programs, using a combination of a manual, prerecorded cassettes, and sample documents. These allow you to learn the system in your office at your own speed. Some systems now offer computer-aided instruction programs or interactive training, which guides you through the learning process on the screen, also at your own pace.

Some companies will give you personal instruction on how to use your word processor. This may come in the form of classes which are given at your office or held at a special training facility of the vendor's, or may be provided by a customer support representative assigned to help you get started.

Early training usually shows you the basics of how to use your word processor. Even a five-day course covering all functions of the system will probably wind up as an introduction. If you're unfamiliar with the system, chances are you'll retain the basics and forget the advanced functions that you won't be ready to use for a few weeks, or maybe even months.

Self-paced and computer-aided training has the advantage of always being there. If you don't remember how to use a function six months down the road, you can go back and review. On the other hand, self-paced training is preset. You don't get the chance to ask your questions—you're shown what the vendor has decided you need to know. If the system you're looking at allows you to train yourself, look at the material. Does it show you how to apply the functions, as well as use them?

Another glitch in self-paced training is that it's easy for operators to be interrupted while training. Phone calls and last-minute projects have a way of intruding. If you or your staff will be using self-paced materials, try to free up some time for them to learn the system without interruptions—preferably away from their desks, in a quiet place.

Installation. This may be a two-part task: installing the hardware (plugging the cables together, putting paper in the printer), then installing the software. If your word-processing software was designed specifically for your hardware, installing the software may be as simple as inserting the disk and pushing one key, or answering a few questions such as how many terminals are hooked up and what kind of printer you have. If you select software which works on a variety of computers, however, such as microcomputer-based word processing, an "install" program will probably have to be run. It may only take five minutes, if you know how to answer the questions. It can take hours if you don't.

Who installs the word processor hardware and software? In the old days, the vendor did. In fact, boxes used to have large warnings plastered on them that if anyone other than a "field service engineer" opened them, the warranty would be voided. This is changing. You may be asked to uncrate the equipment yourself, plug it together following diagrams, run a "diagnostics" diskette, which checks out all the parts of the computer, and then call the vendor's office if you encounter a problem. If you select a system where this will be expected of you, be sure you know who to call, and try to pick a time when that person will be available to set up your computer. You may have no problems and be up and running in thirty minutes or less. Or you could have hours of frustration ahead of you. Often the success of this approach depends on the clarity of the instructions provided, and your willingness to read them. (*Read them!*)

"Down the Road" Support

Advanced Usage. You've had your word processor for two months and have successfully used it for letters and financial reports. Now you want to do a large mass mailing, and you have never used the mail-merge capability before. You haul out your manual to step through it, and begin keying in your list of names and addresses. Three hours later, you realize that you want to sort the list based on the zip code, which you included as part of the address instead of on a separate line. You don't want to retype everything. What's the fastest way to correct your file? The manual doesn't say. Who can help you?

Or you've been using your word processor for four months to write 25-page reports. It still seems awkward, and your hunch is that there are shortcuts you don't know. How do you find them?

Or, the accounting department finally got their business computer, and you're ready to use your communications option to pull some of their figures into your word processor to include in your letters. Instead of numbers, you get gibberish when you try to use the feature. Why doesn't it work?

Your word-processing operator quits, and you hire a new one. Will the vendor help you train the new operator?

There's a good chance that you'll need some help maximizing the use of your word processor several months to a year or more down the road. It's a good idea to plan for this need in the beginning. Will you have a direct contact at the company who can help you? Will there be a charge for additional help? Will someone help you over the phone? Is an 800 number available? Will a representative come to your office if a phone call doesn't answer your question, or will you go to their office?

Troubleshooting. Let's say you're a whiz kid, and that learning to use your word processor was a snap. You like figuring out how to get it to do things the vendor doesn't realize it can handle. But all of a sudden something you've been doing for months doesn't work right. Is something wrong with the disk you've stored your information on? Is there a bug in the software? Did a power failure "zap" your software disk? Is something wrong with the hardware? Are your drives out of alignment? Answering these kinds of questions is called "troubleshooting." Someone at the vendor's office should be able to help you.

Updates—to Software and Documentation. Somewhere down the line more features and capabilities should be available for your word processor. These are called software "updates" or "enhancements." How do you find out about them? How do you acquire them? Is there a charge?

In addition, there may be changes and additions to the documentation for your word processor. These may come with software updates, or the company may decide to rewrite the manual. Will these be made available to you automatically? How do you stay current?

Perhaps the most important question to ask about updates is, "Are some planned?" If you're buying directly from the manufacturing company, your sales representative should know. With the industry changing as fast as it is, updates should be planned. If they're not, is the company phasing out the line of equipment you're looking at? Will their next step be to develop different equipment rather than to enhance what is available? Find out before you commit yourself to a piece of equipment. Be careful, though. If you need a feature which isn't available on the equipment now, but will be an "update in the near future," look out. Software development can take longer than expected, and may be subject to last-minute changes. Make sure your equipment has the fundamentals you need when you buy it.

Upgrades to Hardware. A hardware upgrade usually implies making a change to the machine itself to give it improved capabilities. On old systems, which "hardwired" in word-processing functions, a hardware upgrade was the only way to add more features to the word processor. Today features are usually added through new software, while a hardware upgrade is more likely to add more memory, disk storage space, another printer, another terminal, or communications capabilities. New software may also be necessary to make the hardware upgrade work. Adding some new software capabilities may require a hardware change, too. For example, adding an "equations package" to produce Greek and math symbols may require that a special board be added inside your terminal to generate the new characters. Normally your vendor will make any necessary hardware changes if you upgrade your equipment. But if another company has developed the equipment you want to add, they may not. For example, let's say that when you bought the equipment, you thought you had more disk space than you'd ever need. And one printer was just fine. Nine months down the road you realize you need a 25-megabyte hard disk and a draft printer added to your system. Your sales representative tells you that the manufacturer doesn't have those products, but another company does, and your word processor can be made to work with them. Great, but be sure to see them work together before you buy. And find out who will make sure they work in your office. Will your salesperson help coordinate the additions? Will your service agreement be nullified by adding another company's gear? It's sometimes hard to get service when you have different manufacturers' hardware connected together. Each company blames the problem on the other company's product.

Conversion. Sometimes vendors talk about upgrading "from one word processor to another." This means replacing your existing equipment with a new model, thereby "upgrading" your capabilities. This kind of upgrade can be tricky. The most important question to ask in this situation is whether you can use the documents you already have on disk from your current word processor with the new one. If you can't simply pull the disks out of the old one, put them in the new one, and run them—you need a procedure called "conversion." A conversion moves your stored text from a disk on one word processor to a disk on another, translating special codes as it goes. Conversions can be an incredibly long, arduous, and expensive task which may almost make it seem easier to just retype all of your stored documents. Find out if a conversion will be necessary, if your vendor will help you with it, and how much it will cost before you buy a new system.

Maintenance of Hardware

When some part of your word processor breaks, whether it's the printer, a disk drive, or the computer itself, you're going to need someone to fix it. Most equipment has a warranty for 90 days, but after that it's up to you. You can make arrangements ahead of time by obtaining a "maintenance contract," or you can trust to your luck and pay time and materials when something goes wrong.

Most "direct sales" companies will encourage you to get a maintenance contract, and they almost always have a service branch to carry it out. Computer stores may have hardware technicians who can fix equipment, too, but remember, in most cases there won't be specialists on hand for the one brand of equipment you bought—they may have to keep up on six different brands. Other computer stores don't provide hardware maintenance directly. They may be willing to send your equipment back to the factory for you, or you may have to do that yourself. How long will that take? Hard to tell, but you'd better find out how far away the factory is. And whether "loaner" equipment is available while you wait for yours to be repaired.

How Much Does Maintenance Cost? Maintenance contract costs vary depending on the "response time" you want and how much special equipment you have attached to your system. Roughly speaking, you can figure yearly maintenance at about 1 to 1.5 percent of the cost of the equipment. On a $10,000 processor, that's between $1000 and $1500 per year. This normally entitles you to parts and labor to repair your equipment on a Monday through Friday, 9:00 a.m. to 5:00 p.m. basis. If you want round the clock or weekend service, or a guaranteed response time (someone at your door within two to four hours, ready to fix the equipment), you'll probably pay more. Maintenance contracts for some parts of word-processing equipment will be more expensive than others, too. Printers, for example, tend to develop more problems, so their maintenance may be figured at a higher rate. Annual or semi-annual preventative maintenance checks often are included with service contracts, too.

If you elect to pay time and materials in the event of a breakdown, expect to pay at least $40 per hour and the replacement cost of whatever is broken. As with a limping car you've taken to your mechanic, it's hard to say what the cost will be. You may be pleasantly or unpleasantly surprised. It could be $100, $1500, or more, depending on the problem.

Down Time. How long will it take to fix your word processor? You'll be surprised how dependent and helpless you can feel when the machine you're counting on to print out the proposal for your biggest account on Monday morning refuses to start. Can you afford to have it out of commission for a day or two; a week or two; or do you want it fixed that day?

Loaners or "Swaps." While your word processor is being fixed, can the company loan you another to use? Or "swap" the bad part with a working one while repair is under way? Some companies will provide this service, while others don't stock enough equipment to be able to.

Response Time. What will be the average response time to a distress call from you? "Response time" means the time it takes from your call until someone is on your doorstep to help.

Nearness of the Service Center. How far away is your help? If the service department is two hours away, that in itself will delay the response to your call.

Make Emergency Plans

No matter what your maintenance contract with a vendor says, it's not a bad idea to have a local backup in the form of another business using the same equipment and software you have. When your system has problems, you can use the other person's during off hours and vice versa.

It's also a good idea to have backup copies of your important disks away from your business. These should include software and important documents. If a fire develops in your building, equipment is usually insured and can be replaced. But the time you've spent entering text and data can't, and it may take a while to get copies of the software from the vendor.

How Can You Really Gauge Support?

Despite promises and contracts, how can you really tell whether you'll get the support you need from a company? Use a combination of subjective and objective evidence.

When you settle on a word processor, chances are you trust your sales representative and the company. The "gut feeling" that you'll be supported is important. And a good rapport with the sales and support staff can go a long way toward insuring your good support. After all, they like to work with people they like, too. That's one reason it's important to meet the support staff before you buy. Look for interest, willingness, responsiveness, experience, and intelligence in the staff of a company.

Our experience trying to hook up a strange printer to our computer eventually bore out our initial impression. The person who sold us the system knew what we needed and helped us out. Unfortunately, she was out sick when our problem developed, and wasn't told we were having problems. Once she knew, our problem was solved rapidly. It would have been much nicer if someone else at the store also knew how to solve our problem, which leads us to evaluating objective evidence of support.

How many employees are there in the local office to handle word-processing support and maintenance? How many customers do they work with? The answer to this question can give you a good clue to how responsive a company will be. If there are two word-processing support specialists to help four hundred word-processing installations, one-third of which are for fairly new users, look out! When will they have time to fit you in? If there's a phone hotline in addition to individuals to help you onsite, your chances may improve. Still, find out the approximate ratio of support staff to customers and equipment. Sixty to eighty installed word processors per support person is about right.

Support Lines Within Vendors. There will inevitably be some support issues, whether advanced usage, software bugs, or odd problems with the hardware, that your local support staff can't solve. What backup do they have, to find solutions for you? Is there regional or corporate support for them (or you) to appeal to when the information isn't available locally? In the case of a dealer, whether a systems house or computer store, will the manufacturer help them out when they're stumped? Do they have good contacts within the companies supplying equipment and software? Do they make use of them?

Talk to users, if possible, not just the companies on the list the vendor gives you. Before you settle on equipment, or on a company to buy from, talk to existing users. The vendor you're working with may give you a list of reference accounts. Check them out. Find out how happy they are with the equipment and the support they've been given. Ask about any unexpected surprises they encountered. If possible, talk to some companies with the equipment you're eyeing who aren't on the reference list. Naturally, vendors will give you names of their most satisfied accounts and will probably omit those who had problems. Word processors can be lemons, just like cars. If you find a company that got a lemon and received good support in turning that lemon into a peach, you know you're in good hands. Even if the lemon didn't turn into a peach overnight, the company will have a good perspective on how willing, interested, and experienced the vendor was when it came to helping them.

Finding Extra Support on Your Own. As an "end user," you may get to know your word-processing software and equipment much more intimately than the people at the company that sold it to you. Gradually you'll find your own shortcuts to functions, ways around limiting features, how to avoid quirks in the system. You're not alone. Chances are other users have found their own tidbits. Why not share them? For this reason, "users groups" abound throughout the country. Sometimes vendors initiate user associations, realizing that their own viewpoint will never be quite the same as yours, because you work on the equipment daily. At other times, users have to find one another. You may find a group who all use the same equipment you do, or you may find a general word-processing group who share problems, solutions, and interests.

If your vendor doesn't know of a users group, how do you find one? Try some of the associations listed in magazines, and check your Yellow Pages under "Associations." Some are directly involved in word and information processing. Others are large computer user associations who may have special chapters or committees addressing word-processing needs. You can also start an informal users group on your own. Get to know a few of the reference accounts the vendor sends you to. Maybe they'd be interested in sharing ideas and information.

Final Negotiations: Should You Buy, Lease, or Rent?

To acquire a word processor you don't have to purchase it outright. You have essentially the same options you do when car shopping: you can buy, lease, or rent word processing. The method you use will be determined by your cash flow, tax situation, future plans, and the financial options available for the equipment you want. It's fairly common to be able to purchase or lease equipment; fewer companies provide rental options.

Purchasing Equipment. You may be in a position to pay cash for a word processor, but then again, particularly if you need a multi-user system, you may not. Talk to your bank about financing computers, and talk to the vendors—they may have financing available. Although many of the more powerful microcomputers are now in the price range of cars ($5000–$10,000), not many computer stores offer direct financing as car dealerships often do. Purchasing new equipment will give you a tax credit, and the equipment can then be depreciated. The normal life of a computer is usually set at five years. Whether software qualifies as part of the equipment or not is under debate. The issue at stake is whether software is a tangible product or not. Talk to your accountant about how purchasing, leasing, or renting a word-processing system will affect your taxes. Purchasing on time usually requires a down payment, followed by monthly payments for three to five years. In addition, you'll have a monthly maintenance fee, and may have yearly costs for the software license. We'll talk more about that under "Hidden Costs," below.

Leasing Equipment. Many vendors have arrangements with leasing companies. When you lease equipment, you don't have to make a down payment, although you may have to pay the equivalent of several months' lease upfront. Leases usually are for three to five years, at the end of which time you have an option to buy the equipment for 10 to 15 percent of the original price. You may have the advantage of a tax credit, or you may not, depending on the contract. The company you use for leasing becomes the owner of the equipment; they may take the tax credit, or may make it available to you. Be sure to ask. The total cost of a leased system, if you opt to buy it at the end of your lease, will be greater than if you purchased it. And you'll still be responsible for any maintenance costs.

Renting Equipment. Not all companies offer rental agreements. When they do, the cost per month is usually greater than if you had purchased or leased the same equipment. On the other hand, a portion or all of your rental fee can often be applied toward purchase. So if you don't have the cash now, but expect to in six months, renting may allow you to acquire a word processor sooner. It also gives you a chance to try out the system and make sure it's the right one for you. If you like this line of reasoning, though, be careful. It takes time to train your staff to use the equipment, and its use will make changes in your company procedures. If at the end of a rental you want to try a different system, there will be another learning curve for your operators. And the next system you try may not be compatible with the first, meaning that everything you've stored on disk may have to be retyped into the new equipment. On the other hand, the cost of renting usually includes the cost of maintenance.

Hidden Costs

Whatever the list price, the cost of your word processor will probably be more. A "quote" from each vendor should detail other costs. If not, be sure to get them spelled out.

Shipping Costs. You are normally responsible for any shipping costs incurred. If you buy from an office in Seattle whose equipment is manufactured on Route 128 outside of Boston, you will probably have to pay the freight from Boston to Seattle.

Maintenance. Equipment is usually on warranty for 90 days. After that you can either get a maintenance contract, or opt to pay time and materials when something breaks down. Maintenance contracts are usually 1 to 1.5 percent of the cost of the system per year, paid monthly. So if your word processor costs $10,000, maintenance would be about $1000 to $1500 per year, or $83 to $125 per month. Contract costs can vary depending on the response time you want. If you elect not to get a contract, figure that any maintenance will cost a minimum of $40 per hour, plus parts. A new disk drive can easily cost $400 to $1200 or more, so be careful.

Training. Today many word processors come with self-paced training packages which you can use in your office to learn to operate the system. Two or three days of personal training for one or two of your staff may also be included in the cost of your word processor. Some companies charge for any personal training, while others charge only when you want more than two people trained, or need more than two days' assistance. Personal training can cost from $250 to $750 per day, depending on how many of your staff are included.

Software Licenses. If you elect to purchase a word processor, you may find that although you own the equipment, or hardware, you don't "own" the software. You sign an agreement that "licenses" you to use it on your particular equipment. You are usually allowed to make copies of the program for backup purposes for your equipment only. The license fee you pay may be included in the quoted price, or may be additional. It may be a one-time-only fee, meaning that you never pay for it again, or it may be a renewable license, good for one, two, or three years. Check the wording on your contract carefully. If the software license is $500, but is for one year only, next year you'll have another $500 to pay if you want to keep using the word-processing program on your equipment. Or perhaps the second year's license will be slightly less. At any rate, find out if you will be billed for additional usage. You may have the option to get a one-time-only license for $750, or a two-year license for $400. In that kind of situation, the question is, will you want the same software two years from now? Is the company developing a new version with more capabilities, in which case you may want a limited license. Each company's policies are somewhat different. Ask to have them clarified, and then check the wording on your contract.

Software Updates. Chances are that more features will be available for your equipment within the year after you buy it. How much will you have to pay to acquire new versions of the software? Some companies distribute updated software to their customers at no charge. You may receive updates free in the first year you own the equipment, and then be charged. Sometimes you can get a "software maintenance contract" for a fee, which will entitle you to updates at little or no charge. Most of the time new versions of the software will cost you less than the original version.

Word-Processing Supplies. Whether or not you buy supplies from the company that sells you a word processor, you should consider them when figuring the costs of a word processor. You will at least need paper and ribbons for your printer, and printwheels or "thimbles" if you get a letter-quality printer, and floppy diskettes if your system uses them. A box of 2000 sheets of continuous-feed 8½" × 11" paper costs between $30 and $40 from an office supply store. If you buy in quantity, of course, or direct from the manufacturer, the unit cost per box will go down. Ribbons for a letter-quality printer cost $4 and up on a single-unit basis, and if they're the Mylar kind that are not reusable, you'll go through them pretty fast. Plastic printwheels are in the $12 to $15 range, and may need to be replaced as often as every 4 to 8 weeks, depending on how much you print. Metal printwheels last longer, but cost more, sometimes as much as $40 each. Floppy diskettes, depending on size and density, can cost from $3.50 to $10 each. A box of ten 8" diskettes can be had for between $45 and $80. You'll probably want about 20 diskettes to start off with.

Some vendors require that you use their supplies. The justification is that you're getting quality products which are made to work with the equipment you've purchased. Other vendors will suggest a brand of quality supplies, and still others leave you to your own devices. You'll find word-processing supplies just about anywhere you can buy word processors, and also in many office supply stores. Some stores, such as The Very Last Word in San Francisco, specialize in word-processing supplies, explain the differences to you, and help you insure you get quality products that will work on your system.

As you research your needs and the word-processing solutions available, you may find the list of magazines and reports in Appendix C informative.

7

What It's Like to Start

BEFORE THE SYSTEM ARRIVES: PREPARING YOUR OFFICE AND STAFF

You've made the plunge and said, "Yes, this is the system." The contract is signed, financing is obtained. You're at the end of months of learning about word processing, pinpointing your needs, reading brochures, watching demonstrations, evaluating equipment and companies. You're ready to get back to your day-to-day business, with a new tool in hand. Wait just a minute. You've still got some time to go before word processing is integrated into the daily work flow of your office.

After you sign the order form for a word processor, you may wait anywhere from a week to three months or more for delivery, depending on where you buy it. If you buy from a computer store, your chances of walking out the door with your word processor are greater than if you buy direct from the manufacturer. Even computer stores don't stock a lot of systems, though, so you may have to wait for yours. The waiting period can be put to good use: prepare your office and your staff for the arrival of your word processor.

Is Your Office Ready for Word-Processing Equipment?

Linda Urban used to work for a major word-processing vendor as a trainer. She remembers one firm of accountants in particular: they purchased a word processor and neglected to prepare their office. "They were very cautious and thorough in their approach to word processing. They really checked out the equipment we were selling, and made sure it did each and every function that their office required. I demonstrated the equipment for them several times, using their reports as testing material. After about three months, they ordered one of the machines our company offered. There was a backlog of orders then, so it took several months for delivery, and they were really chomping at the bit. I'll never forget the day their machine arrived. Those C.P.A.s were so excited. Our field service staff went out to uncrate all the boxes and hook it up, only to find that the office (in an old building) had 110 wiring, and the machine had to have 220. Our field service staff was usually pretty good at catching that kind of problem long before delivery, but somehow this one had slipped through their fingers. It took another three weeks for the firm to get an electrician to change the wiring, and the C.P.A.s were livid. That company had been so thorough in making sure the equipment would meet their needs! But they had never thought to scrutinize their office. They hadn't given a thought to wiring, or to where they'd put the equipment once it came in the door."

Do you know where the equipment will go? Will you need new furniture? Can it plug into your existing electrical outlets and work without a hitch, or will you need new wiring, a voltage regulator, or adapters? These questions should be answered and resolved before the word processor arrives. You don't want to uncrate the box and find you can't use the system yet. Some vendors will help you answer these questions by doing a "site prep"—a meeting to prepare and plan for any necessary changes in your office. If this service isn't offered by the vendor, be sure to consider these issues yourself.

PLAN WHERE THE EQUIPMENT WILL GO
- Is the spot you have in mind near a window? If so, are there venetian blinds or drapes that can be closed to prevent glare on the screen from the sun?
- Is there adequate, indirect lighting? As we discussed in Chapter 5, "Making the Change Easier," the lighting around equipment can heighten or lessen eyestrain when working in front of a tube for long hours.
- Have you checked the physical dimensions of the equipment against the space you plan to put it in? Cables are often bulkier than expected, so be sure to allow a few extra inches around and behind the equipment. Some vendors require that there be an extra clearance of about six inches or so behind the gear for ventilation before they'll maintain it. Don't box yourself in.

FURNITURE
- Does the word processor come housed in its own desk, or will you supply the furniture?
- If keyboard and video display screen are in one molded piece, you may want to set them in the typing well or extension of a

desk, or find a table of suitable height. Most standard tables and desks are too high to set a keyboard on for comfortable typing. Sitting comfortably, your arms should be parallel with the table-top your keyboard sits on. Special word- or data-processing desks are manufactured by a range of companies to solve this problem. If the keyboard is detached or movable, you might opt for a desk where the keyboard can be at a good height and the screen slightly higher, on a shelf slightly above the desk top.

- If floppy disk drives are in a separate unit, can they be positioned nearby? If small enough, you'll probably want them on the desk. If they're housed in a stand-up cabinet, you'll want them no more than an arm's length away. If a large hard-disk drive is housed in its own cabinet, you can afford to have it further away, because you won't be changing disks all the time. Find out how long the standard cable between it and the processor is, however. Do you need a longer one?
- Is there room for the printer nearby? Printers pose a paradoxical problem: they're noisy, so you don't want them too close, but it's inconvenient to always go down the hall to retrieve printout. Consider investing in a sound cover if the printer doesn't come with one.
- If you've selected a multiterminal or shared-resource (cluster or network) system, will shared devices such as printers and disks be conveniently placed for all users?

ELECTRICAL NECESSITIES
- Are there enough outlets for the plugs? Do you know how many plugs the equipment will have? You may be surprised to find you'll have two or three plugs to put into the wall for a small stand-alone system.
- Does your office have 110 or 220 wiring? What does the system require?
- Will the equipment come with two-prong or three-prong plugs? If three-prong, are your outlets three-prong? If not, do you have adapters? You may want one of those long "extenders" that turn one outlet into an outlet for 6 to 10 plugs. And while you're at it, you might want the kind that will also protect you against power surges.
- This one's important: What other outlets in your office tie into the same circuit that your word processor will use? Some vendors tell you the equipment requires a "dedicated circuit"—one that isn't used by other outlets, or at least none with high-voltage equipment in use.

Why is this so important? Well, let's say that your copying machine is plugged into an outlet connected to the same circuit your word processor will use. It's conceivable that every time someone makes a copy, the power will fluctuate enough to interrupt the current used by the word processor. Whoever is at work on the word processor may or may not see any difference, the screen might flicker, or it might not. But the data in the memory of your word processor and text being written or read from disk can be affected. You may not know it until you recall a document and find it full of extra characters and gibberish.

SUPPLIES

- When your word processor arrives, will you have the necessary supplies to use it? Most dedicated word processors come with a small amount of paper, one or two ribbons and print elements, and a few diskettes. You'll probably need more of everything quickly. At the least you'll want a large box of paper, some extra ribbons, and ten to twenty diskettes, if your system uses them.

Is Your Staff Ready for Word Processing?

A friend of ours is the manager for a fairly new technical writing department at a large established firm. When she started at the company, there was already a small word-processing center. The center was working to capacity handling the corporate needs for letters and financial reports. When the technical writing department was created, the word-processing center was expected to support the writers, too. The writers produced typed and handwritten drafts of the material, and the word-processing center was to enter the documents into their systems and produce the final drafts. But since the center was understaffed and working at capacity already, these documentation projects became the lowest priority. Sometimes it would take five weeks for a writer to get a draft back; sometimes three months.

Our friend began to ask for a word-processing system for her writers. It seemed only natural for them to create text on a word processor and be able to change it easily, and she wanted management to do a study of their needs and recommend the correct system. Soon thereafter the technical writers were handed a system—a multi-terminal version of the equipment used in the word-processing center with three workstations attached. No study had been done; no one had asked any of the writers or their manager what they wanted or needed. Management's attitude was, "A word processor's just another typewriter, and a typewriter is a typewriter. If you can't use the equipment the word-processing center uses, you must not be very competent."

How did the writers react? "Bitterly," says our friend. "Out of ten writers, one learned to use it. The others tried and refused. They needed a system to create their long documentation projects on, one they could learn quickly and that was easy to use. Then perhaps a word-processing operator could massage the text and put it in the proper format. They didn't want to know all the ins and outs. The system we got works with one page at a time and is very complicated. While it's fine for entering final versions, the way they do in the word-processing center, it is very clumsy for creating text that goes through many changes. Suddenly half of our writers' jobs have become clerical. Instead of spending their time writing and submitting drafts to the word-processing center, they now write and then are supposed to type up the final version on the word processor themselves. The word-processing center in this company is looked down on by corporate management as the lowest of the low. And suddenly the writers are doing this 'lowly' task. How do you think they feel? They're very angry. They keep asking me, 'Is this my job?' They think their creativity has been ruined."

Is the word processor the wrong one for these writers? Probably. We heard legitimate complaints about the capabilities not being what the writers needed. But it's also obvious that they're not interested in trying to make what use they can of the equipment. They were not considered in the decision, not approached, not even asked what tasks they do that a word processor might simplify. And they have no stake in making it a success. They have much stake in making it a failure: their status, their pride, their creativity.

Whether you're a large company establishing a word-processing center, or a small department or company providing a tool for a secretary or professional worker, introducing a word processor to your office is going to affect your staff. Their reaction to it can make word processing in your office a success or a failure. Ideally, your staff should be included in discussions about word processing before you select the equipment (see Chapter 5, "Making the Change Easier"). Whether the staff has been consulted or not, take the interim time before your system arrives to address some of the issues that concern them. Discuss how word processing will be used in your office. Who will be affected by your use of word processing? How will it affect them? What can they expect the equipment to do for them? Your staff may be enthusiastic about automation of the office, or fearful and hostile. You want them on your side, so talk about their concerns and expectations.

Provide as Much Education as You Can Before the Equipment Arrives. Some vendors will provide a "preinstallation" introduction for you and some of your staff. This can be anything from a demonstration similar to the one you saw while selecting the equipment to hands-on training at the vendor's office. If the vendor doesn't offer this, you can certainly ask for it. Two different needs can be filled with this. First, you let your staff see what the equipment looks like and how it works, and you can cut down the necessary training time once the equipment is in your office. The more "hands-on" time you have before you get the system, the less mysterious and foreign the equipment will seem when it arrives.

Realize That Installing a Word Processor Will Affect Current Work. Mary Molloy is one of three legal secretaries in a small law firm in San Francisco. All of their legal briefs, letters, and documents had been done on typewriters until this year, when they decided to get a word processor. They settled on a stand-alone DECMATE system, which would give them good word-processing capabilities immediately and allow them to add on a computerized bookkeeping program in the future.

Mary was one of two of the secretaries who set about learning the equipment as soon as it arrived. Neither of them gave a thought to training—their busy work loads didn't encourage taking days to learn the system without being productive. This didn't prove to be a problem in this office. Mary had used two different word-processing systems before and felt right at home learning another one. "The menus on the screen made it easy to figure out," she said, "and when I had a question I'd dig through the manuals." Her coworker quickly found that the 800 phone number DEC made available could answer most of her questions quickly. And they approached it sensibly—only nonrush projects were done on the DECMATE while they were learning to use it. Last-minute projects were still done on the typewriter.

When we talked to Mary, it had been a month since the law firm had acquired the system. She realized she was still learning to use the advanced features, and seemed quite comfortable using the system. What surprised her was that while learning and using the system had been straightforward, the general work in the office became very confusing.

"Before we got the word processor, I worked for two of the lawyers, and Virginia worked for a different two. We each knew our bosses' specialities and cases. When the word processor arrived, it went on

Virginia's desk. My desk became the typing desk. We hadn't really worked out a schedule for who would use the word processor when, so we sat at whichever desk we needed to. Our bosses became very confused. They didn't know where to put work to be done—should they give it to us directly, or set it on our 'desks'? But whose desk was whose? Word-processing work (long documents, or ones which were expected to be revised) was often handed to whoever was working at the terminal. And we got confused, too. It became very unclear who was responsible for what, and at the end of the day we were never sure who should be making copies of documents we were mailing, and who would make sure the necessary ones got mailed. The office became very disorganized, and it started getting on all of our nerves."

After a month, Mary and Virginia had worked out a system of sorts: each worked on the word processor for half a day. The company now plans to get a second stand-alone so that each secretary will have her own terminal. In the interim, they still have things to work out—how will they organize their documents on the disks? Whose job is it to be sure a copy of a new proposal is placed onto the "master disk" they've created for standard documents? Although they realize that they need to spend some time planning and organizing, it's hard for them to take the time.

We told Mary we thought the confusion they were experiencing was a common problem in offices installing word processing for the first time. She seemed surprised and relieved. She'd expected that there might be problems in learning the new system, but had never been prepared for it to affect the way the work in the office had been distributed.

WHEN THE EQUIPMENT ARRIVES: INSTALLATION AND TRAINING

You've seen the size of the equipment you'll be getting at the vendor's office. You're prepared for the size of the terminals, processor, disk units, and printers. You may be surprised by the size of the boxes. Whether you're in a position to load the pieces into your car yourself and drive them away from a store, or wait for a delivery truck to appear from halfway across the country, the boxes word processors come in may lead you to think you're refurnishing your entire office, or that some mistake has been made. There's probably no mistake. Word-processing and computer components are simply well packed, to prevent damage in transit. Each box may be close to twice the size of the equipment inside.

Depending on the type of equipment and who you buy it from, you may be asked to "uncrate" and connect the word processor yourself, or you may be told not to touch the boxes. The boxes may even be plastered with "Hands Off" messages, warning you that if anyone other than a trained technician opens the boxes, your warranty will be invalid.

If you won't be installing the equipment yourself, call your vendor as soon as it arrives. Most computer companies keep track of your delivery date and notify their local office of the shipping and expected delivery dates. But paperwork can be slowed down and mislaid. Don't expect them to know your floor space is covered with boxes; tell them. They should be out to install the equipment within a day or two.

Installation

"Installation" is the process of unboxing the equipment, hooking it together, running "diagnostics" to make sure all the parts are in working order, and setting up the software to work on the equipment. (There is usually a "diagnostic" program that exercises all the parts of the word processor when it is run.) If everything's in working order, this process can take from an hour to half a day. For larger systems, it may take a few days for a technician to make sure everything's in order. If the diagnostics show something isn't working right, a part didn't arrive, or something is just wrong, installation can take longer. In the event of a missing part or cable, hopefully the local office will have one in stock. If not, the wait can take a few days and be very frustrating. In most cases, the equipment will be up and running without any problems.

If you've selected an "off-the-shelf" word-processing software package to work with your equipment, another type of installation is called for. These types of packages are commonly designed to work with more than one type of computer. To get them to work with yours, an "install" program may have to be run. If at all possible, have your dealer do the installation for you, while you watch. Installation programs ask you questions about your video display screen, computer, and other components. They don't usually take long if you know how to answer the questions. Unfortunately, the questions they ask aren't always clear-cut. If the words on the screen are: "Is the clear to end of line switch set in your video terminal?" will you know how to answer the question? Better to get some help than try to do it yourself and find yourself throwing your hands up in the air.

Learning to Use Your Word Processor: What to Expect

It takes time to learn to use a new tool. Word processors are no exception. And in most cases, the learning time is greater than the training time your vendor has discussed with you. Training usually refers either to "self-paced training" or to personal training provided by the vendor. Either one is just a beginning.

Self-Paced Training in Your Office. Self-paced training packages take you through each step in using your word processor, from turning it on and off through trying out the most advanced features. Usually self-paced training kits are broken down into sequential lessons, which start you out with the easy functions and then build on what you've already learned.

Although "self-paced" implies that you learn at your own speed, the vendor may quote you an approximate time frame in which most users complete the training. This can be anywhere from 90 minutes to two to three days. Use these figures as estimates only. You may zip through the lessons in half the suggested time, or find that you need double the suggested hours. Of course, self-paced training will be easier if you're not interrupted by phone calls or other demands. Try to allow uninterrupted periods of two to three hours at a time for training. You may also find it useful to spend some practice time after each lesson, trying out what you've learned. Even if the steps seem obvious to you, you're going to be absorbing a lot of new information in a short amount of time. The more advanced features will be easier if the early basics have a chance to sink in.

Training from the Vendor. Personal training from the vendor may take one of several forms. You may be asked to go to a scheduled training session at the vendor's office for several consecutive days or half-days. Or a trainer may come out to your office to show you how to use the equipment. In either case, you may be expected to know nothing when this training happens, or you may be asked to go through self-paced training material first and use the personal training session to ask questions and learn details specific to your office.

Basic Training at a Vendor's Office. Vendor training or classes often follow a self-paced training course, with an expert available to answer your questions and speed you on. Although it may seem to you that you could as easily do this on your own ground, you won't have interruptions at a vendor's office as you might at your own. If the vendor's training takes whole days, there should be practice time included for you to review steps and try out the word-processing functions on test documents of your own. If the training is set up in half-day increments, don't rush back to your office to catch up on all your other work. Spend some time practicing what you learned. Take some real work, and create a letter or two on your word processor. See how much you've retained when moved from the vendor's quiet classroom to the hubbub of your own office environment.

Advanced Training from the Vendor. When you're asked to go through self-paced material before receiving personal training, don't rush to your trainer the second you're through with the basics. Try some experiments on your own first. Play around. Experiment. Enter some of the types of documents you'll be producing in your office, and see how you do. You'll get a better idea of where you have questions or problems, and where you need help.

Reactions to Training

There's more to training than learning what buttons to push. Successful training entices the new user to want to learn and experiment. The attitude toward training and toward the word-processing equipment can be crucial.

Dotti Sauer's first exposure to word processing was in 1978, when she took a job as an administrative assistant for an insurance company in San Francisco. She was hired to fill a position vacated by a woman who was being moved to another department against her will. The firm used an IBM Memory Typewriter to fill out standard forms and letters with variable information. Dotti was "trained" on the IBM Memory Typewriter, so to speak, by the woman she was replacing. Dotti's training consisted of watching the other woman use the machine, and hurriedly taking notes of what buttons to push. As she watched, she was told things like, "The machine's kind of quirky. Sometimes it will do this, and then you have to do this."

When the Memory Typewriter was turned over to Dotti, she was hardly thrilled. In fact, she was scared. "The machine would run by itself until it hit a 'stop,'" Dotti explained. "Then I had to type in some information, press a key, and it would go again. The idea that it went by itself was frightening. I didn't know how or why it worked, and didn't understand where the information it typed came from."

Dotti quit after two weeks on the job. The bosses kept telling her to work faster on the machine she didn't understand. There had been no preparation in the office for the changes that were happening, or to train her to use the equipment.

At her next job as an office manager for a small manufacturing firm, Dotti encountered the same model IBM Memory Typewriter. She learned to use it in very little time, and had few problems in the two years she worked for the company. Why such a different experience when her first contact with the machine had been awkward and scary? The company's approach to training new employees was completely different.

"The company had a contract with IBM that included training new operators of the Memory Typewriter. Until the day I could go to training, the previous office manager stayed around. She showed me how to do a few simple things on the Memory machine and gave me the manual to look through. And she was excited. She'd say things like 'Look what this can do!' By the time I went to the class, I'd read part of the manual and tried out some steps, so I could ask questions about what I didn't understand.

"When I went to the class, I felt a little pressured. Here I was in this room full of people, and we all had to learn a certain amount in one and half days. Would I perform well? The pressure wasn't from the company, though, and I gained confidence quickly. We worked through a self-paced manual, but there was someone from IBM present all the time. When I didn't understand something, I could ask for help. I didn't have to figure it all out myself. And the trainer obviously liked the Memory Typewriter. She was very positive. She showed us how much it could do and how easy it was to use. Her attitude rubbed off, and by the end of the first day, I knew I could use that machine."

Training Versus Learning. Completing training doesn't mean you've mastered the equipment. Ideally, training should step you through the basic functions and show you how to apply them to some documents. Training may be completed in 90 minutes, three days, or five half-days. Learning to apply the word-processing functions to your office needs happens gradually over a period of months, and continues for a long time.

Don't expect an immediate increase in productivity in your office. In fact, you may even find a temporary decrease in overall productivity while you and your staff get used to the equipment and learn to use it. That doesn't mean you won't get useful work from your word processor in the first month or two. You probably will. But your chances are much greater if you take it easy and let people learn gradually.

Once you and your staff have been trained, it's important to use what you've learned regularly. Begin by producing simple documents on the word processor—letters, short documents, memos. Gradually add more difficult projects, such as mass mailings, proposals, or statistical typing. If you're reorganizing your office and plan to have a central word-processing center take over many of the typing tasks, implement the change gradually. Don't throw away your typewriters the day the word processors arrive, or hand your new operators stacks of all the office reports the day they're back from training.

Roslyn Heimberg, a freelance word-processing specialist, has been using Xerox word processors for over five years now. She says she's still learning shortcuts and faster ways to set up documents. Ros first learned word processing on a Xerox 800, a "blind" word processor with no display. The company replaced the 800 with a Xerox 850 one-line display, and Ros attended a four-day training class at Xerox. She remembers: "The support was excellent. I was having difficulty with a multicolumn report, and the trainer helped me set it up. Then later there was this [800] phone number in Dallas that I could call when I needed help. There was so much to learn about the 850. I didn't know how much then, because the 850 was so much easier to use than the 800. I used the equipment as soon as I was back at the office, but I didn't know it well enough to be what I consider 'productive' on it for about four months."

Ros went on to become a lead operator in a word-processing center at another firm. As lead operator, not only did she have a good deal of word processing to do, but she was also responsible for setting priorities on all the work, making sure it got done on time, deciding which jobs were "rush," and fielding (angry) staff who needed their work done immediately. Her standards for mastering a word processor are high, because her jobs have demanded it. Anyone in the office could submit work to the word-processing center, so the operators had to be prepared to produce all kinds of documents quickly. That meant knowing the system's capabilities to the fullest extent.

When the word-processing center replaced their one-line display Xerox 850s with full-screen Xerox 860s, Ros was nervous. She was used to the one-line display, and to "mapping the layout of the documents" in her mind. The work load in the center was tremendous. Each operator filled out a daily production log and the center was "graded" monthly on their performance. Training time to learn a new machine was not taken into account. Ros said she expected to hate the 860, and might not have gotten through without the help and encouragement of her officemate, who had worked with display-based word processors before and loved them. Within two weeks she was churning out more work than ever before, and had adjusted to the new machine.

Ros now works on her own as a freelance word-processing specialist. If she were to take a full-time job for one company again, she says she'd be very selective. "I'd look for a pleasant environment. Some word-processing centers are terrible pits. And I'd look to see what might create stress." She also thinks she'd prefer a secretarial or administrative job that included word processing over a job that was straight word processing. And she'd be wary of switching to a different word-processing system today, despite the fact her fears of change proved unfounded before. "I've invested so much time in learning the Xerox!" While working freelance, she's found an informal network of Xerox specialists, too, who share their word-processing secrets and shortcuts that are never found in the manuals.

Using the "Buddy" System. As Ros's experiences show, learning the ins and outs of a sophisticated word processor takes time. It helps to have someone else around who knows the system. Even if you have a very small office, it's a good idea to train more than one person on your word processor. Two or more heads can often figure out how to do something where one may get lost in reference manuals and give up in frustration. If you're self-employed, you may want to find some local companies or individuals who have the same type of equipment or word-processing software you have. Vendors, users groups, or associations can help you locate someone with whom to trade problems and solutions.

Let Word Processing Be Fun. Whether you're fascinated by word processing and computers, or are acquiring a word processor strictly to improve productivity in your business, make it fun for your staff to learn and use the equipment. Making games available on the system is a good way to get true "typewriter addicts" interested in trying out the keyboard and over their fear of a machine that gobbles words without printing them out immediately. When games aren't available, they can be made up.

Jonathan Price remembers his first job at which word processors were provided for the writers: "It was really terrible. We were writing lengthy documents, and they bought a system that worked with one page at a time. It seemed ridiculous, and impossible to learn. We created a document called 'messages,' and wrote in whatever we had to say. Anyone could call up that document, read the messages, and add some of their own. Often it was full of complaints about the equipment. But it kept us using it, and gave us a place to vent our frustrations and let off steam."

PROCEDURES FOR LONG-TERM SUCCESSFUL USE OF YOUR EQUIPMENT

Marty Downey is a freelance editor. One of her largest corporate clients installed a Lanier No Problem Shared System, and Marty was asked to use the word processor to make her editorial comments and revisions of their documents. Having used a word processor before, Marty had no qualms about learning this one. To prepare her, she was sent to a two-day training course at Lanier. The training was easy and pleasant, using a training manual and taped instructions. The material stepped her through the basics, telling her exactly what to do, and requiring no memorization.

Back at her client's office and ready to work, Marty had no immediate questions about using the Lanier. "The training had been very straightforward. I told them, 'Let me just start entering some text and see what comes up.' Then I started going nuts. For practice, they had me enter a long repetitive document used to tell one department how to use a computer program. It was divided into sections with titles such as 'Delete Item,' 'Create Item,' 'Create Maintenance Item,' 'Delete Maintenance Item.' The Lanier required that I give a name to each page of the document. I was told that the standard in the department was to use an abbreviated name of the section as the page name, so I gave names to my pages like 'CRDI,' 'CRDM,' and 'CRDMI.'

"Over a period of two days, I entered about 20 pages. On the third day, I couldn't remember where I'd left off in the original, because the text was so repetitive. I looked at the index [list of documents] on the Lanier, and figured I'd call up the last document I'd entered to see where I left off. There were three rows of page names, so I tried the last one in the third row. It wasn't the right page. Then I realized that the Lanier had alphabetized the names of my pages. But because of the way I'd named them, I couldn't figure out what was what. It took me three hours to find my place. Later I found out the other writers were using numbers for the names of their documents so they wouldn't have this problem. I wish I'd known that when I started. My nickname for the word-processing system has become 'The No Problems Are Shared System.' "

If you want long-term successful usage of your word-processing system, find a way to chart and share the problems you encounter while you're learning the new system, as well as the solutions you work out. This will become the beginning of your internal word-processing procedures, standards, and organization methods. When you're first learning to use a word processor you may not realize the types of procedures and organizational issues you need to plan for. So that you don't have to discover the need for standards and procedures as you go, you'll find some of the most common organizational and procedural issues below.

Supervision and Management

The procedures and organization we're recommending involve planning, time, and work. No matter how small your organization, someone on your staff should be responsible for your word-processing installation. Whether word-processing supervision or management becomes a full-time job in itself will depend upon the size of your organization. The person overseeing word processing should be responsible for the following areas:

Internal Documentation. This includes creating and keeping up-to-date binders or manuals detailing procedures and formats. We'll talk more about the type of information to go in these below.

Setting Priorities. What documents are done first? Is work done on a first-in, first-out basis? Do certain individuals or departments have priority?

Realistic Scheduling. This includes seeing that word-processing work is done in a timely manner and educating the company staff as to what they can expect from the word-processing operators. You'll probably want to set standards for how the work is submitted, determine lead time necessary for different types of documents, and decide whose responsibility it will be to perform tasks such as proofreading text after it is printed.

Maintaining Supplies. Enough word-processing supplies should be kept on hand so that word-processing production doesn't come to a halt for lack of a ribbon.

Vendor Contacts. Work with the word-processing vendor to solve problems with the equipment, whether it is a question of how to use a feature or function, or a malfunction of the hardware.

Document Standards and Formats

If you work in a small company and word processing is used by only one person in your office, you may not be concerned that all letters or sales proposals use the same print format. Or if you're the only word-processing operator, you may know you'll never forget how many lines down to start a letter on your stationery. But if you bring in a temporary worker to do some word processing, can you expect a new person to know? And if you work in a large company, where document formats are standardized, you'll want to be sure any new or temporary word-processing operators follow them.

Start a binder with sample printed copies of the different kinds of documents created on your word processor. Mark them up so that formatting standards are seen immediately. To show standard letter format, for example, you might want to indicate the sizes of all four margins (left, right, top, and bottom); block or indented paragraphs; spacing between addresses, salutations, and the body of the text; print element and pitch to be used for all letters; second-page headings and margins; whether a page number is to be printed on the first page; and any other special requirements you have.

Some word processors allow you to store format lines or instructions separately, apart from the text of documents. If yours does, make use of this feature, and mark on the printed sample where to find the format to be used, or what keys to press to activate it. Or draw a "ruler line" across your printed sample, showing where margins and tabs should be set.

Boilerplate Text

"Boilerplate" is a term used for frequently reused chunks of text that are stored on disk so that you can merge them into another document without retyping them. Boilerplate might include standard paragraphs which you combine to create proposals, general letters which can be personalized, or forms that you fill in regularly.

Make several copies of a boilerplate binder, including printed copies of all standard paragraphs and documents you have on disk. Include the document name the text is stored in, and any key word or phrase which you can use to retrieve it by. This binder will be useful for the word-processing operator, and for whoever "originates" the documents. A manager might use this binder when preparing letters or proposals. The manager could write down the customer's name and address, and then write the numbers or key words of the boilerplate paragraphs included in the letter. The word-processing operator can then easily merge the information together.

If your word processor allows you to enter comments which won't print in your documents, note any special requirements inside the boilerplate text. When you copy that text into a document, you'll have your reminder right in front of you on the screen. For example, if a filled-out form must be printed using 12 pitch, while most other documents in the office are printed using 10, you might want to put a reminder as the first or last line in the document.

Document Naming Conventions

Each word processor has its own limits to document names. You may be able to use up to 20 or 30 characters, with whatever special symbols you want, or you may be limited to 8 characters and not allowed to use any spaces in the name. You may be asked not to use numbers, or told to use numbers. Whatever the restrictions imposed by the word processor, you'll want to come up with your own system of naming documents. This may not seem particularly important when you start out on a word processor and have only 15 or 20 documents stored on your disk. But several months down the road, when you have hundreds of documents, you may forget what text you saved in EX1, EX1A, or ZB25, or even SBLETTER, BRLETTER, or STDLETTER. As Marty found out the hard way, she'd have been better off naming her document pages with numbers than with abbreviations. On a word-processing system that lists documents in the order they're created, she wouldn't have encountered the problem she did. Here are some naming conventions you might want to consider:

- Decide on standard prefixes or suffixes for types of documents. For example, "PROP-" might be the beginning of document names for any proposals, ".LET" might go at the end of all letters, "STD" might begin or end the names of standard, or boilerplate documents.
- If the directory that shows you the names of documents doesn't automatically provide the date the document was created, you might want to make it part of the name. This will help you identify different versions of documents, and how recent they are. Depending on the length you have available, a document name with date might be anything from "Jones Letter, 3/12/84" to "Jones3/2.let." You might also want to add a code to show at what date the document can be safely deleted—say "D3" for "delete in the third month (March)."
- If the directory information doesn't let you identify who created each document, you might consider using your initials somewhere in the name, like this: "Jones Letter, 3/84, LU."

Organizing Your Documents on Disk

It's a good idea to think about how you will organize your documents on disk, so that you can find them quickly and so that you'll always have room on disk to edit them and make changes. Establishing naming conventions will help. In addition, you may want to consider these issues:

- If your system uses floppy disks, how will you know which documents are on each disk? To help you locate documents, store similar ones together. For example, you might have one disk for letters, another for proposals or reports, another for statistical

charts, and another for boilerplate documents. Or you might want to have separate disks for each person who uses the word processor. Of course, after a while you may have several diskettes for each type of document, or each person.
- Some word processors let you print the directory of a disk. If yours does, you might want to print the directory of each disk regularly, keeping the latest copies in a binder. Then name or number each disk, and write the name on the printed directory. This will give you a pretty good cross-referencing system.
- Where will you store your floppies? Usually they come in a box of ten, and initially you'll probably find it easy to store the disks you use right in the box. As you accumulate more of them, however, you might want to consider keeping them somewhere else. You can buy notebooks with plastic sheets that hold floppies, large plastic boxes that will hold up 20 to 50 disks, and a variety of other containers. Ask your word-processing supply company what they have available.
- Always leave enough room on your disk to allow you to make changes to your documents. How much space you need to leave depends on the kind of changes you make and how the system stores text. It can be very frustrating to try to add two sentences to a document and find out that there isn't room on the disk to hold the information. Some systems will warn you when your disk is almost full; others wait until there's no room left and then tell you can't save your text. Somewhere in your word-processing software or operating system should be a way to ask how much space is left on disk: Find it and use it.
- If you have a hard-disk system, the disk is probably broken down into sections, somewhat like the drawers in a file cabinet. Hard disks hold many more documents than floppy disks can, so you have access to more at one time. They will fill up eventually, and you may have to store some of your documents on floppies, copying them back onto the hard disk when you need them. You may want to keep all standard text in one section of the hard disk, and assign other areas of the disk to individual users.
- If you have a multi-user system with a hard disk, you may have "security" features, allowing you to create passwords for each user, and assigning portions of the disk for use. If you have this type of system, you'll want to think carefully about how you organize documents. Be sure that standard files that everyone shares are placed in an area that can be reached easily by all users. You don't want each person to have to keep his own copy

of a long proposal on disk, taking up disk space that could be used for other text. Although the room on disk may seem boundless at first, chances are you'll begin to wish you had more after six months of using the system.

How Long Should You Keep Each Document?

There will come a time when you want and need all the disk space you can get. You'll have to decide what documents to delete, and decide how long to keep a document on disk. Naturally, how long you keep a document depends on whether or not you expect to revise it again, or will need to print another original copy. In most cases, give yourself the benefit of the doubt, and keep it longer than you think you'll need it. How often have you typed a letter for someone and heard him say it looked perfect, only to return the next day to find another paragraph was needed? Ros Heimberg says that when she worked in a word-processing center, they kept all documents on disk for two weeks and then deleted them. Consequently they had to retype many documents, because staff would return with changes long after two weeks. Having seen other centers address this problem differently, Ros says she would now plan to keep most documents for several months.

Creating a Backup Procedure

To safeguard your work, you'll want to make backup copies of your disks. It's a good idea to set aside a specific time for this, to be sure it gets done. Although it may not happen often, your disk drives can malfunction, damaging the text stored on your disk (or sometimes, erasing all of it). Floppy diskettes do wear out over time, and are subject to warping if not properly cared for. And there's also the possibility that you'll simply delete the wrong file. With proper backup procedures, none of these situations should cause you to lose very much stored text.

- Plan to make backup copies daily.
- Have one or two people in charge of making backups—perhaps just before they go home. Or, if you have a floppy-based system and the users have their own disks, you might make them responsible for it. (While writing the manuscript of this book, we backed up each file every time we made a change to it. If this seems like a lot of work, it's not. We simply made it a habit.)

- Have a set of disks (or tapes, if you have a tape drive) just for backup. You can work out a variety of systems. You might make an exact duplicate of each disk, or copy all files altered that day onto a daily backup disk. Some companies have a week's supply of daily backups, and rotate their use.
- If you have a fixed hard disk, with one floppy drive for "archiving," backup will unfortunately be a longer chore. It will take a number of floppy disks to hold all the files present on your hard disk. It's worth the effort, though. If you don't think so, ask around until you find someone who's lost the contents of a hard disk.

Shortcuts and Tips for Using the Word Processor

As you use your word processor more and more, you'll find your own shortcuts and ways to use its functions. Most training guides will show you how to use a word processor's features in the way that's easiest to learn. They may not show you the fastest way, because it takes more understanding of the system. You're bound to stumble on some of these, or discover them tucked away in the reference manual. You may even find that you can do things with the system that the vendor doesn't know are possible. Whatever these little tidbits are, write them down. Combine your notes with those of anyone else using the system, and keep them in a binder.

Along with your shortcuts and notes, include information that new or occasional operators may need to know. Facts such as the need to "format" brand new diskettes before using them, or that writing on diskette labels with anything but a felt-tip pen can damage the disk, should be readily available to everyone who will use the system.

Organizing the Word-Processing Work Load

If you or your staff will be using the word processor to enter other people's work, you'll want to plan how the work is submitted, how priorities should be set, and how you'll distribute the printed copies. How formally you handle this will depend on your office, the number of word-processing operators you have, how many people submit work to be done on the system, and the volume of word-processing work.

Many word-processing centers use forms to help them organize their work load. One form is filled out and attached to any material submitted to the word-processing center, and another is attached to completed work when it is distributed.

WORD PROCESSING SUBMISSION FORM

Name   Phone ext   Dept

Date and time submitted:

Date and time required:

Type of document: Original material   Revision   Doc code:

   Last rev date   Confidential   Rough draft   Final

   Letter   Report   Statistical   Technical   Mass mailing

   Other:

Future needs: Additional revisions expected

Length of time to keep text on disk:

Print requirements: Typestyle   Spacing

   Margins   Header/Footer

   Letter quality needed   Rough draft quality OK

   Other

Additional comments or description:

WORD PROCESSING COMPLETION FORM:

Operator name   Date

Document name assigned to text

Expected deletion date

Document length (lines/pages)

Time spent   Original   Revision

Requests for clarification of original:

Comments:

Despite the changes that come when you acquire a word processor, in most circumstances, you're in for a treat. Word processing is a rapidly growing and exciting technology. Getting the best use of your equipment needs thought and planning. But so do many other advances and changes. Fortunately, many people before you have installed word processing, met with successes and failures, had problems, and found solutions. Learning from their experiences can help insure your own successful word-processing operations.

8

The Office of the Future

When you turn on your word processor, you are plugging into the office of the future: Machines listening to what you say, and typing that automatically—without a misspelling. Or taking a picture right off the television set and putting it into your report. Or recording your thoughts about some letter you've just received, and then sending both across town, so a coworker can hear what you have to say as she reads the letter you're talking about. Or taking charts off the main computer downstairs, and without a moment's hesitation, plugging them into the document you're creating on your word processor. Or distributing your report to every copying machine in the company—or every display screen—at the same time.

In some offices you can do all those things now. In five or ten years, you'll probably be able to do some or all of these things in a lot of companies—probably even yours. The biggest guns in office equipment (IBM, Xerox, AT&T), followed by the leading manufacturers of medium-sized computers (Data General, Hewlett-Packard, Digital Equipment Corporation), plus high-tech vendors like Wang, Honeywell, and Burroughs and dozens of less famous corporations, are retooling their computers, copying machines, printers, word processors, facsimile machines, telephones, and communications gear to create what they call the automated office. Some of the technology is already there. The manufacturers' investment in creating and linking together all this new gear has swollen way beyond sales, which are already running at about $3 billion a year, and should go four times that by 1986.

Why are vendors jockeying so hard for position in a market that's just taking off? And why have Fortune 500 companies like Atlantic

Richfield, Aetna, and Avon Products "automated" their offices? Both vendors and buyers are looking at costs. In 1980 U.S. office workers earned more than 60 percent of the total $1.3 trillion (that's $13,000,000,000,000) paid out in wages and fringe benefits. At first, using the analogy of a production line, some companies figured they could save some of that money by replacing people with machines. In factories, productivity per worker went up when new machines came in. Why not in the office?

Well, because the work's different. Just increasing the number of pieces of paper I turn out does not necessarily mean I'm more productive, when my job is to plan a dam. In fact, few people have been able to document "hard" factory-style savings directly due to automating the office. SRI International surveyed some 4000 offices asking for this kind of proof. They found almost none. Patricia Seybold, who runs the influential newsletter *Seybold Report on Office Systems*, says, "The organizational benefits of word processing, such as making work flow more smoothly, or sending off a bid more quickly, are so intangible that you can't get 'hard' proof of dramatic savings."

But a word processor tied in to my firm's main computer can help me get my work done faster, without waiting for half a dozen other people to return my calls, find a blueprint, send it across town to me, copy it, and return it. The more office machines that are connected, the easier it is for me to do real work. And that's the reason so many executives are intrigued with "OA"—the acronym for Office Automation. They figure it'll cut out the delays while they wait for someone

Three terminals tied to one computer—the first step toward office automation. (Photo courtesy of Data General)

else to do something—and let them think faster. Paul Strassmann, a Xerox vice-president, adds, "We're still deeply rooted in industrial-engineering concepts of efficiency, but office technology doesn't achieve its most powerful effects primarily by mechanizing what people are doing already. Instead, it simplifies tasks, and eliminates unnecessary job steps."

So OA will do more than multiply paper and flip information around. It may change the way we work—who we talk to, how we delegate responsibility, how we find, relay, analyze, reconstruct, and present ideas. At its best OA frees us of drudgery and delay, letting us solve a problem today, rather than next week. In a world where a few hours' headstart can mean millions of dollars in profits, speed is a real benefit.

OA is inevitable, too. Once the competition goes OA, your company will feel the pressure to follow. Automation probably does cut some costs and boost others; but it makes it possible to combine data in ways you never thought of before. OA offers a chance to do what's never been done before, and although no one knows for sure what that might be, a lot of people are eager to find out.

Not everyone. The last person to need office automation is someone who works alone. A poet, say. Someone who doesn't need to know today's news—or even last month's gossip. Someone who doesn't have to get facts and figures from someone else, or send reports to half a dozen people around the world. Someone who rarely talks on the phone, doesn't use television, never makes charts or pictures. Someone who might as well be using a pen.

If you work by yourself now, but want to tap libraries on computers in other countries, and to send reports to people in large offices across town without getting in your car, you'll need to make sure your word processor can "talk" that way.

If you're part of a small-business or professional group, you may want to think seriously about office automation before buying a word processor, particularly if your business is expanding rapidly. The choice will either limit your chances or open them up.

And if you're working in some part of a large corporation, you'll find that someone there is already planning for office automation. Some sooner than others. Some more efficiently, some more economically. But any Fortune 500 company knows it better be planning for OA, or it won't stay in the top 500 much longer. That means that your department's choice of a word processor may have to dovetail with larger plans. Or you may be out in front of them, so you can establish a precedent. The money you spend—and save—will determine whether other departments can move ahead or languish.

Certainly a lot of the people who authorize budgets like the idea of automation. Sales of word processors, often seen as the first step in that direction, have grown at 50 percent a year for the last six years. The next item people are buying: digital telephone switchboards, that let you send any computerized information (numbers or text, say) along the phone lines you already have installed. (In essence, you can call up a computer, and have it send a chart over to your word processor, or you can type a memo to someone upstairs, and send it over the phone line so it will be immediately displayed on her video display—electronic mail.) Sales of these computerized Private Branch Exchanges (abbreviated PBX's) are expected to blossom from $220 million in 1981 to around $4 billion in 1986. In fact, sales of all equipment that could eventually be linked together by OA should grow by 34 percent a year during the same period, according to Dataquest, Inc.

But if your company buys the wrong equipment now, you won't be able to automate much more than text, later. You'll find your word processor can't talk with your computer; your phone lines can't carry messages from your word processor to copiers or printers in distant buildings; your television system won't send anything but static to your facsimile machines, and you'll be getting sales calls from vendors who want you to junk every piece of equipment you own, and start fresh, with a modest million dollar investment.

Since vendors don't have much interest in explaining how this all works—"Just buy our equipment and everything will turn out hunky-dory"—you can keep your options open by learning a little about the technology that makes this new kind of office possible. In this chapter, we'll sketch out some of the ways this electronic office will function. You'll begin to see how much—or how little—automation your office really needs. You'll see how wide a range of systems there are, and how many problems can arise. And throughout, we'll be raising some pointed questions you can bring up, when a salesperson starts making vague promises.

Already the newest copying machines, printers, television cameras, and telephone switchboards can be controlled by microprocessors (little computers). And since all computers code information electronically, we can make them all talk to each other. That's the idea behind the electronic office.

You'll be able to connect every piece of computerized equipment in your company on one network, so that you can move information forward and back in seconds—not days. In contrast, think of the slow, uncoordinated way ideas move around offices today:

- One person hoards a mound of information, doling it out slowly, from a private reserve.
- Reports get stuck on someone's desk for weeks, waiting for an extra fact to come in from a branch.
- News comes in, but gets mislaid in the mailroom.
- You call someone, and miss him; the only message you can leave is so short that you have to wait for him to call you back; but when he does, you're in a meeting. Days pass before you connect.
- The big computer downstairs prints out a report, but to discuss it in your letters, you have to key the whole report in again, to get it on your word-processing system. Or if you're still using typewriters, you have to type it, and retype it, and retype it again, until you've made a perfect copy of what one computer could have sent to another in less than a minute.
- People carry around a lot of information physically—copying it, passing it out, collecting it. A single form takes sixteen signatures—and a month to complete.
- One department starts a study that three other departments have already run—but nobody told anybody else about it.
- The warehouse does not know what the buyers have in mind; the dealers don't know where their shipments are; slips of paper drop on the floor, and millions of dollars get lost.

In this sluggish, uneven movement of information, we see that information developed in one place cannot be readily used by the rest of the company. Information gets through late and garbled. People waste half their days toting and typing what the computer could do. Therefore, the corporation misses opportunities for sales, savings, and profits.

But the automated office should give you almost instantaneous access to whatever information you want, speed up your own "processing" of information drawn from many sources, and zip your messages to their recipients in seconds. By connecting every microprocessor and every large computer in the company, the automated office makes information flow so fast that you can get your work done in half the time. That's why so many major corporations are headed this way, with smaller businesses trailing after.

Here's a rough checklist of functions you'll be able to perform in the electronic office, whether you're the boss, or secretary:

- Send mail instantaneously, from your video display screen to someone else's (electronic mail).

- Set up a computerized tickler file, so that the system reminds you of due dates, meetings, birthdays.
- Look up information in the computer, rather than in the file cabinet, simply by keying in the name of the file, and the particular subject you're studying.
- Find out, from hour to hour, how a given product is selling in a particular store—to see if your television spots are taking effect.
- Use the gigantic memory and computing power of your company's mainframe computer, right from your desk, without waiting hours, days, or weeks for some response.
- Embed spoken comments alongside printed text, to be broadcast when the text is displayed on someone's video screen.
- Turn television pictures into print images.
- Transmit voice, television, data, or text at speeds almost as fast as your computer can think.
- Monitor exactly who has been browsing through your files—and lock out anyone who's got no business there.
- Acknowledge receipt of messages, without being there. (Your computer tells the other computer it got the word.)
- Save telephone, text, and television messages for display when you get back to the office.
- Distribute multiple copies of a report on paper and on video display screens, while filing it on microfiche, or magnetic disk—at the press of a button.

In this way, you'll be able to carry out one job from beginning to end, without putting it off for further information, without waiting for a reply to your letter, without having to reenter and redo what's already been done. More information faster—that's the gist of this small network.

Your word processor, then, might become an all-purpose workstation. Hooked into every other office machine, your workstation will let you circulate rough drafts to half a dozen approvers, and get back comments; file and retrieve any letter you get or send; perform complex calculations; print and distribute. Some people are buying personal computers—with word-processing programs—as their workstations. In one company, an engineer brought his own Apple computer in, to help him do his work. That started a trend; now there are a hundred throughout the company, and they're talking to each other.

It's the network that makes a word processor or personal computer into an "executive workstation." And it's the network that allows electronic mail, and voice mail. In electronic mail, you type a message on your keyboard, and send it to someone else's terminal—outpacing the regular mail. In voice mail, you dial a special number, and talk to a machine that turns your speech into computer code, stores it that way, and alerts the person you were calling that he has a message waiting; when he calls, he gets the reconstructed message. It's as if everyone had an answering machine.

The network—not just the cable connecting all those machines, but the actual free flow of information—forms the basis for all significant office automation. Peter G. W. Keen, a professor at M.I.T.'s Center for Information Systems Research, says, "I think the local area network is the single most important development in communications, data processing, and information management of the eighties. When people don't have to get up and transport papers down the hall ten times a day, that will really change how internal operations are conducted."

WHAT'S POSSIBLE NOW

You can link microfilm systems to a large computer, so that you can file a letter there, then recall it at a flip of a switch. You can now send electronic information over regular phone lines, coaxial cables, and microwaves, so you can do meetings-by-television and high-speed transfer of huge files, from one computer to another. You can go into a computer's data base, and call up any given record within a few seconds; in fact, that record may be a still photograph, a voice you can hear, or a moving picture. In brief, you can do every one of those functions now.

But you can't do them all on the same system, or at least not very often. It's still hard to get one company's computerized equipment to talk to another brand. Many buildings have lousy wiring—so new cable may have to be laid. The regular phone lines have trouble carrying that much information fast enough. And then, the people selling this gear have indulged in a lot of hype. Some have announced products that don't exist except in somebody's mind. Others claim that their equipment will be able to communicate with some other vendor's—but it can't. So far, you can't very often count on putting graphics, television images, voice, and text together on the same line. And the information's not often transmitted at the speed of a computer, so you may have delays that last from a few seconds to a few hours, while you wait for answers.

Still, there are already more than 5000 somewhat automated offices at work in the United States, Canada, Europe, and Japan. These systems don't tie everything together; in fact, they rarely merge more than two forms of information, television and text, say. Dr. W. L. Coggshall, who has been shopping for a network for his own company,

Dataquest, reports on his conversations with the people who work in some of these offices. He says that most people like getting access to data bases that were previously closed to them, or available only after a week's wait; sharing work with others, and passing it along on the system, rather than taking it off and sending it through interoffice mail; evading a lot of manual work (retyping, copying, carrying); and knowing that they can add new employees gradually, as they come on board, without overwhelming the system. They look forward to even more links to mainframe computers, and outside electronic libraries; and, through special carriers, to similar networks in the company offices on other continents.

Who uses the network the most? Accounting people, word-processing operators, writers, lawyers, engineers, and a very few executives. Coggshall suggests that it makes sense to solve a lot of problems for a few highly paid professionals, such as engineers, before trying to do everything for everyone in the company.

The problems? No one liked rewiring a building. Some vendors were slow in delivering equipment, clumsy at training people to use the network. And just deciding which network to buy can give anyone a headache.

As you begin to look at different networks, you'll see that the whole field is a tangle of advertising terms, mixed metaphors, and engineering jargon. You will find a confusing variety of plugs that don't plug in, wires that don't connect, switches that freeze, data that goes haywire. Equipment is available, but the programmers haven't finished the software that makes the machine work. Nothing is standard, although half a dozen groups argue that their idea should be the industry model. Some companies build their networks around huge central computers; others put small computers out along the line. Some companies ignore your phones; others insist on putting television on the same line with your text. You could end up with two or three separate networks—not too efficient—or you could decide that there's no cheap way to tie together all the different machines you've acquired over the years. Even if you have two different machines from the same vendor, they may turn your letter into trash, when you attempt to communicate it from one to another.

Here's what an executive at a very smart, fairly automated company has to say about their own experimental network. "There are serious problems," claims William Mellentin of SRI International. "I cannot get very good output directly from the time-sharing system. It cannot handle tables or graphs. We often use bullet-style charts that would make better reading or viewing if we could output to a photocomposer and if fancy formats were easier. We cannot come back from the Wang printer to our system because of the inability of the system to handle the same formatting codes (such as underlining). Sometimes we have problems of response time because we have a low priority in the system as a test group."

Alexia Martin, of the same company, lists some of the machines people often use in offices:

> Electronic copiers
> Facsimile machines
> Interactive graphics systems
> Large computers
> Micrographics
> Optical Character Readers (OCRs)
> Personal computers
> Photocomposers
> Printers
> Telephones
> Television
> Videodisk players
> Videotape recorders
> Word processors

"Without exception, there is no overall system under which *all* information or services available on the above machines can be accessed in a logically related manner." Not now. Not all of them. Not logically. And not too fast. Some of them, yes, and pretty well. But so far, you can't expect to leap into utopia tomorrow.

One law firm, for instance, has set up a large word processor at the core of their network, storing the basic texts for wills, trusts, employment contracts, leases, limited partnership agreements, profit-sharing plans, real estate sales contracts, stock purchase agreements, so that any lawyer in the firm can call one up, plug in the particulars, and run off a dozen originals, to review with the client. In addition, the lawyer can use his word-processing terminal to talk to the firm's main computer, with its regular accounting programs (accounts receivable, accounts payable, payroll and general ledger), or he can call up a special time-keeping package that lets him enter his hours for a client, and have the billing taken care of automatically. And when a lawyer wants to consult one of the computerized law libraries, he can dial that on the phone, have the citations shown onscreen, then memorized by his own system. All the lawyers schedule their appointments on one universal calendar. And whenever a lawyer takes on a new client, another program in the main computer checks for possible conflict of interest with other clients.

This firm encountered a few problems setting up the system. At first, the word processor's disk storage did not have enough space to remember all the repetitive documents it was supposed to keep on file—so they added some more circuit boards and a different disk, and it could remember more. Furthermore, they had to buy both the main computer and the word processor, and the devices that let both communicate along the phone lines to outside data bases, from one vendor—otherwise, they would have had a hard time making plug-in connections. And the vendor they chose figured they were such a small account that service was limited to some toll-free calls to an 800 number. The cost of the hardware was $70,000. The firm plans to add an Optical Character Reader, ink jet printers, and microfiche filing system later, when the vendor gets those products ready; and much later, a voice message system.

BUYING AN AUTOMATED OFFICE

More than 60 companies claim to sell "automated offices." What exactly do they offer? Let's look at the Datapoint brochure called "The Integrated Electronic Office®." Interesting that they feel compelled to claim such a banal title as a trademark. But the brochure looks fancy: aluminum paper cover, full-color pictures, twelve two-column pages of text. It assumes you have no equipment at all, so you can start from scratch with Datapoint. There's no mention of the fact that you might want to start with some other vendor's word processor, or computer—and have trouble linking up with Datapoint.

"You can get just the processing power you need initially and expand incrementally with predictable expenditures"—through Datapoint, naturally. If you have to send large amounts of data, text, and messages through the network, they suggest their ARC (Attached Resource Computer—another trademark—Local Network). "Your ARC local network can grow without performance degradation to nearly unlimited size . . . in numbers of users and peripherals . . . amount of memory . . . amount of storage."

Now that vagueness suggests what can go wrong with some networks: even if you only use equipment from one vendor, you may not be able to expand very far. You may not be able to connect enough terminals, or computers; you may not be able to add extra memory, or storage for your computers. Or you can add them, but the speed of response goes down. That's what they mean by "performance degradation."

Then they have a switching system that handles the phones and helps you jump from one ARC local network to another. This is called ISX: Information Switching Exchange. It's got a lot of power, since it can support from 100 to 20,000 terminals—that'd be regular phones, word processors, keyboards, electronic mail stations—all from Datapoint.

Integration

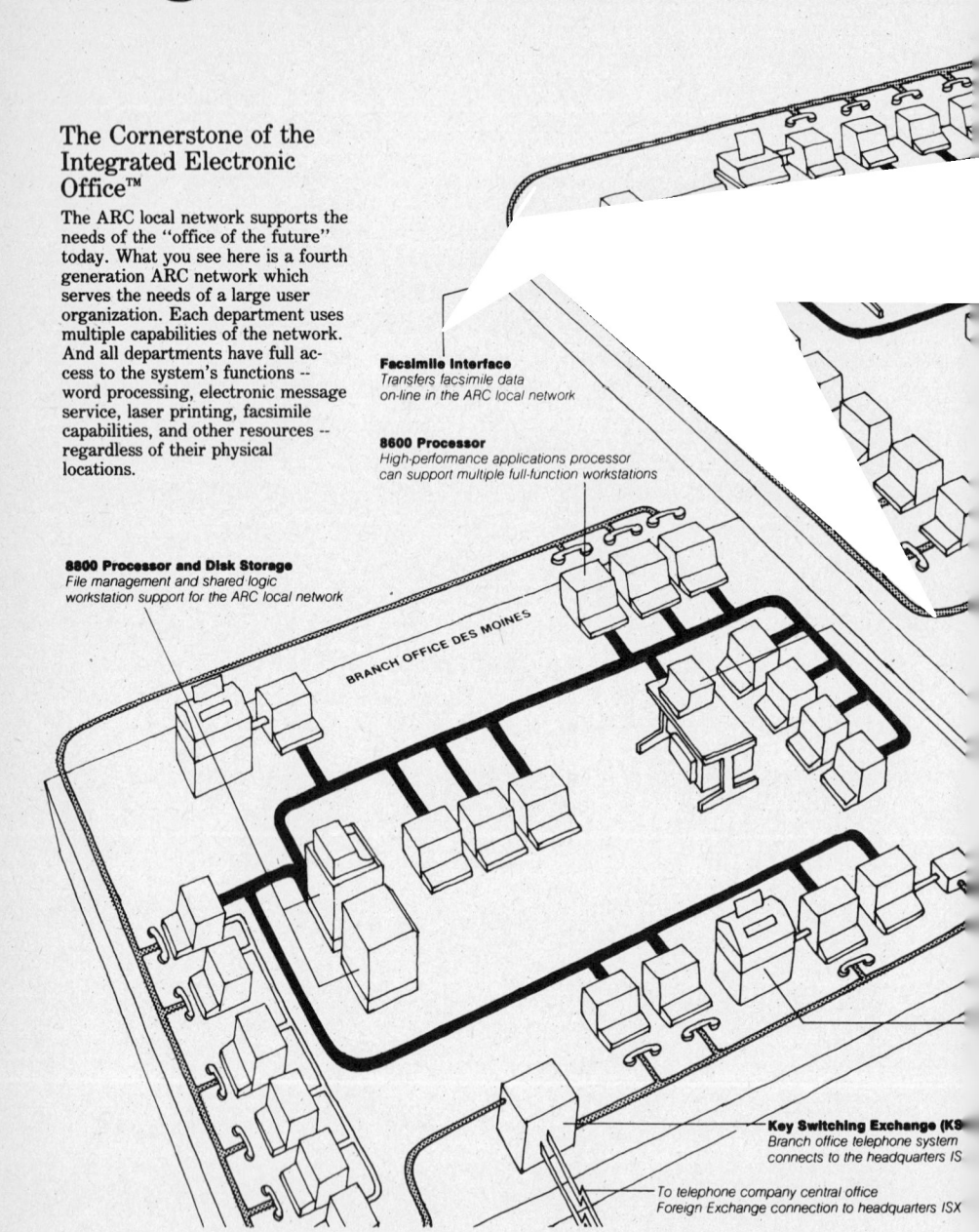

The Cornerstone of the Integrated Electronic Office™

The ARC local network supports the needs of the "office of the future" today. What you see here is a fourth generation ARC network which serves the needs of a large user organization. Each department uses multiple capabilities of the network. And all departments have full access to the system's functions -- word processing, electronic message service, laser printing, facsimile capabilities, and other resources -- regardless of their physical locations.

Facsimile Interface
Transfers facsimile data on-line in the ARC local network

8600 Processor
High-performance applications processor can support multiple full-function workstations

8800 Processor and Disk Storage
File management and shared logic workstation support for the ARC local network

BRANCH OFFICE DES MOINES

Key Switching Exchange (KS
Branch office telephone system connects to the headquarters IS

To telephone company central office
Foreign Exchange connection to headquarters ISX

A diagram of what Datapoint calls an Integrated Electronic Office.™ From a Chicago workstation, information goes to a letter-quality printer, for local copies, then merges with color graphics in the center of the office, and zips over to a laser printer for seventy-five pages a minute. Then the same material is sent over phone lines to the branch office computers, printers, and disk storage. (Diagram courtesy of Datapoint)

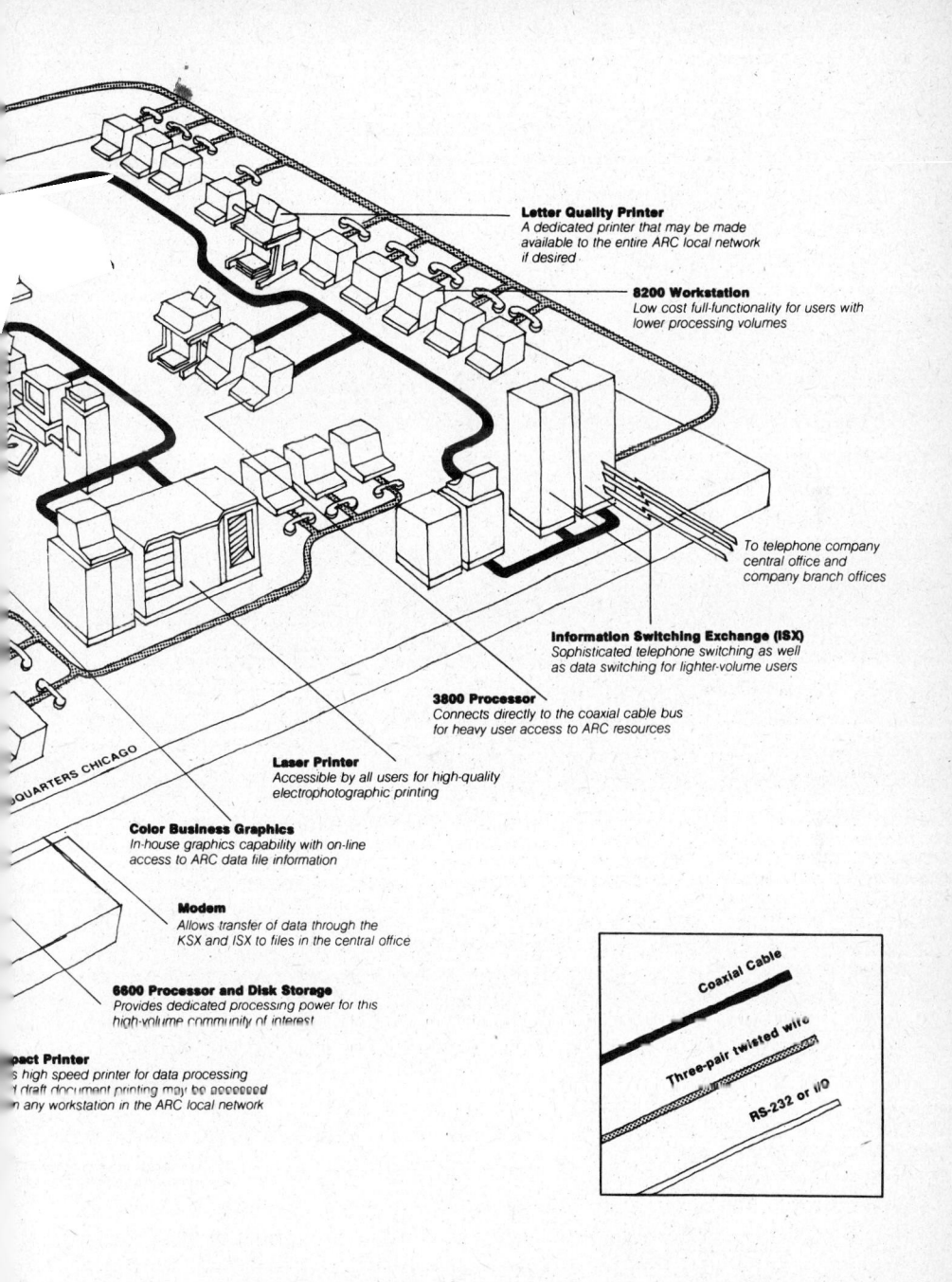

Letter Quality Printer
A dedicated printer that may be made available to the entire ARC local network if desired

8200 Workstation
Low cost full-functionality for users with lower processing volumes

To telephone company central office and company branch offices

Information Switching Exchange (ISX)
Sophisticated telephone switching as well as data switching for lighter-volume users

3800 Processor
Connects directly to the coaxial cable bus for heavy user access to ARC resources

Laser Printer
Accessible by all users for high-quality electrophotographic printing

Color Business Graphics
In-house graphics capability with on-line access to ARC data file information

Modem
Allows transfer of data through the KSX and ISX to files in the central office

6600 Processor and Disk Storage
Provides dedicated processing power for this high-volume community of interest

pact Printer
s high speed printer for data processing
d draft document printing may be accessed
n any workstation in the ARC local network

Coaxial Cable

Three-pair twisted wire

RS-232 or I/O

Forming a Network

The key concept in all such "integrated" offices: the network. A local area network (LAN) connects office equipment within one building, or within a few next-door buildings. A wider network connects the local one with the regular phone lines, lines especially designed to carry a lot of data, microwave relay stations, even satellites, taking your messages out to the rest of the country or the world. An open network can handle equipment from different vendors; a closed one, only the gear from one vendor.

But since there are so many local networks being advertised today, you may wonder how to distinguish between them. How are different networks designed? Which one will serve your office best? And what will that mean for your word processor?

A network's a little like a Welsh town, with bells sounding on every street corner. From above, you hear the intersecting chimes, racing back and forth, enlivening the whole town. Each one brings a little signal from its corner; and if you know what timbre to listen for, you can tell who's ringing now. A network depends on many signals circulating at different frequencies.

How frequently does the surface of your eardrum tremble when a bell sounds? If it goes up and down in one second, we call that a frequency of one hertz. Our vocal cords tend to give off a whole range of these frequencies, mixed together. So the telephone line has been designed to carry a continuous range of frequencies, from 300 hertz to about 3400 hertz—that's enough to reproduce one's voice in a vaguely recognizable way at the other end.

Because the sound waves get represented by analogous electrical frequencies, we call this form of transmission "analog." It's a sliding scale, and scientists use it in analog computers, which measure the rise and fall of tides, or temperatures in a vat of molten steel—any continually changing phenomenon. A stereo transmits at around 20,000 hertz. Your television set requires signals around 4½ million hertz (both sound and pictures move in waves).

By contrast, a bank's computer has a very limited vocal range. It can say yes or no. On or off. One or zero. To express anything on the computer, you must turn your data into a series of answers to yes or no questions—effectively, a stream of ones or zeroes. Since these numbers are called digits, this kind of transmission is called "digital." Electrically, it's a stream of on's and off's. Each pulse is known as a bit—the smallest bit of information known to the computer.

To send information around on a network, it's possible—and sometimes helpful—to turn an analog signal into a digital one, sorting analog waves out into digital bits. If you took pictures of a wave sweeping past the pilings of a pier, then marked each spot where the water cut through the middle of a log, you could represent that curving form as a series of steps, almost like a staircase. Instead of a continuous movement, then, you would have a series of distinct levels, each of which could be translated into a number, so that instead of showing a curve, you would show "2, 2.5, 3, 3.5, 4, 5, 6, 7, 6.5, 6, 5, 4, 3, 2." Those digits could then be sent out as a coded series of on and off impulses. Record companies do this when they record a violin concerto digitally. The phone company sometimes turns your voice into a series of on/off pulses for a long distance call, then reconstructs it at the far end; and your friends recognize it as, more or less, you.

Why would anyone want to digitize your voice? Well, in analog transmissions, the waves sent along the line tend to wobble when static creeps in; every little shock makes them quiver more, and the farther they go, and the more often they're amplified, to keep them going, the worse this tintinnabulation becomes, until you can't really hear a voice any more—just buzzing and ringing. When you send a digital signal—a series of these on/off pulses—you can place repeaters all along that line; they pick up the pulse, recognize it, and reproduce it, so that from that point on, it goes out full strength. The amplifiers on analog lines just amplify the noise along with the wave, whereas these repeaters generate a fresh impulse; and since you've only got two choices, on or off, both crisp or new, you're not so likely to lose any subtle overtones.

The country's turning digital, partly because the signal doesn't fall apart over long distances, partly because computers need to talk to each other directly, and partly because the technology that allows conversion of all analog signals into digital ones has now become so cheap. For instance, you can now turn your phone system into a network carrying digital data—just by buying a digital Private Branch Exchange, or switchboard. Another advantage: in digital transmission, all signals look alike, whether they originate from voice, television, facsimile machines, or your word processor. Just on and off pulses.

That's why whatever starts in your word processor can eventually be reconstructed as a disembodied voice on the phone; or a picture that started live on television can be caught, and framed on your word processor's screen, then printed out in full color, on the first page of your report. Of course, this takes quite a few gizmos, to do the deconstruction and reconstruction. But we already have the gizmos. For instance, we have devices called modems, which turn digital signals into analog ones and turn them back ("modulating" and "demodulating"), and these modems easily fit between your word processor and the phone line, to create a small network.

Speed and Code

Of course, different equipment spits out different ranges of frequencies, and those translate into more or fewer bits per second in the signal. For example, a burglar alarm is either on or off, so it only needs to send one bit per second—once—to alert the police. A fast typist averages 90 words per minute—about eight characters per second; that would require a minimum of 64 bits per second (abbreviated as bps). A stereo needs more than 300,000 bits per second. A television signal takes 92 million bps. Computers communicate at different speeds—microcomputers often send 9600 bps to each other.

The complexity of your message determines how many bps you'll need. If you type the word "word" on your word processor, it'll take approximately 32 bits to send (at 8 bits per character). But if you say it out loud, with a blend of frequencies, you'll need a hundred times as many bits per second to reconstruct your rich tones. To transmit a wide-screen movie with sound might take 100 million bps.

So if you have an electronic typewriter, sending out 17 characters per second, or somewhere around 150 bps, to a computer that normally sends and receives at 9600 bps, you may have a problem—unless you buy another series of black boxes, to translate speeds. And you'll need to make sure that your cables can carry that much information that fast. For instance, phone lines carry 600 bps easily, but they get shaky at 4800 bps, and lose lots of bits along the way at 9600 bps—unless the phone company "conditions" them very carefully. The maximum those wire pairs can handle, on a line called T4, is 274 million bps—but there aren't many T4's around. A satellite can transmit television signals to cable companies at 800 million bps. You probably won't need that much unless your company generates half a dozen television channels at once. But, if you plan a network, you'll want to know how fast all your equipment talks—and whether your current cables can handle that. In this area, you'll sometimes find the word "baud" used. "10 baud" means the equipment can send 10 discrete signals a second. But a few of these signals tell the system, "Here comes a message," or "That's the end of that message," so the baud number is usually a little more than the actual number of bits of information you can send through each second.

Distance matters, too. The farther you have to send a signal, the harder you have to throw it—and the more often you have to insert gear along the line, to freshen it and hurl it forward again. When Xerox studied where information went inside their own company, they found that almost two-thirds of the information traveling around a given organization circulates within a few thousand feet, the area served by one of these local networks. That's one technology. A slightly different kind of wire and signal can be used for short hauls, between two computers in one room, say; and another to go out into the surrounding countryside, for dozens of kilometers; still another, if you want to send a message for more than a hundred kilometers. But you'll need to anticipate expanding beyond those walls. In thinking ahead, one telecommunications consultant, Dixon Doll, says: "The focus should be on looking at all your corporation's requirements for information transfer. What may be a local requirement today may not be a local requirement tomorrow. The purpose of networks in general should be to mask geography." When the network's in and working, you don't have to worry about how far away someone is—but to set the network up, you do.

For instance, if you want to connect your word processor to another in the next room, you might lay down some flat cable with 8, 16, or more separate wires in it. Then you can send signals in parallel, down all the wires; if your system translates "Q" into eight bits, then each would shoot down its own wire. Since your word-processing system doesn't send bits out very fast, the parallelism lets you get more information over a little faster than if you had to send one bit after another, in serial fashion.

And whenever you send a message from your word processor to a printer, the printer has to know exactly where the message begins and ends; in effect, both terminals have to be in sync. If the printer gets out of sync, then it will misinterpret the rush of 1s and 0s, and you'll end up with some well-printed gibberish. There are two main ways that you can establish sync. If you send short messages every once and a while, you'll probably be able to use a cheap but slow transmission speed, in the mode called "asynchronous." This doesn't mean that the terminals get out of sync, just that your messages come at irregular intervals (*you* are out of sync). At the beginning of each character, the system sends a code telling the receiver to start counting; and from then on the sender and the receiver are in sync. But it does this for every character—that is, for every five to eight bits representing a letter, it inserts a start bit and a stop bit. Most personal computers and stand-alone word processors talk to their printers asynchronously—every once and a while—because the method's inexpensive and reliable, even if a little slow.

But if you need greater speed and volume, you'll turn to synchronous transmission. This eliminates the start and stop bits for every character, so less of your transmission time is taken up with announcements like, "Here's the beginning of a character." Instead, a clock in the terminal or in a modem establishes a constant pulse. So a message might consist of a clockbeat, followed by a complex pattern of bits that indicate, "Here comes the whole message," then a few thousand bits making up your text, then a closing message ("That's the end of that message.") All mainframe computers, and almost anything that sends more than 2400 bits per second, work synchronously. In general, then, asynchronous means slow; synchronous, fast.

So if you are thinking about buying a stand-alone word processor now and turning it into one terminal on a cluster later, you may have trouble, since the stand-alone probably transmits asynchronously, but the cluster, with more information to circulate quickly, has to work synchronously. And even though both come from the same vendor, they may not really communicate. Or they may do so occasionally, then drop forty pages out of a document, somewhere in the middle, as happened to a small architectural firm. They first bought a stand-alone, liked it, bought a cluster of six terminals from the same vendor, then discovered that only half of the reports created on the stand-alone could be read on the cluster. The vendor blamed cables; but the problem persisted after all cables got replaced. "We should have traded in that stand-alone—or forced them to convert all our files, so we could use them on the new network," said one architect, too late. Vendors usually deny that this kind of snafu will occur, but it happens more often than it should, and their technicians have a devil of a time getting everything in sync. So, before you believe them, ask for proof that they've succeeded in making this link work—in someone else's company.

Another problem that may come up when you try to get one machine to talk to another: the alphabet—and symbols like $, %, and &—into a series of 1s and 0s. One system, called Baudot, uses 5 bits to do this; another, called the American Standard Code for Information Interchange (ASCII), uses 7 bits per character, and lets you add another bit if you want. This extra bit is often called a checkbit or parity bit. In one system, the sending computer adds up all the 1s in the character, and if the total's odd, puts a 1 here; if even, a 0. Then the computer at the other end does the same calculation to see if it comes up with the same result. If it does, it figures the message got through all right. If not, it sounds an alarm. (This is just one way to figure the checkbit.) These two codes are usually employed for asynchronous transmission. In fact, three-quarters of today's stand-alone word processors speak ASCII. But each manufacturer uses the code slightly differently to express oddments like underlining, hyphens, sub- and superscripts. So even though both claim to understand ASCII, your message may be garbled, going from one vendor's word processor to another. What went in as "co-operate" may come out as "DX$XLCTORC."

Then there's an even more complicated code that's customarily used for fast synchronous transmissions, because although it takes 8 bits to express one character, that means you have the ability to define up to 256 characters, including those ticklish hyphens. Invented for IBM mainframe computers, it's called Extended Binary-Coded Decimal Interchange Code (EBCDIC).

Protocols at War

If you happen to start with a stand-alone word processor, it'll probably be slow and asynchronous, and it'll speak ASCII. But how can it talk to a mainframe computer, used to EBCDIC? Sometimes you can buy a modem that will convert the codes; sometimes you'll have to buy or write a computer program to solve the problem, or add another computer to do the job; sometimes you have to go inside the terminal with a soldering iron.

An accountant we know bought one particular stand-alone word processor mainly because the saleswoman swore it could receive data from the Dow Jones stock quotation service. Alas, instead of getting the latest prices through his phone lines, he got a series of circumflexes, parentheses, and exclamation points. For a few weeks the vendor refused to answer phone calls. Finally the accountant got ahold of an engineer in their company. The engineer just laughed at what the saleswoman had said. Why? The Dow Jones service and the word processor communicate in different codes, at different speeds, with different standards.

Hasn't anyone worked out some standards, so that different machines can be sure of communicating, without glitches? Well, yes and no. One group came up with a set of protocols—agreed-upon conventions for coding data and controlling the flow of messages on your network. But other groups have come up with different protocols.

How "standard" a protocol is depends on how many people vote for it—the voters are individual vendors and representatives of different electronics firms, meeting together as trade associations. In the United States, that's the Electronics Industry Association (EIA). In Europe, it's the Consulting Committee on International Telegraph and Telephone (CCITT). You'll see their initials in front of a lot of protocols—and draft protocols. Usually someone proposes a standard; then they argue over that for a few years. Meanwhile different companies are going off on their own. Finally, after a few more years, and half a dozen votes, almost by accident, an industry standard evolves—often the one that has sold the most.

For communications within your own office, protocols come in layers, from the plug to what you see onscreen. The lowest level defines the physical link (maximum cable length, voltage, resistance, cable type, size, and capacitance) and the accompanying "handshakes" that reassure each machine that the connection has been made correctly. You might have a "plug" with 25 pins, each dedicated to a particular message, such as:

- "I want to send out some data."
- "I am ready to receive."
- "My terminal is on."
- "Here is the sync."
- "I got that sync."

Depending on what machines you're connecting, and how far you're sending messages, you may find your new word processor's ready to use an EIA RS 232C Interface (an interface is just a connection between two pieces of machinery), but your old printer likes EIA RS 422A (no good). Or you might discover that the company that sold you your word processor ignored all industry standards, and came up with its own brand-new protocols, that don't match anyone else's. Just remember that if a machine doesn't get the secret handshake it expects, it won't send or receive anything but static.

That's the physical link. You need to make sure that matches, just to connect your terminal to a printer. The next level makes sure that data flows around the office going to and from the right people. It acts as a busybody mail clerk. It puts a to-and-from address on every message, makes sure that the recipient gets it, and acknowledges receipt, and it rereads the message at the far end to make sure it got there right. So this level says things like:

- "This is Joe's terminal transmitting."
- "I got Al's message."
- "That's the end of my message: what have you got to say for yourself?"
- "I'm busy now; don't bother me."

Sometimes the system manages this with special control characters that indicate this kind of information about the flow of the data. In IBM's Synchronous Data-Link Control (SDLC), every message is sent in a "frame," which is divided into particular hunks. The first one's a flag, warning, "This is the beginning of a message" (that takes 8 bits to say). The next hunk gives the addresses of sender and receiver (another 8 bits). The next field, called "control," tells the head computer how many frames a terminal has sent or received; or tells the terminal to start asking other terminals for information, to send it out, or to send a message a second time, because it got fouled up the first time (8 bits). Then there's a field of almost any length, which carries your message, in a code like EBCDIC. Finally, there's the error-checking field (16 bits), and another flag, indicating that you've ended the whole frame (8 bits). Of course, SDLC is just one of half a dozen data-link protocols that use 8-bit hunks like this. You don't have to know the inner workings of any of these protocols. But you've got to pray that your terminal, and any other device you want to communicate with, both understand the same data-link protocols.

The next level up assumes that you've handed over a complete frame, or block of data, some of which is your message, and some control characters. This protocol routes that frame through the network to its end destination. Instead of handling one message, this level handles them all. A particular computer program shunts the messages around the circuits, like trains in a freight yard. For instance, the CCITT came up with a recommendation called X.25 that tells computers how to send more than one message at a time, around a network.

Higher-level protocols are needed, but beyond this point, not even the trade associations have agreed. So it's every vendor for himself:

- Transport level: This one handles any conversations that jump from one network to another, so that you do not have to worry about that, when you're sitting at your terminal.
- Session level: This helps you to get on the network, have a session, and get off.
- Presentation level: This level translates from ASCII or EBCDIC codes into English, so that you do not have to look at "1011," but "K." This protocol governs what you see.
- Application level: This lets you do whatever task you've chosen, once you log on to the system: you might be retrieving information, sending electronic mail, or doing word processing. This protocol actually governs what you can do in a meaningful way, with all the layers of connection that lie hidden below.

By now you can see how a slight variation on any of these levels can spit static into your connection, or shut it down completely. So how can you be sure that doesn't happen?

Well, you could buy a protocol converter. These black boxes have been designed to translate from one protocol to another. They take an entire frame in on one side, understand it, and then express it in terms the other protocol can understand. Or you could buy a Cluster Controller that does the same thing, while supervising the movement of data around the network. Or you could just dial up one of the public networks that send whole packets of information around the country. That's like making a long distance call to reach your neighbor, but for only a few thousand dollars per terminal per month, you can use their facilities to link synchronous equipment with asynchronous, or connect one of your local networks with another one that observes different protocols.

(A protocol converter that sits between two networks is also called a gateway. Essentially a gateway is a protocol for translating protocols. Sometimes it comes in a box; sometimes it comes as a program. If you have a hundred communications lines going out to regular long distance lines, a gateway server will know what protocol the recipient uses, and, recognizing the address, will translate from your protocols to theirs. A gateway processor makes your terminal look like one of theirs. It's "imitating" or "emulating" one of theirs—hence the term "emulation," which you'll encounter a lot in these discussions. It means that somehow the system can make your network look "just like" the recipient's network—it's "virtually" the same. For instance, Nixdorf Computer Company calls its gateway processor "Virtual Terminal Support.")

This is too much for most small offices, and even hard for a large office to justify. And definitely out of reach—today—for individuals working at home. At the moment, the easiest way around the problem is to set up a local area network in which every terminal, every computer, every single device agrees, from the word go, on the same protocols. The next easiest is to use only a few protocols. (You could use one for fast high-volume work, one for facsimiles talking to each other, and a third for short slow messages.) Always ask what communications protocols your word processor can handle—and get worried if it can't talk to any other equipment you own.

Carriers

If you're part of a small firm, you may not want to lay down lots of new cables around your offices. You might be able to plug into your phone lines instead, and forward memos around the way you do calls. But if you have a lot of information to send around, or if you're in a large office, you may have to take down your ceiling, or lift the carpet, to install coaxial cables. Phone lines and cables are called carriers—they carry your messages.

There are half a dozen types of carriers, some appropriate for a small business, others for an international corporation. The carrier you choose can have a tremendous impact on how much data you can send, how fast, to how many places, with what guarantee of accuracy—and, yes, how much it will all cost.

Telephone Lines. The phone lines can carry more than just talk. Usually these circuits carry waves of electrical frequencies, analogous to the sound waves you put in by speaking; so, as we've seen, this is analog transmission. For your word processor to communicate over the phone lines, you have to convert its digital signals (on and off impulses) into gradually sliding waves. For that, you need the device known as a modem, which was discussed previously. A modem lets you modulate digital pulses into analog waves when you send, and to demodulate them back, when you receive. But you have to go over a lot of switches to go far: twisted pairs of copper wires take your call to a local office. There, you're switched onto a large trunk line, carrying you from switch to switch across the country, until you reach another local office and go back onto one of the short local "loops" to reach your friend. But the lines are noisy, and when the signal gets amplified at each switch, the static does too. So you can't always be sure of getting accurate data over regular phone lines at speeds above 1200 bits per second.

Leased Lines. If you know you're going to be sending a lot of data every day, you might want a leased circuit all your own. Then you don't have to go through all that public switching—which takes time—and you can get the line "conditioned" to carry more than 1200 bits per second. You're still threatened with crosstalk, but you have a better chance of sending accurate data at speeds a computer can absorb: say around 9600 bps, and up.

Coaxial Cable. That's a large cable containing a bunch of copper tubes. Inside of each tube, there's some insulation, and a single wire that conducts electricity. The current runs on the inside of each copper tube, and on the outside of the inner wire. So there's less chance of interference with someone else's conversation. And signals can move along almost as fast as light.

Microwaves. When you're sending messages along a line of sight, you can use microwaves. Where a phone carries only from 300 to 3400 hertz (cycles per second), microwave radio can handle 1000 to 15,000 million hertz, which means you can pack a lot of information into a short time. But a stray bird can wander through your data; rain, heat, thunder, and lightning interfere; and these days, you'll have to spend months setting up a channel that does not accidentally intersect someone else's beam.

Satellite. You can send up a satellite, and transmit several thousand phone conversations a second. Of course, they have to go more than 35 kilometers up, and 35 kilometers down, so sunspots and magnetic storms can disturb reception. On the other hand, you can broadcast your message to hundreds of terminals over the continent. (It'll cost you more than a hundred thousand dollars to send, but only about $10,000 for each receiving dish.)

Optical Fibers. In the future, you'll be able to use optical fibers. These threads of glass carry extremely short pulses of light, that act like the on/off pulses from your word processor. A laser shoots the blips in at frequencies ranging from 1,000,000,000,000,000 to 10,000,000,000,000,000 (10^{14} to 10^{15}) cycles per second: so you have ten thousand times as many frequencies to send on as you would in microwave. By 1990, fiber optics will probably handle most transmissions above 20 million bits per second.

Thinking about costs? The cheapest, slowest, and sloppiest carrier starts at your phone. You've already got phone lines throughout your buildings. If you also have a computerized switchboard, then you have all you need to send a little data around the office, particularly if you don't need it in a hurry, and you don't mind occasional spurts of nonsense, when one computer overhears another on the line. For calls outside of the building, a leased line's more secure—and expensive. If you don't already have coaxial cable installed, as universities and cable TV companies do, then you'll have to rip up ceilings, walls, floors—or put up a whole new building. Expensive, but coaxial cable can carry television signals, graphics, and hundreds of calls without too much static. Even more costly: microwaves, then satellite transmissions, then fiber optics.

But on any of these carriers, you can send more than one message at once, so you get more message for your money. Think of a copper wire as a circuit. Inside any circuit, you can carve out various channels, carrying information. If a line only has one channel in it, then you can only send information in one direction—that mode of operation is called "simplex." But when you have at least two channels within the same circuit, you can send information both ways at the same time. That's called "full duplex." But if you have to wait for the other person to finish before you send, then you're using a sort-of mode, called "half-duplex."

With an ordinary circuit, you can get a lot more channels by using a device called a multiplexer. And that can save you money, because in a lot of installations, your carrier will cost you twice what you pay for the equipment at either end. In a regular phone line, for instance, you have about 3000 different frequencies. If you think of them as radio stations, you can assign different frequencies to different messages; leaving a few blank to act as buffers, you can send several signals, both ways. So you don't use every frequency for a message, since you have to leave some room between channels, but at least you get more information per circuit than you would without this Frequency Division Multiplexing (FDM). Of course, on a regular phone line, you'll have to redo this multiplexing at every switch, and that's expensive.

For a lot more channels, you can slice up time, instead of frequencies. A Time Division Multiplexer takes signals from a whole bunch of slow-speed channels, then combines them, so they can be sent over a high-speed carrier, such as Bell's special T1 Carrier, which handles 1.5 million bits per second. It may pick up one bit from each channel, transmit that, then go back to the beginning, and pick up the next, and so on. Since information comes in so much more slowly than it goes out, the TDM can pick up one bit from each channel, transmit that along with a special framing code to show the TDM at the other end which message this bit came from, then go back to the beginning, and pick up the next bit (that's just arrived), and so on. (A slower version does this character by character. And a smarter version can store any information that comes in too fast, and shift messages from channel to channel, for greater efficiency. That is called an Intelligent TDM.) Because all Time Division Multiplexers help you change speeds, you'll find them most useful if you have a number of stand-alone word processors which transmit slowly at irregular moments, plus some mainframes that send out a steadily synchronized stream of information at top speeds. But in general, with that much information going through, you'll want a wider range of frequencies than you can get in any ordinary phone line.

When they want more frequencies, most people turn to coaxial cable—baseband or broadband. In baseband coaxial cable, you have one channel, but it can handle up to 10 million bits per second, so with multiplexing, you'll be able to send a lot of messages around the building at one time. Baseband's cheaper than broadband (half as much per connection), but it can't go as far (a mile or two, compared to fifty), and it can't handle telephone conversations, so you'll have to keep your phone systems, and you won't be able to attach out-loud comments to electronic messages. Broadband can handle 20 million bits per second, over a much wider range of frequencies (25–40 million hertz), so you can use it for hundreds of messages at once—plus your phone calls, and television pictures. If you want to take a television picture and put it into your reports, you'll need broadband. At the moment, broadband may be more than you need; some consultants argue that it's only cost-effective today if you have at least 250,000 square feet of office space, and a mix of services (television, phone, word processing, regular data processing, say). But if your business is growing fast, broadband lets you multiply the number of people talking to each other, and the range of media you can mix.

Another way of thinking about what kind of circuits you need: do you really need to hold a channel open continuously, or would it be all right to use it in short, fast bursts? A phone call keeps one circuit open continuously, throughout your conversation, and on regular phone lines that's okay. That's what they're designed for. But when you want to talk to your computer, or you want your mainframe computer to talk to your word processor, there's no need to devote the whole carrier, or even a whole channel, to any one communication. You can handle many more messages by cutting them up into short hunks as in Time Division Multiplexing, and sending those in bursts. In this burst mode, you can store some data, when the line's busy, then send it along a few seconds later, when traffic slows down; you can handle information coming in at half a dozen different speeds—from an electronic typewriter, a word processor, a mainframe computer, and several different personal computers. In this way, too, you fill up the line—although one message goes in fits and starts, the channel's always full, so you're not paying for a line while you pause to collect your thoughts, or the other person coughs. If you have a lot of data to send around the office, then, coming from many different machines, you'll probably want to use the burst mode, and you'll probably want a carrier that's a little sturdier than the regular phone lines. That carrier—probably a coaxial cable or a specially conditioned and controlled phone line—could handle both voice and data at once—or it could just deal with your data.

Should a single network handle both voice and data? If you do combine both voice and data on the same carrier, you'll find it a lot easier to make comments out loud on a letter you're transmitting electronically; you'll quickly get into computers outside the company, when you're looking for information; and as long as you don't have too much data that needs high speeds, you can use the existing phone lines to carry data. If you already have a computerized PBX switchboard, then it won't cost you much to add the ability to carry a little data along those phone lines.

But if you have a lot of data swimming around, it could begin to drown out your voice. So you should make sure you've protected your voice traffic, before you combine. And you might consider digitizing the whole network, so you can go into a burst mode. Even your voice would be treated as data, then; the phone company does this already, on some long distance calls. Or you could put both voice and data on a broadband coaxial cable. Of course, if your phone system works well now, you risk fouling it up while you're adding data capacity. And, really, how many people have to make oral notes on a piece of electronic mail (couldn't they type it in?). And when the gear—regular or special phone lines, or broadband coaxial cable—is tuned for data, it doesn't always make voices sound real: data, for instance, can stand slight delays, but few errors, while our ear can stand a slight distortion, but gets confused when the first syllable's cut off of every word. So in a fairly small office, you might prefer to connect everything but the phones, and let the phones continue as a separate network. In a large office, you might save some money by combining, because you'd be making more efficient use of all that cable.

Controlling Your Network

If you work alone you won't need a network. But if you work with even four or five other people, you may want to connect your word processor with the other computer equipment around your office, including other people's terminals. And no matter what kinds of wires you use, you'll need some way to direct traffic through the network.

That's called "control." And there are two main ways to control your network: centralized or decentralized. In a centralized network, a computer sits at the center, controlling who gets what channel, how fast messages will move, what protocol gets translated into what other protocol, depending on where the message is going. That computer's boss. In a decentralized network, control over the line passes from one terminal to another.

The advantages of centralized control:

- You can avoid the expense of putting heavy coaxial cables all over your company.
- You put all the technicians in one place, to fix it.
- You make sure that there's only one computer in charge—not two or three, with differing views of standards and protocols.
- You maintain your large files at one site, so you're sure they're all up to date.
- You only have one operating system to worry about.
- You can keep out anyone who doesn't have the right password.

But if you're using your mainframe computer, or even a large "mini" to control communications, the job may take more and more of its computing power. As a result, people have to wait in line to get into the files; messages slow down; you may have to concoct your own computer programs to make changes; and you may have to tinker with equipment that doesn't understand the boss computer's language. And if the main computer breaks down, you're sunk.

With a decentralized system, you buy a cable and gizmos that connect your terminal to the main line. That way you don't have to change your existing equipment—just buy the right gizmos, called controllers. (Or you may have to buy the vendor's own gear, with the controller built in.) Most people are moving toward decentralized communications, because they like having their own files out next to them, they get faster access to the line, and to other computers, they can create local programs, and if one terminal collapses, the rest of the system can continue unharmed. But those controllers cost a lot, and because they aren't all in one room, it may take a repair crew longer to track down a problem.

What does the physical layout of a network look like? There are three basic shapes for networks: a star, a circle, or a line. You'll hear these crude outlines called "topologies," which is a big word for maps, and "configurations" since they diagram, or "figure" the way you have to arrange equipment to form the networks. And in the same semi-scientific jargon, any piece of equipment that joins the network at some point gets called a "node." In botany, that's the place where a leaf joins the stem. Let's look at a few of the most common layouts, to see which might be best for you.

1. The Star. A computer sits at the center, with one communication line coming out from it to each terminal, or node. To get from one node to another, you have to go through the computer at the core—which is fine in a small system, sometimes slow in a larger one. A familiar example: the main telephone switchboard, or PBX. If you put a real computer at the center, it can translate codes, speeds, and protocols for messages moving from one machine to another.

2. The Loop. A complete circle, including all terminals and a controlling computer. A message for one node just makes the circuit until it reaches the right node. Each node has to have a lot of computing power to recognize its own message ontime. If one terminal breaks, they all go down.

3. The Ring. Another circle, but here the nodes don't link to each other—just to controllers that join to the ring. Information moves around the ring much faster than from terminal to controller. Usually, each node gets its chance, in turn, to send a message, so control passes cyclically among the terminals. (This is called "token passing"—when your token comes around, you get on the ring.)

4. The Bus. One long line, to which every node is connected. Each node has a particular address, and a way of scrutinizing each message for the address; if the message isn't for this node, the node passes it along to the next node. You fight for access, and get it whenever a channel is free, perhaps using a "contention" method, such as CMSA-

CD, in which the Carrier (the cable) Senses Multiple terminals demanding Access, Detects any possible Collisions—and avoids them.

5. Distributed. A mess. No one shape. Many lines from one terminal to others; some terminals only connected with one other; some tied to forty others. You may have three ways to get from one node to another, sometimes none. This is usually the result of tying terminals together to do one task—inventory, say—and then a few years later, tying a different bunch together to do some other job, like payroll. Not very efficient.

Some networks connect every terminal in half a dozen systems—inventory control, say, general ledger, accounts receivable, accounts payable, payroll, order entry, and word processing. If you can move from your own processor into any of those systems without delay, and if someone over in the warehouse can use word processing without any problems, then the system is called "symmetrical," since you can go both ways with equal ease. The systems are peers. But if you can't go directly from one system to another, without detouring through another piece of equipment that acts as a doorman to the other system (a server, it's called), or if you can't even get in the door to the other system, then you are looking at an asymmetrical network—clumsy, slow, and not very open.

If you think that you're going to expand your network later, you'll also want to consider how well each configuration can grow in scale. Can you add a lot of stations, without losing speed? Usually not in a PBX exchange or star; usually so, in a common bus, loop, or ring. With the star, your computer's at the center, and when you add terminals, you draw off your computing power, just to direct traffic; as a result, every message gets slowed down. When talking to your vendor, then, you might ask, in their jargon, "How well does it scale?"

Planning Ahead

We've just gone through the basics of networks, which are the key to any automated office. If you don't have very much computerized office equipment today, but think that you'll be ordering a lot over the next few years, then you'll want to talk to vendors who can offer you a full line of equipment, all supposedly able to hook up to their network. If you've already got equipment from several vendors, you have a harder task, trying to locate one network that can help all your incompatible machines talk to each other. And you may want to defer your decision on a word processor until you have at least a vague idea how your network's going to work. If your company has a mainframe computer, and you think you're going to want more and more access to its files over the next few years, then start with the company that sold you that. You may be able to use that computer to control the network; and if so, you may be backed into buying their word processor. Obviously, moving toward an automated office will take a lot of thought. You'll need to study your own requirements in detail, then shop around.

Before you hire a consultant, or assign someone on your own staff to do a six-month study, ask yourself how much your company could really use a local area network:

- Is my business being cramped because information does not circulate fast enough?
- Do I want to be able to mix the spoken word with the written one, and with numbers spewed out by the main computer?
- Would we be working more efficiently, if I could get information from one machine to another?
- Do we have to reenter, retype, or otherwise repeat entering data?
- Would I like to add pictures to my reports?
- Do I want to distribute memos electronically?
- Do I want to let more people have access to all our computerized files?
- Could meeting by television, rather than traveling, save me money?
- Do I want easy access to the thousands of electronic libraries springing up around the country?

If the answer to some of these questions is "yes," you ought to start looking into local area networks, so you can integrate your office electronically. And you may want to postpone your purchase of a word processor until you have a better idea of the shape that network will take.

But before you go to a vendor, you'll need to do some hard work, analyzing your own situation, with questions like these:

- How many different vendors' machines do I have?
- Does most information flow between all terminals, or just some?
- What speeds do most of my machines transmit and receive at?
- How far apart are they?
- What is the average volume of information circulating in my office on a particular day, measured in bits per second? (Each machine transmits a different number of bits per second.)
- Is this volume fairly steady, day and night? Or does it ebb and flow? What's the peak rate?

- Do some of my machines transmit asynchronously? Or are they all, like mainframe computers, synchronous?
- Do all of my machines use the same code for translating characters into 1s and 0s?
- Do all of my machines use the same protocols for communication? And if so, can they really communicate—or have the vendors fudged a little?
- Is there any protocol converter around that can convert the various protocols my existing equipment can handle?
- Do I need a gateway, to translate from my network's protocols to the protocols of some other network?
- Do I need a leased line, for heavy volumes of data? Or will a regular switched phone line do?
- Which medium seems most reliable, given my budget, for communication beyond the local area network? Regular switched phone lines? My own leased lines? Coaxial cable? Microwave? Satellite transmission? Fiber optics?
- Within my own local area network, which type of multiplexing seems best?
- If I'm thinking about coaxial cable, do I mind that baseband cannot carry voice or television?
- Do I need the 20 million bits per second available on broadband coaxial cable?
- Do I need to use most circuits continuously? Or will burst transmission be more efficient for me?
- Do I prefer centralized control? Or decentralized?
- Which configuration strikes me as best: Star? Loop? Ring? Bus? Distributed?
- Do I want a symmetrical system? Or can I stand one that is asymmetrical?
- How much do I expect to expand this system in the next ten years?

And then, when you've really analyzed your communications needs, you'll be ready to ask the vendors some hard questions. Since many of these advertised networks are still imaginary, or "in pilot mode," you might ask some questions like this:

- How many have actually been installed?
- Exactly what vendor's equipment can be handled on this network? Exactly which machines?
- What are the minimum and maximum distances between nodes in your network?
- Exactly which of your machines actually work on this network? (Today, not next year.)

- How easy will it be for me to add new terminals, or change the location of old ones?
- Who does the troubleshooting, and how many days will the system be down, while I wait for that to be done?
- How fast does this network circulate information?
- How does it handle conversion of codes, protocols, speeds?
- How much does the line cost? The extra hardware and software?
- When exactly will everything I need be available—not just parts of it?
- How much do I really have to know about its nuts and bolts, if I just want to use it? How transparent is it?
- When can I talk to someone who's already using one of these networks in their own company?

So if you think you'll want to fit your word processor into a network, put off buying any word processor for a few more months while you rough out the best network for you. Only then will you have a clear idea of what codes, speeds, protocols, and communications software your word processor will need to join. Of course, any vendor who's got a network you like will have a word processor that works on it; you may settle for that word processor even if it's not ideal, just because the network's more important to your company.

Or you can ignore OA and just pick the word processor you like best, trusting that some small company somewhere will one day create a black box to let your word processor join some network. In general, if you think you might want to head for OA later, but you don't want to run a full-fledged study now, you can go ahead and figure out which word processor you like best—but avoid the weird ones.

Networking means giving information to more people—spreading access around. So you have a right to demand that the vendor choose communications methods that are common, not idiosyncratic. You don't want a plug to be eccentric or original—you want to be able to plug it in.

The View from 2001

As your office gets automated, your word processor lets you do a lot more than writing. Through the same screen and keyboard, you can now do your accounts, maintain your schedule, create graphics, send and receive electronic mail, tell printers to run off your report, and call up data from large computers in other cities. You begin to see your word processor as an entry point to a whole series of computer programs, a way of reaching everyone else on the network, a very fast clerk looking through every record on the big computer, a mailbox.

So your terminal loses its identity as a word processor, becoming an all-purpose workstation, part of the system. In the same way, reports will lose their physical presence, since many will never show up on paper. They are ideas lit up by electrons.

The way that we think about what we do—and the way we do it—will change. Since you can do so much more with a few keystrokes at your desk, you won't have as many occasions to get up, wander down the hall, chat at the copying machine, deliver a report in person, pick up some letters from someone, look out the window. Some people will begin to work at home, so you won't see them, even on payday. (Their pay will be deposited electronically.) Automating the office, then, may mean that you lose some of the sociability—less schmoozing, less gossip, perhaps lower morale.

Some people will be deprived of the chance to make as many decisions about what to do, and when. For instance, the boss could decide to write a program telling you how and when to do your work. The computer would tell him whether you did it on time. This means the system becomes a watchdog barking at you to make sure you meet your quotas, tying you down to your desk, cutting you off from contact with your peers.

If you're at the bottom of the hierarchy, then, the automated office will probably mean that you can turn out more work at first. But if the boss is thoughtless, you may begin to feel so lonely, disgruntled, or pressured that you find subtle ways to foul up the system, which you begin to see as an enemy, not a friend.

If you're a decision-maker, a professional, say, or a middle manager, the automated office will help you do two days' work in a morning. You'll feel less frustration in trying to get the big computer to tell you what you want to know. You'll get and give more information than ever before, since it's so easy. Along the way, you'll learn to read and write onscreen, without bothering with paper and pen. But to keep your secretary from feeling isolated and trapped, you'll have to enrich that job, by passing along some tasks you used to do—making decisions, attending meetings, planning.

By 2001 most of our offices will be automated—plugged into several networks, electronically communicating far more information than we can handle today. We'll look back on today's word processors as crude and limited because they can handle only words; drab, because their screens can only display half a page of text with only one color and a few pictures; clumsy, because they cannot accept information from every other computer program, such as an accounts receivable or general ledger package; dumb, because they are unable to talk to other people's terminals, deaf to news from distant data bases, blind to television images.

In 2001, most of us won't even think of a word processor as a separate machine. Words will be data then, and their processing just another function on the system.

APPENDIX A

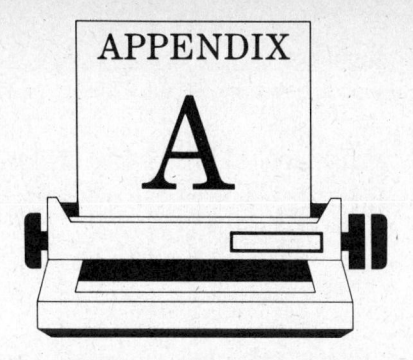

List of Word-Processing Products

Here are some of the most popular word-processing products on the market today. We've asked the vendors to answer some very detailed questions about each one, so you can compare them. Reading through this list, you'll begin to see what a range of equipment is available—and you may spot a few products that you want to try out.

This is just a sampling from a field that is constantly changing. New products keep appearing; old ones disappear, or are improved. Don't reject a system that has forty of the functions you want, but lacks two others. By now the vendor may offer those two as well. And certainly don't make any decision to buy based on this list. Use it to get an idea of what's available and to see which products you'd like to look at and evaluate.

The Problems with "Features" Lists

Word-processing vendors like their products to seem unique, so they tend to come up with special terms for features and functions. Some of these terms have become commonplace in the word-processing industry, but may seem like buzzwords to you. Also, different vendors may use different names for the same function, while some ascribe different meanings to the same terms. To help overcome this confusion, we've defined our terms in an extended key to the list of word-processing products. You'll find it just before the start of the products list.

To poll vendors as to the capabilities of their products, we sent them a questionnaire very similar to the key to the list of word-processing products printed here. We wanted to be sure they understood exactly what we were asking. Most of the people we consulted in vendors' offices were very honest about the strengths and weaknesses of their products. But every vendor knows how to "get around" the lack of a feature. They usually can find some way to accomplish the same function, even if it becomes cumbersome and clumsy, just so they can say their system has this feature. Despite our best efforts to phrase questions in a way that would limit these claims, some vendors were more slippery than expected. We've noted some of these possibly dubious features on the key to the list of word-processing products.

THE BASIC RULE OF THUMB: Don't believe anything until you see it in action. Use this chart (and those in other publications) to help you choose which products to look at. But don't buy on the basis of the information here. There is no substitute for a thorough demonstration of the equipment.

How We Selected Word-Processing Products to Profile

The number of word-processing products on the market today is so large that we knew we'd never be able to include information on all of them. We decided to concentrate on dedicated word processors, hybrid systems designed for both word and data processing, and software packages available for microcomputers. We've also included a couple of examples of electronic or memory typewriters, software for larger computers, and typesetting equipment. If you want a list of additional products available in the latter categories, DataPro Research Corporation has some excellent reports available (1805 Underwood Boulevard, Delran, New Jersey 08075).

The directory of vendor names and addresses in Appendix D includes even more companies with word-processing products than are covered in the list. It is by no means complete. Some vendors did not respond to repeated phone calls and letters. And others refused to call their product a word processor, preferring more glorious terms, such as "Office System." We have probably overlooked some excellent products. (Just because we haven't heard of them does not mean they're bad). And, of course, new products—and improvements of all of these current products—appear every few months. So your best friend may look at this list and cry out, "They don't have my Zotsky system and that's the best word processor since the quill pen."

Remember, this list will give you an excellent view of a wide range of word processors. We've included examples of every major type.

You'll be able to get a sense of what's available, what you want, what you'd like but don't really need.

But you can't make a sensible choice based on a list. Use the list to refine your own shopping list—then get out of the house and go shopping. This list just gives you a glimpse of what's out there.

Here, then, are the questions we asked the vendors. On the right, you'll find references to the pages on which these features are discussed in more detail.

The list of word-processing products is broken down into two groups:

1. Complete systems, including hardware and software.
2. Software that is sold separately to run on one or more computers.

Products are listed alphabetically by vendor. To locate a product directly when you don't know the company name, see the Index.

KEY TO THE LIST OF WORD-PROCESSING PRODUCTS

VENDOR:
MODEL:
TYPE: (Stand-alone, multiterminal, or software only?)

What can your word processor do?		See page
ENTERING TEXT		
Where	Can I enter text anywhere on the screen? (ANYWHERE) Or is the entry line always at the bottom of the screen? (BOTTOM)	76
Word wrap	When the text flows beyond the right margin, does the text automatically return to the next line? (YES or NO) If so, is word wrap always on, or can I turn it on and off? (ON/OFF)	53
Length of document	How long can a document be? Is there a limit to the number of lines, or pages per document? (#L or #P) Or does the length depend on the amount of room on the disk? (DISK)	75
Orientation	Does the system work with one page at a time? (PG) Or does it treat a document as one long scroll of text? (DOC)	75
	NOTE: Some vendors claimed their product was both page- and document-oriented. We're not sure whether this means that they basically work with one page (although the page might be up to 120 lines long) but can link the pages to repaginate or print. Or maybe they can display a full page at a time, or "go to" a specific page.	
EDITING TEXT		
During entry	Can I do both entry and editing of text at the same time? (YES means I can; NO means these two activities are separate)	22-25

What can your word processor do? See page

Insert	*Can I insert new text into old text?* (YES *or* NO) *If so, is this function always* ON? *Or can I turn it* ON *and* OFF?	35
Delete, copy, and move	*Can I delete, copy, and move portions of text?* (YES *or* NO) *Are there special keys provided for different amounts? How much?* (CH = *character,* W = *word,* L = *line,* S = *sentence,* P = *paragraph,* PG = *page,* COL = *column,* VAR = *variable, depending on how much I mark*) *Can I copy and move text from one document to another?* (DOC)	32
	NOTE: *Some vendors use the term "block" to mean that you mark the beginning and ending of text, rather than using specific "amount keys." We've classified these as "variable," or "*VAR*." By "*DOC*," we implied that you could move marked text to and from another document without leaving the current one. Some vendors seem to have ignored our implied meaning, so this might require many steps, including leaving the current document and opening another.*	

MOVEMENT WITHIN DOCUMENT

Cursor	*How far forward and back can I move my cursor directly?* (W = *word,* L = *line,* S = *sentence,* P = *paragraph,* PG = *page,* COL = *column*)	64
	NOTE: *Here we were looking for keys that made cursor movement quick and easy. When there don't seem to be many responses, the products probably use arrow keys, which may "repeat" when you hold them down.*	
Scroll	*Are there keys that let me scroll through my text? If so, how*	28

What can your word processor do?   See page

	much? (L = line, P = paragraph, PG = page, SC = screen's worth, TOP/BOT = to top or bottom of the text)	
Search	How does the system search for a particular hunk of text? (FOR = forward, BACK = backward, IG-ORE CASE = the system can find the text whether it is in upper- or lowercase, EX = can only find text when it appears exactly as I entered it)	25
Search and replace	How can I search for a particular hunk of text and replace it? (FOR = forward, BACK = backward, IGNORE CASE = the system can find the text whether it is upper- or lowercase, EX = can only find text when it appears exactly as I entered it, GLOB = can search and replace globally throughout the document, AUTO = replacement takes place automatically, SEMI-AUTO = stops at each occurrence and waits for my okay to replace)	25

SPECIAL FEATURES AND FORMATS

Alternate character sets	Can I print some parts of the text in an alternate set of characters? (YES or NO)	60
Boilerplate	Can I call in stored words, phrases, or paragraphs, called "boilerplate"? (YES or NO, GLOSSARY = can pull in words and phrases, P = can pull in whole paragraphs)	219
	NOTE: True boilerplating facilities allow you to store frequently used portions of text together in a document or in memory. We distinguished words and phrases from paragraphs because some products make one easy but not the other. Some vendors claim boilerplating facilities when you must store each portion of text in	

LIST OF WORD-PROCESSING PRODUCTS || 265

What can your word processor do?		See page
	a separate document and then "read it in."	
Bold	*Can I have parts of the text printed heavily in boldface?* (YES or NO, SC = *seen onscreen,* PR = *seen only on printout*)	42
Calculate	*Does the system provide me with math functions?* (YES or NO, A = *add,* S = *subtract,* M = *multiply,* D = *divide,* % = *percentages,* OPT = *feature is optional*)	79
Centering	*Can I have the system center portions of my text?* (YES or NO, SC = *seen onscreen,* PR = *seen only on printout*)	32
Center around tab	*Can I center around a tab stop?* (YES or NO)	28
Change case	*Can I change parts of the text from lower- to uppercase, or vice versa, without rekeying?* (YES or NO)	
Control characters	*Do I insert extra characters into the text onscreen to start, end, or change formats? Is this true for* SOME or MOST *formats?*	77
Decimal tabs	*Can I set a special tab that will align the decimal points in numbers?* (YES or NO)	
Dot commands	*Are dot commands such as ".Indent 5" used within the text to set formats? Is this true for* SOME or MOST *formats?*	78
Footnotes	*Is there a special facility to make footnoting easy?* (YES or NO, RENUMBER = *facility to renumber footnotes automatically if one is added or deleted,* REPOSITION = *facility to reposition text automatically if the text reference changes position*)	46
Forced page break	*Can I force the system to make a page break wherever I want?* (YES or NO)	40
Format line	*Does a line appear onscreen indicating left and right margins,*	28

What can your word processor do? See page

	and tab stops, while I am entering text? (YES, NO, *or* ON/OFF)	
Generate index	*Can the system generate an index for my document, if I provide the key words?* (YES *or* NO, OPT = *feature is optional*)	79
Generate table of contents	*Can the system generate a table of contents for my document, based on the headings in my document?* (YES *or* NO, OPT = *function is optional*)	79
Headers and footers	*Can I specify text to be printed on the top and bottom of pages?* (YES *or* NO) *How many lines fit into each header or footer?* (#L, DATE = *current date can appear in header or footer*)	29
Hyphenating	*Will the system automatically hyphenate when it is justifying or wrapping the text?* (AUTO) *Will the system tell me where I could break a word, if I want to?* (USER)	
Letter merge	*Can I merge a list of names and addresses with a form letter?* (YES *or* NO, OPT = *feature is optional*)	79
Line spacing	*Can I request certain line spacing?* (½, *1, 1½, 2, 3, or* OTHER, SC = *seen onscreen,* PR = *seen only on printout*)	
	NOTE: *Some printers let you adjust line spacing in increments of ¹⁄₄₈ inch, or let you select whether you want to print using 6 or 8 lines per inch. Although that isn't quite what we were asking, it's the information some vendors gave us.*	
Lines per page	*Can I set the number of lines to be printed per page?* (YES *or* NO)	
Margin release key	*Can I temporarily release my margins by using a special key?* (YES *or* NO)	

LIST OF WORD-PROCESSING PRODUCTS || 267

What can your word processor do?		See page
Margin width	*How wide can my margins be? (Number of characters, maximum)*	28
Multicolumn	*Can I enter the text in several columns, without losing my ability to edit, reformat, and word wrap?* (YES *or* NO, SC = *seen onscreen,* PR = *seen only on printout*)	
Nonprinting comments	*Can I put comments into the document, but make sure they do not print out?* (YES *or* NO)	
Onscreen	*Can I see the text as it will print out, onscreen?* (YES *or* NO)	76
	NOTE: *This proved to be a loaded question. Some vendors claim "what you see is what you get" when the text onscreen is loaded with extra control characters that aren't interpreted into underlining, boldface, or other special formats until you print. While some vendors gave us a qualified "yes, except for," we could tell others were stretching it. Also, some systems don't display formatted text while you're entering, but do allow you to "preview" it by "printing to the screen."*	
Page breaks	*Can I have the page breaks automatically inserted into the text?* (AUTO) *Or do I have to indicate pages manually?* (USER, SC = *seen onscreen,* PR = *seen only on printout*)	
Page numbers	*Will the system automatically enter page numbers?* (YES *or* NO, ALT = *can alternate on odd/even pages,* RESTART = *can reset page numbers in document,* ROMAN = *page numbers can print as roman numerals, not just arabic*)	39
Paragraph indent	*Can I have new paragraphs automatically indented?* (SC = *seen onscreen,* PR = *seen only on printout*)	28

What can your word processor do?   See page

Programmable key	*Can I assign certain keys to carry out editing or formatting functions?* (YES or NO)	62
	NOTE: *Although this questionnaire asks for word-processing features, we think some vendors answered* YES *to this question when their hardware allows a programmer to assign functions to special keys before you use word processing. This is* not *what we had in mind.*	
Reformat after changes	*After I have changed the text, will my new text be fitted into the old margins automatically?* (AUTO) *Or do I have to do that myself?* (USER)	
Repeat last command	*Can I tell the system to repeat the last command I entered, instead of keying the whole thing in again?* (YES or NO)	
Right justify	*Can I have my text lined up flush right?* (YES, NO, *or* ON/OFF; SC = *seen onscreen,* PR = *seen only in printout*)	
Right justify tabs	*Can I set up tabs that will line up the text on the right, rather than the left?* (YES or NO)	
Sort	*Will the system sort a list for me?* (ALPH = *alphabetically,* NUM = *numerically,* OPT = *optional*)	79
Spelling check	*Can the system check my spelling against a dictionary and highlight my mistakes?* (YES or NO) *How many words are in the dictionary?* (#W, OPT = *function is optional*)	79
Storing formats	*Once I have set up a format, can I store it for later use, separate from a particular text?* (YES or NO)	
Strikeover	*Can I have some characters struck through, so they will appear crossed-out in the text?* (YES or NO, SC = *seen onscreen,* PR = *seen only on printout*)	

What can your word processor do?   See page

Sub/superscript	*Can I have some characters set above and below the line?* (YES or NO, SC = *seen onscreen,* PR = *seen only on printout*)	
Tabs	*Are the tabs set every 5, 8, or 10 characters?* (#CH) *Or are they variable?* (VAR)	28
Underline	*Can I underline text?* (YES *or* NO, SC = *seen onscreen,* PR = *seen only on printout*)	
Variable pitch	*Can I set parts of my text in different pitches?* (YES *or* NO, SC = *seen onscreen,* PR = *seen only on printout*)	
Vertical lines	*How many lines can I have on each page?* (#L) *Is there a fixed number, or can I vary it?* (VAR)	
Widows and orphans	*Does the system automatically avoid leaving one or two lines at the end of one page, or the top of the next?* (AUTO) *Or do I have to put in page breaks to avoid this?* (USER)	

FILES

File names	*How do I create names for the files that hold my documents?* (FREE = *I can use any combination of numbers and letters,* OPSYS = *the operating system dictates the type of name,* #CH = *the maximum number of characters in a file name*)	219
Renaming	*Can I rename a document?* (YES *or* NO)	
Copying and deleting files	*Can I copy from one file to another?* (YES *or* NO) *Can I delete an entire file?* (YES *or* NO)	
Copying disks	*Can I copy an entire disk?* (YES *or* NO)	20
Auto save	*When I'm entering or editing text, does the system automatically save the contents of the document?* (YES *or* NO, USER = *I*	75

What can your word processor do?   See page

	can request that the system save what I've done so far)	
Auto backup	When I open a file and take out my document to work on, does the system automatically make a copy, just in case something happens to the version I am working on? (YES or NO)	
Verify	Can I verify that the text has been stored correctly on the disk? (YES or NO)	
	NOTE: *This question gave rise to a great deal of confusion among some vendors, prompting answers such as "only if you edit the document." We were looking for a function or utility called "verify," which would check the text on disk to make sure it wasn't garbled.*	
Disk directory	Does the system provide me with a list of all the documents on a given disk? (YES or NO, ORDER = I can specify the order these documents appear in, SIZE = directory indicates the size of each document, NAME = directory gives the name of each person who entered material in that document, TITLE = directory indicates name and number of each document, DATE = directory gives date the document was created or edited)	220

PRINTING

Continuous or sheet feed	Will the system print on continuous paper? Will the system print on separate pieces of paper? (CONT, SHEET, or BOTH)	91
Multiple printers	Can I send documents to more than one printer? (YES or NO)	
Queue	Can I send a series of documents to a printer and have them "queued up," so that one prints when another is done? (YES or NO)	

What can your word processor do?		See page
Simultaneous	*Can I print one document while entering or editing another?* (YES or NO)	
Specific pages	*Can I specify exactly which pages of a document to print?* (YES or NO)	
Typefaces	*Can I use more than one typeface (print element) while printing a document?* (YES or NO)	87

HARDWARE

Internal memory	AMOUNT	68
Storage and drives	*What drives are standard with the system? What others are available? How many bytes will each hold? For diskettes, what density are they?* (SD = *single density*, DD = *double density*, QUAD = *quad density*) *How many sides can be used?* (SS = *single-sided*, DS = *double-sided*)	69
Communications	*What communications protocols does the word processor use? What baud rate? Is there customized software to make use of communications?* (OPT = *optional*)	96
	NOTE: *Although many vendors told us protocols and baud rates, few mentioned whether the software to make use of these is accessible through word processing. We hope they were implying that it is.*	
Keyboard	*Is the keyboard attached to the video tube, or detached and movable?* (ATTACHED *or* DETACHED) *Does it have a numeric pad?* (#PAD) *Do some keys have labels, indicating word-processing functions?* (WP KEYS)	61
Video tube	*What colors show up on the screen? What size is it in characters or lines?* (#CH WIDE × #L) *How many tubes can be attached to each system?*	56

What can your word processor do?   See page

Printer(s) — *What printer comes with your word processor? How fast does it print? (#CPS, #WPM, or #LPM) What is the maximum number of printers that can be attached to the system? (#MAX)*   82

DOCUMENTATION AND TRAINING

Documentation — *What kinds of documentation will I get with your word processor?*   191

Training — *What kind of training will you provide me, when I buy your word processor?*   192, 214

Notes — *Anything of relevance not covered by the preceding questions.*

Key to Abbreviations

A = add
ALPH = alphabetically
ALT = on alternate pages
AUTO = done automatically
BACK = backward
BPS = bits per second, an indication of speed of communication
CH = character(s)
COL = column
CPS = characters per second
D = disk
DATE = date document was created or edited
DD = double density
DEDICATED = designed primarily for word processing
DIV = divide
DOC = document
DS = double-sided
EX = exact
FOR = forward
FREE = any combination of numbers and letters
GLOB = globally, that is, throughout the document
HYBRID = designed for both word and data processing
L = line
LPM = lines per minute
LQP = letter-quality printer

M = multiply
NAME = name of writer
NUM = numerically
OPSYS = feature can be done through operating system
OPT = feature is optional
ORDER = you can specify the order
P = paragraph
PG = page
PR = seen only on printout
QUAD = quad density on disk
RESTART = can reset page numbers
ROMAN = prints roman numerals
S = sentence
SC = seen onscreen
SD = single-density disk
SEMI-AUTO = semi-automatic
SHEET = uses cut-sheet paper
SS = single-sided disks
SUB = subtract
TITLE = name of document
TOP/BOT = to top or bottom of the text
USER = user intervention allowed or required
VAR = variable
W = word
WPM = words per minute
? = information not available
= number

For a more detailed explanation of each item on the list, see the preceding Key to the List of Word-Processing Products.

COMPLETE SYSTEMS

VENDOR: A B Dick
MODEL: Magna SL
TYPE: Multiterminal, dedicated

ENTERING TEXT
  Where   ANYWHERE
  Word wrap   YES
  Length of document   DISK
  Orientation   PG

EDITING TEXT
  During entry   YES
  Insert   YES, ON/OFF
  Delete, copy, and move   CH, W, L, S, P, PG, COL, VAR, DOC

MOVEMENT WITHIN DOCUMENT
  Cursor   PG, DOC
  Scroll   TOP/BOTTOM; UP/DOWN
  Search   FOR
  Search and replace   FOR, IGNORE CASE, GLOB, AUTO, SEMI-AUTO

SPECIAL FEATURES AND FORMATS
  Alternate character sets   YES
  Boilerplate   YES, GLOSSARY, P
  Bold   NO
  Calculate   YES A, SUB, M, DIV, %
  Centering   YES, SC
  Center around tabs   YES
  Change case   NO
  Control characters   NO
  Decimal tabs   YES
  Dot commands   NO
  Footnotes   SEMI-AUTOMATIC
  Forced page break   YES
  Format line   YES
  Generate table of contents   NO
  Generate index   NO
  Headers and footers   YES UNLIMITED #L
  Hyphenating   USER
  Letter merge   YES
  Lines per page   YES
  Line spacing   1, 2, 3—SC   ½, 1½—PR
  Margin release key   YES
  Margin width   250
  Multicolumn   YES, SC
  Nonprinting comments   YES
  Onscreen   YES

Page breaks	AUTO, SC
Page numbers	YES, ALT, RESTART
Paragraph indent	YES, SC
Programmable key	YES
Reformat after changes	USER
Repeat last command	YES
Right justify	YES, SC
Right justify tabs	NO
Sort	YES, ALPH, NUM
Spelling check	NO
Storing formats	YES
Strikeover	YES, PR
Sub/superscript	YES, SC
Tabs	VAR
Underline	YES, SC
Variable pitch	NO
Vertical lines	99 MAX, VAR
Widows and orphans	AUTO

FILES

File names	FREE, 20 CH
Renaming	YES
Copy and delete files	YES
Copying disks	YES
Auto save	USER
Auto backup	YES
Verify	YES
Disk directory	YES, TITLE

PRINTING

Continuous or sheet feed	BOTH
Multiple printers	YES
Queue	YES
Simultaneous	YES
Specific pages	YES
Typefaces	YES

HARDWARE

Internal memory	64K
Storage and drives	8″ SS, SD, 300 KB
Communications	ASCII, 300–2400 BPI
Keyboard	DETACHED, WP KEYS
Video tube	GREEN ON BLACK 102 × 66
Printers	QUME SPRINT, 55 CPS

DOCUMENTATION AND TRAINING

Documentation	SKIL PAK & APPLICATIONS MANUAL
Training	2 PER WORKSTATION
NOTES	ALL SOFTWARE & UPDATES FREE; CAN PRIORITIZE PRINT QUEUE

VENDOR: A B Dick
MODEL: Magna III
TYPE: Stand-alone or multiterminal, hybrid

ENTERING TEXT
Where	BOTTOM
Word wrap	YES ON/OFF
Length of document	DISK
Orientation	PG

EDITING TEXT
During entry	YES
Insert	YES, ALWAYS ON
Delete, copy, and move	CH, W, L, S, P, PG, VAR, DOC

MOVEMENT WITHIN DOCUMENT
Cursor	W, L, S, P, PG
Scroll	L, P, PG, SC
Search	FOR, EX
Search and replace	FOR, GLOB, AUTO, SEMI-AUTO

SPECIAL FEATURES AND FORMATS
Alternate character sets	YES
Boilerplate	YES, GLOSSARY, P
Bold	NO
Calculate	YES, A, SUB, M, DIV, %
Centering	YES, SC
Center around tabs	YES
Change case	NO
Control characters	NO
Decimal tabs	YES
Dot commands	NO
Footnotes	NO
Forced page break	YES
Format line	YES
Generate table of contents	NO
Generate index	NO
Headers and footers	YES, UNLIMITED #L
Hyphenating	USER
Letter merge	YES
Lines per page	YES
Line spacing	½, 1, 1½, 2, 3, OTHER, PR
Margin release key	NO
Margin width	401
Multicolumn	SC
Nonprinting comments	YES
Onscreen	YES
Page breaks	AUTO, SC
Page numbers	YES, ALT
Paragraph indent	YES, SC
Programmable key	NO

Reformat after changes	AUTO
Repeat last command	NO
Right justify	YES, SC
Right justify tabs	YES
Sort	YES, ALPH, NUM
Spelling check	NO
Storing formats	YES
Strikeover	YES, PR
Sub/superscript	YES, PR
Tabs	VAR
Underline	YES, SC
Variable pitch	YES, PR
Vertical lines	VARIABLE
Widows and orphans	AUTO

FILES

File names	FREE, 13 CH
Renaming	YES
Copy and delete files	YES
Copying disks	YES
Auto save	USER
Auto backup	YES
Verify	YES
Disk directory	YES, SIZE, NAME, TITLE

PRINTING

Continuous or sheet feed	BOTH
Multiple printers	YES
Queue	YES
Simultaneous	YES
Specific pages	YES
Typefaces	YES

HARDWARE

Internal memory	64K
Storage & drives	5¼″ DS, DD—273KB
Communications	ASCII, 100–1200 BPS
Keyboard	DETACHED, WP KEYS
Video tube	GREEN ON BLACK 80 × 20
Printers	QUME DAISY, 55 CPS

DOCUMENTATION AND TRAINING

Documentation	SKIL/PAK & APPLICATIONS MANUALS
Training	2 PER WORKSTATION

VENDOR: AES Data LTEE/LTD
MODEL: Alphaplus
TYPE: Stand-alone, dedicated

ENTERING TEXT

Where	ANYWHERE
Word wrap	YES

Length of document	DISK
Orientation	PG

EDITING TEXT

During entry	YES
Insert	YES, ON/OFF
Delete, copy, and move	YES, W, L, P, (REMAINDER), DOC

MOVEMENT WITHIN DOCUMENT

Cursor	26 LINES AT A TIME
Scroll	L, SC
Search	FOR, EX, IGNORE CASE
Search and replace	FOR, EX, IGNORE CASE, GLOB, AUTO, SEMI-AUTO

SPECIAL FEATURES AND FORMATS

Alternate character sets	YES
Boilerplate	YES, GLOSSARY, P
Bold	YES, PR
Calculate	YES, A, SUB, M, DIV, %, OPT
Centering	YES, SC
Center around tabs	YES, SC
Change case	YES, LOWER TO UPPER, ONLY IF STORED IN GLOSSARY
Control characters	SOME
Decimal tabs	YES
Dot commands	SOME
Footnotes	YES, REPOSITION
Forced page break	YES
Format line	YES
Generate table of contents	NO
Generate index	NO
Headers and footers	YES, UNLIMITED # L
Hyphenating	USER
Letter merge	YES, OPT, FREE
Lines per page	NO
Line spacing	YES, PR
Margin release key	NO
Margin width	254
Multicolumn	YES, SC
Nonprinting comments	YES
Onscreen	YES
Page breaks	YES, USER, SC
Page numbers	YES, ALT
Paragraph indent	YES, SC
Programmable key	YES
Reformat after changes	YES, AUTO
Reformat to new margins	YES
Repeat last command	YES
Right justify	YES, PR

LIST OF WORD-PROCESSING PRODUCTS ‖ 279

Right justify tabs	YES
Sort	YES, ALPH, NUM, OPT
Spelling check	NO
Storing formats	YES
Strikeover	YES
Sub/superscript	YES, PR
Tabs	VAR
Underline	YES, SC
Variable pitch	YES, PR
Vertical lines	99 LINES
Widows and orphans	YES, AUTO

FILES
File names	FREE, 15 CH
Renaming	YES
Copy and delete files	YES
Copying disks	YES
Auto save	USER
Auto backup	YES
Verify	YES
Disk directory	YES, TITLE

PRINTING
Continuous or sheet feed	BOTH
Multiple printers	NO
Queue	YES
Simultaneous	YES
Specific pages	YES
Typefaces	YES

HARDWARE
Internal memory	64K
Storage and drives	5¼" OR 8", SS OR DS, SD OR DD, 1–4 DISKS
Communications	ASYNCH, SYNCH, 110–9600 BAUD
Keyboard	ATTACHED OR DETACHED, WP KEYS
Video tube	GREEN, 80 × 26
Printers	QUME PRINTER 3/45, 45 CPS WIDE-TRACK PRINTER, 45 CPS

DOCUMENTATION AND TRAINING
Documentation	OPERATOR INSTRUCTION MANUAL
Training	2½ DAYS; FOLLOWUP BY EDUCATION REPRESENTATIVE EVERY 6–8 WEEKS

VENDOR: Algorithmics
MODEL: Algo 2100
TYPE: Stand-alone

ENTERING TEXT
Where	MIDDLE LINE—FIXED
Word wrap	YES

Length of document	DISK
Orientation	DOC

EDITING TEXT

During entry	YES
Insert	YES
Delete, copy, and move	YES, CH, W, L, VAR, DOC

MOVEMENT WITHIN DOCUMENT

Cursor	?
Scroll	L, TOP/BOT
Search	FOR, EX
Search and replace	FOR, EX, GLOB, AUTO, SEMI–AUTO

SPECIAL FEATURES AND FORMATS

Alternate character sets	YES
Boilerplate	YES; EA PORTION STORED IN SEP. DOC
Bold	YES, PR
Calculate	A, SUB, M, DIV, %, OPT
Centering	PR
Center around tabs	YES
Change case	NO
Control characters	MOST
Decimal tabs	YES
Dot commands	MOST
Footnotes	NO
Forced page break	YES
Format line	NO
Generate table of contents	NO
Generate index	NO
Headers and footers	YES, H–6 L, F–2 L
Hyphenating	NO
Letter merge	YES, STD, W/SORT–OPT
Lines per page	YES
Line spacing	½, 1, 1½, 2, 3, OTHER, PR
Margin release key	NO
Margin width	WHATEVER PRINTER WILL ALLOW
Multicolumn	YES, PR
Nonprinting comments	YES
Onscreen	NOT DURING EDIT
Page breaks	AUTO, PR
Page numbers	YES, ALT, RESTART, ROMAN
Paragraph indent	YES, PARA SYMBOL, PR
Programmable key	NO
Reformat after changes	AUTO
Repeat last command	NO
Right justify	YES, ON/OFF, PR
Right justify tabs	YES
Sort	YES, ALPH, NUM, OPT
Spelling check	YES, OPT—SPELLGUARD
Storing formats	YES

LIST OF WORD-PROCESSING PRODUCTS

Strikeover	PR
Sub/superscript	YES, PR
Tabs	VAR
Underline	YES, PR
Variable pitch	YES, PR
Vertical lines	VARIABLE
Widows and orphans	USER

FILES

File names	LETTERS & NUMBERS, 11 CH
Renaming	YES
Copy and delete files	YES
Copying disks	YES
Auto save	NO, USER
Auto backup	YES
Verify	OPSYS
Disk directory	YES, SIZE, TITLE

PRINTING

Continuous or sheet feed	BOTH
Multiple printers	OPT
Queue	OPT
Simultaneous	OPT
Specific pages	YES
Typefaces	YES

HARDWARE

Internal memory	64K
Storage and drives	5¼″ DOUBLE TRACK, 79K EA 8″ SS, DD; 6 MG OR 8.5 MG HARD DISKS
Communications	TTY, ASYNCH ASCII, BISYNCH 3741 300–9600 BPS
Keyboard	DETACHED, #PAD, WP KEYS
Video tube	BLACK ON WHITE OR WHITE ON BLACK, POLARIZING FILTERS IN DIFF. COLORS 80 × 24
Printers	VARIETY OF LQP & DOT MATRIX PRINTERS; 1 MAX PER SYSTEM

DOCUMENTATION AND TRAINING

Documentation	USERS GUIDE, OPERATOR MANUAL
Training	3½ DAYS FOR 2 OPERATORS

VENDOR: Am Varityper
MODEL: Varityper
TYPE: Comp/Edit Phototypesetter

ENTERING TEXT

Where	ANYWHERE
Word wrap	YES
Length of document	DISK
Orientation	DOC

282 || THE DEFINITIVE WORD-PROCESSING BOOK

EDITING TEXT
During entry	YES
Insert	YES
Delete, copy, and move	YES, VAR, DOC

MOVEMENT WITHIN DOCUMENT
Cursor	FULL SCREEN
Scroll	YES, COMPLETE BUFFER, 9K
Search	FOR, EX
Search and replace	FOR, EX, GLOB, AUTO, SEMI-AUTO

SPECIAL FEATURES AND FORMATS
Alternate character sets	YES
Boilerplate	YES
Bold	YES, TYPESETTER
Calculate	NO
Centering	YES, PR (W/IMAGE PREVIEW OPTION)
Center around tabs	YES
Change case	NO
Control characters	YES
Decimal tabs	NO
Dot commands	NO
Footnotes	NO
Forced page break	YES
Format line	YES
Generate table of contents	?
Generate index	NO
Headers and footers	YES
Hyphenating	AUTO
Letter merge	NO
Lines per page	YES, PAGINATION PROGRAM
Line spacing	LEADING IN ½ POINTS
Margin release key	?
Margin width	YES
Multicolumn	YES
Nonprinting comments	YES
Onscreen	YES, W/IMAGE PREVIEW
Page breaks	AUTO, USER, SC
Page numbers	YES
Paragraph indent	YES
Programmable key	YES
Reformat after changes	AUTO
Repeat last command	NO
Right justify	YES
Right justify tabs	YES
Sort	NO
Spelling check	NO
Storing formats	YES
Strikeover	YES, SPECIAL TYPEFACE
Sub/superscript	YES

LIST OF WORD-PROCESSING PRODUCTS || 283

    Tabs   VARIABLE IN 1/18 ENI (SMALL UNIT)
    Underline   YES (W/RULE OR SPECIAL TYPE)
    Variable pitch   YES, IMAGE PREVIEW-SC, OTHERWISE, TYPESET
    Vertical lines   VARIES W/TYPE SIZE—UP TO 130
    Widows and orphans   USER
FILES
    File names   FREE, 8 CH
    Renaming   NO
    Copy and delete files   YES
    Copying disks   YES
    Auto save   YES
    Auto backup   NO
    Verify   YES
    Disk directory   YES, SIZE, TITLE
PRINTING
    Continuous or sheet feed   WITH LINE PRINTER OPTION
    Multiple printers   YES, TYPESETTER
    Queue   NO
    Simultaneous   YES
    Specific pages   NO
    Typefaces   16 TYPEFACES ONLINE; 144 SIZES
HARDWARE
    Internal memory   TO 128K
    Storage and drives   8" SS, DD, 300KB DUAL FLOPPY DRIVES
    Communications   RS232, 110–9600 BPI
    Keyboard   ATTACHED
    Video tube   GREEN ON CHARCOAL, 40 × 64
    Printers   TYPESETTER; LINE PRINTER OPTION WITH T/C
DOCUMENTATION AND TRAINING
    Documentation   FULL MANUAL
    Training   AT BRANCH OFFICES OR CUSTOMER'S OFFICE

VENDOR: Apple Computer, Inc.
MODEL: Apple Writer III for the Apple III computer
TYPE: Personal computer with software

ENTERING TEXT
    Where   ANYWHERE
    Word wrap   ON/OFF
    Length of document   128 CH
    Orientation   DOC
EDITING TEXT
    During entry   YES
    Insert   YES
    Delete, copy, and move   YES, CH, W, P, VAR, DOC

MOVEMENT WITHIN DOCUMENT

Cursor	W, L, P, BEG/END OF TEXT
Scroll	L, TOP/BOT, 12 LINES
Search	FOR, BACK, EX
Search and replace	FOR, BACK, EX, GLOB, AUTO, SEMI-AUTO

SPECIAL FEATURES AND FORMATS

Alternate character sets	YES
Boilerplate	YES, GLOSSARY, P
Bold	YES
Calculate	NO
Centering	PR
Center around tabs	NO
Change case	YES
Control characters	YES, MOST
Decimal tabs	NO
Dot commands	YES, MOST
Footnotes	YES, RENUMBER
Forced page break	YES
Format line	NO
Generate table of contents	NO
Generate index	NO
Headers and footers	YES, 1 LINE, DATE
Hyphenating	NO
Letter merge	YES
Lines per page	YES
Line spacing	1, 2, 3 PR
Margin release key	NO
Margin width	255
Multicolumn	NO
Nonprinting comments	YES
Onscreen	NOT DURING EDIT
Page breaks	AUTO PR
Page numbers	YES, RESTART
Paragraph indent	YES, PR
Programmable key	VIA PROGRAMMING LANGUAGE
Reformat after changes	AUTO
Repeat last command	ONLY ON FIND/REPLACE
Right justify	YES, PR
Right justify tabs	YES
Sort	NO
Spelling check	OPT
Storing formats	YES
Strikeover	YES, PR
Sub/superscript	YES, PR
Tabs	VAR
Underline	YES, PR
Variable pitch	YES, PR

Vertical lines	VAR
Widows and orphans	USER

FILES

File names	OPSYS, 15 CH
Renaming	YES
Copy and delete files	YES
Copying disks	NO
Auto save	USER
Auto backup	NO, BUT NO CHANGE TO DISK UNTIL YOU SAVE
Verify	NO
Disk directory	YES, SIZE, DATE

PRINTING

Continuous or sheet feed	BOTH
Multiple printers	YES
Queue	YES
Simultaneous	NO
Specific pages	YES
Typefaces	YES

HARDWARE

Internal memory	256K/1512K
Storage and drives	5¼" SS, SD, 143K EA, 1 FLOPPY STANDARD, 4 AVAILABLE, HARD DISK AVAILABLE
Communications	NONE
Keyboard	DETACHED, #PAD
Video tube	B/W OR GREEN; 80 × 24 MULTIPLE TUBES ATTACHED
Printers	QUME OR SILENTYPE; 5 MAY BE ATTACHED

DOCUMENTATION AND TRAINING

Documentation	USER MANUAL, REFERENCE CARD
Training	OPTIONAL—PRODUCT TRAINING PACK

VENDOR: Applied Digital Data Systems, Inc.
MODEL: Multivision
TYPE: Stand-alone or multiterminal

ENTERING TEXT

Where	ANYWHERE
Word wrap	YES
Length of document	DISK
Orientation	DOC

EDITING TEXT

During entry	YES
Insert	YES, ALWAYS ON
Delete, copy, and move	YES, VAR, DOC

MOVEMENT WITHIN DOCUMENT

Cursor	ANYWHERE
Scroll	L, PG, SC, TOP/BOTTOM
Search	FOR, BACK
Search and replace	FOR, BACK, EX WITH WILD CARD GLOB, AUTO, SEMI-AUTO

SPECIAL FEATURES AND FORMATS

Alternate character sets	YES
Boilerplate	YES, GLOSSARY, P
Bold	YES, SC
Calculate	NO
Centering	YES, SC
Center around tabs	YES
Change case	NO
Control characters	YES, MOST
Decimal tabs	YES
Dot commands	YES, SOME
Footnotes	NO
Forced page break	YES
Format line	NO
Generate table of contents	NO
Generate index	NO
Headers and footers	YES
Hyphenating	USER
Letter merge	YES
Lines per page	VAR
Line spacing	1, 2, 3
Margin release key	YES
Margin width	155
Multicolumn	YES, SC
Nonprinting comments	NO
Onscreen	ALMOST
Page breaks	AUTO
Page numbers	YES, ALT, RESTART
Paragraph indent	NO
Programmable key	NO
Reformat after changes	AUTO
Repeat last command	NO
Right justify	YES, PR
Right justify tabs	YES
Sort	YES
Spelling check	YES
Storing formats	YES
Strikeover	YES, PR
Sub/superscript	YES, PR
Tabs	VAR
Underline	YES, PR
Variable pitch	NO

LIST OF WORD-PROCESSING PRODUCTS ‖ 287

Vertical lines	VAR
Widows and orphans	USER
FILES	
File names	6 CH
Renaming	YES
Copy and delete files	YES
Copying disks	YES
Auto save	USER
Auto backup	YES
Verify	YES
Disk directory	YES, SIZE, DATE CREATED & DATE EDITED
PRINTING	
Continuous or sheet feed	BOTH
Multiple printers	NO
Queue	NO
Simultaneous	YES
Specific pages	YES
Typefaces	YES
HARDWARE	
Internal memory	64K–256K
Storage and drives	DOUBLE SIDED, DOUBLE OR QUAD DENSITY, BYTES: 358KB/800KB FLOPPY & HARD
Communications	ASYNCH, SYNCH UP TO 9600 BPS
Keyboard	ATTACHED, #PAD, WP KEYS
Video tube	BLACK/WHITE 80 × 24 #8 TUBES POSSIBLE—4
Printers	VARIABLE
DOCUMENTATION AND TRAINING	
Documentation	REFERENCE MANUAL & CARDS
Training	TRAINING MANUAL

VENDOR: ATV Jacquard, Inc.
MODEL: J500 or J100/200/300
TYPE: Stand-alone or multiterminal shared resource

ENTERING TEXT	
Where	ANYWHERE
Word wrap	YES
Length of document	DISK
Orientation	DOC
EDITING TEXT	
During entry	YES
Insert	YES, ON/OFF
Delete, copy, and move	YES, CH, L, VAR, DOC
MOVEMENT WITHIN DOCUMENT	
Cursor	W, L
Scroll	L, UP/DOWN; ON/OFF

Search	FOR, BACK, EX
Search and replace	FOR, BACK, EX, GLOB, AUTO, SEMI-AUTO

SPECIAL FEATURES AND FORMATS

Alternate character sets	YES
Boilerplate	YES, GLOSSARY, P
Bold	YES, PR
Calculate	A, SUB
Centering	YES, SC
Center around tabs	YES
Change case	NO
Control characters	YES
Decimal tabs	YES
Dot commands	NO
Footnotes	NO
Forced page break	YES
Format line	YES, ON/OFF
Generate table of contents	YES
Generate index	YES
Headers and footers	YES, UNLIMITED #L; DATE
Hyphenating	USER (HOT ZONE)
Letter merge	YES
Lines per page	YES
Line spacing	½, 1, 1½, 2, 3, PR
Margin release key	NO
Margin width	450
Multicolumn	YES, SC
Nonprinting comments	YES
Onscreen	YES, EXCEPT FEATURES SUCH AS BOLD & UNDERLINE
Page breaks	AUTO
Page numbers	YES, ALT, RESTART
Paragraph indent	YES, SC
Programmable key	YES
Reformat after changes	YES, AUTO, USER
Repeat last command	YES (AUTO KEY)
Right justify	YES, ON/OFF, PR
Right justify tabs	YES
Sort	BASIC SORT INCLUDED; ADVANCED SORT
Spelling check	NO
Storing formats	YES
Strikeover	YES, SC
Sub/superscript	YES, SC
Tabs	5, VAR
Underline	YES, PR
Variable pitch	YES, PR
Vertical lines	VAR
Widows and orphans	AUTO

LIST OF WORD-PROCESSING PRODUCTS || 289

FILES
    File names   #'S & LETTERS; 8 CH
    Renaming   YES
    Copy and delete files   YES
    Copying disks   YES
    Auto save   YES
    Auto backup   YES
    Verify   YES
    Disk directory   YES, NAME, DATE, TITLE, SIZE

PRINTING
    Continuous or sheet
      feed   BOTH
    Multiple printers   YES
    Queue   YES
    Simultaneous   YES
    Specific pages   YES
    Typefaces   YES

HARDWARE
    Internal memory   J100:128K/256K/512K; J500:128K
    Storage and drives   8" SS/SD, SS/DD; HARD DISKS,
                                   12, 24, 80 MEGABYTES
    Communications   TTY EMULATOR; BSP; 3270 EMULATOR; BSM
                                   SUPPORTS IBM 2780/3780; URJE (SUPPORTS
                                   UNIVAC)
    Keyboard   DETACHED; # PAD, WP KEYS
    Video tube   WHITE ON BLACK OR GREEN
    Printers   DIABLO, QUME, NEC: 45–55 CPS; QUME
                                   WIDE TRACK: 40 CPS

DOCUMENTATION AND TRAINING
    Documentation   USER REF MANUAL & INSTALL MANUAL
                                   SELF-PACED AUDIO/WORKBOOK PROGRAM
    Training   PERSONAL INSTRUCTION; 2 OPERATORS FREE

VENDOR: ATV Jacquard Inc.
MODEL: J425
TYPE: Stand-alone, dedicated

ENTERING TEXT
    Where   ANYWHERE
    Word wrap   YES
    Length of document   100 PG
    Orientation   PG, SOME DOC CAPABILITIES

EDITING TEXT
    During entry   YES
    Insert   YES, ON/OFF
    Delete, copy, and move   YES, CH, W, L, PG, VAR, DOC

MOVEMENT WITHIN DOCUMENT

Cursor	BEG/END LINE, TOP/BOT PAGE, TOP SCREEN, LINE, TAB
Scroll	PAGE
Search	FORWARD, IGNORE CASE, EX
Search and replace	FORWARD, IGNORE CASE, EX, SEMI-AUTO, AUTO

SPECIAL FEATURES AND FORMATS

Alternate character sets	PR; CHANGE PRINT WHEELS
Boilerplate	YES, GLOSSARY, P
Bold	YES, PR
Calculate	A, SUB, M, DIV, CROSS FOOT & EXTEND
Centering	YES, SC
Center around tabs	YES
Change case	NO
Control characters	YES, MOST
Decimal tabs	YES
Dot commands	YES, SPECIAL CODES INSTEAD OF DOTS
Footnotes	YES
Forced page break	YES
Format line	YES
Generate table of contents	NO
Generate index	NO
Headers and footers	YES, UNLIMITED #
Hyphenating	AUTO OR USER
Letter merge	YES
Lines per page	YES
Line spacing	1, 2—SC; 1½ —PR; 8L/INCH—PR
Margin release key	SPECIAL COMMAND
Margin width	253
Multicolumn	YES, SC
Nonprinting comments	YES
Onscreen	YES, W/ FEW EXCEPTIONS
Page breaks	AUTO, SC
Page numbers	YES
Paragraph indent	USER
Programmable key	NO
Reformat after changes	YES, AUTO
Repeat last command	NO
Right justify	YES, PR
Right justify tabs	YES
Sort	YES, OPT
Spelling check	NO
Storing formats	STORE AS SEPARATE DOCUMENT
Strikeover	YES, PR
Sub/superscript	YES, PR
Tabs	5, VAR
Underline	YES, SC

Variable pitch	NO
Vertical lines	VAR; MAX OF 127 LINES/PAGE
Widows and orphans	YES DURING REPAGINATION

FILES

File names	FREE, 20 CH
Renaming	YES
Copy and delete files	YES
Copying disks	YES
Auto save	YES
Auto backup	USER
Verify	NO
Disk directory	YES, SIZE, TITLE, DATE

PRINTING

Continuous or sheet feed	BOTH
Multiple printers	NO
Queue	NO
Simultaneous	YES
Specific pages	NO
Typefaces	YES

HARDWARE

Internal memory	48K
Storage and drives	8" SS, SD; (APPROX 75 PG) DUAL FLOPPY DRIVES
Communications	CMC (IBM COMMUNICATING MAGCARD), IBM 2741, ASCII ASYNCH, J425–J425. 15–1200 BPS
Keyboard	DETACHED, WP KEYS
Video tube	GREEN ON GREEN, 80 × 54; 1 screen/SYSTEM
Printers	QUME SPRINT 3, 55 CPS

DOCUMENTATION AND TRAINING

Documentation	SELF-PACED TRAINING PROGRAM; QUICK REFERENCE GUIDE & MANUAL
Training	AMTRAIN SELF-PACED TRAINING

NOTES MULTICOLUMN CAPABILITIES INCLUDE EASY EDITING & COPY BALANCE OF TEXT & STATISTICAL TYPING

VENDOR: Basic 4 Information Systems Division
MODEL: Dataword II
TYPE: Multiterminal, hybrid

ENTERING TEXT

Where	ANYWHERE
Word wrap	YES
Length of document	DISK
Orientation	PG

EDITING TEXT

During entry	YES
Insert	YES
Delete, copy, and move	YES, W, S, P, PG, VAR, DOC

MOVEMENT WITHIN DOCUMENT

Cursor	PG
Scroll	DOCUMENT
Search	FOR, BACK, EX
Search and replace	FOR, BACK, GLOBAL, AUTO, SEMI-AUTO

SPECIAL FEATURES AND FORMATS

Alternate character sets	NO
Boilerplate	YES, P
Bold	YES, SC
Calculate	YES, OPT
Centering	YES, SC
Center around tabs	YES
Change case	YES
Control characters	NO
Decimal tabs	YES
Dot commands	NO
Footnotes	YES
Forced page break	YES
Format line	YES
Generate table of contents	NO
Generate index	NO
Headers and footers	YES, VAR #L, DATE
Hyphenating	NO
Letter merge	YES
Lines per page	YES
Line spacing	1, 2, SC
Margin release key	NO
Margin width	250
Multicolumn	?
Nonprinting comments	NO
Onscreen	YES
Page breaks	USER, SC
Page numbers	YES
Paragraph indent	NO
Programmable key	NO
Reformat after changes	AUTO
Repeat last command	NO
Right justify	YES, PR
Right justify tabs	NO
Sort	YES, ALPH, NUM, BY PAGE
Spelling check	YES, 50,000
Storing formats	YES
Strikeover	NO
Sub/superscript	YES, SC

LIST OF WORD-PROCESSING PRODUCTS || 293

Tabs	VAR
Underline	YES, SC
Variable pitch	NO
Vertical lines	VAR
Widows and orphans	USER
FILES	
File names	OPSYS
Renaming	YES
Copy and delete files	YES
Copying disks	YES
Auto save	YES
Auto backup	NO
Verify	NO
Disk directory	YES
PRINTING	
Continuous or sheet feed	BOTH
Multiple printers	YES
Queue	YES
Simultaneous	YES
Specific pages	YES
Typefaces	NO
HARDWARE	
Internal memory	AMOUNT: 64K
Storage	?
Drives	?
Communications	?
Keyboard	DETACHED, #PAD, WP KEYS
Video tube	BLUE OR GREEN
Printers	DIABLO, QUME, BFISD 40 CPS, TO 1000 LPM
DOCUMENTATION AND TRAINING	
Documentation	MANUAL
Training	MANUALS, SOME PERSONAL INSTRUCTION AT NO COST

VENDOR: Burroughs Corporation
MODEL: Ofiswriter 400
TYPE: Stand-alone, dedicated

ENTERING TEXT

Where	ANYWHERE
Word wrap	YES, ON/OFF
Length of document	DISK
Orientation	PG

EDITING TEXT

During entry	YES
Insert	YES, ALWAYS ON
Delete, copy, and move	YES, CH, W, L, P, PG, COL, VAR, DOC

MOVEMENT WITHIN DOCUMENT

Cursor	W, L, P, PG, COL
Scroll	UP TO 121 LINES
Search	FOR, BACK, EX
Search and replace	FOR, IGNORE INITIAL CAPS, EX, GLOB, AUTO

SPECIAL FEATURES AND FORMATS

Alternate character sets	YES
Boilerplate	YES, GLOSSARY, P
Bold	YES, SC
Calculate	A, SUB, M, DIV, %, OPT
Centering	YES, SC
Center around tabs	YES
Change case	NO
Control characters	MOST; ONSCREEN OR IN A MENU
Decimal tabs	YES
Dot commands	NO
Footnotes	YES, SEMI-AUTO, REPOSITION W/I PAGE
Forced page break	YES
Format line	NO
Generate table of contents	YES
Generate index	NO
Headers and footers	YES, UNLIMITED # L
Hyphenating	USER
Letter merge	YES
Line spacing	1, 1½, 2, 3, SC
Lines per page	VARIABLE
Margin release key	YES
Margin width	200
Multicolumn	YES, PR
Nonprinting comments	YES
Onscreen	YES
Page breaks	AUTO, USER, SC
Page numbers	YES, RESTART
Paragraph indent	NO
Programmable key	YES
Reformat after changes	AUTO
Repeat last command	IF STORED
Right justify	ON/OFF, PR
Right justify tabs	YES
Sort	YES, ALPH, NUM
Spelling check	NO
Storing formats	YES
Strikeover	NO
Sub/superscript	YES, SC
Tabs	VARIABLE
Underline	YES, SC
Variable pitch	YES, PR
Vertical lines	VAR, UP TO 121
Widows and orphans	AUTO

LIST OF WORD-PROCESSING PRODUCTS || 295

FILES
  File names   FREE
  Renaming   YES
  Copy and delete files   YES
  Copying disks   YES
  Auto save   USER
  Auto backup   USER
  Verify   YES
  Disk directory   YES, ALPH ORDER, SIZE, NAME, TITLE, DATE

PRINTING
  Continuous or sheet feed   BOTH
  Multiple printer   NO
  Queue   YES
  Simultaneous   YES
  Specific pages   YES
  Typefaces   YES

HARDWARE
  Internal memory   64K
  Storage and drives   5¼" DS, DD, 228K 1 OR 2 DRIVES
  Communications   TTY MT 983, 2770/2780/3780, 110 TO 9600 BAUD
  Keyboard   DETACHED; RIGHT SIDE OF KEYBOARD MAY BECOME NUMERIC, WP KEYS
  Video tube   GREEN OR AMBER ON BLACK OR BLACK ON WHITE, 80 × 30 ONE TUBE PER SYSTEM
  Printers   DIABLO 20 CPS, DIABLO 35 CPS, QUME 55 CPS, QUME WIDE TRACK, 40 CPS; MAXIMUM OF 1 ATTACHED

DOCUMENTATION AND TRAINING
  Documentation   MANUAL, QUICK REFERENCE
  Training   SELF-PACED KIT

VENDOR: Cado Systems
MODEL: CAT III
TYPE: Stand-alone

ENTERING TEXT
  Where   ANYWHERE
  Word wrap   YES, ALWAYS ON
  Length of document   DISK
  Orientation   DOC

EDITING TEXT
  During entry   YES
  Insert   YES, ALWAYS ON
  Delete, copy, and move   CH, W, L, S, P, PG, COL, VAR, DOC

MOVEMENT WITHIN DOCUMENT
  Cursor   W, L, S, P, COL
  Scroll   L#, P, PG, TOP/BOT

Search	FOR, IGNORE CASE
Search and replace	FOR, IGNORE CASE, GLOB, AUTO, SEMI-AUTO

SPECIAL FEATURES AND FORMATS

Alternate character sets	YES
Boilerplate	GLOSSARY, P
Bold	YES, PR
Calculate	A, SUB, M, DIV, %
Centering	SC
Center around tabs	YES
Change case	NO
Control characters	MOST
Decimal tabs	YES
Dot commands	NO
Footnotes	YES, REPOSITION
Forced page break	YES
Format line	YES
Generate table of contents	NO
Generate index	NO
Headers and footers	YES, UNLIMITED #L, DATE
Hyphenating	AUTO & GHOST
Letter merge	YES
Lines per page	YES
Line spacing	½, 1, 1½, 2, 3, OTHER, PR
Margin release key	YES
Margin width	160
Multicolumn	SC
Nonprinting comments	YES
Onscreen	YES
Page breaks	AUTO, USER, PR
Page numbers	YES, RESTART
Paragraph indent	YES
Programmable key	NO
Reformat after changes	AUTO
Repeat last command	YES, FOR SEARCH COMMAND
Right justify	YES, SC
Right justify tabs	YES
Sort	YES, ALPH, NUM
Spelling check	YES, OPT
Storing formats	YES
Strikeover	YES, PR
Sub/superscript	YES, PR
Tabs	VAR
Underline	YES, PR
Variable pitch	PR
Vertical lines	VAR
Widows and orphans	AUTO

FILES

File names	FREE, 20 CH
Renaming	YES

Copy and delete files	YES
Copying disks	YES
Auto save	USER
Auto backup	NO
Verify	N/A
Disk directory	YES, TITLE, SIZE

PRINTING

Continuous or sheet feed	BOTH
Multiple printers	YES
Queue	YES
Simultaneous	YES
Specific pages	YES
Typefaces	YES

HARDWARE

Internal memory	96KB
Storage and drives	DD/SS 630KB STD; OPT: 2ND DRIVE, DD/DS 1.26 MB, 5¼" WINCHESTER 7.5 MB/15MG
Communications	ASYNCH, 2770, 2780, 3780 50–9600 BAUD, OPT
Keyboard	DETACHED, #PAD, WP KEYS
Video tube	GREEN PHOSPHOR, 80 × 25, UP TO 3 TERMINALS
Printers	20, 35 OR 55 CPS, MAXIMUM OF 3

DOCUMENTATION AND TRAINING

Documentation	SELF-TEACHING COMPUTER-BASED TUTORIAL
Training	

NOTES TOTAL MIX OF PRINTERS AND EXTRA VIDEO TUBES: 3; PRINTERS MAY BE PURCHASED DIRECTLY

VENDOR: Compal, Inc.
MODEL: 8200 Wordpal & Ez Type
TYPE: Stand-alone or multiterminal, hybrid

ENTERING TEXT

Where	ANYWHERE
Word wrap	YES
Length of document	27,000 CH
Orientation	DOC

EDITING TEXT

During entry	YES
Insert	YES, ON/OFF
Delete, copy, and move	YES, VAR

MOVEMENT WITHIN DOCUMENT

Cursor	ANYWHERE W/I TEXT
Scroll	YES, L, PG, SC

Search	FOR, EX, WILD CARDS
Search and replace	FOR, GLOB, AUTO, SEMI-AUTO

SPECIAL FEATURES AND FORMATS

Alternate character sets	YES
Boilerplate	YES, GLOSSARY, P
Bold	YES, PR
Calculate	A, SUB
Centering	YES, SC
Center around tabs	NO
Change case	YES
Control characters	MOST
Decimal tabs	YES
Dot commands	MOST
Footnotes	YES, RENUMBER, REPOSITION
Forced page break	YES
Format line	YES
Generate table of contents	NO
Generate index	NO
Headers and footers	YES, UP TO 9 L
Hyphenating	AUTO, USER
Letter merge	YES
Lines per page	YES
Line spacing	YES, SC
Margin release key	YES
Margin width	225
Multicolumn	YES, SC
Nonprinting comments	YES
Onscreen	YES
Page breaks	AUTO & USER, SC & PR
Page numbers	YES, ALT, RESTART
Paragraph indent	YES, SC
Programmable key	UP TO 10/DISKETTE
Reformat after changes	AUTO
Repeat last command	YES
Right justify	YES, ON/OFF, SC
Right justify tabs	YES
Sort	OPT
Spelling check	YES, 88,000, OPT
Storing formats	YES
Strikeover	YES, PR
Sub/superscript	YES, PR
Tabs	VAR
Underline	YES, PR
Variable pitch	PR
Vertical lines	VAR 1-99
Widows and orphans	AUTO, ON/OFF

FILES

File names	OPSYS, 10 CH
Renaming	YES

LIST OF WORD-PROCESSING PRODUCTS || 299

Copy and delete files	YES
Copying disks	YES
Auto save	USER
Auto backup	YES
Verify	YES
Disk directory	YES

PRINTING
Continuous or sheet feed	BOTH
Multiple printers	YES
Queue	YES
Simultaneous	YES
Specific pages	YES
Typefaces	YES

HARDWARE
Internal memory	56KB
Storage and drives	315KB–5MB; 2 DISKETTES OR 1 DISKETTE & HARD DISK
Communications	TTY, 3270, 3780, TELEX, FILE TRANSFER
Keyboard	8200—DETACHED, #PAD, WP KEYS EZTYPE—ATTACHED, #PAD, WP KEYS
Video tube	WHITE ON BLACK OR REVERSE, 80 × 24, 1 PER SYSTEM
Printers	NEC SPINWRITER, 35 OR 55 CPS, UP TO 4

DOCUMENTATION AND TRAINING
Documentation	USER'S MANUAL
Training	INITIAL TRAINING IN 3 HOUR INCREMENTS, N/C, RETRAINING

NOTES   HARDWARE MAINTENANCE CONTRACTS AVAILABLE; INCLUDES SOFTWARE ENHANCEMENTS

VENDOR: Compucorp
MODEL: Omega 685
TYPE: Stand-alone, dedicated

ENTERING TEXT
Where	ANYWHERE
Word wrap	YES
Length of document	DISK
Orientation	DOC

EDITING TEXT
During entry	YES
Insert	YES, ON/OFF
Delete, copy, and move	YES, VAR, DOC

MOVEMENT WITHIN DOCUMENT
Cursor	W, L, PG
Scroll	L, P, PG, SC

Search	FOR, IGNORE CASE, ALSO EX
Search and replace	FOR, IGNORE CASE, GLOB, AUTO, SEMI-AUTO

SPECIAL FEATURES AND FORMATS

Alternate character sets	YES
Boilerplate	YES, GLOSSARY, P
Bold	YES, SC
Calculate	A, SUB, M, DIV, %, OPT
Centering	YES, SC
Center arond tabs	YES
Change case	NO
Control characters	NO
Decimal tabs	YES
Dot commands	NO
Footnotes	YES, RENUMBER, REPOSITION
Forced page break	YES
Format line	YES
Generate table of contents	NO
Generate index	NO
Headers and footers	YES, UNLIMITED #L
Hyphenating	YES
Letter merge	YES
Lines per page	YES
Line spacing	½, 1, PR; TO 1/48" IF PRINTER ALLOWS
Margin release key	NO
Margin width	255
Multicolumn	SC
Nonprinting comments	YES
Onscreen	YES
Page breaks	AUTO, USER
Page numbers	YES, ALT
Paragraph indent	NO
Programmable key	YES, "AUTO PILOT" FUNCTION
Reformat after changes	YES
Repeat last command	NO
Right justify	YES, SC
Right justify tabs	YES
Sort	YES
Spelling check	YES, 50,000 W, OPT—"B" PACKAGE
Storing formats	YES
Strikeover	YES, PR
Sub/superscript	YES, SC
Tabs	VAR
Underline	YES, SC
Variable pitch	YES, PR
Vertical lines	VAR
Widows and orphans	AUTO

FILES

File names	FREE 35 CH
Renaming	YES

Copy and delete files   YES
Copying disks   YES
Auto save   YES, USER
Auto backup   NO
Verify   ?
Disk directory   YES, SIZE, NAME, TITLE, DATE

PRINTING
Continuous or sheet
  feed   BOTH
Multiple printers   YES
Queue   YES
Simultaneous   YES
Specific pages   YES
Typefaces   YES

HARDWARE
Internal memory   64–192K
Storage & drives   5¼", 150K–5MG
Communications   TO 9600 BPS, TTY, 2780, 3780
Keyboard   DETACHED, #PAD, WP KEYS
Video tube   B/W, 80 × 20 OR 80 × 60
Printers   ANY DAISY WHEEL OR RS232 PRINTER

DOCUMENTATION AND TRAINING
Documentation   MANUAL, QUICK REFERENCE GUIDE
Training   ON-HAND MSR TRAINING

VENDOR: Compugraphic
MODEL: MCS 8400
TYPE: Phototypesetter

ENTERING TEXT
Where   ANYWHERE
Word wrap   YES
Length of document   160,000 CH
Orientation   PG

EDITING TEXT
During entry   YES
Insert   YES
Delete, copy, and move   YES, CH, W, L, P, PG

MOVEMENT WITHIN DOCUMENT
Cursor   PG
Scroll   L, P, PG, SC, T/B
Search   IGNORE CASE
Search and replace   IGNORE CASE, EX, GLOB, AUTO &
                          SEMI-AUTO

SPECIAL FEATURES AND FORMATS
Alternate character
  sets   YES
Boilerplate   YES, GLOSSARY, P

Bold	YES, SC
Calculate	NO
Centering	YES, SC
Center around tabs	YES
Change case	YES
Control characters	MOST
Decimal tabs	NO
Dot commands	NO
Footnotes	NO
Forced page break	YES
Format line	YES
Generate table of contents	NO
Generate index	NO
Headers and footers	YES
Hyphenating	AUTO, USER
Letter image	YES
Lines per page	VARIABLES
Line spacing	½, 1, 1½, 2, 3
Margin release key	YES
Margin width	70 PICA
Multicolumn	YES, SC
Nonprinting comments	NO
Onscreen	YES
Page breaks	USER, SC
Page numbers	YES
Paragraph indent	YES, SC
Programmable key	YES
Reformat after changes	USER
Repeat last command	YES
Right justify	YES, SC
Right justify tabs	YES
Sort	NO
Spelling check	NO
Storing formats	YES
Strikeover	YES, SC
Sub/superscript	YES
Tabs	VAR
Underline	YES
Variable pitch	YES
Vertical lines	YES
Widows and orphans	USER

FILES

File names	FREE, 12 CH
Renaming	YES
Copy and delete files	YES
Copying disks	YES
Auto save	NO
Auto backup	NO
Verify	NO
Disk directory	YES

LIST OF WORD-PROCESSING PRODUCTS || 303

PRINTING
Continuous or sheet feed	BOTH
Multiple printers	YES
Queue	YES
Simultaneous	YES
Specific pages	YES
Typefaces	YES

HARDWARE
Internal memory	?
Storage and drives	?
Communications	?
Keyboard	?
Video tube	?
Printers	?

DOCUMENTATION AND TRAINING
Documentation	?
Training	?

VENDOR: CPT Corporation
MODEL: 8100
TYPE: Stand-alone, dedicated

ENTERING TEXT
Where	STATIONARY TYPING LINE
Word wrap	YES, ON/OFF
Length of document	3½–4 PG (12,000 CH)
Orientation	PG W/SOME DOC CHARACTERISTICS

EDITING TEXT
During entry	YES
Insert	YES
Delete, copy, and move	YES, CH, W, L, P, PG, DOC

MOVEMENT WITHIN DOCUMENT
Cursor	LENGTH OF SCREEN—240 CH
Scroll	W, L, P, PG
Search	IGNORE CASE
Search and replace	IGNORE CASE, GLOB, AUTO, SEMI-AUTO

SPECIAL FEATURES AND FORMATS
Alternate character sets	YES
Boilerplate	YES, GLOSSARY, P
Bold	YES, PR
Calculate	A, SUB, M, DIV, %
Centering	YES, SC
Center around tabs	NO
Change case	YES
Control characters	NO
Decimal tabs	YES

Dot commands	NO
Footnotes	YES, RENUMBER, REPOSITION
Forced page break	YES
Format line	YES
Generate table of contents	NO
Generate index	?
Headers and footers	YES, UNLIMITED #L
Hyphenating	AUTO, USER
Letter merge	YES
Lines per page	YES
Line spacing	1, 2, 3—SC, 1½, 1¼, PR
Margin release key	YES
Margin width	240
Multicolumn	YES, SC
Nonprinting comments	YES
Onscreen	YES, THROUGH "DIRECT PRINTING"
Page breaks	AUTO
Page numbers	YES, ALT, RESTART
Paragraph indent	YES
Programmable key	YES
Reformat after changes	YES
Repeat last command	YES, W/PROGRAM KEY
Right justify	YES, PR
Right justify tabs	RIGHT JUSTIFY COLS, BUT NOT W/TABS
Sort	YES, ALPH, NUM
Spelling check	YES, 10,000 W
Storing formats	YES
Strikeover	YES, SC
Sub/superscript	YES, PR
Tabs	VAR
Underline	YES, SC
Variable pitch	YES, PR
Vertical lines	VARIABLE
Widows and orphans	AUTO, USER

FILES

File names	FREE, 10 CH
Renaming	YES
Copy and delete files	YES
Copying disks	YES
Auto save	USER
Auto backup	NO, ORIG ALWAYS RESIDENT ON DISK
Verify	YES
Disk directory	YES, TITLE LINE FOR ADD'L INFO

PRINTING

Continuous or sheet feed	BOTH
Multiple printers	YES
Queue	YES
Simultaneous	YES

Specific pages	YES
Typefaces	YES

HARDWARE
Internal memory	128K
Storage	8″ SS, SD, 300KB
Drives	DUAL DISK DRIVES
Communications	ASYNCH OR BISYNCH 300–1200 BPS
Keyboard	DETACHED, #PAD, WP KEYS
Video tube	WHITE ON BLACK, 240 × 54 (HORIZONTAL SCROLL)
Printers	DIABLO, QUME, OR RICOH

DOCUMENTATION AND TRAINING
Documentation	OPERATOR'S MANUAL, SPECIFIC TO SYSTEM & SOFTWARE PURCHASED
Training	3 DAYS "BASICS" CLASS, ADDITIONAL FOR SPEC. SOFTWARE

NOTES WINDOW AT BOTTOM—"PREVIEW"—CAN BE USED TO VIEW & SELECT TEXT IN OTHER DOCUMENTS

VENDOR: Datapoint
MODEL: Datapoint
TYPE: Stand-alone multiterminal, hybrid

ENTERING TEXT
Where	ANYWHERE
Word wrap	YES
Length of document	DISK OR 9999 L PER PG
Orientation	DOC

EDITING TEXT
During entry	YES
Insert	YES, ON/OFF
Delete, copy, and move	YES, VAR, DOC

MOVEMENT WITHIN DOCUMENT
Cursor	PG
Scroll	CURSOR KEYS MOVE THROUGHOUT DOC
Search	FOR, IGNORE CASE
Search and replace	FOR, IGNORE CASE, GLOB, AUTO, SEMI-AUTO

SPECIAL FEATURES AND FORMATS
Alternate character sets	YES, CHANGE PRINT WHEEL
Boilerplate	YES, SOME GLOSSARY, P
Bold	YES, PR
Calculate	YES, OPT, FREE
Centering	YES, SC
Center around tabs	YES
Change case	NO
Control characters	ALL, DISPLAYED ONLY ON REQUEST

Decimal tabs	YES
Dot commands	NO
Footnotes	NO
Forced page break	YES
Format line	YES
Generate table of contents	NO
Generate index	NO
Headers and footers	YES, 1 L
Hyphenating	NO
Letter merge	YES
Lines per page	YES
Line spacing	SC—1, 2, 3, 4, 5, 6
Margin release key	NO
Margin width	140
Multicolumn	NO
Nonprinting comments	NO
Onscreen	YES
Page breaks	AUTO, SC
Page numbers	YES, ALT, RESTART
Paragraph indent	YES, SC
Programmable key	YES
Reformat after changes	AUTO
Repeat last command	SOME COMMANDS
Right justify	YES, ON/OFF, SC
Right justify tabs	YES
Sort	YES
Spelling check	NO
Storing formats	YES
Strikeover	YES, SEEN IN HIGHLIGHT MODE
Sub/superscript	YES, SEEN IN HIGHLIGHT MODE
Tabs	VAR
Underline	YES, SEEN IN HIGHLIGHT MODE
Variable pitch	YES, PR
Vertical lines	VARIABLE, UP TO 9999
Widows and orphans	USER

FILES

File names	FREE, OPSYS
Renaming	YES
Copy and delete files	YES
Copying disks	YES
Auto save	USER
Auto backup	YES
Verify	YES, "SCAN"
Disk directory	YES, ORDER, SIZE, NAME, TITLE—NO #, DATE

PRINTING

Continuous or sheet feed	BOTH
Multiple printers	YES
Queue	YES

Simultaneous   YES
Specific pages   YES
Typefaces   YES

HARDWARE
Internal memory   60–256K
Storage and drives   FLOPPIES: SSSD, SSDD, OR DSDD ¼ MB, ½ MB, 1 MB, UP TO 08 MB HARD DISKS: 10 MB, 20 MB, 67 MB, 135 MB
Communications   2780, 3770, 2770, 3780, 3741, 3270 DCT—2000–UNIVAC, TTY, HASP, DIRECT CHANNEL INTERFACE TO IBM, MLDCIC, UNIVAC UNISCOPE, HONEYWELL VIP, HONEYWELL GI–15
Keyboard   DETACHABLE KEYBOARD #PAD, WP KEYS
Video tube   AMBER OR GREEN, 80 × 24 # DEPENDS ON SYSTEM; 8600 SUPPORTS 3, 8800 SUPPORTS 12
Printers   30 CPS, 45 CPS, MATRIX + LINE PRINTERS, LASER; 3 TO A PROCESSOR W/I A NETWORK—UNLIMITED

DOCUMENTATION AND TRAINING
Documentation   SIMPLIFIED USER'S GUIDE + SUPR. GUIDE
Training   MUST ATTEND 1-WEEK COURSE
Options   DATA-PROCESSING SOFTWARE AT NO CHARGE

VENDOR: Data Terminals & Communications
MODEL: 210A/B
TYPE: Stand-alone or multiterminal

ENTERING TEXT
Where   ANYWHERE
Word wrap   YES
Length of document   DISK
Orientation   DOC

EDITING TEXT
During entry   YES
Insert   YES, ON/OFF
Delete, copy, and move YES, VAR, DOC

MOVEMENT WITHIN DOCUMENT
Cursor   PG
Scroll   TOP/BOT
Search   EX
Search and replace   EX

SPECIAL FEATURES AND FORMATS
Alternate character
  sets   YES
Boilerplate   NO

Bold	YES, PR
Calculate	YES, OPT
Centering	PR
Center around tabs	NO
Change case	NO
Control characters	MOST
Decimal tabs	NO
Dot commands	MOST
Footnotes	NO
Forced page break	YES
Format line	NO
Generate table of contents	NO
Generate index	YES
Headers and footers	YES
Hyphenating	AUTO
Letter merge	YES
Lines per page	YES
Line spacing	VAR, PR
Margin release key	NO
Margin width	?
Multicolumn	YES, PR
Nonprinting comments	YES
Onscreen	YES
Page breaks	AUTO, SC
Page numbers	NO
Paragraph indent	NO
Programmable key	NO
Reformat after changes	AUTO
Repeat last command	YES
Right justify	NO
Right justify tabs	YES
Sort	ALPH, BY FILE NAME
Spelling check	NO
Storing formats	YES
Strikeover	NO
Sub/superscript	YES, PR
Tabs	VAR
Underline	YES
Variable pitch	YES
Vertical lines	VAR
Widows and orphans	USER

FILES

File names	FREE
Renaming	YES
Copy and delete files	YES
Copying disks	YES
Auto save	USER
Auto backup	NO
Verify	YES
Disk directory	YES, TITLE

LIST OF WORD-PROCESSING PRODUCTS || 309

PRINTING
Continuous or sheet feed	BOTH
Multiple printers	YES
Queue	YES
Simultaneous	YES
Specific pages	YES
Typefaces	YES

HARDWARE
Internal memory	64K RAM 2K ROM
Storage and drives	5¼" DS, DD, 300K EA, 2 FLOPPIES PLUS 2 WINCHESTER, 10 MG EA
Communications	EIA 50–19.2K BPS
Keyboard	ATTACHED, #PAD, WP KEYS
Video tube	OPTIONAL COLORS, 80 × 24; 4 TUBES/PROCESSOR
Printers	DTC-383 OPTIONAL; 20–40 CPS, 4 MAX

DOCUMENTATION AND TRAINING
Documentation	USER MANUAL + EXT BASIC
Training	2-DAY USER TRAINING

VENDOR: Delta Data Systems Corp.
MODEL: Easyone
TYPE: Stand-alone, hybrid

ENTERING TEXT
Where	ANYWHERE
Word wrap	YES
Length of document	DISK
Orientation	DOC

EDITING TEXT
During entry	YES
Insert	YES, ON/OFF
Delete, copy, and move	YES, VAR, DOC

MOVEMENT WITHIN DOCUMENT
Cursor	L
Scroll	SC, TOP/BOT
Search	FOR, BACK, IGNORE CASE, EX
Search and replace	FOR, BACK, IGNORE CASE, GLOB, AUTO, SEMI-AUTO

SPECIAL FEATURES AND FORMATS
Alternate character sets	NOT YET
Boilerplate	YES, GLOSSARY, P
Bold	YES, SC
Calculate	A, SUB, M, DIV, %
Centering	YES, SC
Center around tabs	YES

Change case	YES
Control characters	MOST
Decimal tabs	YES
Dot commands	NO
Footnotes	NOT YET
Forced page break	YES
Format line	NO
Generate table of contents	NOT YET
Generate index	NOT YET
Headers and footers	YES, UNLIMITED # L
Hyphenating	USER
Letter merge	YES
Lines per page	YES
Line spacing	1, 2, 3, PR
Margin release key	YES
Margin width	UNLIMITED
Multicolumn	YES, SC
Nonprinting comments	NO
Onscreen	YES
Page breaks	AUTO, USER, SC, PR
Page numbers	YES, ALT, RESTART
Paragraph indent	YES, SC
Programmable key	YES
Reformat after changes	AUTO
Repeat last command	YES
Right justify	YES, SC
Right justify tabs	YES
Sort	ALPH, NUM
Spelling check	YES, # DEPENDS ON DISK SPACE AVAIL
Storing formats	YES
Strikeover	YES
Sub/superscript	YES, PR
Tabs	8, VAR
Underline	YES, SC
Variable pitch	YES, PR
Vertical lines	VAR
Widows and orphans	AUTO

FILES

File names	FREE
Renaming	YES
Copy and delete files	YES
Copying disks	YES
Auto save	USER
Auto backup	NO
Verify	YES
Disk directory	YES

PRINTING

Continuous or sheet feed	BOTH
Multiple printers	NO

LIST OF WORD-PROCESSING PRODUCTS || 311

    Queue   NO
    Simultaneous   NO
    Specific pages   YES
    Typefaces   NO

HARDWARE
    Internal memory   64K
    Storage and drives   8″ FLOPPY, 5¼″ WINCHESTER, DS, DD
    Communications   TTY, 9600 BAUD, $1000
    Keyboard   DETACHED, # PAD, WP KEYS
    Video tube   P31 GREEN PHOSPHOR, 80 × 24,
                                          1 TUBE/SYSTEM
    Printers   QUME, 45 CPS, MAXIMUM/SYSTEM—1

DOCUMENTATION AND TRAINING
    Documentation   OPERATING REFERENCE MANUAL,
                                          WORD-PROCESSING OPERATOR'S MANUAL &
                                          GUIDE, CP/M SET
    Training   OPERATOR TRAINING, ONE ON ONE

VENDOR: Dictaphone Corporation
MODEL: Dual Display
TYPE: Stand-alone or multiterminal, dedicated

ENTERING TEXT
    Where   ANYWHERE
    Word wrap   YES
    Length of document   254 PG
    Orientation   DOC

EDITING TEXT
    During entry   NO
    Insert   YES, ON/OFF
    Delete, copy, and move   YES, VAR, DOC

MOVEMENT WITHIN DOCUMENT
    Cursor   PG ANYWHERE IN DOC AND PAGE
    Scroll   L, P, PG, SC, TOP/BOT
    Search   FOR, IGNORE CASE, EX
    Search and replace   FOR, IGNORE CASE, EX, GLOB, AUTO,
                                          SEMI-AUTO

SPECIAL FEATURES AND FORMATS
    Alternate character
      sets   YES
    Boilerplate   YES, GLOSSARY, P
    Bold   YES, SC
    Calculate   A, SUB, M, DIV
    Centering   YES, SC
    Center around tabs   YES
    Change case   NO
    Control characters   NO
    Decimal tabs   YES
    Dot commands   NO

Footnotes	YES, RENUMBER, REPOSITION
Forced page break	YES
Format line	YES, ON/OFF
Generate table of contents	YES
Generate index	YES
Headers and footers	YES, 6 L, DATE
Hyphenating	AUTO, USER
Letter merge	YES
Lines per page	YES
Line spacing	½, 1, 1½, 2, 3, SC
Margin release key	NO
Margin width	316
Multicolumn	YES, PR
Nonprinting comments	YES
Onscreen	YES
Page breaks	AUTO, SC
Page numbers	YES, ALT
Paragraph indent	SC
Programmable key	NO
Reformat after changes	AUTO
Repeat last command	YES
Right justify	YES, ON/OFF, SC
Right justify tabs	YES
Sort	YES, ALPH, NUM
Spelling check	NO
Storing formats	YES, IN "LIBRARY"
Strikeover	YES, PR
Sub/superscript	YES, SC
Tabs	VAR
Underline	YES, SC
Variable pitch	YES, SC
Vertical lines	VARIABLE
Widows and orphans	AUTO

FILES

File names	FREE, 32 CH
Renaming	YES
Copy and delete files	YES
Copying disks	YES
Auto save	AUTO, USER
Auto backup	YES
Verify	YES
Disk directory	YES

PRINTING

Continuous or sheet feed	BOTH
Multiple printers	YES
Queue	YES
Simultaneous	YES

LIST OF WORD-PROCESSING PRODUCTS || 313

    Specific pages   YES
    Typefaces   YES

HARDWARE
Internal memory	96KB
Storage and drives	SS, DD—250K; DS, DD—500K
Communications	ASYNCH ASCII, 50–4800 BPS, OPT
Keyboard	DETACHED, WP KEYS
Video tube	GREEN ON CHARCOAL, 102 × 66, MAX OF TUBES/SYSTEM
Printers	RICOH 1600/DIABLO HYTYPE II, 40 CPS; MAXIMUM/SYSTEM—3

DOCUMENTATION AND TRAINING
Documentation	COMPLETE OPERATOR'S MANUAL PLUS CASSETTE AUDIO/VISUAL SELF-PACED PACKAGE
Training	3 FULL DAYS OUR OFFICE PLUS 1 FOLLOW-UP DAY OUR OFFICE ADVANCED APPLICATIONS

VENDOR: Digital Equipment Corporation
MODEL: Decword/DP
TYPE: Multiterminal, hybrid

ENTERING TEXT
Where	BOTTOM
Word wrap	YES
Length of document	DISK
Orientation	DOC

EDITING TEXT
During entry	YES
Insert	YES, ALWAYS ON
Delete, copy, and move	CH, L, S, P, PG, TAB, DOC, OTHERS

MOVEMENT WITHIN DOCUMENT
Cursor	CH, L, S, P, PG, DOC, TAB, OTHERS
Scroll	L, P, PG, SC, TOP/BOT
Search	FOR, BACK, IGNORE CASE, EX
Search and replace	FOR, BACK, IGNORE CASE, SEMI-AUTO (VERSION 1.2—GLOB & AUTO)

SPECIAL FEATURES AND FORMATS
Alternate character sets	YES
Boilerplate	YES, GLOSSARY, P
Bold	YES, PR (VERSION 1.2—SC)
Calculate	A, SUB, M, DIV
Centering	YES, SC
Center around tabs	NO
Change case	YES

Control characters	NO
Decimal tabs	YES
Dot commands	NO
Footnotes	YES, RENUMBER, "FOOTNOTE CONTINUED"
Forced page break	YES
Format line	ON/OFF
Generate table of contents	YES
Generate index	YES
Headers and footers	YES, UNLIMITED #L, DATE
Hyphenating	USER
Letter merge	YES
Lines per page	YES
Line spacing	VARIABLE, PR (SYMBOL INDICATED ON RULER)
Margin release key	NO
Margin width	132
Multicolumn	VIA "USER-PROGRAMMED FUNCTION KEYS"
Nonprinting comments	YES
Onscreen	YES, W/SOME EXCEPTIONS
Page breaks	AUTO, USER, SC
Page numbers	YES, ALT, RESTART
Paragraph indent	YES, SC
Programmable key	YES, "USER DEFINED KEYS"
Reformat after changes	AUTO
Repeat last command	WITH "USER DEFINED KEYS"
Right justify	YES, PR
Right justify tabs	YES
Sort	YES, ALPH, NUM
Spelling check	YES, 10,000 W, MODIFIABLE
Storing formats	YES
Strikeover	YES, SYMBOL—SC
Sub/superscript	YES, PR, IN VIEW MODE—SC
Tabs	VAR
Underline	YES, SC
Variable pitch	YES, SYMBOL-SC
Vertical lines	VAR
Widows and orphans	USER

FILES

File names	FREE, 50 CH
Renaming	YES
Copy and delete files	YES
Copying disks	YES
Auto save	USER
Auto backup	YES
Verify	YES
Disk directory	YES, ORDER, TITLE

PRINTING

Continuous or sheet feed	BOTH
Multiple printers	YES

LIST OF WORD-PROCESSING PRODUCTS | 315

Queue	YES
Simultaneous	YES
Specific pages	YES
Typefaces	YES

HARDWARE

Internal memory	256K (MINIMUM)
Storage and drives	HARD DISKS—RL01–5MB, RL02—10MB, OTHERS DEPENDING ON PDP-11 CONFIGURATION
Communications	ASCII, UP TO 9600 BPS DECNET
Keyboard	DETACHED, WP KEYS
Video tube	BLACK & WHITE, 80 × 24
Printers	LQP—40 CPS LA34—30 CPS LA120—180 CPS #MAX 1–40, DEPENDING ON CPU SIZE

DOCUMENTATION AND TRAINING

Documentation	MANAGER, USER & ADVANCED USER BINDERS
Training	COMPUTER-BASED INSTRUCTION LECTURE/LAB, ADVANCED AND SYSTEM MANAGER

VENDOR: Digital Equipment Corporation
MODEL: DECMATE
TYPE: Stand-alone, hybrid

ENTERING TEXT

Where	BOTTOM
Word wrap	YES
Length of document	DISK
Orientation	DOC

EDITING TEXT

During entry	YES
Insert	YES, ALWAYS ON
Delete, copy, and move	CH, W, L, S, P, PG, VAR, DOC

MOVEMENT WITHIN DOCUMENT

Cursor	W, L, S, P, PG
Scroll	L, P, PG, SC, TOP/BOT
Search	FOR, BACK, EX UPPER; IGNORE LOWER
Search and replace	FOR, BACK, EX UPPER; IGNORE LOWER; GLOB, AUTO, SEMI-AUTO

SPECIAL FEATURES AND FORMATS

Alternate character sets	YES
Boilerplate	YES, GLOSSARY, P
Bold	YES, SC
Calculate	A, SUB, M, DIV, %, FORMULAS
Centering	YES, SC
Center around tabs	YES
Change case	YES

Control characters	NO
Decimal tabs	YES
Dot commands	NO
Footnotes	NO
Forced page break	YES
Format line	YES
Generate table of contents	NO
Generate index	NO
Headers and footers	YES, VARIABLE #L
Hyphenating	NO
Letter merge	YES, OPT
Lines per page	YES
Line spacing	½, 1, 1½, 2, 3, OTHER, PR
Margin release key	NO
Margin width	158
Multicolumn	YES, SC
Nonprinting comments	YES
Onscreen	YES, EXCEPT VERTICAL SPACING
Page breaks	YES, SC
Page numbers	YES, RESTART
Paragraph indent	YES, SC
Programmable key	YES
Reformat after changes	AUTO
Repeat last command	NO
Right justify	YES, PR
Right justify tabs	YES
Sort	ALPH, NUM, OPT
Spelling check	NO
Storing formats	YES
Strikeover	YES, SYMBOLS ON SCREEN
Sub/superscript	YES, PR, SC-VIA "VIEW MODE"
Tabs	VAR
Underline	YES, SC
Variable pitch	NO
Vertical lines	VARIABLE
Widows and orphans	USER

FILES

File names	FREE, 71 CH
Renaming	YES
Copy and delete files	YES
Copying disks	YES
Auto save	YES
Auto backup	NO
Verify	YES
Disk directory	YES, SIZE, TITLE, DATE

PRINTING

Continuous or sheet feed	BOTH
Multiple printers	VIA COM LINE OR SHARED PRINTER SWITCH

LIST OF WORD-PROCESSING PRODUCTS || 317

    Queue   YES
    Simultaneous   YES
    Specific pages   YES
    Typefaces   YES

HARDWARE
    Internal memory   64KB
    Storage and drives   8" SS, SD—256K; SS, DD—512KB UP TO 4 DRIVES/SYSTEM
    Communications   SERIAL ASYNCH ASCII, UP TO 4800 BPS
    Keyboard   DETACHED, #PAD, WP KEYS
    Video tube   BLACK-ON-WHITE OR WHITE-ON-BLACK 80 OR 132 × 24 CH
    Printers   LQP—35 CPS, LA—34 DOT MATRIX—30 CPS (DESK TOP); LA120 HIGH-SPEED DOT MATRIX—2160 CPS; 2 MAX

DOCUMENTATION AND TRAINING
    Documentation   OWNER'S GUIDE, USER'S MANUALS FOR SOFTWARE, PRINTER MANUAL
    Training   AUDIO-PRINT AND SELF-PACED MANUALS/CASSETTES; OPT ONE-ON-ONE INSTRUCTION CAN BE PURCHASED

VENDOR: Durango Systems
MODEL: 700, 800, 900 series
TYPE: Multiterminal

ENTERING TEXT
    Where   ANYWHERE
    Word wrap   NO
    Length of document   DISK
    Orientation   DOC

EDITING TEXT
    During entry
    Insert   YES
    Delete, copy, and move   YES, VAR, DOC

MOVEMENT WITHIN DOCUMENT
    Cursor   YES, TOP/BOT
    Search   FOR, EX
    Search and replace   FOR, EX, GLOB, AUTO/SEMI-AUTO

SPECIAL FEATURES AND FORMATS
    Alternate character sets YES
    Boilerplate   NO
    Bold   NO
    Calculate   NO
    Centering   YES, PR
    Center around tabs   NO
    Change case   NO

Control characters	YES
Decimal tabs	NO
Dot commands	MOST
Footnotes	NO
Forced page break	YES
Format line	NO
Generate table of contents	NO
Generate index	NO
Headers and footers	YES, L=1
Hyphenating	NO
Letter merge	YES
Lines per page	?
Line spacing	YES, PR
Margin release key	NO
Margin width	?
Multicolumn	NO
Nonprinting comments	YES
Onscreen	YES
Page breaks	AUTO, PR
Page numbers	YES, RESTART
Paragraph indent	YES, PR
Programmable key	NO
Reformat after changes	AUTO
Repeat last command	AUTO
Right justify	YES, SC/PR
Right justify tabs	NO
Sort	NO
Spelling check	NO
Storing formats	YES
Strikeover	YES, PR
Sub/superscript	YES/PR
Tabs	VAR
Underline	YES, PR
Variable pitch	YES, PR
Vertical lines	26 ON CRT
Widows and orphans	USER

FILES

File names	?
Renaming	YES
Copy and delete files	COPY, DELETE
Copying disks	YES
Auto save	USER
Auto backup	YES
Verify	YES
Disk directory	YES, ORDER, TITLE, DATE

PRINTING

Continuous or sheet feed	BOTH
Multiple printers	YES

LIST OF WORD-PROCESSING PRODUCTS || 319

    Queue   YES
    Simultaneous   NO
    Specific pages   YES
    Typefaces   YES (LETTER QUALITY, MATRIX, HIGH RES)

HARDWARE
    Internal memory   ?
    Storage   5¼″ DUAL-DENSITY, DOUBLE-SIDED, 1MGB PLUS UP TO 28MGB FIXED DISK
    Drives   MPI DISKETTES; RMS DISK
    Communications   ASYNCH/SYNCH, RS232; 1200 BAUD
    Keyboard   ATTACHED, # PAD, WP KEYS
    Video tube   GREEN, 26 LINES × 80 CH
    Printers   DURANGO, 185CPS

DOCUMENTATION AND TRAINING
    Documentation   USER GUIDE
    Training   SELF-INSTRUCTION; USER GUIDE

VENDOR: Exxon Office Systems
MODEL: The Intelligent Typewriter
TYPE: One-line display

ENTERING TEXT
    Where   ONE LINE DISPLAY
    Word wrap   YES
    Length of document   10,000 CH
    Orientation   DOC

EDITING TEXT
    During entry   YES
    Insert   YES, ALWAYS ON
    Delete, copy, and move YES, CH, W, L, S, P, PG, VAR, DOC

MOVEMENT WITHIN DOCUMENT
    Cursor   W, L, S, P, PG, COL
    Scroll   L, P, PG, TOP/BOT
    Search   FOR, BACK, EX
    Search and replace   FOR, BACK, EX, GLOB, AUTO

SPECIAL FEATURES AND FORMATS
    Alternate character
      sets   NO
    Boilerplate   YES, P
    Bold   YES
    Calculate   NO
    Centering   YES, PR
    Center around tabs   YES
    Change case   NO
    Control characters   NO
    Decimal tabs   YES
    Dot commands   NO
    Footnotes   NO

Forced page break	YES
Format line	YES
Generate table of contents	NO
Generate index	YES
Headers and footers	YES
Hyphenating	USER
Letter merge	YES
Lines per page	SET INCHES OF TEXT
Line spacing	VARIABLE, PR
Margin release key	YES
Margin width	156
Multicolumn	YES
Nonprinting comments	NO
Onscreen	NO
Page breaks	AUTO, USER, PR
Page numbers	NO
Paragraph indent	NO
Programmable key	NO
Reformat after changes	AUTO
Repeat last command	NO
Right justify	YES, PR
Right justify tabs	YES
Sort	NO
Spelling check	NO
Storing formats	YES
Strikeover	YES, PR
Sub/superscript	YES, SC
Tabs	VAR
Underline	YES, SC
Variable pitch	NO
Vertical lines	VAR
Widows and orphans	USER

FILES

File names	FREE
Renaming	YES
Copy and delete files	YES
Copying disks	NO
Auto save	USER
Auto backup	NO
Verify	NO
Disk directory	YES, SIZE, TITLE

PRINTING

Continuous or sheet feed	BOTH
Multiple printers	NO
Queue	NO
Simultaneous	NO
Specific pages	NO
Typefaces	YES

HARDWARE
  Internal memory   10,000 CH
  Storage and drives   5¼″ SS, SD, 60KB 2 DISK DRIVES
  Communications   ASYNCH; TO EXXON WORD PROCESSORS
  Keyboard   ONE-LINE DISPLAY ATTACHED TO
                                KEYBOARD; WP KEYS
  Video tube   RED, 20 CH
  Printers   24CPS; ONE PER SYSTEM

DOCUMENTATION AND TRAINING
  Documentation   ?
  Training   SELF-STUDY AND CSR SUPPORT

VENDOR: Exxon Office Systems
MODEL: 1200, 1400 & 1800 Word Processors
TYPE: Stand-alone, dedicated

ENTERING TEXT
  Where   ANYWHERE
  Word wrap   YES, ON/OFF
  Length of document   4,094 CH
  Orientation   PG

EDITING TEXT
  During entry   YES
  Insert   YES, ON/OFF
  Delete, copy, and move   YES, VAR, DOC

MOVEMENT WITHIN DOCUMENT
  Cursor   W, L, S, P, PG, COL
  Scroll   L, P, PG, SC
  Search   FOR, IGNORE CASE, EX
  Search and replace   FOR, IGNORE CASE, GLOB, AUTO

SPECIAL FEATURES AND FORMATS
  Alternate character
    sets   YES
  Boilerplate   YES
  Bold   YES, PR
  Calculate   A, SUB, M, % (1800 ONLY)
  Centering   YES, SC
  Center around tabs   NO
  Change case   NO
  Control characters   NO
  Decimal tabs   YES
  Dot commands   NO
  Footnotes   YES, RENUMBER, REPOSITION
  Forced page break   YES
  Format line   YES, ON/OFF
  Generate table of con-
    tents   NO
  Generate index   NO
  Headers and footers   YES, VARIABLE #L

Hyphenating	USER
Letter merge	YES
Lines per page	YES
Line spacing	VAR, PR
Margin release key	NO
Margin width	UNLIMITED
Multicolumn	YES, SC
Nonprinting comments	YES
Onscreen	YES, EXCEPT SUB/SUPERS
Page breaks	AUTO, USER, SC
Page numbers	YES, ALT, RESTART
Paragraph indent	YES, SC
Programmable key	NO
Reformat after changes	AUTO
Repeat last command	NO
Right justify	YES, ON/OFF, PR
Right justify tabs	NO
Sort	YES, ALPH, NUM, OPT
Spelling check	NO
Storing formats	NO
Strikeover	YES, PR
Sub/superscript	YES, SC
Tabs	VAR
Underline	YES, SC
Variable pitch	YES, PR
Vertical lines	VAR
Widows and orphans	AUTO

FILES

File names	?
Renaming	?
Copy and delete files	YES
Copying disks	YES
Auto save	NO
Auto backup	YES
Verify	YES
Disk directory	NO

PRINTING

Continuous or sheet feed	BOTH
Multiple printers	YES
Queue	NO
Simultaneous	YES
Specific pages	YES
Typefaces	NO

HARDWARE

Internal memory	24K
Storage and drives	8″ SS, SD, 250KB DUAL DRIVES
Communications	TTY, ASYNCH, BSC, 66.5–9600 BPS
Keyboard	ATTACHED, WP KEYS

Video tube   GREEN, 96 OR 160 × 64
Printers   QUME, 40CPS, 2 PER SYSTEM

DOCUMENTATION AND TRAINING
Documentation   MANUAL, TRAINING KIT
Training   SELF-PACED

VENDOR: Exxon Office Systems
MODEL: 500 Series Information Processor
TYPE: Stand-alone, dedicated

ENTERING TEXT
Where   ANYWHERE
Word wrap   YES
Length of document   DISK
Orientation   DOC

EDITING TEXT
During entry   YES
Insert   YES, ON/OFF
Delete, copy, and move   YES, VAR

MOVEMENT WITHIN DOCUMENT
Cursor   W, L, S, P, PG, COL
Scroll   TOP/BOT
Search   FOR, IGNORE CASE, EX
Search and replace   FOR, IGNORE CASE, EX, GLOB, AUTO, SEMI-AUTO

SPECIAL FEATURES AND FORMATS
Alternate character sets   NO
Boilerplate   YES, GLOSSARY, P
Bold   YES, PR
Calculate   A, SUB, M, DIV, %
Centering   YES, SC
Center around tabs   YES
Change case   NO
Control characters   NO
Decimal tabs   YES
Dot commands   NO
Footnotes   YES, RENUMBER, REPOSITION
Forced page break   YES
Format line   YES
Generate table of contents   NO
Generate index   YES
Headers and footers   YES
Hyphenating   USER
Letter merge   YES
Lines per page   YES
Line spacing   VAR, PR

Margin release key	NO
Margin width	256
Multicolumn	
Nonprinting comments	YES
Onscreen	YES
Page breaks	AUTO, USER, SC
Page numbers	YES, ALT
Paragraph indent	?
Programmable key	NO
Reformat after changes	AUTO
Repeat last command	NO
Right justify	YES, SC
Right justify tabs	YES
Sort	YES, ALPH, NUM
Spelling check	YES, 50,000 W
Storing formats	YES
Strikeover	YES
Sub/superscript	YES, PR
Tabs	VAR
Underline	YES, PR
Variable pitch	NO
Vertical lines	99
Widows and orphans	USER

FILES

File names	FREE, 32 CH
Renaming	YES
Copy and delete files	YES
Copying disks	YES
Auto save	USER
Auto backup	NO
Verify	NO
Disk directory	YES, SIZE, NAME, TITLE, DATE

PRINTING

Continuous or sheet feed	BOTH
Multiple printers	?
Queue	YES
Simultaneous	YES
Specific pages	YES
Typefaces	YES

HARDWARE

Internal memory	64 OR 128K
Storage and drives	5¼", DS, DD, 600KB EA, DUAL-DISK DRIVES
Communications	ASYNCH, 110–9600 BPS
Keyboard	DETACHED, # PAD, WP KEYS
Video tube	WHITE ON BLACK, 80 × 24
Printers	35 CPS

DOCUMENTATION AND TRAINING

Documentation	?
Training	?

LIST OF WORD-PROCESSING PRODUCTS || 325

VENDOR: Fortune Systems Corporation
MODEL: F 32:16 W/FOR:Word Software
TYPE: Multiterminal (1–14 terminals), hybrid

ENTERING TEXT
Where	ANYWHERE
Word wrap	YES
Length of document	128 PG
Orientation	DOC

EDITING TEXT
During entry	YES, LIMITED
Insert	YES, ON/OFF
Delete, copy, and move	CH, W, L, S, P, PG, COL, VAR, DOC

MOVEMENT WITHIN DOCUMENT
Cursor	W, L, S, P, PG, COL
Scroll	L, P, PG, SC, TOP/BOT
Search	FOR, BACK, IGNORE CASE
Search and replace	FOR, BACK, IGNORE CASE, GLOB, AUTO, SEMI-AUTO

SPECIAL FEATURES AND FORMATS
Alternate character sets	YES
Boilerplate	YES, GLOSSARY, P
Bold	YES, SC
Calculate	A, SUB, M, DIV
Centering	YES, SC
Center around tabs	YES, SC
Change case	NO
Control characters	NO
Decimal tabs	YES
Dot commands	NO; CODES ARE INVISIBLE
Footnotes	NO
Forced page break	YES
Format line	YES
Generate table of contents	YES, OPT
Generate index	YES, OPT
Headers and footers	YES, UNLIMITED #L, DATE
Hyphenating	AUTO, USER
Letter merge	YES, OPT
Lines per page	YES
Line spacing	YES, PR
Margin release key	NO
Margin width	250
Multicolumn	YES, SC
Nonprinting comments	YES
Onscreen	YES
Page breaks	AUTO, USER, SC
Page numbers	YES
Paragraph indent	YES, SC

Programmable key	VIA GLOSSARY
Reformat after changes	AUTO
Repeat last command	NO
Right justify	YES, ON/OFF, PR
Right justify tabs	NO
Sort	YES, OPT
Spelling check	YES, 30,000 W STD; 100,000 W OPT
Storing formats	YES
Strikeover	YES, SC
Sub/superscript	YES, PR
Tabs	VAR
Underline	YES, SC
Variable pitch	YES, PR
Vertical lines	VAR
Widows and orphans	USER

FILES

File names	FREE, 8 CH
Renaming	YES
Copy and delete files	YES
Copying disks	YES
Auto save	YES
Auto backup	YES
Verify	?
Disk directory	YES, AUTHOR, OPERATOR, TITLE, DATE

PRINTING

Continuous or sheet feed	BOTH
Multiple printers	YES
Queue	YES
Simultaneous	YES
Specific pages	YES
Typefaces	YES

HARDWARE

Internal memory	128KB-1MB
Storage and drives	5¼" FLOPPIES, DS, DD, 800KB (UP TO 4); 5, 10, OR 20MB HARD DISKS (UP TO 4)
Communications	RS232—TO 19,200 BPS ETHERNET
Keyboard	DETACHED, # PAD, WP KEYS
Video tube	B/W, 80 × 24 OR COLOR BIT MAPPED
Printers	?

DOCUMENTATION AND TRAINING

Documentation	?
Training	NONE

NOTES   UNIX OPERATING SYSTEM

VENDOR: Hewlett-Packard
MODEL: HP Word on HP3000
TYPE: Multiterminal, hybrid

ENTERING TEXT
Where	ANYWHERE
Word wrap	YES
Length of document	DISK
Orientation	DOC

EDITING TEXT
During entry	YES
Insert	YES, ON/OFF
Delete, copy, and move	YES, CH, W, L, S, P, VAR, FROM DOC

MOVEMENT WITHIN DOCUMENT
Cursor	W, L, S, P, PG, 1ST PG, LAST PG, TOP/BOT
Scroll	LINE, W/REPEATING CAPABILITY
Search	FOR, BACK, IGNORE CASE, EX
Search and replace	FOR, BACK, IGNORE CASE, EX, AUTO, SEMI-AUTO

SPECIAL FEATURES AND FORMATS
Alternate character sets	YES, BOLD & ITALICS
Boilerplate	ONLY BY PAGE
Bold	YES, SC
Calculate	NO
Centering	YES, SC
Center around tabs	YES
Change case	NO
Control characters	NO
Decimal tabs	YES
Dot commands	NO
Footnotes	NO
Forced page break	YES
Format line	YES
Generate table of contents	NO
Generate index	NO
Headers and footers	YES, 10 LINES, DATE
Hyphenating	AUTO
Letter merge	YES, USING HPWORD + HP3000 DATABASE & QUERY
Lines per page	YES
Line spacing	1, 1½, 2, 3
Margin release key	NO
Margin width	132
Multicolumn	NO
Nonprinting comments	NO
Onscreen	YES, W/SOME EXCEPTIONS
Page breaks	AUTO, SC
Page numbers	YES

Paragraph indent	YES, SC
Programmable key	NO
Reformat after changes	AUTO
Repeat last command	NO
Right justify	YES, SC
Right justify tabs	YES
Sort	USING HP 3000 QUERY FACILITY
Spelling check	NO
Storing formats	BY SAVING AS SEP DOCUMENTS
Strikeover	NO
Sub/superscript	YES, PR
Tabs	VAR
Underline	YES, SC
Variable pitch	YES, PR
Vertical lines	VAR
Widows and orphans	AUTO

FILES

File names	FREE, 8 CH
Renaming	YES
Copy and delete files	YES
Copying disks	YES, W/ HP3000 FACILITIES
Auto save	YES
Auto backup	NO
Verify	?
Disk directory	?

PRINTING

Continuous or sheet feed	BOTH
Multiple printers	YES
Queue	YES
Simultaneous	YES
Specific pages	YES
Typefaces	YES

HARDWARE

Internal memory	DEPENDS ON HP3000; FROM 258K TO 8 MB
Storage and drives	FROM 20 MB THROUGH 404MB
Communications	ASYNCH, UP TO 9600 BAUD
Keyboard	DETACHED, #PAD FOR DP ONLY, SYNTACTIC KEYS
Video tube	WHITE ON BLACK, 132 × 21, # TUBES/SYSTEM DEPENDS ON PROCESSOR; GREEN VIDEO AVAILABLE
Printers	LQP, LINE PRINTERS TO 1000 LPM, AND LASER PRINTER AT 45 PAGES/MINUTE

DOCUMENTATION AND TRAINING

Documentation	QUICK REFERENCE GUIDE AND REFERENCE GUIDE
Training	SELF-PACED TRAINING PACKAGE; 4-DAY TRAINING; MORE TIME AVAILABLE

NOTES   FUNCTION KEYS LABELED ON BOTTOM LINE OF SCREEN

LIST OF WORD-PROCESSING PRODUCTS ‖ 329

VENDOR: Honeywell
MODEL: Infowriter
TYPE: Stand-alone or multiterminal, dedicated

ENTERING TEXT
Where	ANYWHERE
Word wrap	YES
Length of document	DISK OR 999 PG
Orientation	PG

EDITING TEXT
During entry	YES
Insert	YES, ON/OFF
Delete, copy, and move	YES, CH, W, S, DOC

MOVEMENT WITHIN DOCUMENT
Cursor	PG, TOP/BOT, LEFT/RIGHT
Scroll	L, P, PG, SC, TOP/BOT, ARROW KEYS & HOME
Search	FOR, IGNORE CASE
Search and replace	FOR, IGNORE CASE, GLOB, AUTO, SEMI-AUTO

SPECIAL FEATURES AND FORMATS
Alternate character sets	YES
Boilerplate	YES, GLOSSARY, P
Bold	YES, SC
Calculate	A, SUB, M, DIV, %
Centering	YES, SC
Center around tabs	YES
Change case	NO
Control characters	NO
Decimal tabs	YES
Dot commands	NO
Footnotes	YES, RENUMBER
Forced page break	YES
Format line	YES
Generate table of contents	YES, USER-PROGRAMMABLE
Generate index	YES, USER-PROGRAMMABLE
Headers and footers	YES, UNLIMITED #L, DATE, LEFT ONLY
Hyphenating	USER
Letter merge	YES
Lines per page	YES
Line spacing	YES, PR
Margin release key	YES
Margin width	160
Multicolumn	YES, SC
Nonprinting comments	YES
Onscreen	NO
Page breaks	AUTO, USER, SC
Page numbers	YES, RESTART
Paragraph indent	YES, SC
Programmable key	YES

Reformat after changes — AUTO
Repeat last command — YES, IF COMMANDS IN GLOSSARY
Right justify — YES, PR
Right justify tabs — NO
Sort — YES, ALPH, NUM
Spelling check — NO
Storing formats — YES
Strikeover — YES, SC
Sub/superscript — YES, PR
Tabs — VAR
Underline — YES, SC
Variable pitch — YES, PR
Vertical lines — VAR
Widows and orphans — AUTO

FILES
File names — FREE, 9 CH
Renaming — YES
Copy and delete files — YES
Copying disks — YES
Auto save — YES
Auto backup — NO
Verify — YES
Disk directory — ORDER, NAME, TITLE, DATE

PRINTING
Continuous or sheet feed — BOTH
Multiple printers — NO
Queue — YES
Simultaneous — YES
Specific pages — YES
Typefaces — YES

HARDWARE
Internal memory — 128K
Storage and drives — 5¼" DS, DD
Communications — HONEYWELL PVE/VIP IBM 3270, VIP 7700R, TO 9600 BPS
Keyboard — DETACHED, WP KEYS
Video tube — GREEN ON BLACK, 80 × 24
Printers — LQP—35 OR 55 CPS, OR LINE PRINTER, ONE PER SYSTEM, CAN BE SHARED

DOCUMENTATION AND TRAINING
Documentation — SET-UP GUIDES, SELF-INSTRUCTION, USER REF GUIDE, QUICK REFERENCE, OFFICE-PLANNING GUIDE
Training — SELF-INSTRUCTION DOCUMENTATION; TOLL-FREE NUMBER; COURSES OFFERED

VENDOR: IBM Corporation
MODEL: Displaywriter
TYPE: Stand-alone, dedicated

ENTERING TEXT
  Where   ANYWHERE
  Word wrap   YES, ON/OFF
  Length of document   DISK
  Orientation   DOC OR PG

EDITING TEXT
  During entry   YES
  Insert   YES, ON/OFF
  Delete, copy, or move   YES, VAR, DOC—FULL PG ONLY

MOVEMENT WITHIN DOCUMENT
  Cursor   W, L, S, P, PG, COL
  Scroll   L, P, SC, PG
  Search   FOR, IGNORE CASE, EX
  Search and replace   FOR, EX, GLOB, AUTO, SEMI-AUTO UP TO 3 REPLACEMENTS AT ONE TIME

SPECIAL FEATURES AND FORMATS
  Alternate character sets   YES
  Boilerplate   YES, GLOSSARY, P
  Bold   NO
  Calculate   A, SUB, M, DIV, %, AVERAGE
  Centering   YES, SC
  Center around tabs   YES
  Change case   NO
  Control characters   YES, MOST
  Decimal tabs   YES
  Dot commands   NO
  Footnotes   YES, RENUMBER, REPOSITION (TEXTPACK 6)
  Forced page break   YES
  Format line   YES
  Generate table of contents   NO
  Generate index   NO
  Headers and footers   YES, 256 CH, DATE
  Hyphenating   AUTO, USER
  Letter merge   YES
  Lines per page   YES
  Line spacing   1, 1½, 2, 3, OTHER; SC W/FULL-PAGE SCREEN
  Margin release key   NO
  Margin width   450
  Multicolumn   YES, SC
  Nonprinting comments   NO
  Onscreen   YES
  Page breaks   AUTO, SC
  Page numbers   YES, ALT, RESTART

Paragraph indent	YES, SC
Programmable key	YES
Reformat after changes	AUTO
Repeat last command	YES
Right justify	ON/OFF, PR
Right justify tabs	YES
Sort	YES, ALPH, NUM, W/TEXTPACK 4 OR 6
Spelling check	YES, 11 LANGUAGE DICTIONARIES
Storing formats	YES
Strikeover	YES, SC
Sub/superscript	YES, SC
Tabs	VAR
Underline	YES, SC
Variable pitch	YES, PR
Vertical lines	VAR
Widows and orphans	AUTO

FILES

File names	FREE, 44 CH
Renaming	YES
Copy and delete files	YES
Copying disks	YES
Auto save	YES, USER
Auto backup	NO
Verify	YES
Disk directory	YES, S TITLE

PRINTING

Continuous or sheet feed	BOTH
Multiple printers	YES, VIA COMMUNICATIONS
Queue	YES
Simultaneous	YES
Specific pages	YES
Typefaces	YES

HARDWARE

Internal memory	128K–320K
Storage and drives	8″ SD, 284K OR DD, 985K, 2 FLOPPY DRIVES
Communications	ASYNCHRONOUS, TTY, 2741, CMC 110–1200 BPS; BINARY SYNCHRONOUS 2770, 2780, 3780, 600–4800 BPS; OTHERS
Keyboard	DETACHED, WP KEYS
Video tube	GREEN ON GRAY, 80 × 25 OR 100 × 66
Printers	15.5 CPS ELEMENT PRINTER, 40 OR 60 CPS PRINT WHEEL PRINTER

DOCUMENTATION AND TRAINING

Documentation	SELF-PACED TRAINING, CUSTOMER SET-UP AND PROBLEM DETERMINATION MANUALS
Training	SELF-PACED WITH PRE- AND POST-TRAINING TEXT SEMINARS

VENDOR: IBM Corporation
MODEL: 5520 Information System
TYPE: Multiterminal, dedicated

ENTERING TEXT
Where	ANYWHERE
Word wrap	YES, ON/OFF
Length of document	DISK
Orientation	PG

EDITING TEXT
During entry	YES
Insert	YES
Delete, copy, and move	YES, COL, VAR, DOC

MOVEMENT WITHIN DOCUMENT
Cursor	W, L, P, PG
Scroll	L, P, PG, SC
Search	FOR, IGNORE, EX
Search and replace	FOR, IGNORE, EX, GLOB, AUTO, SEMI-AUTO

SPECIAL FEATURES AND FORMATS
Alternate character sets	YES
Boilerplate	YES, GLOSSARY, P
Bold	YES, PR
Calculate	A, SUB, M, DIV, %
Centering	YES, SC
Center around tabs	YES
Change case	NO
Control characters	NO
Decimal tabs	YES
Dot commands	NO
Footnotes	NO
Forced page break	YES
Format line	YES
Generate table of contents	NO
Generate index	NO
Headers and footers	YES, VAR #L, DATE
Hyphenating	USER
Letter merge	YES
Lines per page	YES
Line spacing	YES, PR
Margin release key	YES
Margin width	172
Multicolumn	NO
Nonprinting comments	NO
Onscreen	NO
Page breaks	AUTO, SC
Page numbers	YES, ALT, RESTART

Paragraph indent	YES, SC
Programmable key	NO
Reformat after changes	AUTO
Repeat last command	YES, WITH SELECTED FUNCTIONS
Right justify	YES, ON/OFF, PR
Right justify tabs	YES
Sort	YES, ALPH, NUM
Spelling check	NO
Storing formats	YES
Strikeover	YES, SC
Sub/superscript	YES, PR
Tabs	5, VAR
Underline	YES, SC
Variable pitch	YES, PR
Vertical lines	VARIABLE, TO 131 LINES
Widows and orphans	AUTO

FILES

File names	FREE, 30 CH
Renaming	YES
Copy and delete files	BOTH
Copying disks	NO
Auto save	YES, ON PAGE BASIS
Auto backup	OPTIONAL FOR SELECTED FUNCTIONS
Verify	YES
Disk directory	YES, NAME, TITLE, DATE, SIZE

PRINTING

Continuous or sheet feed	BOTH
Multiple printers	YES
Queue	YES
Simultaneous	YES
Specific pages	YES
Typefaces	YES

HARDWARE

Internal memory	?
Storage and drives	FIXED HARD DISKS: 29MB, 65MB, 130 MB; DISKETTES: 1MB, DS, DD; UP TO 23 DISKETTES MAY BE LOADED AT ONE TIME
Communications	2770 BISYNCH, SDLC, 1200–9600 BPS
Keyboard	DETACHED, WPKEYS
Video tube	LIGHT GREEN ON DARK GREEN 80 × 24, UP TO 18 PER SYSTEM
Printers	5258 INKJET, 5219 IMPACT, 6670 LASER, 60–92CPS; 12 MAX

DOCUMENTATION AND TRAINING

Documentation	PROBLEMS DETERMINATION, OPERATIONAL MAINTENANCE, EDUCATIONAL, LIBRARY
Training	CLASSROOM AND/OR PROGRAMMED INSTRUCTIONS AVAILABLE FOR A FEE

VENDOR: Intelligent Systems Corporation
MODEL: 8364 W/Color-Coded Word Processing
TYPE: Stand-alone, hybrid

ENTERING TEXT
Where	BOTTOM
Word wrap	YES
Length of document	DISK
Orientation	DOC

EDITING TEXT
During entry	YES
Insert	YES, ALWAYS ON
Delete, copy, and move	YES, CH, W, L, S, P, PG, DOC

MOVEMENT WITHIN DOCUMENT
Cursor	W, L, S, P, PG
Scroll	L, P, PG, SC, TOP/BOT
Search	FOR, EX
Search and replace	FOR, EX, GLOB, AUTO, SEMI-AUTO

SPECIAL FEATURES AND FORMATS
Alternate character sets	NO
Boilerplate	YES, GLOSSARY, P
Bold	YES, SC
Calculate	A, SUB, M, DIV, %
Centering	YES, SC
Center around tabs	YES
Change case	YES
Control characters	NO
Decimal tabs	YES
Dot commands	NO
Footnotes	NO
Forced page break	YES
Format line	YES
Generate table of contents	NO
Generate index	NO
Headers and footers	YES, UNLIMITED #L
Hyphenating	NO
Letter merge	YES
Lines per page	YES
Line spacing	YES, PR
Margin release key	YES
Margin width	80
Multicolumn	NO
Nonprinting comments	NO
Onscreen	YES
Page breaks	AUTO, USER, SC
Page numbers	YES, RESTART
Paragraph indent	YES, SC

Programmable key	NO
Reformat after changes	AUTO
Repeat last command	NO
Right justify	YES, PR
Right justify tabs	NO
Sort	NO
Spelling check	YES, OPT
Storing formats	YES
Strikeover	NO
Sub/superscript	YES, PR
Tabs	VAR
Underline	YES, SC
Variable pitch	NO
Vertical lines	VAR
Widows and orphans	USER

FILES

File names	26 CH
Renaming	YES
Copy and delete files	YES
Copying disks	YES
Auto save	USER
Auto backup	YES
Verify	YES
Disk directory	YES, TITLE

PRINTING

Continuous or sheet feed	BOTH
Multiple printers	NO
Queue	YES, UP TO 20 DOC
Simultaneous	YES
Specific pages	YES
Typefaces	NO

HARDWARE

Internal memory	?
Storage and drives	SS OR DS, DD—1MG DUAL FLOPPY DRIVES
Communications	RS 232 110–9600 BPS
Keyboard	ATTACHED # PAD WP KEYS
Video tube	8 COLORS, 80 × 48, 1 TUBE/SYSTEM
Printers	NEC SPINWRITER, 55 CPS, BIDIRECTIONAL; 1 PER SYSTEM

DOCUMENTATION AND TRAINING

Documentation	MANUAL
Training	TRAINING IS OPTIONAL

LIST OF WORD-PROCESSING PRODUCTS || 337

VENDOR: Itek Graphic Systems
MODEL: Quadritek
TYPE: Phototypesetting

ENTERING TEXT
  Where   ANYWHERE
  Word wrap   YES
  Length of document   DISK
  Orientation   PG
EDITING TEXT
  During entry   NO
  Insert   YES
  Delete, copy, and move   YES
MOVEMENT WITHIN DOCUMENT
  Cursor   PG
  Scroll   L, P, PG, SC, TOP/BOT
  Search   FOR, EX
  Search and replace   FOR, EX, GLOB, AUTO
SPECIAL FEATURES AND FORMATS
  Alternate character
    sets   YES
  Boilerplate   YES, GLOSSARY, P
  Bold   YES, PR
  Calculate   NO
  Centering   YES, SC
  Center around tabs   NO
  Change case   NO
  Control characters   MOST
  Decimal tabs   YES
  Dot commands   YES
  Footnotes   YES, REPOSITION
  Forced page break   YES
  Format line   YES
  Generate table of con-
    tents   NO
  Generate index   NO
  Headers and footers   YES
  Hyphenating   AUTO, USER
  Letter merge   YES, OPT
  Lines per page   YES
  Line spacing   VARIABLE, SC
  Margin release key   YES
  Margin width   65
  Multicolumn   YES, SC
  Nonprinting comments   YES
  Onscreen   YES
  Page breaks   AUTO, SC
  Page numbers   YES, ALT
  Paragraph indent   YES, SC
  Programmable key   NO

Reformat after changes	AUTO
Repeat last command	YES
Right justify	YES
Right justify tabs	YES
Sort	YES, OPT
Spelling check	YES, 20,000 W OPT
Storing formats	YES
Strikeover	YES, SC
Sub/superscript	YES, SC
Tabs	VAR
Underline	YES, SC
Variable pitch	YES, SC
Vertical lines	?
Widows and orphans	USER

FILES
File names	FREE, 8 CH
Renaming	YES
Copy and delete files	YES
Copying disks	YES
Auto save	YES, USER
Auto backup	YES
Verify	YES
Disk directory	YES, ORDER

PRINTING
Continuous or sheet feed	BOTH
Multiple printers	NO
Queue	NO
Simultaneous	YES
Specific pages	YES
Typefaces	YES

HARDWARE
Internal memory	96K
Storage and drives	8″ SS, SD, 244KB EA, 1–4 DRIVES
Communications	DATA COMM INTERFACE, ASCII, SERIAL, TTY, RS232, 300–1200 BPS
Keyboard	DETACHED, WP KEYS
Video tube	GREEN, 65 × 16
Printers	QUADPRINT

DOCUMENTATION AND TRAINING
Documentation	?
Training	21 HOURS, NO CHARGE

NOTES
MULTIPLE-APPLICATION PHOTOTYPESETTING EQUIPMENT

VENDOR: Lanier
MODEL: EZ-1
TYPE: Stand-alone, dedicated

ENTERING TEXT
Where	ANYWHERE
Word wrap	YES
Length of document	DISK
Orientation	DOC

EDITING TEXT
During entry	YES
Insert	YES, ALWAYS ON
Delete, copy, and move	YES, CH, W, L, S, P, PG, VAR, DOC

MOVEMENT WITHIN DOCUMENT
Cursor	W, L, S
Scroll	L, P, PG, SC, TOP/BOT
Search	FOR, IGNORE CASE, EX
Search and replace	FOR, IGNORE CASE, EX, GLOB, AUTO, SEMI-AUTO

SPECIAL FEATURES AND FORMATS
Alternate character sets	YES
Boilerplate	YES, GLOSSARY, P
Bold	YES, PR
Calculate	YES, OPT
Centering	YES, SC
Center around tabs	NO
Change case	YES
Control characters	NO
Decimal tabs	YES
Dot commands	NO
Footnotes	YES, REPOSITION
Forced page break	YES
Format line	YES
Generate table of contents	YES
Generate index	YES
Headers and footers	YES, UNLIMITED #L
Hyphenating	USER
Letter merge	YES
Lines per page	YES
Line spacing	VARIABLE, PR
Margin release key	NO
Margin width	150
Multicolumn	YES, SC
Nonprinting comments	YES
Onscreen	YES, EXCEPT PITCH AND SPACING
Page breaks	AUTO, SC
Page numbers	YES, ALT
Paragraph indent	YES, VIA APPLICATION

Programmable key	YES
Reformat after changes	AUTO
Repeat last command	NO
Right justify	YES, PR
Right justify tabs	YES
Sort	YES, ALPH, NUM, OPT
Spelling check	YES, 88,000 W, OPT
Storing formats	YES
Strikeover	NO
Sub/superscript	YES, SC
Tabs	VARIABLE
Underline	YES, SC
Variable pitch	YES, PR
Vertical lines	UNLIMITED
Widows and orphans	YES, AUTO

FILES

File names	FREE, 24 CH
Renaming	YES
Copy and delete files	YES
Copying disks	YES
Auto save	USER
Auto backup	USER
Verify	NO
Disk directory	YES, SIZE, TITLE

PRINTING

Continuous or sheet feed	BOTH
Multiple printers	YES (SWITCH)
Queue	VIA APPLICATION
Simultaneous	YES
Specific pages	YES
Typefaces	YES

HARDWARE

Internal memory	128–224K
Storage and drives	5¼" 140K, 5¼" 600K, WINCHESTER—5 MG FLOPPY OR RIGID
Communications	ASCII OR 3780 VARIABLE BAUD RATE
Keyboard	DETACHED, # PAD, WP KEYS
Video tube	GREEN ON CHARCOAL, 80 × 24
Printers	VARIOUS PRINTERS, FROM 20–40 CPS; 4 ATTACHED VIA PRINT SWITCH

DOCUMENTATION AND TRAINING

Documentation	OPERATORS MANUAL AND HANDBOOK
Training	2-DAY AUDIO TRAINING COURSE W/FIELD FOLLOW-UP

LIST OF WORD-PROCESSING PRODUCTS ∥ 341

VENDOR: Lanier
MODEL: No Problem
TYPE: Stand-alone, dedicated

ENTERING TEXT
  Where   ANYWHERE
  Word wrap   YES
  Length of document   DISK
  Orientation   PG

EDITING TEXT
  During entry   YES
  Insert   YES, ON/OFF
  Delete, copy, and move   YES, CH, W, L, S, P, PG, COL, VAR, DOC

MOVEMENT WITHIN DOCUMENT
  Cursor   TO MARGINS, TOP/BOT OF PG
  Scroll   L, P, PG, SC, TOP/BOT
  Search   FOR, IGNORE CASE, EX
  Search and replace   FOR, IGNORE CASE, EX, GLOB, AUTO, SEMI-AUTO

SPECIAL FEATURES AND FORMATS
  Alternate character sets   YES
  Boilerplate   YES
  Bold   YES, PR
  Calculate   YES
  Centering   YES, SC
  Center around tabs   YES
  Change case   NO
  Control characters   SOME
  Decimal tabs   YES
  Dot commands   NO
  Footnotes   WITH SUPER NO-PROBLEM
  Forced page break   YES
  Format line   YES
  Generate table of contents   YES
  Generate index   WITH SUPER NO-PROBLEM
  Headers and footers   YES, DATE
  Hyphenating   USER
  Letter merge   YES, OPT
  Lines per page   YES
  Line spacing   VARIABLE, PR
  Margin release key   YES
  Margin width   254
  Multicolumn   YES, SC
  Nonprinting comments   YES
  Onscreen   YES
  Page breaks   AUTO
  Page numbers   YES, ALT, RESTART
  Paragraph indent   YES, SC

Programmable key	YES
Reformat after changes	AUTO
Repeat last command	NO
Right justify	YES, PR
Right justify tabs	YES
Sort	YES, ALPH, NUM, OPT
Spelling check	NO
Storing formats	YES
Strikeover	YES, PR
Sub/superscript	YES, PR
Tabs	VAR
Underline	YES, SC
Variable pitch	YES, PR
Vertical lines	99
Widows and orphans	AUTO

FILES

File names	ALPH OR NUM, 12 CH
Renaming	YES
Copy and delete files	YES
Copying disks	YES
Auto save	NO
Auto backup	NO
Verify	YES
Disk directory	YES

PRINTING

Continuous or sheet feed	BOTH
Multiple printers	NO
Queue	YES
Simultaneous	YES
Specific pages	YES
Typefaces	YES

HARDWARE

Internal memory	N/A
Storage and drives	5¼" SS, SD, 70KB MINI-FLOPPY DRIVE
Communications	SYNCH, ASYNCH, 24–4800 BPS
Keyboard	ATTACHED, # PAD, WP KEYS
Video tube	GREEN ON GREEN, 80 × 26
Printers	45CPS CHARACTER PRINTER, 1 OR 2 PER SYSTEM

DOCUMENTATION AND TRAINING

Documentation	OPERATORS MANUAL
Training	FULL

LIST OF WORD-PROCESSING PRODUCTS || 343

VENDOR: Lexor Corporation
MODEL: Lexoritor
TYPE: Stand-alone, dedicated

ENTERING TEXT
  Where   ANYWHERE
  Word wrap   YES
  Length of document   DISK
  Orientation   DOC

EDITING TEXT
  During entry   YES
  Insert   YES, ON/OFF
  Delete, copy, and move   YES, UP TO 45,000 CH

MOVEMENT WITHIN DOCUMENT
  Cursor   ANYWHERE
  Scroll   TOP/BOT, SC, L, PG
  Search   FOR, EX, WILD CARDS AVAILABLE
  Search and replace   FOR, EX, WILD CARDS, GLOB, AUTO

SPECIAL FEATURES AND FORMATS
  Alternate character
    sets   YES
  Boilerplate   YES, GLOSSARY, P
  Bold   YES, PR
  Calculate   A, SUB, M, DIV, %, TRIG, AVG, OPT
  Centering   YES, PR
  Center around tabs   NO
  Change case   NO
  Control characters   ALL
  Decimal tabs   YES
  Dot commands   ALL
  Footnotes   NO
  Forced page break   YES
  Format line   YES, ON/OFF
  Generate table of con-
    tents   NO
  Generate index   NO
  Headers and footers   HEADERS, 1 LINE
  Hyphenating   AUTO, 100% ACCURATE
  Letter merge   YES, OPT
  Lines per page   YES
  Line spacing   YES, PR
  Margin release key   YES
  Margin width   255
  Multicolumn   YES, PR
  Nonprinting comments   YES
  Onscreen   OPT
  Page breaks   AUTO, SC, PR
  Page numbers   YES, RESTART; OPT: RENUMBER
  Paragraph indent   YES, PR
  Programmable key   NO

Reformat after changes	AUTO
Repeat last command	REPEAT ACTION REQUESTED AS PART OF COMMAND
Right justify	YES, PR
Right justify tabs	OPT
Sort	ALPH, NUM, OPT
Spelling check	YES, 25,000 W, OPT
Storing formats	YES
Strikeover	YES, PR
Sub/superscript	YES, PR
Tabs	VAR
Underline	YES, PR (SC AS SYMBOL ONLY)
Variable pitch	YES, PR
Vertical lines	VARIABLE
Widows and orphans	USER

FILES

File names	OPSYS, 8 CH
Renaming	YES
Copy and delete files	YES
Copying disks	YES
Auto save	USER
Auto backup	ORIGINAL ALWAYS PROTECTED
Verify	AUTO
Disk directory	YES, ORDER, SIZE, NAME

PRINTING

Continuous or sheet feed	BOTH
Multiple printers	YES
Queue	YES
Simultaneous	YES
Specific pages	YES
Typefaces	YES

HARDWARE

Internal memory	64K
Storage and drives	5¼″ SS OR DS, DD, 160/320K 2 DRIVES
Communications	ASYNCH, ASCII, 150–4800 BAUD; OPT
Keyboard	DETACHED, #PAD, WP KEYS
Video tube	BLACK ON WHITE OR GREEN; WHITE OR GREEN ON BLACK; 80 × 24; UP TO 4 PER SYSTEM
Printers	LQP'S: 20, 35, 55 CPS AVAILABLE; MAXIMUM OF 4

DOCUMENTATION AND TRAINING

Documentation	TRAINING/REFERENCE MANUAL
Training	ON SITE

VENDOR: Megadata Corporation
MODEL: Series 8000
TYPE: Stand-alone

ENTERING TEXT
Where	BOTTOM
Word wrap	YES
Length of document	DISK
Orientation	DOC

ENTERING TEXT
During entry	YES
Insert	YES, ALWAYS ON
Delete, copy, and move	YES, VAR, (UP TO 1 SCREEN), DOC

MOVEMENT WITHIN DOCUMENT
Cursor	FORWARD ONLY: W, S, P; BACKWARD, CH ONLY
Scroll	L, P
Search	FOR, EX
Search and replace	FOR, EX, GLOB, AUTO, SEMI-AUTO

SPECIAL FEATURES AND FORMATS
Alternate character sets	YES
Boilerplate	YES, GLOSSARY, P
Bold	YES
Calculate	NO
Centering	YES, SC
Center around tabs	NO
Change case	NO
Control characters	NO
Decimal tabs	YES
Dot commands	NO
Footnotes	YES
Forced page break	YES
Format line	YES
Generate table of contents	NO
Generate index	NO
Headers and footers	YES
Hyphenating	HOT ZONE
Letter merge	YES
Lines per page	YES
Line spacing	½, 1, 1½, 2, 3, PR
Margin release key	NO
Margin width	200
Multicolumn	YES, SC
Nonprinting comments	NO
Onscreen	NO
Page breaks	AUTO & USER
Page numbers	YES

Paragraph indent	YES, SC
Programmable key	NO
Reformat after changes	AUTO
Repeat last command	NO
Right justify	YES, PR
Right justify tabs	NO
Sort	NO
Spelling check	NO
Storing formats	NO
Strikeover	YES, SC
Sub/superscript	YES, PR
Tabs	5, VAR
Underline	YES
Variable pitch	YES, 10, 12, 15
Vertical lines	VARIABLE
Widows and orphans	AUTO

FILES

File names	8CH
Renaming	YES
Copy and delete files	YES
Copying disks	YES
Auto save	YES, USER
Auto backup	NO
Verify	NO
Disk directory	YES, SIZE, NAME, TITLE, DATE, TIME

PRINTING

Continuous or sheet feed	BOTH
Multiple printers	NO
Queue	YES
Simultaneous	YES
Specific pages	STARTING & ENDING PAGES
Typefaces	YES

HARDWARE

Internal memory	64K-256K
Storage and drives	5¼″ OR 8″ FLOPPIES; SS OR DS, SD OR DD DUAL 5¼″ OR 8″ DRIVES, 5¼″ WINCHESTER
Communications	83B STANDARD. ALL OTHERS OPTIONAL. SOFTWARE HOURS = COST
Keyboard	DETACHED, #PAD, WP KEYS
Video tube	LIGHT GREEN ON DARK GREEN; 80 × 24 4 TERMINALS TO ONE PRINTER
Printers	NEC 5500 (55 CPS); EXTEL (30 CPS); TWO PRINTERS TO ONE TERMINAL

DOCUMENTATION AND TRAINING

Documentation	WP INSTRUCTION MANUAL
Training	ONE OPERATOR TRAINED FREE OF CHARGE

NOTES

MEGADATA CORP. IS AN APPLICATION-ORIENTED TERMINAL

LIST OF WORD-PROCESSING PRODUCTS ‖ 347

MANUFACTURER SPECIALIZING IN THE UNUSUAL; VERY FLEXIBILE AS FAR AS PROTOCOLS, FUNCTIONS, AND CONFIGURATIONS

VENDOR: Microdata Corporation
MODEL: Wordmate for the Reality and Sequel Computers
TYPE: Multiterminal

ENTERING TEXT
Where	ANYWHERE
Word wrap	YES
Length of document	DISK
Orientation	DOC

EDITING TEXT
During entry	YES
Insert	YES, ALWAYS ON
Delete, copy, and move	YES, CH, W, L, S, PG, VAR, DOC

MOVEMENT WITHIN DOCUMENT
Cursor	W, CH, L, S, PG, TOP/BOT
Scroll	L, P, PG, TOP/BOT
Search	FOR, EX
Search and replace	FOR, EX, IGNORE CASE, GLOB, AUTO, SEMI-AUTO

SPECIAL FEATURES AND FORMATS
Alternate character sets	YES
Boilerplate	YES, P
Bold	YES
Calculate	NO
Centering	YES, SC
Center around tabs	YES
Change case	YES
Control characters	ONLY FOR UNDERLINING
Decimal tabs	YES
Dot commands	NO
Footnotes	NO
Forced page break	YES
Format line	YES, ON/OFF
Generate table of contents	NO
Generate index	NO
Headers and footers	YES, DATE
Hyphenating	USER
Letter merge	YES
Lines per page	YES
Line spacing	YES, 1, 2, 3, 4
Margin release key	NO

Margin width	80
Multicolumn	NO
Nonprinting comments	YES
Onscreen	YES, THROUGH "OUTPUT" COMMAND
Page breaks	AUTO
Page numbers	YES, RESTART
Paragraph indent	YES, SC
Programmable key	NO
Reformat after changes	YES, AUTO
Repeat last command	NO
Right justify	YES, ON/OFF, SC
Right justify tabs	YES
Sort	YES
Spelling check	NO
Storing formats	YES
Strikeover	NO
Sub/superscript	YES, PR
Tabs	VAR
Underline	YES, PR
Variable pitch	YES, PR
Vertical lines	VAR
Widows and orphans	AUTO

FILES

File names	FREE, 15 CH
Renaming	YES
Copy and delete files	YES
Copying disks	NO
Auto save	USER
Auto backup	VIA "RESTORE"
Verify	YES
Disk directory	YES, ORDER, TITLE, AUTHOR, TYPIST, DATE

PRINTING

Continuous or sheet feed	BOTH
Multiple printers	YES
Queue	YES
Simultaneous	YES
Specific pages	YES
Typefaces	YES

HARDWARE

Internal memory	64K–1MB
Storage and drives	TAPE DRIVES
Communications	RS-232C ASYNCH, FULL OR HALF DUPLEX. 300–9600 BPS
Keyboard	DETACHED, #PAD, WP KEYS
Video tube	WHITE ON BLACK OR BLACK ON WHITE 80 × 24; MANY TUBES/SYSTEM
Printers	NEC 3515 (33CPS) OR LINE PRINTER; UP TO 10 PRINTERS/SYSTEM

LIST OF WORD-PROCESSING PRODUCTS ‖ 349

DOCUMENTATION AND TRAINING
  Documentation   GENERAL DESCRIPTION MANUAL, OPERATOR'S MANUAL, TECHNICAL MANUAL
  Training   ONE-DAY CLASSES, SELF-TEACH

VENDOR: Mohawk Data Sciences
MODEL: Series 21
TYPE: Multiterminal, hybrid

ENTERING TEXT
  Where   ANYWHERE
  Word wrap   YES
  Length of document   DISK
  Orientation   DOC

EDITING TEXT
  During entry   YES
  Insert   YES, ON/OFF
  Delete, copy, and move YES, W, L, S, P, COL, DOC

MOVEMENT WITHIN DOCUMENT
  Cursor   TAB TO TAB, L
  Scroll   YES, SET FROM 1 TO 99 LINES & CHANGEABLE
  Search   FOR, BACK, EX
  Search and replace   FOR, BACK, EX, GLOB, AUTO

SPECIAL FEATURES AND FORMATS
  Alternate character sets NO
  Boilerplate   YES, GLOSSARY, P
  Bold   NO
  Calculate   A, SUB, M, DIV, %; PROGRAMMABLE MATH
  Centering   YES, SC
  Center around tabs   NO
  Change case   NO
  Control characters   NO
  Decimal tabs   YES
  Dot commands   NO
  Footnotes   NO
  Forced page break   YES
  Format line   YES
  Generate table of contents NO
  Generate index   NO
  Headers and footers   YES, HEADERS—9 L, FOOTERS—1 L, DATE
  Hyphenating   NO
  Letter merge   YES
  Lines per page   YES
  Line spacing   1, 2, 3, PR

Margin release key	NO
Margin width	132
Multicolumn	NO
Nonprinting comments	YES
Onscreen	YES, EXCEPT 2 & 3 SPACING
Page breaks	USER
Page numbers	YES, RESTART
Paragraph indent	NO
Programmable key	NO
Reformat after changes	USER
Repeat last command	NO
Right justify	YES, SC
Right justify tabs	NO
Sort	THROUGH SERIES 21 UTILITY, "SORTM"
Spelling check	NO
Storing formats	YES
Strikeover	DEPENDENT ON PRINTER
Sub/superscript	NO
Tabs	VAR
Underline	YES, PR
Variable pitch	NO
Vertical lines	UP TO 66
Widows and orphans	USER—"COMMAND GROUP"

FILES

File names	FREE
Renaming	YES
Copy and delete files	YES
Copying disks	YES
Auto save	NO
Auto backup	NO
Verify	NO
Disk directory	YES; SIZE, "KEYWORDS"

PRINTING

Continuous or sheet feed	BOTH
Multiple printers	YES
Queue	YES
Simultaneous	YES
Specific pages	NO, BUT FROM SCREEN AT ANY POINT
Typefaces	NO

HARDWARE

Internal memory	96K FOR 1 CRT, 128 FOR 2, 160 FOR 3 OR 4
Storage and drives	8″ SS FLOPPIES, 242K EA; 4 DRIVES/SYSTEM 5, 19, 20 MG INTEGRATED DISKS, 26–156MB FIXED/REMOVABLE
Communications	3780
Keyboard	ATTACHED, SPECIAL # PAD
Video tube	GREEN, 80 × 24
Printers	2141 PRINTER, 45CPS, 5 MAX ON SYSTEM

LIST OF WORD-PROCESSING PRODUCTS ∥ 351

DOCUMENTATION AND TRAINING
    Documentation   WORD 21 SIMPLIFIED OPERATOR'S GUIDE, OPERATOR'S GUIDE, POCKET GUIDE
    Training   1 OPERATOR FREE; ADDITIONAL OPERATORS $60/HR; PACKAGE FOR INTERNAL TRAINING

VENDOR: Monroe Systems for Business
MODEL: OC8820 with Superword
TYPE: Stand-alone, small-business system, hybrid

ENTERING TEXT	
Where	ANYWHERE
Word wrap	YES, ON/OFF
Length of document	DISK
Orientation	DOC
EDITING TEXT	
During entry	YES
Insert	YES, ON/OFF
Delete, copy, and move	YES, VAR, DOC
MOVEMENT WITHIN DOCUMENT	
Cursor	L, CH
Scroll	L, SC, TOP/BOT
Search	FOR, BACK, IGNORE CASE, EX
Search and replace	FOR, BACK, IGNORE CASE, EX, GLOB, AUTO, SEMI-AUTO
SPECIAL FEATURES AND FORMATS	
Alternate character sets	YES
Boilerplate	YES, BY STORING AS SEPARATE DOCUMENT
Bold	YES, PR
Calculate	NO
Centering	YES, SC
Center around tabs	NO
Change case	NO
Control characters	SOME
Decimal tabs	YES
Dot commands	SOME
Footnotes	OPTIONAL
Forced page break	YES
Format line	YES, ON/OFF
Generate table of contents	OPTIONAL
Generate index	OPTIONAL
Headers and footers	YES, 1 LINE
Hyphenating	USER
Letter merge	OPT
Lines per page	YES
Line spacing	1, 2, 3, SC

Margin release key	YES
Margin width	240
Multicolumn	NO
Nonprinting comments	YES
Onscreen	YES, EXCEPT FOR UNDERLINE & BOLD
Page breaks	AUTO, SC
Page numbers	YES, ALT, RESTART
Paragraph indent	NO
Programmable key	NO
Reformat after changes	USER
Repeat last command	FOR SOME COMMANDS
Right justify	YES, ON/OFF, SC
Right justify tabs	VIA DECIMAL TAB
Sort	NO
Spelling check	YES, OPT
Storing formats	YES
Strikeover	YES, PR
Sub/superscript	YES, PR
Tabs	5, VAR
Underline	YES, PR
Variable pitch	PR
Vertical lines	VARIABLE
Widows and orphans	USER

FILES

File names	OPSYS, 8 CH + 3 CH EXT
Renaming	YES
Copy and delete files	YES
Copying disks	YES
Auto save	USER
Auto backup	YES
Verify	NO
Disk directory	YES, TITLE

PRINTING

Continuous or sheet feed	BOTH
Multiple printers	NO
Queue	NO
Simultaneous	YES
Specific pages	YES
Typefaces	YES

HARDWARE

Internal memory	128K
Storage and drives	5¼" DD, SD, 320KB DUAL MINI FLOPPIES; HARD DISK IN FUTURE
Communications	TTY, OPT. 2780/3780, 3276
Keyboard	ATTACHED, #PAD, WP KEYS
Video tube	AMBER ON GRAY, 80 × 24
Printers	LQP—35CPS, DOT MATRIX—135CPS ATTACH ONLY ONE

LIST OF WORD-PROCESSING PRODUCTS || 353

DOCUMENTATION AND TRAINING
   Documentation   TUTORIAL TRAINING GUIDE, REFERENCE MANUAL, REFERENCE CARD
   Training   1 HR INSTALL TRAINING; TUTORIAL, 2 HRS APPLICATIONS TRAINING

VENDOR: NBI
MODEL: System 3000, 3000S, OASYS 8/64
TYPE: 3000—Stand-alone; OASYS—Multiterminal, dedicated

ENTERING TEXT
   Where   ANYWHERE
   Word wrap   YES, ALWAYS ON
   Length of document   DISK
   Orientation   DOC

EDITING TEXT
   During entry   YES
   Insert   YES, ALWAYS ON
   Delete, copy, and move   YES, VAR, DOC

MOVEMENT WITHIN DOCUMENT
   Cursor   W, L, PG, COL
   Scroll   L, PG, REPEAT, TOP/BOT
   Search   FOR, EX, IGNORE CASE
   Search and replace   FOR, EX, IGNORE CASE, GLOB, AUTO, SEMI-AUTO

SPECIAL FEATURES AND FORMATS
   Alternate character sets   YES
   Boilerplate   YES, GLOSSARY, P
   Bold   YES, PR
   Calculate   A, SUB, M, DIV, %, OPT
   Centering   YES, SC
   Center around tabs   YES
   Change case   NO
   Control characters   MOST, FORMAT SQUARE
   Decimal tabs   YES
   Dot commands   NO
   Footnotes   YES, RENUMBER, REPOSITION
   Forced page break   YES
   Format line   TABS ONLY
   Generate table of contents   YES, STD
   Generate index   YES, STD
   Headers and footers   YES, UNLIMITED #L
   Hyphenating   USER
   Letter merge   YES, STD
   Lines per page   YES

Line spacing	½, 1, 1½, 2, 3, OTHER, PR
Margin release key	NO
Margin width	238
Multicolumn	YES, SC
Nonprinting comments	YES
Onscreen	YES
Page breaks	AUTO, USER, SC
Page numbers	YES, RESTART, ROMAN
Paragraph indent	YES
Programmable key	YES, STORED KEYSTROKES, OPT
Reformat after changes	AUTO
Repeat last command	NO
Right justify	YES, PR
Right justify tabs	YES
Sort	YES, ALPH, NUM, OPT
Spelling check	NO
Storing formats	YES
Strikeover	YES, PR
Sub/superscript	YES, #'S-SC, LETTERS-PR
Tabs	VAR
Underline	YES, SC
Variable pitch	YES, PR
Vertical lines	126
Widows and orphans	AUTO

FILES

File names	FREE, 10 CH
Renaming	YES
Copy and delete files	YES
Copying disks	YES
Auto save	YES, AUTO
Auto backup	NO
Verify	RECOVERY PROGRAM
Disk directory	YES, SIZE, TITLE, DATE, NAME

PRINTING

Continuous or sheet feed	BOTH
Multiple printers	YES
Queue	YES
Simultaneous	YES
Specific pages	YES
Typefaces	YES

HARDWARE

Internal memory	SYSTEM 3000–64K
Storage and drives	SYSTEM 3000: 8", SS OR DS, SD OR DD; 1 OR 2 8" DRIVES; OASYS 8: 2, R OR 10 MG HARD DISKS; OASYS 64: 33, 66, OR 132 MG
Communications	BISYNCH: 2780, 3780, 2770 RJE 300–9600 BAUD, ASYNCH TTY EMULATION OPT
Keyboard	DETACHED, # PAD, WP KEYS

LIST OF WORD-PROCESSING PRODUCTS ‖ 355

  Video tube   WHITE ON BLACK, 80 × 16
  Printers   DIABLO 630, QUME 55, WIDE TRACK, TWIN TRACK, DRAFT PRINTERS
DOCUMENTATION AND TRAINING
  Documentation   OPERATOR'S GUIDE, SPECIAL FEATURES GUIDE, IMPLEMENTATION GUIDE FOR 8/64, 3000 AT A GLANCE, 8 AT A GLANCE
  Training   PERSONAL; 5½ DAYS; 2 OPERATORS PER KEYBOARD
NOTES   OUTLINING—STANDARD DOCUWRITER: ENTRY-LEVEL STAND-ALONE WORD PROCESSOR W/ LIMITED FUNCTIONS

VENDOR: NCR
MODEL: Worksaver
TYPE: Stand-alone or multiterminal, hybrid

ENTERING TEXT
  Where   ANYWHERE
  Word wrap   YES
  Length of document   DISK
  Orientation   DOC
EDITING TEXT
  During entry   YES
  Insert   YES, ON/OFF
  Delete, copy, and move   L, P, PG, VAR, DOC
MOVEMENT WITHIN DOCUMENT
  Cursor   L, PG, BEGIN, END OF L
  Scroll   SC, TOP/BOT
  Search   FOR, IGNORE CASE, EX
  Search and replace   FOR, IGNORE CASE, EX, GLOB, AUTO
SPECIAL FEATURES AND FORMATS
  Alternate character
    sets   YES
  Boilerplate   YES, GLOSSARY, PARA
  Bold   YES, SC
  Calculate   NO
  Centering   YES, SC
  Center around tabs   YES
  Change case   NO
  Control characters   NO
  Decimal tabs   YES
  Dot commands   NO
  Footnotes   NO
  Forced page break   YES
  Format line   YES

Generate table of contents	NO
Generate index	NO
Headers and footers	YES, DATE
Hyphenating	USER
Letter merge	YES
Lines per page	VAR
Line spacing	ALL, SC
Margin release key	NO
Margin width	256
Multicolumn	NO
Nonprinting comments	NO
Onscreen	YES
Page breaks	AUTO, SC
Page numbers	YES, ALT, RESTART
Paragraph indent	YES
Programmable key	YES
Reformat after changes	AUTO
Reformat to new margins	AUTO, USER
Repeat last command	YES
Right justify	YES, SC
Right justify tabs	YES, SC
Sort	NO
Spelling check	NO
Storing formats	YES
Strikeover	YES, PR
Sub/superscript	YES, SC
Tabs	VAR
Underline	YES, SC
Variable pitch	YES, PR
Vertical lines	VAR
Widows and orphans	AUTO

FILES

File names	FREE, 30 CH
Renaming	YES
Copy and delete files	YES
Copying disks	YES
Auto save	YES, USER
Auto backup	NO
Verify	N/A
Disk directory	YES, ORDER, SIZE, DATE

PRINTING

Continuous or sheet feed	BOTH
Multiple printers	YES
Queue	YES
Simultaneous	YES
Specific pages	YES
Typefaces	YES

HARDWARE

Internal memory	256K–1M
Storage and drives	5¼" DS, DD FLOPPIES; 8" SS, DD (512K); HARD DISKS—5, 10, 20, 40, 120 MG
Communications	2780/3780 ASYNCH TTY; ASYNCH DOC TRANSFER; 3270 BYSYNCH; 2780/3780 DOC TRANSFER; X.25; SNA, OPTIONAL PBS
Keyboard	DETACHED, # PAD, WP KEYS
Video tube	GREEN/GRAY, 28 × 80–100 SYSTEM; 34 × 80 OR 34 × 132—200 SYSTEM
Printers	NEC, 20, 35 OR 55 CPS; ONE WP, ONE DP PRINTER WITH STAND-ALONE

DOCUMENTATION AND TRAINING

Documentation	OWNER'S MANUAL, REFERENCE MANUAL, PRINTER MANUAL, INSTALL MANUAL, 800#
Training	3 DAYS CLASSROOM TRAINING; 1 OPERATOR PER WORKSTATION; $250 FOR ADD'L DAYS

NOTES
UP TO 6 EDIT WINDOWS

VENDOR: Nixdorf Computer Corporation
MODEL: 8840/5
TYPE: Multiterminal

ENTERING TEXT

Where	ANYWHERE
Word wrap	YES
Length of document	DISK
Orientation	DOC

EDITING TEXT

During entry	YES
Insert	YES
Delete, copy, and move	CH, W, L, S, P, PG, DOC

MOVEMENT WITHIN DOCUMENT

Cursor	PG
Scroll	L
Search	FOR, BACK, EX
Search and replace	FOR, BACK, EX, GLOD, AUTO, SEMI-AUTO

SPECIAL FEATURES AND FORMAT

Alternate character sets	NO
Boilerplate	YES, GLOSSARY, P
Bold	YES, SC
Calculate	A, SUB, M, DIV, %, OPT
Centering	SC
Center around tabs	NO
Change case	NO
Control characters	MOST
Decimal tabs	YES

Dot commands	MOST
Footnotes	YES
Forced page break	YES
Format line	YES
Generate table of contents	YES
Generate index	NO
Headers and footers	YES
Hyphenating	USER
Letter merge	YES
Lines per page	YES
Line spacing	YES, PR
Margin release key	NO
Margin width	125-10 PI, 153-12PI
Multicolumn	NO
Nonprinting comments	YES
Onscreen	YES
Page breaks	AUTO, SC, PR
Page numbers	YES, RESTART
Paragraph indent	YES, SC
Programmable key	NO
Reformat after changes	AUTO
Repeat last command	NO
Right justify	ON/OFF
Right justify tabs	NO
Sort	YES, ALPH, NUM
Spelling check	NO
Storing formats	YES
Strikeover	NO
Sub/superscript	YES, SC
Tabs	VAR
Underline	YES, SC
Variable pitch	YES, PR
Vertical lines	VAR
Widows and orphans	AUTO

FILES

File names	FREE
Renaming	YES
Copy and delete files	YES
Copying disks	YES
Auto save	USER
Auto backup	NO
Verify	YES
Disk directory	YES, SIZE, NAME, TITLE, DATE

PRINTING

Continuous or sheet feed	BOTH
Multiple printers	YES
Queue	YES
Simultaneous	YES

Specific pages	YES
Typefaces	YES

HARDWARE

Internal memory	64K
Storage and drives	5MB & FLOPPY 5 MB & 1 FLOPPY STD; OPTIONAL FLP
Communications	NONE
Keyboard	DETACHED, WP KEYS
Video tube	GRAY/WHITE, 80 × 24; 4 CAN BE ATTACHED
Printers	45CPS LQP, 300LPM LINE PRINTER; 2 PRINTERS MAX

DOCUMENTATION AND TRAINING

Documentation	OPERATOR'S GUIDE, SUPERVISOR'S GUIDE, SELF-TEACHING
Training	FREE FOR 1 PERSON PER WORKSTATION

VENDOR: North Star Computers
MODEL: Northword for Horizon or Advantage
TYPE: Stand-alone or multiterminal, hybrid

ENTERING TEXT

Where	ANYWHERE
Word wrap	YES
Length of document	DISK
Orientation	DOC

EDITING TEXT

During entry	YES
Insert	YES, ON/OFF
Delete, copy, and move	YES, VAR UP TO 24 LINES, DOC

MOVEMENT WITHIN DOCUMENT

Cursor	L, PG VERTICAL MOVE
Scroll	L, SC
Search	FOR, EX
Search and replace	FOR, EX, SEMI-AUTO

SPECIAL FEATURES AND FORMATS

Alternate character sets	YES
Boilerplate	YES, P
Bold	YES, PR
Calculate	NO
Centering	YES, SC
Center around tabs	NO
Change case	NO
Control characters	NO
Decimal tabs	NO
Dot commands	MOST
Footnotes	NO

Forced page break	YES
Format line	NO
Generate table of contents	NO
Generate index	NO
Headers and footers	YES, 150 CH; DATE
Hyphenating	NO
Letter merge	YES
Lines per page	YES
Line spacing	YES, PR
Margin release key	NO
Margin width	160
Multicolumn	NO
Nonprinting comments	YES
Onscreen	YES
Page breaks	AUTO, SC
Page numbers	YES, RESTART
Paragraph indent	NO
Programmable key	YES, ON ADVANTAGE MODEL
Reformat after changes	AUTO
Repeat last command	NO
Right justify	YES, SC
Right justify tabs	NO
Sort	NO
Spelling check	NO
Storing formats	NO
Strikeover	YES
Sub/superscript	NO
Tabs	VAR
Underline	YES, PR
Variable pitch	YES, PR
Vertical lines	VARIABLE
Widows and orphans	AUTO

FILES

File names	15 CH
Renaming	YES
Copy and delete files	YES
Copying disks	YES
Auto save	AUTO W/ESCAPE, USER
Auto backup	NO
Verify	NO
Disk directory	YES, ALPH ORDER IS AUTO, TITLE

PRINTING

Continuous or sheet feed	BOTH
Multiple printers	YES
Queue	YES
Simultaneous	YES
Specific pages	SPECIFY STARTING PAGE
Typefaces	NO

LIST OF WORD-PROCESSING PRODUCTS

HARDWARE
    Internal memory   64K
    Storage and drives   5¼″ QUAD (DS, DD FLOPPIES 2 STANDARD, 360KB EA; 5 & 18MB HARD DISKS
    Communications   NONE
    Keyboard   ATTACHED, # PAD, WP KEYS (ADVANTAGE MODEL ONLY)
    Video tube   ADVANTAGE: GREEN; BOTH: 80 × 24 UP TO 5 TUBES ON THE HORIZON
    Printers   ANY SERIAL OR PARALLEL LQP OR DOT MATRIX—SPEED VARIES; 3 MAX

DOCUMENTATION AND TRAINING
    Documentation   USER MANUAL
    Training   THROUGH DEALERS

VENDOR: Olivetti
MODEL: ET 351
TYPE: Stand-alone, one-line display

ENTERING TEXT
    Where   ONE LINE DISPLAY
    Word wrap   YES
    Length of document   DISK
    Orientation   DOC

EDITING TEXT
    During entry   YES
    Insert   YES, ON
    Delete, copy, and move   YES, VAR, DOC

MOVEMENT WITHIN DOCUMENT
    Cursor   FORWARD TO END, BACKWARD UP TO 2,000 CHS
    Scroll   L, P, PG, TOP/BOT
    Search   FOR, EX
    Search and replace   FOR, EX, GLOB, SEMI-AUTO

SPECIAL FEATURES AND FORMATS
    Alternate character sets   YES
    Boilerplate   YES, GLOSSARY, P
    Bold   YES, SC
    Calculate   NO
    Centering   PR
    Center around tabs   NO
    Change case   NO
    Control characters   YES
    Decimal tabs   YES
    Dot commands   NO
    Footnotes   NO
    Forced page break   YES

Format line	NO
Generate table of contents	NO
Generate index	NO
Headers and footers	NO
Hyphenating	USER
Letter merge	YES
Lines per page	YES
Line spacing	YES, PR
Margin release key	YES
Margin width	10 & PS* = 132 CH, 12 = 158, 15 = 198
Multicolumn	YES, PR
Nonprinting comments	YES
Onscreen	NO
Page breaks	AUTO, SC
Page numbers	YES, RESTART
Paragraph indent	YES
Programmable key	NO
Reformat after changes	AUTO
Repeat last command	NO
Right justify	YES, PR
Right justify tabs	ONE AT RIGHT MARGIN
Sort	NO
Spelling check	NO
Storing formats	YES
Strikeover	YES, SC
Sub/superscript	YES, SC
Tabs	VAR
Underline	YES, SC
Variable pitch	YES, PR
Vertical lines	VAR
Widows and orphans	USER

FILES

File names	FREE, UP TO 6 CH
Renaming	YES
Copy and delete files	YES
Copying disks	YES
Auto save	USER
Auto backup	NO
Verify	NO
Disk directory	YES, NAME, DESCRIPTION, PROTECT STATUS

PRINTING

Continuous or sheet feed	BOTH
Multiple printers	NO
Queue	YES
Simultaneous	NO
Specific pages	NO
Typefaces	YES

HARDWARE
Internal memory	64K
Storage and drives	5¼″ SS, SD, 73K RECORDABLE
Communications	TTY, UP TO 9600 BAUD
Keyboard	ATTACHED TO PRINTER; WP KEYS
Video tube	GREEN ON BLACK; 1 LINE, 40 CH
Printers	OLIVETTI; UP TO 30 CPS

DOCUMENTATION AND TRAINING
Documentation	ONE MANUAL
Training	DEPENDS ON DEALER SELLING SYSTEM

VENDOR: Olympia
MODEL: Stand-alone
TYPE: Electronic typewriter extension (hardware and software)

ENTERING TEXT
Where	ANYWHERE
Word wrap	YES
Length of document	DISK
Orientation	PG

EDITING TEXT
During entry	YES
Insert	YES, ON/OFF
Delete, copy, and move	YES, CH, W, L, S, P, PG, COL, VAR

MOVEMENT WITHIN DOCUMENT
Cursor	W, L, S, P, PG, COL
Scroll	L, P, PG, SC, TOP/BOT
Search	FOR, BACK, IGNORE CASE
Search and replace	FOR, BACK, IGNORE CASE, GLOB, AUTO, SEMI-AUTO

SPECIAL FEATURES AND FORMATS
Alternate character sets	YES
Boilerplate	YES, GLOSSARY, P
Bold	YES, SC
Calculate	NO
Centering	YES, SC
Center around tabs	YES
Change case	YES
Control characters	SOME
Decimal tabs	YES
Dot commands	SOME
Footnotes	YES
Forced page break	YES
Format line	YES
Generate table of contents	YES

Generate index	YES
Headers and footers	YES
Hyphenating	AUTO
Letter merge	YES
Lines per page	YES
Line spacing	½, 1, 1½, 2, 3, OTHER, SC
Margin release key	YES
Margin width	240
Multicolumn	YES, SC
Nonprinting comments	YES
Onscreen	YES
Page breaks	AUTO, SC
Page numbers	YES, ALT, RESTART
Paragraph indent	YES
Programmable key	YES
Reformat after changes	YES, USER
Repeat last command	YES FOR BLOCK COPY
Right justify	YES, SC
Right justify tabs	YES
Sort	NO
Spelling check	YES, 20,000 W + 2000 ADDITIONAL
Storing formats	YES
Strikeover	YES, SC
Sub/superscript	YES, SC
Tabs	5
Underline	YES, SC
Variable pitch	YES, PR
Vertical lines	VAR
Widows and orphans	USER

FILES

File names	FREE, 8 CH
Renaming	YES
Copy and delete files	YES
Copying disks	YES
Auto save	USER
Auto backup	YES, IF USER REQUESTS
Verify	YES
Disk directory	YES, TITLE

PRINTING

Continuous or sheet feed	BOTH
Multiple printers	NO
Queue	?
Simultaneous	NO
Specific pages	YES
Typefaces	YES

HARDWARE

Internal memory	64K
Storage	5¼", SS OR DS, SD 175K OR 350K
Drives	1 DISK DRIVE

Communications	NONE
Keyboard	ELECTRONIC TYPEWRITER
Video tube	GREEN ON BLACK, 80 × 24
Printers	ELECTRONIC TYPEWRITER

DOCUMENTATION AND TRAINING

Documentation	OPERATION GUIDE AND REFERENCE MANUAL
Training	APPROXIMATELY 1 HOUR; FOLLOW-UP TRAINING AT DISCRETION OF LOCAL DEALER

VENDOR: Ontel
MODEL: OP 1/15
TYPE: Stand-alone or multiterminal

ENTERING TEXT

Where	ANYWHERE
Word wrap	YES
Length of document	DISK
Orientation	PG

EDITING TEXT

During entry	YES
Insert	YES, ALWAYS ON
Delete, copy, and move	YES, VAR

MOVEMENT WITHIN DOCUMENT

Cursor	W, L, S, P, PG, COL
Scroll	L, P, PG, SC, TOP/BOT
Search	YES, IGNORE CASE
Search and replace	FOR, IGNORE CASE, EX, AUTO, SEMI-AUTO

SPECIAL FEATURES AND FORMATS

Alternate character sets	YES
Boilerplate	YES
Bold	YES
Calculate	YES
Centering	YES
Center around tabs	YES
Change case	YES
Control characters	YES
Decimal tabs	YES
Dot commands	NO
Footnotes	YES
Forced page break	YES
Format line	YES
Generate table of contents	NOT YET
Generate index	NOT YET
Headers and footers	YES
Hyphenating	USER

Letter merge	YES
Lines per page	YES
Line spacing	YES
Margin release key	YES
Margin width	160
Multicolumn	YES
Nonprinting comments	NO
Onscreen	YES
Page breaks	YES
Page numbers	YES
Paragraph indent	YES
Programmable key	YES
Reformat after changes	AUTO
Repeat last command	NO
Right justify	YES
Right justify tabs	YES
Sort	YES, ALPH, NUM
Spelling check	NO
Storing formats	YES
Strikeover	YES
Sub/superscript	YES
Tabs	VAR
Underline	YES
Variable pitch	YES
Vertical lines	90
Widows and orphans	YES

FILES

File names	OPSYS
Renaming	YES
Copy and delete files	YES
Copying disks	YES
Auto save	YES
Auto backup	YES
Verify	YES
Disk directory	YES, SIZE, NAME, TITLE, DATE

PRINTING

Continuous or sheet feed	BOTH
Multiple printers	YES
Queue	YES
Simultaneous	YES
Specific pages	YES
Typefaces	YES

HARDWARE

Internal memory	64K
Storage	8″ SS SD, SS DD, OR DS, DD; 5¼″ DS DD OR QUAD DENS
Drives	5¼″ 5 MB HARD DISK, 10 & 96MG
Communications	OPT

LIST OF WORD-PROCESSING PRODUCTS || 367

Keyboard	ATTACHED OR DETACHABLE # PAD, WP KEYS
Video tube	GREEN, 80 × 24
Printers	2 PER SYSTEM

DOCUMENTATION AND TRAINING

Documentation	
Training	OEM SALES

VENDOR: Philips Information Systems
MODEL: Micom 2001E
TYPE: Stand-alone, dedicated

ENTERING TEXT

Where	ANYWHERE
Word wrap	YES
Length of document	94 LINES
Orientation	PG ON SCREEN; DOC IN FILES

EDITING TEXT

During entry	YES
Insert	YES, ALWAYS ON
Delete, copy, and move	YES, W, S, P, L, R (REMAINDER), DOC

MOVEMENT WITHIN DOCUMENT

Cursor	W, L, S, P, PG, COL
Scroll	L, P, PG, SC, TOP/BOT
Search	EX, IGNORE CASE
Search and replace	EX, IGNORE CASE, SEMI-AUTO, GLOB UP TO 94 SEARCHES

SPECIAL FEATURES AND FORMATS

Alternate character sets	YES
Boilerplate	YES
Bold	YES, PR
Calculate	YES, A, SUB, M, DIV, %
Centering	YES, SC
Center around tabs	YES
Change case	YES
Control characters	NO
Decimal tabs	YES
Dot commands	NO
Footnotes	YES
Forced page break	YES
Format line	NO
Generate table of contents	YES
Generate index	YES
Headers and footers	YES, OPT
Hyphenating	USER

Letter merge	YES
Lines per page	YES
Line spacing	YES, PR
Margin release key	YES
Margin width	250
Multicolumn	YES, SC
Nonprinting comments	YES
Onscreen	NO
Page breaks	YES, AUTO, USER, SC
Page numbers	YES, ALT, RESTART, ROMAN
Paragraph indent	YES, SC
Programmable key	NO
Reformat after changes	YES, AUTO
Repeat last command	YES
Right justify	YES, PR
Right justify tabs	YES
Sort	YES, ALPH, NUM
Spelling check	YES, 76,000, OPT
Storing formats	YES
Strikeover	NO
Sub/superscript	YES, SC
Tabs	VAR
Underline	YES, SC
Variable pitch	YES, SC
Vertical lines	94 MAX WITH 80 COLUMN WIDTH
Widows and orphans	AUTO

FILES

File names	FREE
Renaming	YES
Copy and delete files	YES
Copying disks	YES
Auto save	YES
Auto backup	YES
Verify	YES
Disk directory	YES, SIZE, NAME, TITLE, DATE

PRINTING

Continuous or sheet feed	BOTH
Multiple printers	NO
Queue	YES
Simultaneous	YES
Specific pages	YES
Typefaces	YES

HARDWARE

Internal memory	128K
Storage and drives	8″ FLOPPY, SS, SD, 127K
Communications	2780/3780, 3270, 3276, VT52, "MICONET II" (INTERNAL), ASYNCH 50–9600 BPS, SYNCH 1200–4800
Keyboard	ATTACHED, #PAD OPT, WP KEYS

Video tube	GREEN ON BLACK, 80 × 31
Printers	45 CPS QUME, 40 CPS PHILIPS 1 MAXIMUM (OPTIONAL)

DOCUMENTATION AND TRAINING

Documentation	REFERENCE MANUAL AND OPERATOR'S MANUAL
Training	TWO OPERATORS PER KEYBOARD

VENDOR: Prolink
TYPE: Multiterminal, hybrid

ENTERING TEXT

Where	ANYWHERE
Word wrap	YES
Length of document	DISK
Orientation	DOC

EDITING TEXT

During entry	YES
Insert	YES, ALWAYS ON
Delete, copy, and move	YES, VAR

MOVEMENT WITHIN DOCUMENT

Cursor	?
Scroll	TOP/BOT
Search	FOR, EX, IGNORE CASE
Search and replace	FOR, EX, IGNORE CASE, GLOB, AUTO, SEMI-AUTO

SPECIAL FEATURES AND FORMATS

Alternate character sets	YES
Boilerplate	YES
Bold	YES, SC
Calculate	NO
Centering	SC
Center around tabs	?
Change case	NO
Control characters	NO
Decimal tabs	YES
Dot commands	?
Footnotes	?
Forced page break	YES
Format line	NO
Generate table of contents	NO
Generate index	NO
Headers and footers	YES
Hyphenating	?
Letter merge	?
Lines per page	YES

Line spacing	YES, SC
Margin release key	NO
Margin width	240
Multicolumn	YES, SC
Nonprinting comments	NO
Onscreen	YES
Page breaks	AUTO, SC
Page numbers	YES, ALT, RESTART, ROMAN
Paragraph indent	SC
Programmable key	YES
Reformat after changes	AUTO
Repeat last command	NO
Right justify	YES, SC
Right justify tabs	YES
Sort	?
Spelling check	?
Storing formats	YES
Strikeover	SC
Sub/superscript	SC
Tabs	VAR
Underline	YES, SC
Variable pitch	SC
Vertical lines	?
Widows and orphans	AUTO

FILES

File names	?
Renaming	YES
Copy and delete files	YES
Copying disks	YES
Auto save	YES
Auto backup	NO
Verify	?
Disk directory	?

PRINTING

Continuous or sheet feed	BOTH
Multiple printers	YES
Queue	YES
Simultaneous	YES
Specific pages	YES
Typefaces	?

HARDWARE

Internal memory	?
Storage and drives	21–35MB DISKS
Communications	?
Keyboard	DETACHED KEYBOARD, # PAD
Video tube	GREEN, 240 × 33
Printers	SUPPORTS MANY PRINTERS SUCH AS DIABLO, QUME

LIST OF WORD-PROCESSING PRODUCTS || 371

DOCUMENTATION AND TRAINING
   Documentation   ?
   Training   ?

VENDOR: Raytheon
MODEL: Lexitron VT 2303
TYPE: Stand-alone

ENTERING TEXT

Where	OPTIONAL
Word wrap	ON/OFF
Length of document	DISK
Orientation	PG

EDITING TEXT

During entry	YES
Insert	ON/OFF
Delete, copy, and move	YES, CH, W, L, S, P, PG, COL, VAR, DOC

MOVEMENT WITHIN DOCUMENT

Cursor	W, L, S, P, PG
Scroll	L, P, PG, TOP/BOT
Search	FOR, IGNORE CASE
Search and replace	GLOB, AUTO, SEMI-AUTO

SPECIAL FEATURES AND FORMATS

Alternate character sets	YES
Boilerplate	YES, GLOSSARY, P
Bold	YES, PR
Calculate	A, SUB, M, DIV, %, OPT
Centering	YES, SC
Center around tabs	YES
Change case	YES
Control characters	NO
Decimal tabs	YES
Dot commands	NO
Footnotes	YES
Forced page break	?
Format line	YES
Generate table of contents	YES
Generate index	NO
Headers and footers	YES
Hyphenating	USER
Letter merge	YES
Lines per page	YES
Line spacing	YES, PR
Margin release key	YES
Margin width	316
Multicolumn	YES, SC

Nonprinting comments	YES
Onscreen	YES
Page breaks	AUTO, SC
Page numbers	YES
Paragraph indent	NO
Programmable key	YES
Reformat after changes	AUTO
Repeat last command	NO
Right justify	YES, PR
Right justify tabs	NO
Sort	ALPH, NUM, OPT
Spelling check	NO
Storing formats	YES
Strikeover	YES, SC
Sub/superscript	YES, PR
Tabs	VAR
Underline	YES, SC
Variable pitch	YES, SC
Vertical lines	220
Widows and orphans	AUTO

FILES

File names	FREE
Renaming	YES
Copy and delete files	BOTH
Copying disks	YES
Auto save	NO
Auto backup	NO
Verify	?
Disk directory	ORDER, SIZE, NAME, TITLE, DATE

PRINTING

Continuous or sheet feed	BOTH
Multiple printers	YES
Queue	YES
Simultaneous	YES
Specific pages	NO
Typefaces	YES

HARDWARE

Internal memory	393K
Storage and drives	5¼" SS OR DS, DD, 2 DISKS, 161K OR 322 K CH APPROXIMATELY 320 PGES STORAGE
Communications	2741, ASCII, BISYNCH PT–PT, TWX, TELEX, 3270, 2770, 2780
Keyboard	ATTACHED WP KEYS
Video tube	GREEN ON GREEN 126 × 25
Printers	QUME 45–55 CPS 4 MAX

DOCUMENTATION AND TRAINING

Documentation	REFERENCE MANUAL
Training	1 OPERATOR TRAINED FREE W/4 HRS SUPPORT

VENDOR: Rothenberg Information Systems, Inc.
MODEL: Word Processing 1/65
TYPE: Stand-alone

ENTERING TEXT
Where	ANYWHERE
Word wrap	YES, ON/OFF
Length of document	DISK
Orientation	DOC

EDITING TEXT
During entry	YES
Insert	YES, ON/OFF
Delete, copy, and move	YES, CH, W, L, S, P, PG, COL, VAR, DOC

MOVEMENT WITHIN DOCUMENT
Cursor	W, L, S, P, PG, COL
Scroll	L, P, PG, SC, TOP/BOT
Search	FOR, BACK, IGNORE CASE
Search and replace	FOR, BACK, IGNORE CASE, GLOB, AUTO, SEMI-AUTO

SPECIAL FEATURES AND FORMATS
Alternate character sets	YES
Boilerplate	YES, GLOSSARY, P
Bold	YES, SC
Calculate	A, SUB, M, DIV %, OPT
Centering	YES, SC
Center around tabs	NO
Change case	YES
Control characters	SOME
Decimal tabs	YES
Dot commands	SOME
Footnotes	YES
Forced page break	YES
Format line	YES, ON/OFF
Generate table of contents	YES
Generate index	YES
Headers and footers	YES, VAR #L
Hyphenating	USER
Letter merge	YES
Lines per page	YES
Line spacing	½, 1, 1½, 2, 3, OTHER, SC
Margin release key	YES
Margin width	255
Multicolumn	SC
Nonprinting comments	YES
Onscreen	YES
Page breaks	AUTO, SC
Page numbers	YES, ALT, RESTART
Paragraph indent	SC

Programmable key	YES
Reformat after changes	USER
Repeat last command	YES
Right justify	YES, ON/OFF, SC
Right justify tabs	NO
Sort	YES, ALPH, NUM
Spelling check	YES, 50,000 W, OPT
Storing formats	YES
Strikeover	YES, PR
Sub/superscript	YES, PR
Tabs	5, VAR
Underline	YES, PR
Variable pitch	YES, PR
Vertical lines	VARIABLE
Widows and orphans	USER

FILES

File names	OPSYS
Renaming	YES
Copy and delete files	YES
Copying disks	YES
Auto save	YES
Auto backup	YES
Verify	YES
Disk directory	YES, ORDER, SIZE, TITLE

PRINTING

Continuous or sheet feed	BOTH
Multiple printers	YES
Queue	YES
Simultaneous	YES
Specific pages	YES
Typefaces	YES

HARDWARE

Internal memory	64K
Storage and drives	8″ SS, SD; DS, SD; DS, DD; 300K, 600K, 1200K EA; 10–150 MB HARD DISKS; DUAL 8″ FLOPPIES STANDARD
Communications	ASYNCH, BISYNCH, SYNCH, SDLC 300–9600 BPS
Keyboard	ATTACHED, # PAD, WP KEYS
Video tube	WHITE ON GREEN, 80 × 24
Printers	DIABLO 630

DOCUMENTATION AND TRAINING

Documentation	MANUAL
Training	CLASSROOM OR ON/SITE—8 HRS.

VENDOR: Royal Busineses Machines
MODEL: Omniwriter, Wordpac Level
TYPE: Stand-alone, dedicated

ENTERING TEXT
Where	ANYWHERE
Word wrap	YES
Length of document	DISK
Orientation	DOC

EDITING TEXT
During entry	YES
Insert	YES, ALWAYS ON
Delete, copy, and move	YES, CH, W, L, P, PG, COL, REMAINDER, DOC

MOVEMENT WITHIN DOCUMENT
Cursor	CH, W, L, P, REMAINDER, OR VIA ARROWS
Scroll	CH, W, L, P, REMAINDER, OR VIA ARROWS
Search	FOR, IGNORE CASE
Search and replace	FOR, IGNORE CASE, GLOB, AUTO, SEMI-AUTO

SPECIAL FEATURES AND FORMATS
Alternate character sets	YES
Boilerplate	YES, GLOSSARY
Bold	YES, PR
Calculate	NO
Centering	YES, SC
Center around tabs	YES
Change case	NO
Control characters	NO
Decimal tabs	YES
Dot commands	NO
Footnotes	NO
Forced page break	YES
Format line	YES
Generate table of contents	YES
Generate index	NO
Headers and footers	YES, UP TO 160 CH, DATE
Hyphenating	USER
Letter merge	YES
Lines per page	YES
Line spacing	YES, SC OR PR
Margin release key	YES
Margin width	255
Multicolumn	YES, SC
Nonprinting comments	NO
Onscreen	YES
Page breaks	AUTO, SC OR PR
Page numbers	YES, RESTART
Paragraph indent	SC OR PR
Programmable key	NO

Reformat after changes	AUTO
Repeat last command	SOME
Right justify	YES, SC
Right justify tabs	YES
Sort	NO
Spelling check	NO
Storing formats	YES
Strikeover	YES, PR
Sub/superscript	YES, PR
Tabs	10, VAR
Underline	YES, SC
Variable pitch	YES, PR
Vertical lines	VARY
Widows and orphans	AUTO

FILES

File names	FREE, 8 CH
Renaming	YES
Copy and delete files	YES
Copying disks	YES
Auto save	USER
Auto backup	YES
Verify	NO
Disk directory	YES, SIZE, TITLE, DATE

PRINTING

Continuous or sheet feed	BOTH
Multiple printers	NO
Queue	NO
Simultaneous	YES
Specific pages	YES
Typefaces	YES

HARDWARE

Internal memory	96K
Storage and drives	5¼″ DS, DD, 320KB; MPI DRIVES—2 DRIVES
Communications	TTY, 110 TO 19,200 PBI, OPT
Keyboard	DETACHED, WP KEYS
Video tube	GREEN ON CHARCOAL—80 × 24
Printers	"CORRESPONDENCE"—140 WPM "HIGH SPEED"—45 CPS, ONE PER TERMINAL

DOCUMENTATION AND TRAINING

Documentation	OPERATOR MANUAL
Training	PERSONAL OR CLASSROOM TRAINING, CHOICE OF TWO SELF-PACED KITS

LIST OF WORD-PROCESSING PRODUCTS || 377

VENDOR: Royal Business Machines
MODEL: Omniwriter, Textpac Level
TYPE: Stand-alone or multiterminal

ENTERING TEXT
   Where   ANYWHERE
   Word wrap   YES
   Length of document   DISK
   Orientation   DOC

EDITING TEXT
   During entry   YES
   Insert   YES, ALWAYS ON
   Delete, copy, and move   YES, CH, W, L, P, PG, COL, REMAINDER, DOC

MOVEMENT WITHIN DOCUMENT
   Cursor   CH, W, L, P, REMAINDER, OR VIA ARROWS
   Scroll   CH, W, L, P, REMAINDER, OR VIA ARROWS
   Search   FOR, IGNORE CASE
   Search and replace   FOR, IGNORE CASE, GLOB, AUTO, SEMI-AUTO

SPECIAL FEATURES AND FORMATS
   Alternate character
     sets   YES
   Boilerplate   YES, GLOSSARY, P
   Bold   YES, PR
   Calculate   A, SUB, M, DIV
   Centering   YES, SC
   Center around tabs   YES
   Change case   NO
   Control characters   NO
   Decimal tabs   YES
   Dot commands   NO
   Footnotes   NO
   Forced page break   YES
   Format line   YES
   Generate table of
     contents   YES
   Generate index   YES
   Headers and footers   YES, UP TO 160 CH, DATE
   Hyphenating   USER
   Letter merge   YES
   Lines per page   YES
   Line spacing   YES, SC OR PR
   Margin release key   YES
   Margin width   255
   Multicolumn   YES, SC
   Nonprinting comments   YES
   Onscreen   YES
   Page breaks   AUTO, SC OR PR
   Page numbers   YES, RESTART
   Paragraph indent   SC OR PR
   Programmable key   YES

Reformat after changes	AUTO
Repeat last command	SOME
Right justify	YES, SC OR PR
Right justify tabs	YES
Sort	ALPH, NUM
Spelling check	NO, BUT WORKING ON IT
Storing formats	YES
Strikeover	YES, PR
Sub/superscript	YES, PR
Tabs	10, VAR
Underline	YES, SC
Variable pitch	YES, PR
Vertical lines	VARY
Widows and orphans	AUTO

FILES

File names	FREE, 8 CH
Renaming	YES
Copy and delete files	YES
Copying disks	YES
Auto save	USER
Auto backup	YES
Verify	NO
Disk directory	YES, SIZE, NAME, TITLE, DATE

PRINTING

Continuous or sheet feed	BOTH
Multiple printers	YES
Queue	YES
Simultaneous	YES
Specific pages	YES
Typefaces	YES

HARDWARE

Internal memory	128K
Storage and drives	5¼" DS, DD, 320KB; MPI DRIVES—2 DRIVES
Communications	TTY, 110 TO 19,200 BPS, OPT
Keyboard	DETACHED, # PAD, WP KEYS
Video tube	GREEN ON CHARCOAL—80 × 24
Printers	"CORRESPONDENCE"—140 WPM; "HIGH SPEED"—45 CPS, ONE FOR 3 TERMINALS

DOCUMENTATION AND TRAINING

Documentation	OPERATOR MANUAL
Training	YOUR CHOICE: PERSONAL OR CLASSROOM TRAINING; CHOICE OF TWO SELF-PACED KITS

LIST OF WORD-PROCESSING PRODUCTS || 379

VENDOR: Savin Corporation
MODEL: Information System Series 1000 & 2000
TYPE: Stand-alone or multiterminal, hybrid

ENTERING TEXT
Where	ANYWHERE
Word wrap	YES
Length of document	DISK
Orientation	PG

EDITING TEXT
During entry	YES
Insert	YES, ON/OFF
Delete, copy, and move	YES, CH, W, L, S, P, PG, COL, VAR, DOC

MOVEMENT WITHIN DOCUMENT
Cursor	W, L, S, P, PG, COL
Scroll	L, P, PG, SC, TOP/BOT
Search	FROM CURSOR TO END OF DOC
Search and replace	TO END OF DOC; IGNORE CASE, GLOB, AUTO, SEMI-AUTO

SPECIAL FEATURES AND FORMATS
Alternate character sets	NO
Boilerplate	YES, P
Bold	YES, SC
Calculate	A, SUB, M, DIV, %
Centering	YES, SC
Center around tabs	YES
Change case	NO
Control characters	NO
Decimal tabs	YES
Dot commands	NO
Footnotes	YES, REPOSITION
Forced page break	YES
Format line	YES
Generate table of contents	NO
Generate index	?
Headers and footers	YES
Hyphenating	USER
Letter merge	NO
Lines per page	?
Line spacing	1, 1½, 2, SC
Margin release key	NO
Margin width	132
Multicolumn	?
Nonprinting comments	NO
Onscreen	YES
Page breaks	AUTO, SC
Page numbers	YES, ALT
Paragraph indent	SC

Programmable key   ?
Reformat after changes   AUTO
Repeat last command   NO
Right justify   YES, SC
Right justify tabs   YES
Sort   ALPH, NUM, TO COME
Spelling check   YES
Storing formats   YES
Strikeover   YES, SC
Sub/superscript   YES, SC
Tabs   VAR
Underline   YES, SC
Variable pitch   YES, SC
Vertical lines   VAR
Widows and orphans   AUTO

FILES
File names   ALPH/NUM—TO 46 CH
Renaming   YES
Copy and delete files   YES
Copying disks   YES
Auto save   USER
Auto backup   YES
Verify   YES
Disk directory   YES, DATE

PRINTING
Continuous or sheet
  feed   BOTH
Multiple printers   YES
Queue   YES
Simultaneous   YES
Specific pages   YES
Typefaces   ?

HARDWARE
Internal memory   256K–640K
Storage and drives   8″ 5MB SS DD; 8″ WINCHESTER—
                             10 OR 20 MB
Communications   ASYNCH, 1200
Keyboard   DETACHED, # PAD, REPLACEABLE TOUCH
                             PANEL
Video tube   GREEN ON BLACK, 80 TO 132 × 34
Printers   SAVIN 1045 PRINT STATION, 45CPS

DOCUMENTATION AND TRAINING
Documentation   USER GUIDE
Training   PAL (PROGRAM-AIDED LEARNING)

VENDOR: Scientific Data Systems
MODEL: SDS 420
TYPE: Stand-alone, multiterminal, or network

ENTERING TEXT
Where	ANYWHERE
Word wrap	YES
Length of document	DISK
Orientation	DOC

EDITING TEXT
During entry	YES
Insert	YES, ALWAYS ON
Delete, copy, and move	YES, VAR, DOC

MOVEMENT WITHIN DOCUMENT
Cursor	W, L, S, P, PG, COL
Scroll	L, P, SC, TOP/BOT
Search	FOR, BACK, EX
Search and replace	FOR, BACK, EX, GLOB, AUTO, SEMI-AUTO

SPECIAL FEATURES AND FORMATS
Alternate character sets	YES
Boilerplate	YES, GLOSSARY, P
Bold	YES, PR
Calculate	A, SUB, M, DIV, %
Centering	YES, SC
Center around tabs	YES
Change case	YES
Control characters	NO
Decimal tabs	YES
Dot commands	NO
Footnotes	NO
Forced page break	YES
Format line	YES
Generate table of contents	YES
Generate index	NO
Headers and footers	YES, UNLIMITED #L, DATE
Hyphenating	USER
Letter merge	YES
Lines per page	YES
Line spacing	YES, PR
Margin release key	YES
Margin width	254
Multicolumn	YES, SC
Nonprinting comments	YES
Onscreen	NO
Page breaks	AUTO
Page numbers	YES, ALT, RESTART, ROMAN
Paragraph indent	YES, SC
Programmable key	?

Reformat after changes	AUTO
Repeat last command	NO
Right justify	YES, PR
Right justify tabs	YES
Sort	YES, ALPH, NUM
Spelling check	FUTURE
Storing formats	YES
Strikeover	YES, PR
Sub/superscript	YES, PR
Tabs	VAR
Underline	YES, SC
Variable pitch	YES, PR
Vertical lines	VAR
Widows and orphans	AUTO

FILES

File names	FREE, 6 CH
Renaming	YES
Copy and delete files	YES
Copying disks	YES
Auto save	YES
Auto backup	YES
Verify	?
Disk directory	YES

PRINTING c

Continuous or sheet feed	BOTH
Multiple printers	NO
Queue	YES
Simultaneous	YES
Specific pages	YES
Typefaces	YES

HARDWARE

Internal memory	64K
Storage and drives	DUAL-DISKETTE DRIVES, SD OR DD WINCHESTER-TYPE RIGID DISK DRIVES (UP TO 2), 31 MB EACH
Communications	RS232
Keyboard	DETACHED, # PAD, WP KEYS
Video tube	WHITE ON BLACK OR GREEN BACKGROUND 80 × 25; UP TO 25 TERMINALS TO A LOCAL-AREA NETWORK
Printers	DIABLO, TALLY, INFOSCRIBE, NEC

DOCUMENTATION AND TRAINING

Documentation	MANUALS
Training	PROVIDED BY DISTRIBUTORS

LIST OF WORD-PROCESSING PRODUCTS || 383

VENDOR: Shasta General Systems
MODEL: Parrot
TYPE: Stand-alone, hybrid

ENTERING TEXT
Where	ANYWHERE
Word wrap	YES
Length of document	DISK
Orientation	DOC

EDITING TEXT
During entry	YES
Insert	YES, ON/OFF
Delete, copy, and move	YES, VAR, DOC

MOVEMENT WITHIN DOCUMENT
Cursor	L, PAGE#, LINE #
Scroll	L, PG, SC
Search	FOR, IGNORE CASE
Search and replace	FOR, IGNORE CASE, GLOB, AUTO, SEMI-AUTO; UP TO 5 DIFFERENT WORDS AT ONE TIME

SPECIAL FEATURES AND FORMATS
Alternate character sets	YES
Boilerplate	YES, P
Bold	YES, SC
Calculate	NO
Centering	YES, SC
Center around tabs	YES
Change case	NO
Control characters	SOME
Decimal tabs	YES
Dot commands	NO
Footnotes	YES, RENUMBER, REPOSITION
Forced page break	YES
Format line	YES
Generate table of contents	NO
Generate index	NO
Headers and footers	ON PARROT II ONLY, UNLIMITED
Hyphenating	USER
Letter merge	YES
Lines per page	YES
Line spacing	YES, UP TO 3½; PR
Margin release key	YES
Margin width	132
Multicolumn	NO
Nonprinting comments	YES
Onscreen	YES
Page breaks	AUTO, SC
Page numbers	YES, RESTART

Paragraph indent	SC
Programmable key	NO
Reformat after changes	AUTO
Repeat last command	NO
Right justify	ON/OFF, PR
Right justify tabs	YES
Sort	NO
Spelling check	NO
Storing formats	YES
Strikeover	YES
Sub/superscript	YES, PR
Tabs	VAR
Underline	YES, PR
Variable pitch	YES, PR
Vertical lines	VAR
Widows and orphans	AUTO; ON/OFF

FILES

File names	FREE, 24 CH
Renaming	YES
Copy and delete files	YES
Copying disks	YES
Auto save	YES
Auto backup	YES
Verify	YES
Disk directory	YES, SIZE, NAME, TITLE, DATE

PRINTING

Continuous or sheet feed	BOTH
Multiple printers	NO
Queue	YES
Simultaneous	YES
Specific pages	YES
Typefaces	YES

HARDWARE

Internal memory	64K
Storage and drives	2 5¼" (96KB) OR 2 8" (318KB) OR 2 5¼" QUAD (720KB) OR 5¼" WINCHESTER (5MB)
Communications	OPTIONAL
Keyboard	DETACHED, # PAD, WP KEYS
Video tube	WHITE ON BLACK, 80 × 24
Printers	45 CPS DAISY WHEEL OR 180 CPS DOT MATRIX; 1 PER SYSTEM

DOCUMENTATION AND TRAINING

Documentation	TRAINING GUIDE, REFERENCE MANUAL
Training	ON-SITE OR CLASSROOM

VENDOR: Syntrex Inc.
MODEL: Aquarius II—stand-alone
TYPE: Gemini—shared resource

ENTERING TEXT
  Where   ANYWHERE
  Word wrap   YES
  Length of document   DISK
  Orientation   DOC

EDITING TEXT
  During entry   YES
  Insert   YES, ON/OFF
  Delete, copy, and move   YES, CH, W, S, P, DOC

MOVEMENT WITHIN DOCUMENT
  Cursor   W, S, P
  Scroll   FOR OR BACK, ON/OFF
  Search   FOR, BACK, IGNORE CASE, EX
  Search and replace   FOR, BACK, IGNORE CASE, EX, GLOB, AUTO, SEMI-AUTO

SPECIAL FEATURES AND FORMATS
  Alternate character sets   YES
  Boilerplate   YES, GLOSSARY, P
  Bold   YES, SC
  Calculate   A, SUB, M, DIV, %
  Centering   YES, SC
  Center around tabs   YES
  Change case   NO
  Control characters   NO
  Decimal tabs   YES
  Dot commands   NO
  Footnotes   YES, RENUMBER, REPOSITION
  Forced page break   YES
  Format line   ON/OFF
  Generate table of contents   NO
  Generate index   YES
  Headers and footers   YES, VARIABLE LINES, DATE
  Hyphenating   USER
  Letter merge   YES, OPT
  Lines per page   YES
  Line spacing   ALL, PR
  Margin release key   NO
  Margin width   200
  Multicolumn   NO
  Nonprinting comments   NO
  Onscreen   YES
  Page breaks   AUTO, USER, SC
  Page numbers   YES, ALT, ROMAN
  Paragraph indent   SC

Programmable key	YES W/KEYSTROKE MEMORY
Reformat after changes	AUTO
Repeat last command	NO
Right justify	YES, ON/OFF, SC
Right justify tabs	YES
Sort	ALPH, NUM, OPT
Spelling check	YES, 87,000 + 30,000 FOR YOU, OPT
Storing formats	YES
Strikeover	YES, SC
Sub/superscript	YES, PR
Tabs	5, VAR
Underline	YES, SC
Variable pitch	SC
Vertical lines	VAR
Widows and orphans	AUTO, USER

FILES

File names	FREE, 20 CH + 1 LINE DESCRIPTION
Renaming	YES
Copy and delete files	YES
Copying disks	YES
Auto save	YES C
Auto backup	VARIABLE; UP TO USER
Verify	NO
Disk directory	YES, SIZE, NAME, TITLE, DATE

PRINTING

Continuous or sheet feed	BOTH
Multiple printers	YES
Queue	NO
Simultaneous	YES
Specific pages	YES
Typefaces	YES

HARDWARE

Internal memory	AQUARIUS—128K; GEMINI—256K
Storage and drives	2 5¼″ DISKS, DS, DD; 360K; FLOPPY-TANDEM OR WINCHESTER
Communications	ASCII, STATION TO STATION
Keyboard	DETACHED, WPKEYS
Video tube	GRAY & WHITE, 80 × 24
Printers	ELECTRONIC TYPEWRITER—20 CPS; QUME—55 CPS

DOCUMENTATION AND TRAINING

Documentation	SELF-TEACHING REFERENCE GUIDE
Training	SELF-PACED + 2–3 DAYS PERSONAL TRAINING

NOTES

SOLD DIRECT & THROUGH DEALERS

LIST OF WORD-PROCESSING PRODUCTS || 387

VENDOR: Technology International Corp.
MODEL: Editpak 1000
TYPE: Stand-alone, dedicated

ENTERING TEXT
Where	ANYWHERE
Word wrap	YES, ON/OFF
Length of document	DISK—NO LIMIT
Orientation	PG

EDITING TEXT
During entry	YES
Insert	YES, ON/OFF
Delete, copy, and move	YES, CH, W, L, P, PG, DOC

MOVEMENT WITHIN DOCUMENT
Cursor	UNLIMITED
Scroll	TOP/BOT
Search	FOR, EX
Search and replace	FOR, EX, GLOB, AUTO

SPECIAL FEATURES AND FORMATS
Alternate character sets	YES
Boilerplate	YES, P
Bold	YES
Calculate	NO
Centering	YES, SC
Center around tabs	YES
Change case	NO
Control characters	NO
Decimal tabs	YES
Dot commands	MOST
Footnotes	NO
Forced page break	YES
Format line	YES
Generate table of contents	NO
Generate index	NO
Headers and footers	YES, UNLIMITED LINES, DATE
Hyphenating	USER
Letter merge	YES
Lines per page	NO
Line spacing	SC
Margin release key	YES
Margin width	UNLIMITED
Multicolumn	YES, SC
Nonprinting comments	YES
Onscreen	YES
Page breaks	USER, SC
Page numbers	NO
Paragraph indent	SC
Programmable key	NO

Reformat after changes	AUTO
Repeat last command	NO
Right justify	YES, ON/OFF, SC
Right justify tabs	YES
Sort	NO
Spelling check	NO
Storing formats	NO
Strikeover	YES, SC
Sub/superscript	NO
Tabs	5, 10 THEREAFTER
Underline	YES, SC
Variable pitch	SC
Vertical lines	99 OR LESS
Widows and orphans	USER

FILES

File names	OPSYS
Renaming	NO
Copy and delete files	DELETE
Copying disks	YES
Auto save	USER
Auto backup	NO
Verify	YES
Disk directory	NO

PRINTING

Continuous or sheet feed	BOTH
Multiple printers	YES
Queue	NO
Simultaneous	NO
Specific pages	YES
Typefaces	YES

HARDWARE

Internal memory	8K
Storage and drives	5¼", SS, DD, 150K SINGLE OR DUAL DRIVES
Communications	RS232
Keyboard	DETACHED, # PAD, WP KEYS
Video tube	GREEN ON BLACK, 80 × 21 ONE PER SYSTEM
Printers	SEVERAL OPTIONS

DOCUMENTATION AND TRAINING

Documentation	?
Training	TWO 4-HOUR SESSIONS AT DEALER'S FACILITY; FOLLOW-UP AS NEEDED

LIST OF WORD-PROCESSING PRODUCTS || 389

VENDOR: Texas Instruments
MODEL: TIPE-990
TYPE: Software for TI 990-based minis

ENTERING TEXT
Where	ANYWHERE
Word wrap	YES, ON/OFF
Length of document	DISK
Orientation	DOC

EDITING TEXT
During entry	YES
Insert	YES, ALWAYS ON
Delete, copy, and move	YES, VAR, DOC

MOVEMENT WITHIN DOCUMENT
Cursor	W, L, PG, COL
Scroll	L, PG, SC, TOP/BOT
Search	FOR, IGNORE CASE
Search and replace	FOR, IGNORE CASE, GLOB, AUTO, SEMI-AUTO

SPECIAL FEATURES AND FORMATS
Alternate character sets	YES
Boilerplate	YES, P
Bold	YES, PR
Calculate	NO
Centering	YES, SC
Center around tabs	NO
Change case	NO
Control characters	MOST
Decimal tabs	YES
Dot commands	NO
Footnotes	NO
Forced page break	YES
Format line	YES
Generate table of contents	NO
Generate index	NO
Headers and footers	YES, UNLIMITED LINES
Hyphenating	NO
Letter merge	YES
Lines per page	YES
Line spacing	PR
Margin release key	YES
Margin width	240
Multicolumn	NO
Nonprinting comments	NO
Onscreen	NO
Page breaks	AUTO, SC
Page numbers	YES, ALT, RESTART
Paragraph indent	NO
Programmable key	NO

Reformat after changes	AUTO
Repeat last command	NO
Right justify	ON/OFF, PR
Right justify tabs	NO
Sort	NO
Spelling check	NO
Storing formats	YES
Strikeover	NO
Sub/superscript	YES, PR
Tabs	VAR
Underline	YES, PR
Variable pitch	NO
Vertical lines	VAR, TO 99
Widows and orphans	AUTO

FILES
File names	OPSYS, 8 CH
Renaming	YES
Copy and delete files	YES
Copying disks	YES
Auto save	USER
Auto backup	YES
Verify	NO
Disk directory	YES, NAME, SIZE, TITLE, DATE

PRINTING
Continuous or sheet feed	BOTH
Multiple printers	YES
Queue	YES
Simultaneous	YES
Specific pages	YES
Typefaces	YES, PRINTWHEEL CHANGE

HARDWARE
Internal memory	VARIES DEPENDING ON COMPUTER
Storage and drives	RANGE OF DISKS AVAILABLE
Communications	3780/2780, 3270, SNA OPT
Keyboard	DETACHED, #PAD, WPKEYS
Video tube	2 COLORS, 80 × 21; 1–30 TUBES ATTACHED, DEPENDING ON SYSTEM AND APPLICATION
Printers	VARIETY: FROM 40CPS TO 600LPM; LQP IS 45 CPS

DOCUMENTATION AND TRAINING
Documentation	TUTORIAL USER'S GUIDE, REFERENCE MANUAL AND REFERENCE CARD
Training	TUTORIAL MANUAL

VENDOR: Toshiba
MODEL: EW100
TYPE: Stand-alone

ENTERING TEXT
Where	BOTTOM
Word wrap	YES
Length of document	DISK
Orientation	DOC

EDITING TEXT
During entry	YES
Insert	YES
Delete, copy, and move	YES, VAR, DOC

MOVEMENT WITHIN DOCUMENT
Cursor	PG
Scroll	SC
Search	FOR, IGNORE CASE
Search and replace	FOR, IGNORE CASE, GLOB, AUTO, SEMI-AUTO

SPECIAL FEATURES AND FORMATS
Alternate character sets	NO
Boilerplate	YES, GLOSSARY, P
Bold	YES, SC
Calculate	YES, A, SUB, M, DIV, %
Centering	YES, SC
Center around tabs	NO
Change case	NO
Control characters	YES
Decimal tabs	YES
Dot commands	NO
Footnotes	NO
Forced page break	YES
Format line	YES
Generate table of contents	NO
Generate index	NO
Headers and footers	YES
Hyphenating	USER
Letter merge	YES
Lines per page	NO
Line spacing	½, 1, 1½, 2, PR
Margin release key	NO
Margin width	132 AT 10 PITCH, 158 AT 12 PITCH
Multicolumn	YES, SC
Nonprinting comments	YES
Onscreen	YES, EXCEPT FOR LINE SPACING
Page breaks	USER, SC
Page numbers	YES
Paragraph indent	YES, SC
Programmable key	YES

Reformat after changes	AUTO
Repeat last command	NO
Right justify	YES, PR
Right justify tabs	NO
Sort	YES, ALPH, NUM
Spelling check	NO
Storing formats	YES
Strikeover	NO
Sub/superscript	YES, PR
Tabs	5
Underline	YES, SC
Variable pitch	YES, PR
Vertical lines	VAR
Widows and orphans	USER

FILES

File names	OPSYS
Renaming	YES
Copy and delete files	YES
Copying disks	YES
Auto save	YES
Auto backup	NO
Verify	NO
Disk directory	YES, SIZE, NAME, TITLE, DATE

PRINTING

Continuous or sheet feed	BOTH
Multiple printers	NO
Queue	YES, UP TO 8 DOCUMENTS
Simultaneous	YES
Specific pages	YES
Typefaces	YES

HARDWARE

Internal memory	64K
Storage and drives	MODEL II: SS, SD, 280K EA MODEL IV; DS, DD, 1MB EA 2 DRIVES/SYSTEM
Communications	TTY, 9600 BPS, WHIZLINK, OPT
Keyboard	DETACHED, WP KEYS
Video tube	GREEN, 80 × 24
Printers	RICOH: 45CPS; 1 PRINTER

DOCUMENTATION AND TRAINING

Documentation	GETTING STARTED BOOK WITH EQUIPMENT; FAMILIARIZATION DISK
Training	PROGRAMMED INSTRUCTION COURSE FOR BEGINNERS & ADVANCED

VENDOR: Vector Graphic
MODEL: 4/20 & 4/30
TYPE: Stand-alone, hybrid Memorite III software

ENTERING TEXT
   Where   ANYWHERE
   Word wrap   YES
   Length of document   APPROX 418 LINES, OR 10–15 PG
   Orientation   DOC

EDITING TEXT
   During entry   YES
   Insert   YES, ON/OFF
   Delete, copy, and move   YES, CH, W, L, S, P, PG, COL, DOC

MOVEMENT WITHIN DOCUMENT
   Cursor   W, L, S, P, PG, COL
   Scroll   L, P, PG, SC, TOP/BOT
   Search   FOR, BACK, EX, IGNORE CASE
   Search and replace   FOR, BACK, EX, IGNORE CASE, GLOB, AUTO, SEMI-AUTO

SPECIAL FEATURES AND FORMATS
   Alternate character sets   YES
   Boilerplate   YES, GLOSSARY, P
   Bold   YES, PR
   Calculate   YES, OPT
   Centering   YES, PR
   Center around tabs   NO
   Change case   NO
   Control characters   YES
   Decimal tabs   YES
   Dot commands   NO
   Footnotes   YES, RENUMBER, REPOSITION
   Forced page break   YES
   Format line   YES
   Generate table of contents   NO
   Generate index   NO
   Headers and footers   YES, 10 LINES
   Hyphenating   AUTO, USER
   Letter merge   YES
   Lines per page   YES
   Line spacing   YES, PR
   Margin release key   NO
   Margin width   25" WIDE
   Multicolumn   YES, PR
   Nonprinting comments   YES
   Onscreen   NO
   Page breaks   AUTO, USER, SC
   Page numbers   YES, ALT, RESTART
   Paragraph indent   PR

Programmable key — YES
Reformat after changes — AUTO
Repeat last command — NO
Right justify — YES, ON/OFF, PR
Right justify tabs — YES
Sort — ALPH, NUM, STD
Spelling check — YES, 30,000 WORDS, STD
Storing formats — YES
Strikeover — YES, PR
Sub/superscript — YES, PR
Tabs — VAR
Underline — YES, PR
Variable pitch — YES, PR
Vertical lines — VARIABLE
Widows and orphans — USER

FILES
File names — FREE, 8 CH
Renaming — YES
Copy and delete files — YES
Copying disks — YES
Auto save — USER
Auto backup — YES
Verify — YES
Disk directory — YES, ORDER, SIZE, NAME, TITLE, DATE

PRINTING
Continuous or sheet feed — BOTH
Multiple printers — YES
Queue — NO
Simultaneous — YES; EXTENDED CP/M REQUIRED
Specific pages — YES
Typefaces — YES

HARDWARE
Internal memory — 128–256KB
Storage and drives — DUAL 5¼" DS, QUAD DENS OR SINGLE FLOPPY + 5MG HARD DISK INTEGRATED INTO VECTOR 4 TERMINAL
Communications — ASYNCH—9600 BPS; SYNCH—EMULATE 2780, 3780 & 3270
Keyboard — DETACHED, # PAD
Video tube — WHITE ON GREEN, 80 × 24
Printers — NEC IMPACT 770, 55 CPS M200 MATRIX PRINTER—350 CPS, 2 MAX

DOCUMENTATION AND TRAINING
Documentation — USER'S MANUAL, HARDWARE MANUAL, REFERENCE GUIDE
Training — THROUGH DEALER NETWORK

VENDOR: Wang Laboratories, Inc.
MODEL: Wang Text Processing Systems
TYPE: Stand-alone or multiterminal, dedicated or hybrid

ENTERING TEXT
Where	ANYWHERE
Word wrap	YES
Length of document	120 PG
Orientation	DOC

EDITING TEXT
During entry	YES
Insert	YES
Delete, copy, and move	YES, VAR, DOC

MOVEMENT WITHIN DOCUMENT
Cursor	FOR/BACK THROUGHOUT PAGE
Scroll	NEXT SCR, PREV SCR, GO TO PAGE
Search	FOR, EX
Search and replace	FOR, EX, GLOB, AUTO, SEMI-AUTO

SPECIAL FEATURES AND FORMATS
Alternate character sets	YES
Boilerplate	YES, GLOSSARY, P
Bold	NO
Calculate	YES, VIA MATH PAC
Centering	YES, SC
Center around tabs	NO
Change case	NO
Control characters	NO
Decimal tabs	YES
Dot commands	NO
Footnotes	YES, REPOSITION
Forced page break	YES
Format line	YES
Generate table of contents	YES, OIS SYSTEMS ONLY
Generate index	YES, OIS SYSTEMS ONLY
Headers and footers	YES, UNLIMITED #L
Hyphenating	USER
Letter merge	YES
Lines per page	YES
Line spacing	¼, ½, 1, 1 ½, 2, 3
Margin release key	NO
Margin width	158
Multicolumn	YES, SC
Nonprinting comments	YES
Onscreen	YES
Page breaks	USER, SC
Page numbers	YES, RESTART

Paragraph indent	YES, SC
Programmable key	NO
Reformat after changes	AUTO
Repeat last command	NO
Right justify	YES, PR; ON-SCREEN, OPTIONAL
Right justify tabs	NO
Sort	ALPH, NUM, OPT ON WP, STD ON OIS SYSTEMS
Spelling check	YES, 80,000 W, OPT ON OIS SYSTEMS ONLY
Storing formats	YES, IN GLOSSARY
Strikeover	YES
Sub/superscript	YES, PR
Tabs	VAR
Underline	YES, SC
Variable pitch	NO
Vertical lines	VARIABLE
Widows and orphans	USER

FILES

File names	FREE, 25 CH
Renaming	YES
Copy and delete files	YES
Copying disks	YES
Auto save	YES
Auto backup	NO
Verify	?
Disk directory	YES, ORDER, NAME, TITLE, DATE, AUTHOR

PRINTING

Continuous or sheet feed	BOTH
Multiple printers	YES
Queue	YES
Simultaneous	YES
Specific pages	YES
Typefaces	YES

HARDWARE

Internal memory	96K AND UP
Storage and drives	5 ¼" DS, DD; 8" HARD DISKS TO 275MB
Communications	RS232 ASYNCH, × 25, 2741/TTY, WPS, 2780/3780, 3271 BSC, 3274 BSC, 3274 SDLC/SNA, WANGNET, OTHERS; SOME MODELS DETACHED, OTHERS ATTACHED
Keyboard	KEYBOARDS, WPKEYS
Video tube	GREEN ON GRAY 80 × 24
Printers	RANGE OF LQP AND DOT MATRIX

DOCUMENTATION AND TRAINING

Documentation	SOFTWARE AND USER REFERENCE MANUALS, PRE-INSTALL MATERIAL, LEARNER'S KIT, OTHERS
Training	VARIES W/SYSTEM; COMBINATION OF CLASSROOM AND SELF-PACED TRAINING

VENDOR: Wordplex
MODEL: System 7
TYPE: Multiterminal

ENTERING TEXT
   Where   ANYWHERE
   Word wrap   YES
   Length of document   252 PG
   Orientation   PG

EDITING TEXT
   During entry   YES
   Insert   YES, ALWAYS ON
   Delete, copy, and move   YES, CH, W, L, P, PG, COL, DOC, REMAINDER OF PAGE

MOVEMENT WITHIN DOCUMENT
   Cursor   PG
   Scroll   SC, TOP/BOT
   Search   FOR, EX
   Search and replace   FOR, EX, GLOB, SEMI-AUTO BY PAGE

SPECIAL FEATURES AND FORMATS
   Alternate character sets   NO
   Boilerplate   YES, P
   Bold   NO
   Calculate   NO
   Centering   YES, SC
   Center around tabs   NO
   Change case   NO
   Control characters   SOME
   Decimal tabs   YES
   Dot commands   NO
   Footnotes   NO
   Forced page break   YES
   Format line   YES
   Generate table of contents   NO
   Generate index   NO
   Headers and footers   NO
   Hyphenating   NO
   Letter merge   YES
   Lines per page   YES
   Line spacing   1 OR 2, PR
   Margin release key   NO
   Margin width   128
   Multicolumn   YES, WITH LIMITATIONS
   Nonprinting comments   NO
   Onscreen   YES
   Page breaks   USER
   Page numbers   YES, RESTART
   Paragraph indent   NO

Programmable key	NO
Reformat after changes	AUTO
Repeat last command	NO
Right justify	YES, SC
Right justify tabs	NO
Sort	YES, ALPH, NUM
Spelling check	NO
Storing formats	YES
Strikeover	NO
Sub/superscript	YES, PR
Tabs	VAR
Underline	YES, SC
Variable pitch	VARY ON PAGE OR DOCUMENT BASIS
Vertical lines	RECORD—128 LINES, PRINT—83 LINES
Widows and orphans	AUTO

FILES

File names	FREE, 12 CH
Renaming	YES
Copy and delete files	YES
Copying disks	YES
Auto save	USER
Auto backup	NO, BUT PREVIOUS PAGE REVISIONS KEPT
Verify	YES
Disk directory	YES, ORDER, SIZE, TITLE, DATE

PRINTING

Continuous or sheet feed	BOTH
Multiple printers	YES
Queue	YES
Simultaneous	YES
Specific pages	YES
Typefaces	ON PAGE BASIS

HARDWARE

Internal memory	128K
Storage and drives	UP TO 4 80MB DISKS; 300MB OPTIONAL
Communications	BISYNCH 2780; WORDPLEX POINT TO POINT (ASYNCH, ASCII, 9600 BPI)
Keyboard	DETACHED, WP KEYS
Video tube	GREEN ON NONREFLECTIVE GRAY 80 × 24
Printers	DAISY WHEEL: 35, 40, 45, 55 CPS; LINE PRINTER: 300, 600 LPM; MAX 12 CH PR, 1 LINE

DOCUMENTATION AND TRAINING

Documentation	OPERATOR'S MANUALS, SUPERVISOR'S MANUAL, COMMAND SUMMARIES
Training	CLASSROOM TRAINING BY MANUFACTURER

LIST OF WORD-PROCESSING PRODUCTS || 399

VENDOR: Xerox
MODEL: 8000 Series "Star"
TYPE: Information system network

ENTERING TEXT
  Where   ANYWHERE
  Word wrap   YES
  Length of document   MEMORY; 10 MB & UP
  Orientation   DOC

EDITING TEXT
  During entry   YES
  Insert   YES, ALWAYS ON
  Delete, copy, and move   YES, VAR, DOC

MOVEMENT WITHIN DOCUMENT
  Cursor   ANYWHERE ON SCREEN VIA MOUSE
  Scroll   DONE W/MOUSE
  Search   FOR, EX, IGNORE CASE, WILD CARD
  Search and replace   FOR, IGNORE CASE, EX, GLOB, AUTO, SEMI-AUTO

SPECIAL FEATURES AND FORMATS
  Alternate character sets   OVER 20 FONTS
  Boilerplate   YES
  Bold   YES, SC, ALSO VARY POINT SIZE
  Calculate   YES
  Centering   YES, SC
  Center around tabs   YES
  Change case   NO
  Control characters   ONLY PAGE END
  Decimal tabs   YES
  Dot commands   NO
  Footnotes   NO, TO COME
  Forced page break   YES
  Format line   NO
  Generate table of contents   NO
  Generate index   NO
  Headers and footers   YES, UNLIMITED LINES, DATE
  Hyphenating   NO
  Letter merge   YES
  Lines per page   YES
  Line spacing   YES, SC
  Margin release key   NO NEED TO
  Margin width   14"
  Multicolumn   YES, SC
  Nonprinting comments   NO
  Onscreen   YES
  Page breaks   AUTO, SC
  Page numbers   YES, ALT, RESTART, ROMAN

Paragraph indent   YES, SC
Programmable key   NO
Reformat after changes   AUTO
Repeat last command   YES, "AGAIN" KEY
Right justify   YES, SC
Right justify tabs   YES
Sort   ALPH, NUM, OPT
Spelling check   NO
Storing formats   YES
Strikeover   NO
Sub/superscript   YES, SC
Tabs   5, VAR
Underline   YES, SC
Variable pitch   YES, SC
Vertical lines   UNLIMITED—FROM 6 TO 24 POINT
Widows and orphans   AUTO

FILES
File names   FREE
Renaming   YES
Copy and delete files   YES
Copying disks   YES
Auto save   YES
Auto backup   YES
Verify   ?
Disk directory   YES, SIZE, TITLE, DATE

PRINTING
Continuous or sheet
  feed   CONT-CHAR, SHEET-LASER PRINTERS
Multiple printers   YES
Queue   YES
Simultaneous   YES
Specific pages   NO
Typefaces   YES

HARDWARE
Internal memory   256K
Storage and drives   RIGID 10 TO 300 MB FLOPPY 8" DS DD WINCHESTER
Communications   FROM 30 TO 9600 BPS; 3270—TTY–PT TO PT, TO 860/820/850 WORD PROCESSORS NETWORK TO NETWORK
Keyboard   DETACHED, WP KEYS
Video tube   11–14" SCREEN
Printers   ANY NUMBER OF PRINTERS—UP TO APPROXIMATELY 1000; LASER PRINTER—12 PGS/MINUTE

DOCUMENTATION AND TRAINING
Documentation   ONLINE
Training   ONLINE TRAINING, VERY INTERACTIVE HELP KEY

NOTES
USES A "MOUSE" AND A SMALL POINTER

VENDOR: XMark
MODEL: 2000-15-S
TYPE: Stand-alone or multiterminal

ENTERING TEXT
Where	ANYWHERE
Word wrap	YES
Length of document	DISK
Orientation	PG

EDITING TEXT
During entry	YES
Insert	YES, ALWAYS ON
Delete, copy, and move	YES, CH, W, L, S, P, PG, COL, VAR, DOC

MOVEMENT WITHIN DOCUMENT
Cursor	W, L, S, P, PG, COL
Scroll	L, P, PG, SC, TOP/BOT
Search	FOR, BACK, IGNORE CASE, EX
Search and replace	FOR, BACK, IGNORE CASE, EX, GLOB, SEMI-AUTO

SPECIAL FEATURES AND FORMATS
Alternate character sets	YES
Boilerplate	YES, GLOSSARY, P
Bold	YES, SC
Calculate	A, SUB, M, DIV, %
Centering	YES
Center around tabs	YES
Change case	YES
Control characters	SOME
Decimal tabs	YES
Dot commands	SOME
Footnotes	YES
Forced page break	YES
Format line	YES
Generate table of contents	NO
Generate index	?
Headers and footers	YES, 2 LINES
Hyphenating	YES
Letter merge	YES
Lines per page	YES
Line spacing	YES
Margin release key	YES
Margin width	80, 130 OR 160
Multicolumn	YES, SC
Nonprinting comments	YES
Onscreen	YES
Page breaks	AUTO
Page numbers	YES
Paragraph indent	YES

Programmable key	YES
Reformat after changes	AUTO
Repeat last command	YES
Right justify	YES
Right justify tabs	NO
Sort	YES, OPT
Spelling check	NO
Storing formats	YES
Strikeover	NO
Sub/superscript	YES
Tabs	VARIABLE
Underline	YES
Variable pitch	YES
Vertical lines	90
Widows and orphans	USER

FILES

File names	FREE
Renaming	YES
Copy and delete files	YES
Copying disks	YES
Auto save	NO, USER
Auto backup	YES
Verify	YES
Disk directory	YES

PRINTING

Continuous or sheet feed	BOTH
Multiple printers	YES
Queue	YES
Simultaneous	YES
Specific pages	YES
Typefaces	YES

HARDWARE

Internal memory	64K
Storage and drives	1.2 MB DUAL MINI-DISKETTE DRIVE; DUAL 8″ DRIVE (600KB); 10 MG HARD DISK (5MG FIXED, 5MG REMOVABLE)
Communications	38.4K ASYNCH, 50K BPS, SYNCH
Keyboard	DETACHED, # PAD, WP KEYS
Video tube	WHITE ON BLACK OR BLACK ON WHITE 80 × 25
Printers	55 CPS NEC PRINTER; OTHERS AVAILABLE

DOCUMENTATION AND TRAINING

Documentation	MANUALS
Training	TWO 4-HOUR SESSIONS FOR ONE OPERATOR ADDITIONAL TRAINING

SOFTWARE

VENDOR: ABC Sales
MODEL: Lazywriter
TYPE: Software for Radio Shack TRS-80 MODEL I and III

ENTERING TEXT
Where	BOTTOM
Word wrap	YES
Length of document	MEM & DISK
Orientation	DOC

EDITING TEXT
During entry	YES, BUT LIMITED
Insert	YES, ON
Delete, copy, and move	YES, CH, W, L, S, P

MOVEMENT WITHIN DOCUMENT
Cursor	W, L, S, P
Scroll	L, P, SC, TOP/BOT
Search	FOR, IGNORE CASE
Search and replace	FOR, IGNORE CASE, GLOB, AUTO, SEMI-AUTO

SPECIAL FEATURES AND FORMATS
Alternate character sets	YES
Boilerplate	NO
Bold	YES, PR
Calculate	NO
Centering	YES, PR
Center around tabs	NO
Change case	YES
Control characters	YES, MOST
Decimal tabs	NO
Dot commands	YES (W/ ">" SYMBOL)
Footnotes	NO
Forced page break	YES
Format line	NO
Generate table of contents	NO
Generate index	NO
Headers and footers	YES, UNLIMITED # LINES
Hyphenating	USER
Letter merge	NO
Lines per page	YES
Line spacing	DEPENDENT ON PRINTER
Margin release key	NO
Margin width	256
Multicolumn	NO
Nonprinting comments	YES
Onscreen	NO

Page breaks	YES, SC W/ SPECIAL FORMATTING FUNCTION
Page numbers	YES, ALT, RESTART
Paragraph indent	YES, SC
Programmable key	YES
Reformat after changes	USER
Repeating last command	NO
Right justify	YES, PR
Right justify tabs	YES
Sort	NO
Spelling check	OPT; SPELLING PROGRAMS AVAILABLE FROM OTHER VENDORS
Storing formats	NO
Strikeover	YES, PR
Sub/superscript	YES, PR
Tabs	VAR
Underline	YES, PR
Variable pitch	YES, PR
Vertical lines	VAR
Widows and orphans	USER

FILES

File names	OPSYS
Renaming	YES
Copy and delete files	YES
Copying disks	YES, THROUGH OPSYS
Auto save	USER
Auto backup	NO
Verify	YES
Disk directory	YES

PRINTING

Continuous or sheet feed	BOTH
Multiple printers	NO
Queue	NO, BUT LINK AVAILABLE
Simultaneous	DEPENDS ON OPSYS
Specific pages	PRINT TO OR FROM CURSOR
Typefaces	YES

DOCUMENTATION AND TRAINING

Documentation	MANUAL, NEWSLETTER
Training	LEARN ON OWN; CALL WITH QUESTIONS |//
NOTES:	REQUIRES 32K MEMORY AT LEAST ONE DISK DRIVE, PRINTER; CP/M VERSION TO BE RELEASED

VENDOR: Data General Corporation
MODEL: Comprehensive Electronic Office
TYPE: Software for Data General Eclipse

ENTERING TEXT
Where	ANYWHERE
Word wrap	YES
Length of document	DISK
Orientation	DOC

EDITING TEXT
During entry	YES
Insert	ON/OFF
Delete, copy, and move	CH, W, VAR, DOC

MOVEMENT WITHIN DOCUMENT
Cursor	W, L, S, P, PG, COL
Scroll	L, P, PG, SC, TOP/BOT, CONT
Search	FOR, IGNORE CASE, EX
Search and replace	FOR, IGNORE CASE, EX, GLOB, AUTO, SEMI-AUTO

SPECIAL FEATURES AND FORMATS
Alternate character sets	NO
Boilerplate	YES, GLOSSARY, P
Bold	YES, SC
Calculate	YES
Centering	YES, SC
Center around tabs	NO
Change case	NO
Control characters	MOST
Decimal tabs	YES
Dot commands	NO
Footnotes	YES
Forced page break	YES
Format line	YES
Generate table of contents	NO
Generate index	YES
Headers and footers	YES, 7L, DATE
Hyphenating	AUTO, USER
Letter merge	YES
Lines per page	YES
Line spacing	1, 1 ½, 2, 3
Margin release key	YES
Margin width	162
Multicolumn	NO
Nonprinting comments	YES
Onscreen	YES (VIEW MODE)
Page breaks	AUTO PR, USER SC
Page numbers	YES, ALT
Paragraph indent	YES, SC

Programmable key	YES
Reformat after changes	AUTO
Repeat last command	NO
Right justify	YES, PR
Right justify tabs	YES
Sort	YES
Spelling check	YES, 91,000 W, OPT
Storing formats	YES
Strikeover	NO
Sub/superscript	PR
Tabs	VAR
Underline	YES, SC
Variable pitch	NO
Vertical lines	VAR
Widows and orphans	USER

FILES

File names	FREE, 75 CH
Renaming	YES
Copy and delete files	BOTH
Copying disks	YES
Auto save	YES, USER
Auto backup	YES
Verify	NO
Disk directory	YES, ORDER (BY USER), NAME, TITLE, DATE

PRINTING

Continuous or sheet feed	BOTH
Multiple printers	YES
Queue	YES
Simultaneous	YES
Specific pages	YES
Typefaces	NO

DOCUMENTATION AND TRAINING

Documentation	ONLINE AND MANUALS
Training	ON-SITE, CLASSROOM, AND SELF-PACED INSTRUCTION

NOTES   COMMUNICATIONS: 2780/3780, 3270, X-25, SNA, 300–192KB; TEMPLATE FOR FUNCTION KEYS; PRINTER: NEC 5515, 55CPS

VENDOR: Data Processing Design, Inc.
MODEL: Word-11
TYPE: Multiterminal software for Digital Equipment Computers with RSTS/E, RSX-11M, PWS, VAY/VMS

ENTERING TEXT

Where	BOTTOM
Word wrap	YES

Length of document   DISK
Orientation   DOC

EDITING TEXT
During entry   YES
Insert   YES, ALWAYS ON
Delete, copy, and move   CH, W, L, S, P, PG, VAR, DOC

MOVEMENT WITHIN DOCUMENT
Cursor   ONLY ON BOTTOM LINE
Scroll   L, P, PG, SC, TOP/BOT, AND MORE
Search   FOR, BACK, IGNORE CASE, EX
Search and replace   FOR, BACK, IGNORE CASE, EX, AUTO SEMI-AUTO

SPECIAL FEATURES AND FORMATS
Alternate character sets   YES
Boilerplate   YES, GLOSSARY, P
Bold   YES, SC
Calculate   TOTALS DURING EDIT, OTHERS W/LIST PROC.
Centering   YES, SC
Center around tabs   NO
Change case   YES
Control characters   NO
Decimal tabs   YES
Dot commands   NO
Footnotes   YES, RENUMBER, REPOSITION
Forced page break   YES
Format line   YES
Generate table of contents   YES
Generate index   YES
Headers and footers   YES
Hyphenating   "HOT ZONE"
Letter merge   YES
Lines per page   YES
Line spacing   YES, PR
Margin release key   NO
Margin width   131
Multicolumn   NO
Nonprinting comments   YES
Onscreen   YES
Page breaks   AUTO, SC
Page numbers   ALT, RESTART
Paragraph indent   YES
Programmable key   YES
Reformat after changes   AUTO
Repeat last command   NO
Right justify   YES, PR
Right justify tabs   YES
Sort   YES, ALPH, NUM
Spelling check   YES, 32,000 W
Storing formats   YES

Strikeover	YES
Sub/superscript	YES
Tabs	VAR
Underline	YES, SC
Variable pitch	YES, PR
Vertical lines	VAR
Widows and orphans	USER

FILES

File names	FREE
Renaming	YES
Copy and delete files	YES
Copying disks	YES
Auto save	YES
Auto backup	YES
Verify	WITH OPERATING SYSTEM
Disk directory	TITLE, DOC#, WILD CARD LOOK UP

PRINTING

Continuous or sheet feed	BOTH
Multiple printers	YES
Queue	YES
Simultaneous	YES
Specific pages	YES
Typefaces	YES

DOCUMENTATION AND TRAINING

Documentation	USER'S GUIDE, POCKET GUIDE, MANAGER'S GUIDE
Training	2 DAYS ON-SITE, TRAVEL COST ONLY

NOTES   COMMUNICATIONS: ASYNCH TO 9600 BAUD

VENDOR: Datasoft
MODEL: Text Wizard
TYPE: Software on various microcomputers

ENTERING TEXT

Where	ANYWHERE
Word wrap	YES
Length of document	30K
Orientation	DOC

EDITING TEXT

During entry	YES
Insert	YES, ON/OFF
Delete, copy, and move	YES, VAR

MOVEMENT WITHIN DOCUMENT

Cursor	?
Scroll	TOP/BOT, + 512 CH
Search	FOR, EX
Search and replace	FOR, EX, SEMI-AUTO

SPECIAL FEATURES AND FORMATS

Alternate character sets	IF PRINTER ALLOWS
Boilerplate	YES, P
Bold	YES, PR
Calculate	NO
Centering	YES, PR
Center around tabs	NO
Change case	NO
Control characters	YES
Decimal tabs	YES
Dot commands	NO
Footnotes	NO
Forced page break	YES
Format line	YES
Generate table of contents	NO
Generate index	NO
Headers and footers	YES, 1 LINE
Hyphenating	NO
Letter merge	NO
Lines per page	YES
Line spacing	YES, PR
Margin release key	NO
Margin width	?
Multicolumn	NO
Nonprinting comments	YES
Onscreen	NO
Page breaks	AUTO, USER, PR
Page numbers	YES
Paragraph indent	YES, SC
Programmable key	NO
Reformat after changes	AUTO
Repeat last command	YES
Right justify	YES, ON/OFF, PR
Right justify tabs	YES
Sort	NO
Spelling check	NO
Storing formats	YES
Strikeover	YES, PR
Sub/superscript	YES, PR
Tabs	5
Underline	YES, PR
Variable pitch	NO
Vertical lines	
Widows and orphans	USER

FILES

File names	OPSYS
Renaming	YES, VIA OPERATING SYSTEM
Copy and delete files	YES

Copying disks   YES, VIA OPERATING SYSTEM
Auto save   USER
Auto backup   NO
Verify   NO
Disk directory   YES, SIZE

PRINTING
Continuous or sheet
  feed   BOTH
Multiple printers   NO
Queue   NO, BUT YOU MAY "CHAIN" FILES
Simultaneous   NO
Specific pages   NO
Typefaces   NO

DOCUMENTATION AND TRAINING
Documentation   ?
Training   ?

VENDOR: Designer Software
MODEL: Palantir Tier 1 & Tier 2
TYPE: Software for various microcomputers

ENTERING TEXT
Where   ANYWHERE
Word wrap   YES
Length of document   DISK
Orientation   DOC

EDITING TEXT
During entry   YES
Insert   YES, ON/OFF
Delete, copy, and move   VAR, DOC

MOVEMENT WITHIN DOCUMENT
Cursor   W, L, S, P, PG, COL
Scroll   L, P, PG, SC, TOP/BOT
Search   FOR, BACK, IGNORE CASE, EX
Search and replace   FOR, BACK, IGNORE CASE, EX, AUTO,
                           SEMI-AUTO

SPECIAL FEATURES AND FORMATS
Alternate character
  sets   YES
Boilerplate   YES, GLOSSARY, P
Bold   YES, SC
Calculate   YES, OPT
Centering   YES, SC
Center around tabs   NO
Change case   NO
Control characters   NO
Decimal tabs   YES
Dot commands   NO

Footnotes	TIER 1—NO, TIER 2—YES, RENUMBER, REPOSITION
Forced page break	YES
Format line	YES
Generate table of contents	NO
Generate index	NO
Headers and footers	YES, UNLIMITED #L
Hyphenating	YES, AUTO USER
Letter merge	YES, OPT
Lines per page	YES
Line spacing	PR
Margin release key	YES
Margin width	255
Multicolumn	TIER 2 ONLY, PR
Nonprinting comments	YES
Onscreen	YES
Page breaks	AUTO, USER, SC
Page numbers	YES, ALT, RESTART
Paragraph indent	NO
Programmable key	YES
Reformat after changes	AUTO
Repeat last command	NO
Right justify	YES, SC
Right justify tabs	YES
Sort	NO
Spelling check	OPT—SPELLGUARD, AVAILABLE FROM ISA
Storing formats	YES
Strikeover	YES, SC
Sub/superscript	YES, PR
Tabs	VAR
Underline	YES, SC IF TERMINAL CAPABLE, OTHERWISE PR ONLY
Variable pitch	YES, SC
Vertical lines	VAR
Widows and orphans	AUTO

FILES

File names	OPSYS
Renaming	YES
Copy and delete files	YES
Copying disks	NO
Auto save	USER
Auto backup	YES
Verify	NO
Disk directory	YES

PRINTING

Continuous or sheet feed	BOTH
Multiple printers	YES
Queue	TIER 2 ONLY

Simultaneous	YES—DEPENDS ON HARDWARE
Specific pages	YES
Typefaces	YES

DOCUMENTATION AND TRAINING

Documentation	MANUALS
Training	TRAINING DEPENDS ON DEALER

VENDOR: Hayden Book Company
MODEL: Apple Pie Editor and Formatter
TYPE: Software for Apple II with 48K RAM

ENTERING TEXT

Where	ANYWHERE
Word wrap	YES, ON/OFF
Length of document	MEMORY
Orientation	DOC

EDITING TEXT

During entry	YES
Insert	YES, ON/OFF
Delete, copy, and move	YES, CH, W, L, VAR

MOVEMENT WITHIN DOCUMENT

Cursor	W, L
Scroll	L, SC, TOP/BOT
Search	FOR, BACK, WILD CARDS
Search and replace	FOR, BACK, EX, GLOB, AUTO, SEMI-AUTO

SPECIAL FEATURES AND FORMATS

Alternate character sets	NO
Boilerplate	NO, BUT CAN APPEND FILES
Bold	YES, PR
Calculate	NO
Centering	YES, PR
Center around tabs	NO
Change case	YES
Control characters	NO
Decimal tabs	NO
Dot commands	MOST
Footnotes	NO
Forced page break	YES
Format line	YES, ON/OFF
Generate table of contents	NO
Generate index	NO
Headers and footers	YES
Hyphenating	NO
Letter merge	YES
Lines per page	YES
Line spacing	VARIABLE, PR

Margin release key	NO
Margin width	VARIABLE
Multicolumn	NO
Nonprinting comments	YES
Onscreen	NOT DURING EDIT
Page breaks	AUTO, PR
Page numbers	YES, RESTART
Paragraph indent	YES, PR
Programmable key	NO
Reformat after changes	AUTO
Repeat last command	NO
Right justify	YES, ON/OFF, PR
Right justify tabs	NO
Sort	NO
Spelling check	NO, BUT COMPATIBLE W/OTHER SPELLING PROGRAMS
Storing formats	YES
Strikeover	YES, PR
Sub/superscript	NO
Tabs	VARIABLE
Underline	YES, PR
Variable pitch	INCREMENTAL SPACING, PR
Vertical lines	VAR
Widows and orphans	AUTO

FILES

File names	OPSYS
Renaming	YES
Copy and delete files	YES
Copying disks	YES
Auto save	NO
Auto backup	NO
Verify	OPSYS
Disk directory	YES

PRINTING

Continuous or sheet feed	BOTH
Multiple printers	WITH OPTION
Queue	WITH OPTION
Simultaneous	WITH OPTION
Specific pages	YES
Typefaces	DEPENDS ON PRINTER

DOCUMENTATION AND TRAINING

Documentation	MANUAL INCLUDES TUTORIAL, REFERENCE, & ADVANCED TOPICS, 157 PAGES
Training	SELF-TRAINING

VENDOR: Information Unlimited Software
MODEL: Easy Writer Professional
TYPE: Software for IBM PC, Apple II, IIe, other microcomputers

ENTERING TEXT
Where	ANYWHERE
Word wrap	YES
Length of document	3–4 PG, 12,235 CH/FILE
Orientation	DOC

EDITING TEXT
During entry	YES
Insert	YES, ON/OFF
Delete, copy, and move	CH, W, L, VAR

MOVEMENT WITHIN DOCUMENT
Cursor	L
Scroll	L, SC, TOP/BOT
Search	FOR, EX
Search and replace	FOR, EX, AUTO, SEMI-AUTO

SPECIAL FEATURES AND FORMATS
Alternate character sets	USER DEFINABLE
Boilerplate	NO
Bold	YES, PR
Calculate	NO
Centering	YES, SC
Center around tabs	NO
Change case	NO
Control characters	MOST
Decimal tabs	NO
Dot commands	YES
Footnotes	NO
Forced page break	YES
Format line	YES, ON/OFF
Generate table of contents	NO
Generate index	NO
Headers and footers	YES 3 L
Hyphenating	NO
Letter merge	OPT
Lines per page	YES
Line spacing	YES, WHOLE NUMBERS
Margin release key	NO
Margin width	132
Multicolumn	NO
Nonprinting comments	NO
Onscreen	YES
Page breaks	AUTO, USER, PR
Page numbers	YES, ALT, RESTART
Paragraph indent	YES, SC
Programmable key	YES
Reformat after changes	USER

Repeat last command	NO
Right justify	YES, ON/OFF, SC
Right justify tabs	NO
Sort	OPT, EASY MAILER
Spelling check	NO
Storing formats	NO
Strikeover	NO
Sub/superscript	YES, PR
Tabs	VAR
Underline	YES, PR
Variable pitch	YES
Vertical lines	VAR
Widows and orphans	USER

FILES

File names	FREE, 10 CH
Renaming	NO
Copy and delete files	DELETE
Copying disks	YES
Auto save	USER
Auto backup	NO
Verify	NO
Disk directory	YES, SIZE, TITLE

PRINTING

Continuous or sheet feed	BOTH
Multiple printers	NO
Queue	NO
Simultaneous	NO
Specific pages	YES
Typefaces	YES

DOCUMENTATION AND TRAINING

Documentation	USER MANUAL, REFERENCE CARDS
Training	CUSTOMER PHONE SUPPORT OTHER THAN DEALER

NOTES   REQUIRES 48K RAM

VENDOR: Information Unlimited Software
MODEL: Easy Writer II
TYPE: Software for IBM PC

ENTERING TEXT

Where	ANYWHERE
Word wrap	YES
Length of document	DISK
Orientation	PG

EDITING TEXT

During entry	YES
Insert	YES, ON/OFF
Delete, copy, and move	CH, W, L, S, P, PG, VAR, DOC

MOVEMENT WITHIN DOCUMENT

Cursor	W, L, S, P, PG
Scroll	PG
Search	FOR, BACK, IGNORE, EX
Search and replace	FOR, BACK, IGNORE, GLOB, AUTO, SEMI-AUTO

SPECIAL FEATURES AND FORMATS

Alternate character sets	NO
Boilerplate	YES
Bold	YES, SC
Calculate	NO
Centering	YES, SC
Center around tabs	NO
Change case	NO
Control characters	NO
Decimal tabs	YES
Dot commands	NO
Footnotes	NO
Forced page break	YES
Format line	YES
Generate table of contents	NO
Generate index	NO
Headers and footers	YES, UNLIMITED #L
Hyphenating	NOW
Letter merge	YES; ONE AT A TIME
Lines per page	YES
Line spacing	YES
Margin release key	NO
Margin width	132
Multicolumn	NO
Nonprinting comments	NO
Onscreen	YES
Page breaks	AUTO, SC
Page numbers	YES, RESTART
Paragraph indent	NO
Programmable key	NO
Reformat after changes	USER
Repeat last command	NO
Right justify	YES, ON/OFF, SC
Right justify tabs	NO
Sort	NO
Spelling check	YES, 88,710 W, OPT
Storing formats	YES
Strikeover	YES, SC
Sub/superscript	YES, PR
Tabs	VAR
Underline	YES, SC
Variable pitch	YES, PR

LIST OF WORD-PROCESSING PRODUCTS ‖ 417

    Vertical lines   200
    Widows and orphans   USER
FILES
    File names   FREE, 50 CH
    Renaming   YES
    Copy and delete files   YES
    Copying disks   YES
    Auto save   YES
    Auto backup   NO
    Verify   YES
    Disk directory   YES, SIZE, NAME, TITLE, DATE
PRINTING
    Continuous or sheet
       feed   BOTH
    Multiple printers   YES, NOT SIMULTANEOUS
    Queue   YES
    Simultaneous   YES
    Specific pages   YES
    Typefaces   YES
DOCUMENTATION AND TRAINING
    Documentation   MANUAL & TUTORIAL DISK
    Training   NONE; PHONE SUPPORT AVAILABLE

VENDOR: Lexisoft
MODEL: Spellbinder
TYPE: Software for CP/M systems

ENTERING TEXT
    Where   ANYWHERE
    Word wrap   YES
    Length of document   DISK
    Orientation   DOC
EDITING TEXT
    During entry   NO
    Insert   YES, S, ON/OFF
    Delete, copy, and move   CH, W, L, S, P, PG, COL, VAR, DOC
MOVEMENT WITHIN DOCUMENT
    Cursor   W, L, S, P, PG, COL
    Scroll   L, P, PG, SC, TOP/BOT
    Search   FOR, IGNORE CASE
    Search and replace   FOR, IGNORE CASE, GLOB, AUTO, SEMI-AUTO
SPECIAL FEATURES AND FORMATS
    Alternate character
       sets   YES
    Boilerplate   YES, GLOSSARY, P
    Bold   YES, PR
    Calculate   A, SUB, M

Centering	SC
Center around tabs	NO
Change case	YES
Control characters	SOME
Decimal tabs	YES
Dot command	SOME
Footnotes	NO
Forced page break	YES
Format line	YES
Generate table of contents	NO
Generate index	YES
Headers and footers	YES, 50 L, DATE
Hyphenating	USER
Letter merge	YES
Lines per page	YES
Line spacing	YES, OTHER, PR
Margin release key	YES
Margin width	25.4"
Multicolumn	YES, PR
Nonprinting comments	YES
Onscreen	YES
Page breaks	AUTO, SC, PR
Page numbers	YES, ALT, RESTART
Paragraph indent	YES, SC
Programmable key	YES
Reformat after changes	AUTO
Repeat last command	YES
Right justify	YES, ON/OFF, SC
Right justify tabs	?
Sort	YES, ALPH, NUM
Spelling check	YES, 20,000 W, OPT
Storing formats	YES
Strikeover	YES, PR
Sub/superscript	YES, PR
Tabs	BOTH
Underline	YES, PR
Variable pitch	YES, PR
Vertical lines	254 LINES
Widows and orphans	USER

FILES

File names	OPSYS
Renaming	YES
Copy and delete files	YES
Copying disks	YES
Auto save	NO, USER
Auto backup	YES
Verify	YES
Disk directory	YES

PRINTING
Continuous or sheet feed	BOTH
Multiple printers	YES
Queue	YES
Simultaneous	NO
Specific pages	YES
Typefaces	YES

DOCUMENTATION AND TRAINING
Documentation	TUTORIAL MANUAL, REFERENCE MANUAL
Training	PROVIDED BY DEALER

VENDOR: Micropro International
MODEL: WordStar Version 3.0
TYPE: Software for CP/M systems

ENTERING TEXT
Where	ANYWHERE
Word wrap	YES
Length of document	DISK
Orientation	DOC

EDITING TEXT
During entry	YES
Insert	YES, ON/OFF
Delete, copy, and move	YES, VAR, DOC

MOVEMENT WITHIN DOCUMENT
Cursor	CH, W, L, SC, MARKER, DOC
Scroll	L, SC, CONT
Search	FOR, BACK, EX, IGNORE CASE, WILD CARD
Search and replace	FOR, BACK, EX, IGNORE CASE, WILD CARD, AUTO, SEMI-AUTO

SPECIAL FEATURES AND FORMATS
Alternate character sets	YES
Boilerplate	INDIVIDUAL DOCUMENTS ONLY
Bold	YES
Calculate	NO
Centering	YES
Center around tabs	NO
Change case	NO
Control characters	YES
Decimal tabs	YES
Dot commands	YES
Footnotes	NO
Forced page break	YES
Format line	YES
Generate table of contents	NO

Generate index | NO
Headers and footers | YES, 1 LINE
Hyphenating | YES, USER
Letter merge | YES, MAILMERGE, OPT
Lines per page | YES
Line spacing | YES
Margin release key | YES
Margin width | 255
Multicolumn | NO
Nonprinting comments | YES
Onscreen | YES
Page breaks | AUTO
Page numbers | YES, ODD/EVEN
Paragraph indent | YES
Programmable key | NO
Reformat after changes | USER
Repeat last command | NO
Right justify | YES, SC
Right justify tabs | NO
Sort | NO
Spelling check | YES, OPT
Storing formats | YES
Strikeover | YES, PR
Sub/superscript | YES, PR
Tabs | 5, VAR
Underline | YES, PR
Variable pitch | YES
Vertical lines | VAR
Widows and orphans | USER

FILES
File names | OPSYS
Renaming | YES
Copy and delete files | YES
Copying disks | NO
Auto save | USER
Auto backup | YES
Verify | NO
Disk directory | YES, TITLE

PRINTING
Continuous or sheet feed | BOTH
Multiple printers | NO
Queue | NO
Simultaneous | YES
Specific pages | YES
Typefaces | YES

DOCUMENTATION AND TRAINING
Documentation | USER'S MANUAL; TRAINING MANUAL (OPT), REF CARDS & KEY TOPS
Training | UP TO DEALER

NOTES | REQUIRES 48K RAM

LIST OF WORD-PROCESSING PRODUCTS || 421

VENDOR: Northern Telecom
MODEL: Omniword
TYPE: Software only for NT Models 503/445/585

ENTERING TEXT
Where	LINE 11 OF CRT
Word wrap	YES
Length of document	10,000 LINES
Orientation	DOC

EDITING TEXT
During entry	YES
Insert	YES, ALWAYS ON
Delete, copy, and move	YES, CH, W, L, S, COL, VAR, DOC

MOVEMENT WITHIN DOCUMENT
Cursor	1, 10 OR 20 LINES, LINE #
Scroll	L, SC, TOP/BOT
Search	FOR, EX
Search and replace	FOR, EX, GLOB, AUTO, SEMI-AUTO

SPECIAL FEATURES AND FORMATS
Alternate character sets	?
Boilerplate	YES, GLOSSARY, P
Bold	SHADOW PRINT, PR
Calculate	NO
Centering	YES, SC
Center around tabs	YES
Change case	YES
Control characters	MOST
Decimal tabs	YES
Dot commands	MOST
Footnotes	NO
Forced page break	YES
Format line	YES
Generate table of contents	NO
Generate index	NO
Headers and footers	YES, 1 LINE
Hyphenating	USER
Letter merge	YES
Lines per page	YES
Line spacing	1, 1½, 2, 3, PR
Margin release key	YES
Margin width	160
Multicolumn	NO
Nonprinting comments	YES
Onscreen	YES
Page breaks	AUTO
Page numbers	YES, ALT, RESTART
Paragraph indent	YES, SC
Programmable key	NO
Reformat after changes	USER

Repeat last command	YES, PR
Right justify	YES, PR
Right justify tabs	YES
Sort	VIA DP FUNCTION
Spelling check	NO
Storing formats	YES
Strikeover	NO
Sub/superscript	YES, PR
Tabs	VAR
Underline	YES, PR
Variable pitch	YES, PR
Vertical lines	VARY
Widows and orphans	USE SR

FILES

File names	FREE, UP TO 8 CH
Renaming	YES
Copy and delete files	YES
Copying disks	YES
Auto save	USER
Auto backup	NO
Verify	VIA DATA PROCESSING
Disk directory	YES, ORDER, TITLE, NAME, DATE, SIZE, OTHERS

PRINTING

Continuous or sheet feed	BOTH
Multiple printers	NO
Queue	NO, BUT OTHER PROCEDURES ALLOW MULTIPLE DOCS
Stimultaneous	NO
Specific pages	YES
Typefaces	YES

DOCUMENTATION AND TRAINING

Documentation	USER GUIDE, REFERENCE GUIDE; SUPERVISOR'S GUIDE—PROVIDED AT CLASS
Training	CLASSES AVAILABLE

VENDOR: Para Research
MODEL: Para Text
TYPE: Software for IBM System 34 and System 38

ENTERING TEXT

Where	ANYWHERE
Word wrap	YES
Length of document	DISK
Orientation	DOC

EDITING TEXT
During entry	YES
Insert	YES
Delete, copy, and move	YES, VAR

MOVEMENT WITHIN DOCUMENT
Cursor	PG
Scroll	SC
Search	EX
Search and replace	EX, GLOB, SEMI-AUTO

SPECIAL FEATURES AND FORMATS
Alternate character sets	NO
Boilerplate	YES
Bold	NO
Calculate	A, M
Centering	YES, SC
Center around tabs	YES
Change case	YES, LOWER TO UPPER
Control characters	NO
Decimal tabs	YES
Dot commands	NO
Footnotes	NO
Forced page break	YES
Format line	NO
Generate table of contents	NO
Generate index	NO
Headers and footers	YES, 6 LINES, DATE
Hyphenating	NO
Letter merge	YES
Lines per page	YES
Line spacing	1, 2, 3, PR
Margin release key	YES
Margin width	74
Multicolumn	YES, SC
Nonprinting comments	NO
Onscreen	NO
Page breaks	USER, SC
Page numbers	YES, RESTART
Paragraph indent	NO
Programmable key	YES
Reformat after changes	AUTO
Repeat last command	NO
Right justify	YES, ON/OFF, SC
Right justify tabs	NO
Sort	YES, ALPH, NUM
Spelling check	YES, OPT, 50,000 W
Storing formats	YES
Strikeover	NO
Sub/superscript	NO

Tabs	VAR
Underline	YES, PR
Variable pitch	YES, PR
Vertical lines	VAR
Widows and orphans	USER

FILES

File names	FREE
Renaming	YES
Copy and delete files	YES
Copying disks	YES
Auto save	YES
Auto backup	YES
Verify	YES
Disk directory	YES, SIZE, NAME, TITLE, DATE

PRINTING

Continuous or sheet feed	BOTH
Multiple printers	YES
Queue	YES
Simultaneous	YES
Specific pages	YES
Typefaces	NO

DOCUMENTATION AND TRAINING

Documentation	USER'S MANUAL
Training	AVAILABLE FOR COST

VENDOR: Peachtree Software
MODEL: Peachtext (previously "Magic Wand")
TYPE: Software for CP/M systems

ENTERING TEXT

Where	ANYWHERE
Word wrap	ON/OFF
Length of document	DISK
Orientation	DOC

EDITING TEXT

During entry	YES
Insert	YES, ALWAYS ON
Delete, copy, and move	YES, CH, W, L, S, P, PG, COL, VAR

MOVEMENT WITHIN DOCUMENT

Cursor	W, L, S, P, PG, COL
Scroll	L, SC, TEXT IN MEMORY
Search	FOR, EX
Search and replace	FOR, EX, AUTO, SEMI-AUTO, GLOBAL ON TEXT IN MEMORY

SPECIAL FEATURE AND FORMATS

Alternate character sets	YES
Boilerplate	YES

Bold	YES, PR
Calculate	A, SUB
Centering	YES, PR
Center around tabs	YES
Change case	NO
Control characters	YES
Decimal tabs	NO
Dot commands	ALL
Footnotes	NO
Forced page break	YES
Format line	NO
Generate table of contents	YES
Generate index	YES
Headers and footers	YES, VAR #L, DATE
Hyphenating	AUTO
Letter merge	YES
Lines per page	YES
Line spacing	OTHER, PR
Margin release key	NO
Margin width	132
Multicolumn	YES, PR
Nonprinting comments	YES
Onscreen	LIMITED BY CRT
Page breaks	AUTO, PR
Page numbers	YES, ALT, RESTART
Paragraph indent	YES, PR
Programmable key	NO
Reformat after changes	AUTO
Repeat last command	SEARCH AND REPLACE ONLY
Right justify	YES, ON/OFF, PR
Right justify tabs	YES
Sort	NO
Spelling check	YES, 20,000 W & USER EXPANDABLE, OPT
Storing formats	YES
Strikeover	YES, PR
Sub/superscript	YES, PR
Tabs	VAR, BY COLUMN OR WORD
Underline	YES, PR
Variable pitch	YES, PR
Vertical lines	VAR
Widows and orphans	AUTO

FILES

File names	OPSYS
Renaming	YES
Copy and delete files	YES
Copying disks	YES
Auto save	YES, USER
Auto backup	YES
Verify	YES
Disk directory	YES

426 || THE DEFINITIVE WORD-PROCESSING BOOK

PRINTING
Continuous or sheet feed	BOTH
Multiple printers	NO
Queue	NO
Simultaneous	YES
Specific pages	YES
Typefaces	YES, IF PRINTER CAN

DOCUMENTATION AND TRAINING
Documentation	SELF-TUTORING MANUAL, REFERENCE CARD
Training	CLASSROOM TRAINING AVAILABLE AT EXTRA COST

VENDOR: Perfect Software
MODEL: Perfect Writer
TYPE: Software for CP/M, PCDOS, and MSDOS operating systems

ENTERING TEXT
Where	ANYWHERE
Word wrap	YES, ON/OFF
Length of document	DISK
Orientation	DOC

EDITING TEXT
During entry	YES
Insert	YES, ON/OFF
Delete, copy, and move	YES, CH, W, L, S, P, VAR, DOC

MOVEMENT WITHIN DOCUMENT
Cursor	W, L, S, P, DOC
Scroll	L, SC
Search	FOR, BACK, IGNORE CASE
Search and replace	FOR, IGNORE CASE, GLOB, AUTO, SEMI-AUTO

SPECIAL FEATURES AND FORMATS
Alternate character sets	YES
Boilerplate	YES, GLOSSARY, P
Bold	YES, SC
Calculate	YES
Centering	YES, SC
Center around tabs	NO
Change case	YES
Control characters	SOME
Decimal tabs	YES
Dot commands	NO
Footnotes	YES, RENUMBER, REPOSITION
Forced page break	YES
Format line	YES, ON/OFF
Generate table of contents	YES

Generate index	YES
Headers and footers	YES, 2 LINES
Hyphenating	USER
Letter merge	YES
Lines per page	YES
Line spacing	YES, PR
Margin release key	YES
Margin width	?
Multicolumn	YES, SC
Nonprinting comments	YES
Onscreen	YES
Page breaks	USER, SC
Page numbers	YES, ALT, RESTART
Paragraph indent	YES, SC
Programmable key	YES
Reformat after changes	YES
Repeat last command	YES
Right justify	YES
Right justify tabs	YES
Sort	NO
Spelling check	YES, 50,000 W, OPT
Storing formats	YES
Strikeover	YES, PR
Sub/superscript	YES, SC
Tabs	8, VAR
Underline	YES, SC
Variable pitch	YES, PR
Vertical lines	?
Widows and orphans	YES

FILES

File names	FREE
Renaming	YES
Copy and delete files	YES
Copying disks	NO
Auto save	YES
Auto backup	YES
Verify	YES
Disk directory	YES, SIZE, TITLE

PRINTING

Continuous or sheet feed	BOTH
Multiple printers	YES
Queue	YES
Simultaneous	UNDER DEVELOPMENT
Specific pages	YES
Typefaces	YES

DOCUMENTATION AND TRAINING

Documentation	USER MANUAL
Training	

VENDOR: Radio Shack, A Division of Tandy Corporation
MODEL: SCRIPSIT 2.0
TYPE: Software for TRS-80

ENTERING TEXT
Where	ANYWHERE
Word wrap	YES
Length of document	DISK
Orientation	PG

EDITING TEXT
During entry	NO
Insert	YES, ON/OFF
Delete, copy, and move	YES, CH, W, S, P, DOC

MOVEMENT WITHIN DOCUMENT
Cursor	PG
Scroll	L, P, PG, SC, TOP/BOT
Search	FOR, IGNORE CASE
Search and replace	FOR, IGNORE CASE, GLOB, AUTO, SEMI-AUTO

SPECIAL FEATURES AND FORMATS
Alternate character sets	YES
Boilerplate	YES
Bold	YES, PR
Calculate	YES, OPT
Centering	YES, SC
Center around tabs	NO
Change case	NO
Control characters	SOME
Decimal tabs	YES
Dot commands	?
Footnotes	NO
Forced page break	YES
Format line	YES
Generate table of contents	NO
Generate index	NO
Headers and footers	YES, UNLIMITED #L, DATE
Hyphenating	AUTO W/DICT. DISK; USER
Letter merge	YES
Lines per page	YES
Line spacing	YES, PR
Margin release key	NO
Margin width	156
Multicolumn	YES, PR
Nonprinting comments	YES
Onscreen	NO
Page breaks	AUTO, USER, SC
Page numbers	YES, ALT
Paragraph indent	YES, SC
Programmable key	YES

Reformat after changes   AUTO
Repeat last command   YES
Right justify   YES, PR
Right justify tabs   YES
Sort   YES, OPT
Spelling check   YES, OPT
Storing formats   YES
Strikeover   YES, PR
Sub/superscript   YES, PR
Tabs   VAR
Underline   YES
Variable pitch   YES, PR
Vertical lines   84
Widows and orphans   USER

FILES
File names   FREE
Renaming   YES
Copy and delete files   YES
Copying disks   YES
Auto save   USER
Auto backup   NO
Verify   YES
Disk directory   YES, SIZE, NAME, TITLE, DATE

PRINTING
Continuous or sheet
  feed   BOTH
Multiple printers   YES
Queue   YES
Simultaneous   YES
Specific pages   YES
Typefaces   NO

DOCUMENTATION AND TRAINING
Documentation   USER'S GUIDE AND TRAINING MANUAL
Training   TRAINING MANUAL

VENDOR: Select Information Systems
MODEL: Select Word Processing
TYPE: Software for CP/M systems

ENTERING TEXT
Where   ANYWHERE
Word wrap   YES, ON/OFF
Length of document   DISK
Orientation   DOC

EDITING TEXT
During entry   YES
Insert   YES
Delete, copy, and move   YES, VAR

MOVEMENT WITHIN DOCUMENTS

Cursor	CH, L, SC, PG, BEG/END, # OF LINES, CH, OR SCREENS
Scroll	CH, L, SC, PG, BEG/END, # OF LINES, CH, OR SCREENS
Search	FOR, BACK, EX
Search and replace	FOR, BACK, EX, GLOB, AUTO, SEMI-AUTO

SPECIAL FEATURES AND FORMATS

Alternate character sets	YES
Boilerplate	YES, WHOLE DOCUMENTS
Bold	YES, PR
Calculate	YES
Centering	YES, SC
Center around tabs	NO
Change case	NO
Control characters	YES
Decimal tabs	NO
Dot commands	NO, "BACKSLASH" FROM MENU
Footnotes	NO
Forced page break	YES
Format line	YES, SHOWING MARGINS
Generate table of contents	OPT, SUPPLIED BY ORTHOCODE
Generate index	OPT, SUPPLIED BY ORTHOCODE
Headers and footers	YES, UNLIMITED #L
Hyphenating	NO
Letter merge	YES
Lines per page	YES
Line spacing	1, 1¼, 2, PR
Margin release key	NO
Margin width	132
Multicolumn	NO
Nonprinting comments	YES
Onscreen	YES
Page breaks	AUTO, SC
Page numbers	YES, RESTART
Paragraph indent	YES, SC
Programmable key	NO
Reformat after changes	AUTO
Repeat last command	SOMETIMES
Right justify	YES, SC
Right justify tabs	NO
Sort	NO
Spelling check	YES, 20,000 W; UNLIMITED ADDITIONS
Storing formats	YES
Strikeover	NO
Sub/superscript	YES, PR
Tabs	5, VAR
Underline	YES, PR

Variable pitch	YES, PR
Vertical lines	VARIABLE
Widows and orphans	USER

FILES
File names	OPSYS
Renaming	YES
Copy and delete files	YES
Copying disks	THROUGH OPSYS
Auto save	YES, USER
Auto backup	YES
Verify	YES
Disk directory	YES, SIZE, TITLE

PRINTING
Continuous or sheet feed	BOTH
Multiple printers	NO
Queue	NO
Simultaneous	NO
Specific pages	YES
Typefaces	YES

DOCUMENTATION AND TRAINING
Documentation	MANUAL + STEP-BY-STEP ONSCREEN HELP (90% OF MANUAL)
Training	SELF-PACED INTERACTIVE TRAINING ONSCREEN

VENDOR: Sofsys
MODEL: Executive Secretary
TYPE: Software for Apple II, IBM PC

ENTERING TEXT
Where	ANYWHERE
Word wrap	YES
Length of document	16,000 CH
Orientation	DOC

EDITING TEXT
During entry	NO
Insert	YES
Delete, copy, and move	YES, VAR, DOC

MOVEMENT WITHIN DOCUMENT
Cursor	W, L, PG, LINE #
Scroll	L, SC, TOP/BOT
Search	FOR, EX
Search and replace	FOR, EX, SEMI-AUTO

SPECIAL FEATURES AND FORMATS
Alternate character sets	YES
Boilerplate	YES, GLOSSARY, P

Bold	YES, PR
Calculate	NO
Centering	YES, PR
Center around tabs	NO
Change case	NO
Control characters	NO
Decimal tabs	YES
Dot commands	MOST
Footnotes	NO
Forced page break	YES
Format line	NO
Generate table of contents	NO
Generate index	YES
Headers and footers	HEADERS, UNLIMITED #L, DATE
Hyphenating	NO
Letter merge	YES
Lines per page	YES
Line spacing	VARIABLE, PR
Margin release key	NO
Margin width	250
Multicolumn	YES, PR
Nonprinting comments	YES
Onscreen	YES, BUT NOT DURING EDIT
Page breaks	AUTO
Page numbers	YES, ALT, RESTART
Paragraph indent	YES, SC
Programmable key	NO
Reformat after changes	AUTO
Repeat last command	SOME
Right justify	YES, PR
Right justify tabs	YES
Sort	YES, ALPH, NUM
Spelling check	YES, 10,000–25,000 W, OPT
Storing formats	YES
Strikeover	YES, PR
Sub/superscript	YES, PR
Tabs	5, 8, 17, VAR
Underline	YES, PR
Variable pitch	YES, PR
Vertical lines	99
Widows and orphans	AUTO

FILES

File names	FREE, 15 CH
Renaming	YES
Copy and delete files	YES
Copying disks	YES
Auto save	USER
Auto backup	NO
Verify	YES
Disk directory	YES, TITLE

PRINTING
Continuous or sheet feed	BOTH
Multiple printers	YES
Queue	NO
Simultaneous	NO
Specific pages	STARTING PAGE
Typefaces	YES

DOCUMENTATION AND TRAINING
Documentation	USER MANUAL
Training	TELEPHONE HAND-HOLDING

APPENDIX B

Jobs in Word Processing

The more people buy word processors, the more new jobs appear—designing, manufacturing, selling, demonstrating, operating, and managing. Here are some of the careers opening up in this field:

Jobs in Companies That Use Word-Processing Equipment

When a company first gets a word processor, they need people to operate it. Often these will be existing employees, at least to start. As the use of word processing increases, the company comes to depend on the equipment and grows to expect the fast turnaround and high quality of documents that a word processor can produce. More use is made of the equipment, and more equipment may be acquired. A variety of jobs arise. Salary ranges for these jobs vary in different parts of the country. The salaries shown here are those common in large cities such as San Francisco, New York, Houston, and Los Angeles. In general, jobs in New York City pay the most, while jobs in smaller cities and towns pay lower wages.

Jobs in Word-Processing Centers

Word-Processing Operator. This is the person who actually uses the equipment to enter and edit text, often doing nothing else. Some companies break this job down into half a dozen different levels, from "trainee" to "senior word-processing specialist." You'll also hear this position called "word-processing specialist," or simply "word processor." A trainee position may pay $950–$1200 per month, while highly experienced operators might command from $1200 to $1400 or $1500 per month. Experienced word-processing operators can make from $10 to $13 per hour through temporary agencies.

Lead Operator. An experienced word-processing operator. Sometimes this may be a status title, conferring the company's confidence in your being the "lead," or best, person in the word-processing center. Most of the time it implies added responsibility for the work load of the center: prioritizing and scheduling work, making sure it gets done on time, talking with the staff who submit work to the center. What is it like to be a word-processing operator? Our interview with Ros Heimberg in Chapter 7, "What It's Like to Start," will give you an idea. The salary range for lead operators can be from $1400 to $1700 or even $1800 per month.

Proofreader. Good word-processing operators are fast, but they aren't always great spellers or accurate typists. Therefore someone needs to proofread the finished documents. This responsibility may be left to the operator and the person who originated the document, or the word-processing supervisor may assign someone to spend all day proofreading. Proofreaders do not have to have any particular skill in using word-processing equipment. Their wages are usually lower than word-processing operators'.

Supervisors and Managers. A wide range of tasks fall to word-processing supervisors and managers. There may be one person in charge, or there may be several levels of supervision and management. As the use of word processing grows in a company, some of these responsibilities may become full-time jobs in their own right. Here are some of the tasks handled by supervisors and managers:

- Coordinate and distribute incoming work.
- Keep "internal documentation" (procedures, tips on using the equipment, copies of boilerplate forms) up-to-date.
- Analyze productivity of the center and look for ways to improve it.
- Evaluate the word-processing operators.
- See that new operators are adequately trained.
- Establish document formats and standards.
- Assist operators with difficult documents.
- Set expectations of the staff who submit work to the word-processing center.
- Deal with the word-processing vendor when assistance or maintenance is needed.
- Establish a word-processing budget.
- Keep abreast of new developments in the field of word processing and recommend new equipment.

Word-processing supervisors and managers earn from $1400 to $1700 or $1800 per month. The top end of the salary range for these jobs may be up to $2100 or more.

Related Jobs Outside of the Word-Processing Center

Trainer. A highly experienced word-processing operator, this person takes on the responsibility of training new operators and assisting existing operators when they don't know how to do something on the equipment. A trainer may need to be familiar with a wide range of equipment. These individuals can earn from $18,000 to $30,000 per year.

Implementation Specialists. An expert in the word-processing field, this person helps departments evaluate their word-processing needs, select appropriate equipment, and insure that installation and training go smoothly. Usually responsible for any needs analysis or feasibility studies undertaken in the company. This person is an "internal consultant," and is usually quite well paid, earning as much as $35,000 to $40,000 a year.

Decentralized Word Processing

Although some large companies tend to install word processing in one center and hire personnel strictly to do word processing, others don't. Many companies integrate the use of word processing into existing jobs. In these companies, word processors become another tool to be used by employees. This is most common in secretarial and clerical positions. While shorthand used to be a required skill for secretarial applicants in many firms, today operation of a word processor is becoming more important. Some companies will train you to use their equipment. Other companies want experience. Where do you get it? More and more junior colleges, adult education groups, and business schools are offering courses. See the end of Appendix C, "Where to Learn More," for more information.

Jobs in Word-Processing and Computer Companies

Companies that design, manufacture, distribute, sell, and support word-processing equipment are chock-full of jobs. Some relate specifically to word processing, while others are the same types of jobs that keep any company going—accountants, bookkeepers, secretaries, receptionists, managers. So if you're interested in working for a word-processing company, you needn't necessarily go out and study word processing company, you needn't necessarily go out and study word processing. The companies themselves can give you a good education, and they often promote from within if you're willing to work your way up through the ranks. Many word-processing and computer companies have their corporate headquarters in what is known as the Silicon Valley in northern California, or off Route 128 in New England. Others are found in Colorado, Florida, Georgia, Texas, and other states. (See the directory of word-processing companies in Appendix D for corporate addresses.)

Product Line Jobs

These jobs are usually placed in or near the corporate headquarters of a company. Development of new products, enhancements to existing ones, and support of the staff in branch offices usually come from the "product line."

Engineers. These are hardware and software specialists who design, build, and modify the word-processing equipment—everything from wiring together new memory circuits to building prototypes of new video display terminals, to writing the operating-system programs that make all the parts work together. Salary range: $25,000 to $50,000, and more.

Designers. There are two types of design in developing a word processor: "functional design," which specifies what the equipment should be able to do and what steps the end-user will go through to accomplish each task; and "systems design," which plans how programs will be written to make the equipment work. Systems design is usually the responsibility of the engineers, systems analysts, and programmers. Functional design may be determined by a team of experts in word processing who know what is already available on the market and are intimately familiar with what it's like to use word processing.

Programmers. Programmers write the code, or programs, that make computers able to do word processing. A range of programmers may be found in any product line. They work with the staff who develop the design for the hardware and software. Salary range: $20,000 to $35,000, and more.

Managers. There are usually a wide range of managers in a word-processing product line: product managers, marketing managers, public relations managers. These people make sure that design and marketing of the equipment fit corporate goals for the product. Salary range: $30,000 to $50,000, and more.

Marketing Positions. Marketing staff decide how the equipment will be marketed. They develop and oversee advertising and sales campaigns, press releases, and product imagery. Gauging new advances in the word-processing market, they may call the shots as to what features must be included in the new release of a product, and what features can wait. They set the retail price for equipment, and sales goals for the entire company. Salary range: $25,000 to $40,000.

Product Line Support Staff. The support staff in a word-processing product line provides information to employees in branch offices and other departments of the company. They find answers to questions and solutions to problems for the sales force, trainers, and dealers across the country. Their responsibilities may cover anything from figuring out a way to use their word processor for a specific task that a large customer needs, to quoting delivery dates of equipment, finding a lost or delayed shipment, or fixing "bugs" that turn up in the system at a customer's office. Salary range: approximately $20,000 to $30,000, and more.

Competitive Analysts. Some word-processing vendors have staff whose sole responsibility is to find out what the competition is doing. This means knowing other equipment in depth, keeping up with new announcements and advancements in the field, and trying to predict what's coming next. Salary range: similar to Marketing.

Writers. Writers in a word-processing company write the training material, user guides, and reference manuals that are distributed with word-processing equipment and software. They may also write advertising copy and press releases. Writers earn about $18,000 to $40,000 in salaried positions. Freelance writers can earn $15 to $40 per hour.

Jobs "In the Field"

These are jobs at branch offices, distributorships, or dealerships of word-processing companies—"in the field," not in corporate offices.

Sales. Some companies hire people with word-processing backgrounds and teach them to sell. Others hire people with sales experience and teach them about word processing. Some are salaried jobs, but most are commission-based. A good salesperson on commission can earn from $25,000 to $60,000, and more.

Support. Word-processing support jobs often have titles such as "MSR" (Marketing Support Representative), or "WPSS" (Word-Processing Support Specialist). These positions provide backup for the sales force. An MSR typically demonstrates the equipment to customers, does training, and helps customers figure out how to get maximum use from their equipment. Salary range: about $16,000 to $28,000.

Trainers. Companies who offer classroom training often have some of their staff dedicated to teaching, or training. These positions are similar to support, or MSR, positions, but have less ongoing contact with customers.

Field Service. The field service staff physically install and repair word-processing equipment.

Jobs in Computer and Retail Stores

Computer stores, office equipment stores, even department stores are beginning to sell word processors. Sales, support, and service are as necessary to these companies as they are to word-processing manufacturers. Selling office equipment and microcomputers means learning more than word processing. Because of the range of equipment often sold in retail stores, the staff must acquire a broad background in small-business computing, of which word processing is only one part.

RELATED JOBS AND COMPANIES

In addition to jobs in companies who use word processing and in companies who manufacture, sell, and support word processing, a variety of other types of companies have sprung up around this industry.

Consultants and Freelance Workers

Individuals with a good background in word processing are taking off on their own and offering services to both word-processing manufacturers and word-processing users. Some may work for a company that offers a range of services; others work on their own.

Word-Processing Consultants. Specialists in the field, consultants help businesses do feasibility studies and select word-processing equipment. They may also provide customized training and help a company set up internal procedures. Paid on an hourly basis, consultants make from $25 to $75 per hour.

Freelance Word-Processing Operators. Experienced operators work on a contract basis for a range of companies, filling in when an employee is out sick or on vacation, or just pitching in when a rush job is imminent. Usually these people know one or two types of word-processing equipment extremely well. Through agencies, these people earn $10 to $13 per hour. On their own, they make up to $20 per hour.

Teachers. Classes in word processing are sprouting up across the country. Junior colleges as well as business, adult, and vocational schools often offer courses in word-processing concepts and hands-on training.

Other Jobs Word-Processing Skills Can Lead To

As more and more companies use word processing, it becomes a skill invaluable in many jobs, and not only because you're familiar with the concepts and uses of word processing. Once you've learned to use one word processor, it's easier to learn the next one. It's also easier to learn to use other computer software. Menus, function keys, "prompts," or messages on the screen from the computer to you are used in software designed to do other jobs in addition to word processing. The menus will have different options, and the function keys will be for different tasks, but your general interaction with the computer will be similar.

If companies really do opt to try the "electronic office," as computer vendors are encouraging them to do, almost everyone in a firm will have some contact with computers, and many will work directly with video display screens and keyboards. One of the biggest stumbling blocks in learning to use a computer for any application is overcoming the fear of it and recognizing it as a tool to make use of rather than to be used by. Once you've used a computer for one task, such as word processing, it's easier to use a computer for other tasks.

Word processing is one computerized application in a rapidly growing field. And where word processors were once treated as "glorified typewriters," having no connection with data processing, this is no longer the case. Personnel with computer experience are in great demand. Word processing can be a stepping stone into a field with a tremendous range of jobs, both in companies who make use of computers and computer software, and in companies who develop, sell, and support them.

APPENDIX C

What to Read

Word Processing in a Large Office

These books assume you are thinking about automating the way you originate text, process words, and distribute the results. They seem to be written for someone who wants to run a word-processing center in a big company.

Cecil, Paula B. *Management of Word Processing Operations*. Benjamin/Cummings, 1980.

———. *Word Processing in the Modern Office*. Benjamin/Cummings, 1980.

Fielden, Rosemary, and Rosen, Arnold. *Word Processing*. Prentice-Hall, 1982.

McCabe, Helen M., and Popham, Estelle L. *Word Processing: A Systems Approach to the Office*. Harcourt Brace Jovanovich, 1977.

Thursland, Arthur L. *Work Measurement: A Guidebook to Word-Processing Management*. International Information/Word Processing Association, revised edition, 1980.

Word-Processing Careers

If you're interested in pursuing a career in word processing—particularly in an office—these books may give you some ideas.

Bergerud, M., and Gonzalez, J. *Word Processing Concepts and Careers*. John Wiley and Sons, 1978.

Konkel, Gilbert J., and Peck, Phyllis J. *Your Future in Word Processing*. Richards Rosen Press, 1981.

International Information/Word Processing Association. *Salary Survey Results, II/WPA*.

Reports on Word Processing

Expensive, but helpful if you are making a thorough search, these reports study every function on many products in great technical detail, often with monthly updates; free telephone inquiry is sometimes included.

Electronic Office Management and Technology. Auerbach Publishers, 6560 North Park Drive, Pennsauken, NJ 08109.

Guide to Word Processing Systems. Computer Guides, Ltd., 30–31 Islington Green, London N1 8BJ, England.

Office Systems Reports. Auerbach Publishers, 6560 North Park Drive, Pennsauken, NJ 08109.

The Seybold Report on Word Processing. Seybold, Jonathan, Box 644, Media, PA 19063.

Word Processing. Datapro Research Corporation, 1805 Underwood Boulevard, Delran, NJ 08075.

Magazines

Written for people who know their way around an office but don't always know too much about word processing or computers, these magazines and newsletters will help you learn more. Some require more computer experience and knowledge than others.

Administrative Management. Geyer-McAllister Publications, New York.

Asian Computer Monthly. Computer Publications Ltd., Hong Kong.

Business Week. McGraw-Hill, New York.

Byte. Byte Publications, Subsidiary of McGraw-Hill, Martinsville, New Jersey.

Canadian Datasystems. MacLean Hunter Ltd., Toronto.

Computer World. CW Communications, Framingham, Massachusetts.

Computer World, Australia. CW Communications, Sydney.

Computer World, España. CW Communications, Framingham, Massachusetts.

Creative Computing. Creating Computing, Morristown, New Jersey.

Data Cast. Wireless Digital, Woodside, California.

Desktop Computing, Wayne Green, Inc., Peterborough, New Hampshire.

Fortune. Time-Life Inc., Chicago.

Information and Word Processing. Geyer-McAllister Publications, New York.

Infoworld: News for Microcomputer Users. Popular Computing, Inc., Framingham, Massachusetts.

Interface Age. McPheters, Wolfe, and Jones, Cerritos, California.

Le Monde Informatique. CW Communications, Framingham, Massachusetts.

MIS Week: "The Newspaper for Information Management." Fairchild Publications, New York.

Office. Office Publications, Stamford, Connecticut.

Personal Computer World. Sportscene Publishers Ltd., London.

Personal Computing. Hayden Publishing Company, Inc., Rochelle Park, New Jersey.

Popular Computing. Byte Publications, Peterborough, New Hampshire.

Small Business Computer's Magazine. Creative Computing, Morris Plains, New Jersey.

Today's Office. Hearst Business Publications, Garden City, New York.

Which Word Processor? EMAP/ECC Publications, London.

Word Processing and Information Systems. Geyer-McAllister Publications, New York.

Words. International Information/Word Processing Association, Willow Grove, Pennsylvania.

Where to Learn More

If you want to learn how to operate a word processor, or how to set up a word-processing center, you'll probably find courses on these topics in your local community college. Look through the catalogs of adult extension courses at larger universities, too.

If you work in a large corporation, ask your training people for news of upcoming seminars and workshops, such as those offered by the American Management Association (135 West 50th Street, New York, NY 10020) or Datapro Research (1805 Underwood Boulevard, Delran, NJ 08075). You'll see major conventions advertised in magazines such as *The Office*. Keep an eye out for trade shows, too; you won't get much chance to use equipment there, but you will get to ask questions and to watch razzle-dazzle demonstrations.

If you can't find any courses nearby, you might call the International Information/Word Processing Association, 1015 North York Road, Willow Grove, PA 19090, (215) 657-6300, for their current directory of word-processing education.

APPENDIX D

Directory of Vendors

Hardware Vendors

AB DICK COMPANY
5700 West Touhy
Nilese, IL 60648

ADLER ROYAL
Division of Triumph-Adler
1600 Route 22
Union, NJ 07083

AES DATA
570 McCaffery Street
Montreal, Quebec
H4T 1N1 Canada

ALGORITHMICS
177 Worcester Road
Wellesley, MA 02181

AM VARITYPER
11 Mount Pleasant Avenue
East Hanover, NJ 07936

APPLE COMPUTER INC.
10260 Bandley Drive
Cupertino, CA 95014

APPLIED DIGITAL DATA SYSTEMS INC.
100 Marcus Blvd.,
Hauppauge, NY 11788

ATV JACQUARD INC.
2921 So. Daimler
Santa Ana, CA 92771

AXXA
21201 Oxnard St
Woodland Hills, CA 91367

BASIC FOUR INFORMATION SYSTEMS
14101 Myford Road
Tustin, CA 92680

BURROUGHS CORPORATION
30 Main Street
Danbury, CT 06810

CADO SYSTEMS
2771 Toledo Street
Torrence, CA 90503

COMMODORE BUSINESS MACHINES
333 Scott Boulevard
Santa Clara, CA 95051

COMPAL COMPUTER SYSTEMS
6300 Varial Avenue, Suite E
Woodland Hills, CA 91367

COMPTEK RESEARCH INC.
One Technology Center
45 Oak Street
Buffalo, NY 14203

COMPUCORP
2211 Michigan Avenue
Santa Monica, CA 90404

COMPUGRAPHIC
26120 Eden Landing Road
Hayward, CA 94545

CPT CORPORATION
8100 Mitchell Road
Minneapolis, MN 55440

DATA GENERAL CORPORATION
4400 Computer Drive
Mail Stop C228
Westboro, MA 01581

DATAPOINT CORPORATION
9725 Datapoint Drive
San Antonio, TX 78284

DATA TERMINALS AND
COMMUNICATIONS
590 Division Street
Campbell, CA 95008

DELTA DATA SYSTEMS CORPORATION
2595 Metropolitan Drive
Trevose, PA 19047

DICTAPHONE
120 Old Post Road
Rye, NY 10580

DIGITAL EQUIPMENT CORPORATION
Word Processing Group
Continental Boulevard
Merrimack, NH 03054

DURANGO SYSTEMS, INC.
3003 North First Street
San Jose, CA 95134

EXXON OFFICE SYSTEMS
777 Longridge Road
Stamford, CT 06904

FORTUNE SYSTEMS CORPORATION
1510 Industrial Road
San Carlos, CA 94070

FOUR PHASE
10700 North DeAnza Boulevard
Cupertino, CA 95014

HEWLETT-PACKARD
19420 Homestead
Cupertino, CA 94304

HONEYWELL INFORMATION SYSTEMS
200 Smith Street
Waltham, MA 02154

IBM CORPORATION
National Marketing Division
P.O. Box 2150
Atlanta, GA 30055

INTELLIGENT SYSTEMS CORPORATION
Intercolor Drive
225 Technology Park
Atlanta, Norcross, GA 30092

ITEK CORPORATION
875 Mahler Road, Suite 105
Burlingame, CA 94010

LANIER BUSINESS PRODUCTS
1700 Chantilly Drive, NE
Atlanta, GA 30324

LEADING EDGE PRODUCTS
225 Turnpike St.
Canton, MA 02021

LEXOR CORPORATION
7100 Havenhurst Avenue
Van Nuys, CA 91406

MEGADATA CORPORATION
35 Orville Drive
Bohemia, NY 11716

MICRODATA CORPORATION
Box 19501
Irvine, CA 92713

MOHAWK DATA SCIENCES
7 Century Drive
Parsippany, NJ 07054

MONROE SYSTEMS FOR BUSINESS
The American Road
Morris Plains, NJ 07950

NBI
P.O. Box 9001
1695 38th Street
Boulder, CO 80301

NCR CORPORATION
World Headquarters
Dayton, OH 45479

NIXDORF COMPUTER
168 Middlesex Turnpike
Burlington, MA 01803

NORTHERN TELECOM INC.
Data Park
P.O. Box 1222
Minneapolis, MN 55440

NORTH STAR COMPUTERS, INC.
14440 Cataline Street
San Leandro, CA 94577

OLIVETTI CORPORATION
155 White Plains Road
Tarrytown, NY 10590

OLYMPIA USA, INC.
P.O. Box 22
Somerville, NJ 08876

ONLINE BUSINESS SYSTEMS, INC.
115 Sansome Street
San Francisco, CA 94104

ONTEL CORPORATION
250 Crossways Park Drive
Woodbury, NY 11797

PHILIPS INFORMATION SYSTEMS
4040 McEwen
Dallas, TX 75234

POINT FOUR DATA CORPORATION
2569 McCabe Way
Irvine, CA 92714

PRIME COMPUTER, INCORPORATED
Prime Park
Natick, MA 01760

PROLINK CORPORATION
5757 Central Avenue
Boulder, CO 80301

Q1 CORPORATION
125 Ricefield Lane
Hauppauge, NY 11788

RADIO SHACK,
A DIVISION OF TANDY CORPORATION
One Tandy Center
Fort Worth, TX 76102

RAYTHEON CORPORATION
1840 De Havilland Drive
Thousand Oaks, CA 91359

ROTHENBERG INFORMATION SYSTEMS
Mountain View Plaza
440 Castro Street
Mountain View, CA 94041

ROYAL BUSINESS MACHINES
150 New Park Avenue
Hartford, CT 06106

SAVIN CORPORATION
Columbus Avenue
Valhalla, NY 10595

SCIENTIFIC DATA SYSTEMS
Venice, CA 90291

SHASTA GENERAL SYSTEMS
1329 Moffett Park Drive
Sunnyvale, CA 94086

SONY CORPORATION
9 West 57th Street
New York, NY 10010

SPERRY UNIVAC DIVISION
SPERRY RAND CORP.
P.O. Box 500
Blue Bell, PA 19422

SYNTREX
246 Industrial Way West
Eatontown, NJ 07724

TECHNOLOGY INTERNATIONAL
200 W. Landstreet Rd.
P.O. Box 13457
Orlando, FL 32859

TEXAS INSTRUMENTS
Digital Systems Division,
Mail Stop 2
P.O. Box 2909
Austin, TX 78769

TOSHIBA AMERICA
Information Processing Division
2441 Michelle Drive
Tustin, CA 92680

VECTOR GRAPHIC, INC.
500 North Ventu Park Rd.
Thousand Oaks, CA 91320

WANG LABORATORIES, INC.
1 Industrial Avenue
Lowell, MA 01851

WORDPLEX
141 Triunfo Road
Westlake Village, CA 91361

XEROX CORPORATION
1341 West Mockingbird Lane
Dallas, TX 75247

XMARK CORPORATION
3176 Pullman Street, 119
Costa Mesa CA 92626

ZENITH DATA SYSTEMS
1000 Milwaukee Avenue
Glenview, IL 60025

Word-Processing Software Vendors for Large Computers

ACS AMERICA, INC.
633 Third Avenue
New York, NY 10017

ADAPT, INC.
450 Sansome Street
San Francisco, CA 94111

AMERICAN FRANKLIN CORPORATION
Data Services
#1 Franklin Square
Springfield, IL 62713

APPLIED BUSINESS SYSTEMS
4350 Upper Soda Road
Dunsmuir, CA 96025

APPLIED DATA RESEARCH, INC.
Route 206 and Orchard Rd., CN-8
Princeton, NJ 08540

BASIC BUSINESS CONTROL SYSTEMS,
INC.
4330 Stafford S.W.
Wyoming, MI 49508

DIRECTORY OF VENDORS || 447

BELL-NORTHERN RESEARCH LTD.
P.O. Box 3511, Station C
Ottawa, Canada K1Y 4H7

BOWNE TIME SHARING, INC.
160 Water Street
New York, NY 10038

BUNDY COMPUTER SYSTEMS, INC.
729 Woodbriar Lane
St. Charles, MO 63301

CALIFORNIA SYSTEMS ASSOCIATES
2845 Mesa Verde Drive East, Ste. 3
Costa Mesa, CA 92626

CASCADE DATA, INC.
6300 28th Street, SE
Grand Rapids, MI 49506

COMARCO, INC.
Computer Text Division
227 W. Hueneme Road
Oxnard, CA 93030

COMPAC SYSTEMS, INC.
59 E. Cunningham Drive
Palatine, IL 60067

COMPLETE COMPUTER SYSTEMS
159 Gilbratar Road
Horsham, PA 19044

COMPUSOURCE CORP.
14580 Midway
Dallas, TX 75734

COMPUTER DESIGNED SYSTEMS
10911 Olson Memorial Hwy.
Minneapolis, MN 55441

COMPUTERM CORPORATION
10420 S.W. Hawthorn Lane
Portland, OR 97225

COMPUTERPLAN INTERNATIONAL, INC.
40 Grove Street
Wellesley, MA 02181

COMPUTER RESOURCES, INC. (CRI)
2570 El Camino Real
Mountain View, CA 94040

COMPU-TOME, INC.
688 South Sunset Avenue
West Covina, CA 91790

CULLINANE CORPORATION
Database Systems
400 Blue Hill Drive
Westwood, MA 02090

CYBERTEK COMPUTER PRODUCTS, INC.
6133 Bristol Parkway
Culver City, CA 90230

DATA PROCESSING DESIGN, INC.
181 W. Orangethorpe Avenue, Ste. F
Placentia, CA 92370

DELPHI DATA SYSTEMS, INC.
7716 Morgan Avenue South
Minneapolis, MN 55423

DIGI LOG BUSINESS SYSTEMS, INC.
905 Sheehy Drive
Horsham, PA 19044

ECD CORPORATION
196 Broadway
Cambridge, MA 02139

EEC SYSTEMS
315 Goodman's Hill Road
Sudbury, MA 01776

HARTLEY COMPUTER, INC.
1109 Inverness Drive
Englewood, CO 80112

MITCHELL HUMPHREY & CO.
77100 Carondelet, Suite 504
St. Louis, MO 63105

INFORMATION PROCESSING
TECHNIQUES CORP.
1070 East Meadow Circle
Palo Alto, CA 94303

INTERACTIVE SYSTEMS CORP.
1212 7th Street
Santa Monica, CA 90401

INTERMETRICS, INC.
701 Concord Avenue
Cambridge, MA 02138

LA SALLE COMPUTING, INC.
P.O. Box 116
Blue Bell, PA 19422

MARC ANALYSIS RESEARCH CORP.
260 Sheridan Avenue, Suite 200
Palo Alto, CA 94306

MARYLAND COMPUTER SERVICES, INC.
2010 Rock Spring Road
Forrest Hill, MD 21050

SCOTT R. MCENTREE & ASSOCIATES
P.O. Box 37
Encinitas, CA 92024

MVT MICROCOMPUTER SYSTEMS, INC.
9241 Reseda Blvd., #203
Northridge, CA 91324

NORTHERN TELECOM
P.O. Box 1222
Minneapolis, MN 55440

THE OFFICE MANAGER, INC.
P.O. Box 66596
127 S.W. 156th Street
Seattle, WA 98166

OHIO SCIENTIFIC, INC.
1333 S. Chillicothe Road
Aurora, OH 44202

ON-LINE BUSINESS SYSTEMS, INC.
115 Sansome Street
San Francisco, CA 94104

OPTIMUM SYSTEMS, INC.
5615 Fishers Lane
Rockville, MD 20852

JERRY OTT, ASSOCIATES
1936 Contra Costa Blvd.
Pleasant Hill, CA 94523

PARA RESEARCH, INC.
Whistlestop Mall
Rockport, MA 01966

PERKIN-ELMER
2 Crescent Place
Oceanport, NJ 07757

POINT FOUR DATA CORPORATION
2569 McCabe Way
Irvine, CA 92714

PROFESSIONAL COMPUTER RESOURCES, INC.
2021 Midwest Road
Oak Brook, IL 60521

QL SYSTEMS LTD.
Ste. 1018, Tower B
112 Kent Street
Ottawa, Ontario, Canada K1P 5P2

REDSHAW, INC.
103 Yost Blvd.
Pittsburgh, PA 15221

SATELLITE SOFTWARE INTERNATIONAL
116 N. State Street
Orem, UT 84057

SOFTWARE CLEARING HOUSE
6188 Cleves Warsaw
Cincinnati, OH 45238

SOFTWARE RESOURCES
P.O. Box 25210
Houston, TX 77005

SYSTEMS RESEARCH, INC.
2400 Science Parkway
Okemos, MI 48864

TECHNICAL ANALYSIS CORP.
120 West Wieuca Road N.E.
Atlanta, GA 30342

THERMEON CORPORATION
131 N. Tustin Avenue
Tustin, CA 92680

UNIQUE AUTOMATION PRODUCTS
17922 Sky Park Circle, Suite L
Irvine, CA 92714

WAGNER DATA SYSTEMS
230 Dakota
San Antonio, TX 78203

WESTERN ELECTRIC
Guilford Center
P.O. Box 25000
Greensboro, NC 27420

WESTINGHOUSE ELECTRIC CORPORATION
2040 Ardmore Blvd.
Pittsburgh, CA 15221

Vendors of Local Area Networks

AMDAX CORPORATION
1600 Wilbur Place
Bohemia, NY 11716

BURROUGHS CORPORATION
Burroughs Place
Detroit, MI 48232

CONTROL DATA CORPORATION
P.O. Box O
HQW O9G
Minneapolis, MN 55440

CORVUS SYSTEMS, INC.
7584 Trade Street
San Diego, CA 92121

DATAPOINT CORPORATION
9725 Datapoint Drive
San Antonio, TX 78284

THE DESTEK GROUP
1923 Landings Drive
Mountain View, CA 94043

DIGITAL EQUIPMENT CORPORATION
Continental Boulevard
Merrimack, NH 03054

ELECTROSOUND SYSTEMS, INC.
725 Broadway Avenue
Holbrook, NY 17412

INTERACTIVE SYSTEMS/3M
3980 Varsity Drive
Ann Arbor, MI 48104

LOGICA VTS LTD.
86 Newman Street
London W1A 4SE England

NESTAR SYSTEMS, INC.
2585 East Bayshore Road
Palo Alto, CA 94303

NETWORK SYSTEMS CORPORATION
7600 Boone Avenue
Minneapolis, MN 55428

PROLINK CORPORATION
5757 Central Avenue
Boulder, CO 80301

PROTEON ASSOCIATES, INC.
24 Crescent Street
Waltham, MA 02154

SYTEK, INC.
1153 Bordeaux Drive
Sunnyvale, CA 94086

UNGERMANN-BSS, INC.
2560 Mission College Boulevard
Santa Clara, CA 95050

WANG LABORATORIES
One Industrial Avenue
Lowell, MA 01851

XEROX CORPORATION
P.O. Box 470065
Dallas, TX 75247

ZILOG, INC.
10460 Bubb Road
Cupertino, CA 95014

Vendors of Dial-Up Word Processing

ADP FIRST DATA CORPORATION
40 Second Avenue
Waltham, MA 02154

ALPHATEXT LIMITED
240 Catherine Street
Ottawa, Ontario, Canada K2P 2G8

ANALYSIS & PROGRAMMING
CORPORATION (APC)
Beloit Computer Center
423 State Street
Beloit, WI 53511

BOWNE TIME SHARING INC.
345 Hudson Street
New York, NY 10014

COMSHARE LIMITED
42 James Street South
Suite 33
Hamilton, Ontario, Canada L8P 2Y4

CYBERSHARE LIMITED
550 Berry Street
Winnipeg, Manitoba, Canada
R3H OR9

ON-LINE SYSTEMS, INC.
115 Evergreen Heights Drive
Pittsburgh, PA 15229

OPTIMUM SYSTEMS INCORPORATED
2801 Northwestern Parkway
Santa Clara, CA 95051

PROPRIETARY COMPUTER
SYSTEMS, INC.
16625 Saticoy Street
Van Nuys, CA 91406

RAPIDATA, INC.
20 New Dutche Lane
Fairfield, NJ 07006

I.P. SHARP ASSOCIATES, LTD.
Suite 1400
145 King Street West
Toronto, Ontario, Canada M5H IJ8

STANFORD RESEARCH INSTITUTE
Augment Research Center
333 Ravenswood Avenue
Menlo Park, CA 94025

UNIVERSITY COMPUTING COMPANY
P.O. Box 6171
Dallas, TX 75222

WANG COMPUTER SERVICES
Division of Wang Laboratories, Inc.
836 North Street
Tewksbury, MA 01876

Glossary

Accounts payable program. An accounting program that functions on your word processor or microcomputer as your record of accounts payable.

Accounts receivable program. An accounting program that functions on your word processor or microcomputer as your record of accounts receivable.

Acoustic coupler. A crude version of the communications device known as a modem. You telephone another computer, and when you hear a high-pitched tone on the line, place your receiver into two rubber-cushioned holes in the acoustic coupler, which takes signals from your computer and translates them into terms the phone line can handle. At the other end, another modem translates them back, for the other computer to receive information. An acoustic coupler allows static into the line, though, so most people prefer a modem that has a jack that can plug directly into the phone line. See **Modem.**

Action paper. Paper that makes a "carbon" of whatever you type. Used to analyze the number of errors, retypings, and half-done pages that crop up before a final perfect page emerges.

Adjust. A word-processing function that lets you move text left and right, or to the center; it sometimes allows you to establish margins, too.

Advance. Move forward in the text.

Alignment. The process of lining up your text so that it fits within some preestablished guidelines, or form. Also, in printing, making all lines parallel.

ALOHA. A way for terminals to gain access to a channel, by contending with each other.

Alphanumerics. Characters—either letters or numbers.

Alternate character sets. Different typefaces. Some printers offer alternate character sets, but your word processor must have the right programming to take advantage of the capability.

Alternate key (ALT). A special key that is pressed before another key to indicate an alternate use of the second key. Sometimes the alternate meaning will be printed on the front of letter and number keys. For instance, pressing an alternate key might tell the word processor you do not mean the letter "D," but the function described on the front of that key, "Delete." See also *Control key, ESC, Function keys.*

Ampere. Minimum unit of electrical current.

Amplifier. An amplifier takes a weakening signal, and makes it louder, but it also tends to make the static louder, too. Used on phone lines.

Analog transmission. A way of transmitting signals inside one computer, or along phone lines. A sound wave is represented by analogous electrical frequencies, on the phone; hence, when you talk on the line, you are making an analog transmission.

Application. A program that applies the computer to a particular job. For instance, one computer can handle several applications programs—an accounting application, a forecasting application, and a word-processing application.

Application level. A protocol governing the way you can move through a network and use a particular computer program or system—known as an application.

ARC. Attached Resource Computer Local Network,™ a local network sold by Datapoint.

Arrow. A key with an arrow on it. When you press the DOWN ARROW key, the cursor moves down the text.

ASCII. A code for turning characters and symbols into patterns of 1s and 0s for the computer to use. The American Standard Code for Information Interchange uses 7 bits (on/off pulses) per character, plus an optional bit at the end, for the computer to check for errors.

Asymmetrical. A network is considered asymmetrical when you cannot move easily from one computer program to another, or when one person can enter your system, but you cannot enter his or hers.

Asynchronous transmission. A form of transmission, substantially slower than synchronous, used on smaller computers and standalone word processors. The computer (or modem) puts in a special bit (on/off pulse) at the beginning and end of the 5, 7, or 8 bits that express a given character; that way, the computer (or modem) on the other end recognizes the completed character. This system establishes synchrony between the two computers, but it does so character by character. Why is it called asynchronous, then? Because it's used when you don't send a constant stream of data through the line—just an occasional memo. It means you aren't a metronome.

Attributes. A term used to describe the special display capabilities of a video display screen. For instance, the ability to show underlining on the screen is a screen attribute.

Audio monitor. A speaker in a modem that allows you to hear the modem making a phone connection with another modem—or the operator saying, "I'm sorry, that number's been changed." The monitor is useful, because then you don't keep having the modem try to make the call, assuming the line is busy.

Auto backup. A function that makes sure that when you remove text from a file, there is still a backup version retained, in case you foul up the one onscreen. That way you can always go back to your original.

Automated office. A general term for an office in which information can flow electronically from your word processor to almost any other piece of office equipment, and back.

Automatic answering. A feature on some modems, allowing them to answer any call from another computer automatically, without waiting for a go-ahead from you.

Automatic dial. A function on some modems, allowing them to make calls late at night, when the rates are cheaper and you aren't around.

Automatic time stamp. A feature in some modems that puts a time and date on any message sent or received.

Auto save. A function that automatically saves whatever text you enter on your word processor. Many systems require you to press some buttons to do this—and if you forget, you may lose the whole text.

Backspace. A key that lets you back up one space. Often it erases the character you've backed up over and lets you type a new one in on the spot.

Baseband. A form of coaxial cable, with one channel carrying about 10 million bits (on/off pulses) a second.

Baud. Signals per second. A way of measuring how much information you can send along a line, to or from a computer. But since some of these signals are used to direct traffic, a baud rate is not directly equivalent to the number of bits per second of the text going through.

Baudot. A code for translating characters and symbols into on/off pulses. This code uses five bits for each.

Bells and whistles. Attractive features that make a word processor as blatant and attention-getting as a steam calliope. Usually used disparagingly by competitors, this phrase implies that all those fancy features aren't really necessary—just flashy extras.

Bidirectional printing. Method used by a printer that prints one line from left to right, then drops down and does the next line backwards, from right to left—thus saving the time that would have gone into a carriage return to the left.

Binary system. A number system using only two digits, 1 and 0. Each position represents a power of 2. The first position is 2^0, or 1. If you put a 1 there, the number means 1. A zero, and it means 0. The second position represents 2^1, or a decimal 2. Put a 1 here, and it means 2. Hence, binary 10 equals decimal 2. Third position is 2^2, or 4. Hence, binary 100 equals decimal 4. To make a decimal 3, you would use binary 11, which means 1×2^0 (or $1 \times 1 = 1$) + 1×2^1 (or 1×2); that is, 1+2. Binary coding is used extensively in computers, since digital computers use on/off signals, which correspond to 1s and 0s.

Bit. The smallest piece of information a digital computer can deal with: a single on or off impulse.

Bit mapped. A method for displaying text and images on screen—much sharper than conventional displays.

Black box. A thingamajig—a joking term for a mysterious machine that can accomplish electronic miracles without our knowing how it does anything. For instance, some companies offer black boxes that translate from one word processor to another.

Boilerplate. Previously stored words, phrases, or paragraphs. Stock answers, stock contractual terms, or form letters would all be considered boilerplate. You can set up a pile of boilerplate on your word processor, then call it into a letter when you need it, without retyping.

Bold. Text that has been printed extra dark.

BPS. Bits Per Second. A way of measuring how fast a machine can send or receive information, or how fast a circuit can carry it. One bit is one on or off pulse, equivalent to a 1 or 0 in a digital computer.

Broadband. A form of coaxial cable, with several channels carrying around 20 million bits per second.

BSC. Binary-Synchronous Communications, a protocol from IBM, for making a data link between different computers.

Buffer. A temporary storage bin in the computer. If information's coming in too fast for the computer to digest, it puts the material in a buffer until ready to absorb some more.

Bug. An irritating little troublemaker—some unknown factor that is causing a computer program to turn out garbage instead of results. Programmers spend much of their time tracking down and eradicating bugs. But the word processor you buy may still have a few lying in wait.

Bundled. A computer grouped together with disk drives, video terminal, programs, and other items, sold as one unit instead of one item at a time. "Bundled software" means that the software programs are included with the computer and its peripherals when you buy it.

Burst mode. Instead of holding a channel open continuously, as in a phone conversation, you bunch together a lot of information, then send it very fast, in a burst.

Bus. A circuit to which all the terminals and controllers are attached in a local area network. Referred to sometimes as a "common bus."

Byte. A group of eight bits of information, which the computer uses together. One byte holds enough bits (on/off pulses) to represent one character.

Calculate. Perform math functions, such as adding, subtracting, multiplying, dividing, figuring percentages. Some word processors do, some don't.

Capacitance. A way of measuring how much charge can go over a circuit.

Carriage return. On a manual typewriter, you push the carriage back to the left, so you can go on typing the next line. On most electric typewriters, the type element itself slides back to the left, while the carriage stays in place. "Carriage return," then, has come to mean the ability—even on a word processor—to go back from the end of one line to start typing at the beginning of the next. Of course, on your word processor there is no carriage, and the return is electronic.

Cartridge disk. A hard disk that can be removed from the disk drive. To make these easy to move around, they are packaged in a "cartridge."

CCITT. The Consulting Committee on International Telegraph and Telephone, a European association of electronics firms. They have recommended several standards and protocols to each other, so that one company's equipment will plug into or communicate with another's.

Centering. Moving a phrase of text to a point midway between the margins, at the press of a button—or several buttons. In some systems, you can arrange to have text centered around a tab stop, too, as for the heading of a column.

Change case. A function in which you can have the word processor automatically change text from lowercase to uppercase, or vice versa.

Channel. The highway for your messages; there are often several channels with a given electrical circuit.

Character. A letter or number. The word *character* is used to refer to both.

Character generator. The combination of hardware and software that creates the image of each character and displays it onscreen.

Character set. The typeface. Some word processors allow you to print out your work in several different typefaces. Some even let you see them onscreen.

Check bit. A bit (on or off pulse, equal to 1 or 0) put at the end of a message, so that the receiving system can make sure it got the message accurately. One way it does this is as follows: the sending computer checks the number of 1s in the message. If the total is odd, it puts a 1 at the end; if even, a 0. Then the computer on the other end performs the same calculation and makes sure it gets the same result. If it does, it assumes everything's correct. If not, there's an error, and it requests retransmission.

Circuit. The physical carrier of electric signals.

Cluster. A group of independent word processors connected by cables to allow them to share documents on the same disks, use the same printer, or send messages back and forth.

CMSA-CD. A way for terminals to gain access to a channel, by contending with each other. The Carrier (the cable) Senses Multiple terminals demanding Access, then Detects any possible Collisions—and avoids them.

Coaxial cable. A large cable that can carry a number of different channels. The cable holds a number of copper tubes; inside each tube, there is some insulation, then a copper wire. This prevents crosstalk and interference.

Code. The text that is written to develop programs is called "code." In word processing, "code" means the special keys pressed to instruct the computer how to format text.

Command. An instruction given to the system.

Communications. Sending and receiving information, as between your word processor and someone else's.

Communications software. A program that you run when you want to send information to or receive information from another word processor or computer. Communications software works in conjunction with special hardware such as modems, telling the computer what to do with them.

Compatible. Two pieces of equipment are said to be compatible if information can move from one to the other, and back, without error.

Competitive analyst. In a company selling word processors, a person who studies the competition's word processors.

Components. The individual parts of a word processor, such as the computer, memory, printer, keyboard, screen, and disk drive.

Computer. The guts of your word processor. Sometimes "computer" is used to refer to the central processing unit (CPU), sometimes to the whole computer system (CPU and other units).

Computer processor. The part of the computer that actually processes signals sent to it, performing calculations and sending information to other devices.

Computer-ese. The technical lingo spoken by experienced computer users, programmers, and others.

Concurrent printing. The ability to enter and edit one document while printing out another document at the same time.

Concurrent word and data processing. The ability to do both word and data processing on the same computer at the same time.

Configuration. Layout of a network—the physical arrangement. Or the particular combination of hardware used in a computer installation.

Connect time. The amount of time a terminal is connected to a computer, sending or receiving information.

Contention. A way for terminals to gain access to a channel, by competing with each other. You get on only when the channel is free. For example, see ***CMSA-CD*** and ***ALOHA.***

Continuous paper. Computer paper that comes folded in one long sheet.

Control. In a local area network, control refers to the way you direct traffic through the system. Centralized control means you have a computer at the center, and every message goes there first before being dispatched to the recipient. Decentralized control means that control passes among the terminals along the line.

Control characters. In an electronic message, control characters tell the system what kind of data to expect in the message, where to send it, and how to translate it. On your word processor, a control character may show up on your video screen, indicating what the printer should do with a certain section: for instance, a star in front of a line might mean that the printer should underline the line. Some systems show you these control characters; others use them, but keep them invisible.

Control key. Often labeled CTRL or CNTRL, the control key acts as a special kind of shift key. When you hold it down and press another key, an instruction goes to the computer telling it how to control the text that follows. For instance, you might press the control key at the same time you press the letter "D," and the computer would understand that you do not mean to type the letter, but to perform the function that begins with D—delete.

Control key sequences. The order in which keys get pressed to request a function. For example, the control key followed by the letter "S" might save a document. Often the sequence consists of only two keys; sometimes it may be as many as three or four keystrokes in a row.

Controller. A device that controls the flow of data from a terminal to the main line of a network.

Conversion. Converting the material on your disk so that some other word processor can read the disk—a tricky process, not always successful. Used also to mean the whole endeavor of getting rid of your old word processor and bringing in a new one.

Copy. To copy is to take text from one document or page and duplicate it somewhere else. Copying does not eliminate the text in the original position; moving does. Copy also refers to the material you enter into your word processor—text.

Copying disks. Taking text from one magnetic disk and putting it on another disk, without erasing the first one.

CP/M. Control Program for Microcomputers, an operating system developed and trademarked by Digital Research to work with microprocessors, specifically the Z80, 8080, and 8086. Many computer programs have been written to work with CP/M-based microcomputers. When CP/M is available on your word processor, it means that you can use many of these other programs on the system, allowing it to be much more than a word processor.

CPU. The Central Processing Unit in your computer.

Create a document. To make a place on a disk for a new document, and to begin entering text.

Critical success factors. The things your office has to do to prove it is a success.

CRT. Cathode Ray Tube, or video display screen. A cathode gun sprays electrons at the surface of the screen, like a ray gun; when an electron hits a dot on the screen, the dot lights up, and you see a period.

CTRL key. Abbreviation for *Control key.*

Cursor. The lighted or blinking line, square, or triangle that marks your position in text on a video display screen. Shows you where you are about to enter the next character. The cursor moves along, just ahead of you.

Customize. To tailor especially for you.

Cut sheets. Separate sheets of paper, thought of as cut apart when compared to the continuous roll or folded sheet of conventional computer paper.

Daisy wheel. A type element, consisting of a circle of characters on the ends of metal or plastic stems. The daisy wheel spins around and plonks characters against the ribbon, creating an inked impact on the paper.

Data. Information. Sometimes used to refer to numbers, as opposed to text. But in general, any information that can move through the word processor is called data, as distinguished from commands, or housekeeping messages.

Data base. An electronic file, such as a record of every product you sell, with the price, the current sales figures, the stores it's selling in, the pack size, the weight, the shipping point. Data-base management, a computer program, allows you access to any record by specifying some part of it. For instance, I could ask the computer to print out every item shipped from Omaha. There are thousands of public data bases you can dial up on the phone.

Data link. In communications, a connection at the level of data—not just a physical plug.

DBMS. Data-Base-Management System, a type of computer program allowing you to organize your files so that you can retrieve information in many different ways.

Dead key. A key that lets you type something without advancing, so you can then type a second character on top of the first.

Dealer. A store or company that sells computer products and software made by other companies.

Decentralized word processing. An arrangement in which various word processors get placed all around your company, as opposed to putting them all in one room and calling it a word-processing center.

Decibel. A measure of sound. Ordinary conversation registers at about 60 decibels. Anything louder than 80 decibels can hurt you.

Decimal tabs. Tab settings on which the word processor can automatically line up all the decimal points in a column of numbers, making it easier to add them up.

Dedicated word processor. A computer designed first and foremost to do word processing. "Dedicated" may also indicate that the system is limited to word processing, but that is not always so.

Default. The standard setting that you get if you don't enter a change.

Delete. Wipe out or erase. In some word processors, you can delete a word, then change your mind and call it back. In others, once a word's gone, it's gone.

Density. The density of a floppy disk indicates how compactly it can store information. Single-density was the initial standard; double-density can store twice as much on the same size disk; quad-density, four times that much.

Descender. The part of a letter, or character, that descends below the line. Sometimes omitted on crude video display screens and printers.

Detached keyboard. A keyboard connected to the video screen by a cable—not molded to it. A detached keyboard lets you move around more—it's usually more comfortable to work with.

Diagnostic. A disk or program that you or a technician can use to diagnose what is going wrong with your word processor.

Digital transmission. A way of recording data on a computer, or transmitting it from one computer to another, using a series of on/off pulses, equivalent to 1s or 0s. Since those are digits, we call this method "digital." Other computers are called "analog computers," because they think in fluctuating electrical waves, which are the analogs of phenomena in the outside world, such as sound waves.

Digitize. To turn analog (or wave) signals into digital signals, which are a series of on/off pulses.

Directory. A list of documents or files on a disk.

Direct sales. A vendor who sells a word processor directly to you, rather than going through a dealer or another manufacturer.

Disk. A magnetic recording medium—round slices of plastic, like phonograph records, encased in square cardboard sleeves. Disks store your text.

Disk converter. A machine or a process that takes the material on one disk—with the standards and protocols of one vendor—and translates that into code your word processor can understand. The disk isn't converted; the material is. Useful when you've dropped one vendor's line and want to use your old disks on your new machine, without rekeying every document. See also *Conversion.*

Display. What you see onscreen. Usually, your text is displayed on a video screen.

Distributed network. A decentralized arrangement for a local area network, as when some terminals are linked to only one other terminal, some to three or four, one or two to all.

Distributor. A company that distributes products developed and manufactured by a different company.

Document. A complete text, whether one page or a hundred. A report or a letter, a budget or a proposal. Some word processors limit the number of pages or lines in each document.

Document analysis. Part of a feasibility study. You find out what types of documents your office is handling, and what problems they present, so that you'll know what kind of word processor you need.

Documentation. Manuals, training disks, reference guides, brochures—anything that describes your word processor and the way it works.

Document merge. To combine parts of two documents to create a third, as when you take an address from one list and a form letter from another. Or to combine whole documents.

Document-oriented. Describes a word processor designed to help you handle text that's longer than a few pages. A document-oriented word processor allows you to make changes throughout the whole document at the push of a button, whereas a page-oriented word processor generally lets you work only on a page at a time.

DOS. Disk Operating System, a computer program that tells the disk drive how to read, write, and communicate with the central processing unit in your word-processing system.

Dot command. A command used by some word processors to define the format of a line—for instance, ".i5" might mean to indent the following line by five spaces when printing.

Dot leader. A function that lets you put a string of periods down, without typing every one.

Dot matrix. A method of printing, using dots in a grid known as a matrix. The greater the number of dots, the more fully formed the character will be.

Down time. The time when your word processor is "down," not working.

Drive. The turntable that drives your magnetic disks around and around, while the information on them is read. It's usually enclosed in a plastic box.

Dumb terminal. A keyboard and video display terminal, or other device that can send or receive information, but cannot do any processing (or thinking).

EBCDIC. Extended Binary-Coded Decimal Interchange Code, a code for translating characters and symbols into on/off pulses, or bits. Used on large, high-speed computers. Since it uses 8 bits per character, it can define up to 256 different characters, including underlines and sub- and superscripts.

Edit. To enter or change text.

Editor. The program that lets you type your text into the computer, then organize and change it. A text editor is a program that was originally designed to help programmers write and rewrite lines of programming code—not very helpful for long documents.

Efficiency. It's supposed to increase when you use word processing. Whether it does or not depends on what you measure—you'll probably turn out more paper faster. But whether you get more real work done depends on your choice of machine and your design of the job.

EIA. The Electronics Industry Association, a group of electronics firms in the United States. They have created a number of standards, so that different companies' machines will be able to plug into one another. For instance, the EIA RS 232C Interface.

Electronic mail. Communication from your video display screen to someone else's. The receiving terminal may store your message, to be displayed when the recipient comes back from lunch.

Electronics Industry Association. See ***EIA.***

Electronic typewriter. A typewriter with electronic signals guiding the letter from the key you press up onto the page. (Electric typewriters do this mechanically.) Most electronic typewriters have a little memory—some can recall a few lines, or even a page of text. And most can perform some very simple word-processing functions on those short passages.

Electronic worksheet. A program designed to automate work normally done on a spreadsheet: entry of headings, columns or rows of numbers, and calculations using the numbers.

Electrostatic printer. A printer that sets up electrostatic charges, to draw ink dust, or liquid ink, to the page, forming characters.

Elite. A typeface that fits 12 characters into an inch—smaller and closer together than pica.

Emulation. Imitation. When your terminal "emulates" another, it can pass for that one without any further tinkering.

End user. The ultimate user of the word processor—you. Vendors employ this term.

Enhancement. An improvement on the program that currently runs your word processor.

Enter. To put in text.

Entry. The process of entering text: typing on the keyboard and seeing the text appear onscreen.

Entry line. The line on which you actually enter text onscreen.

Ergonomic. Describes word processors designed to work in a way that does not hurt you. Such word processors take into account human factors, so you'll feel comfortable and healthy using them.

ESC. A key with the abbreviation for "escape." What it means varies from one program to another. In one, when you press this key, you escape from the normal mode of typing, so that when you type the letter "E," it does not appear as "E" onscreen, but instead you Exit the document. The ESC key helps you to activate special functions, or to escape to a menu filled with options.

Escape key. See *ESC.*

Executive workstation. A video display screen and keyboard designed for use by executives. May include a computer processor and disk drives. Usually implies access to some kind of network, linking the executive to the main company data bases and to other executives.

Facsimile machine. A machine that can send copies of drawings or letters across long distances, using phone lines or other carriers.

Fan-folded computer paper. Conventional computer paper. It comes in one long sheet, folded up. When you hold one side tight and riffle the other to let air in, it looks vaguely like an Oriental fan.

FCC. The Federal Communications Commission. They make the rules for most communications using public phone lines, microwaves, satellite transmission, and fiber optics.

FDM. Frequency Division Multiplexing, a way of dividing up the available frequencies on a channel so that you can send different messages on different ranges of frequencies—in effect multiplying the number of channels.

Feasibility study. A study carried out to see if it will be feasible—possible—to improve productivity in an office. Usually such a study involves examining how you carry out the work now, designing a system to do that better, costing that out, and concluding that, yes, it is feasible.

Feature. A task your word processor can perform. A sales term for "function."

Feature war. A battle between vendors over whose word processor offers the fanciest features.

Feeder. A device that feeds regular typing paper—cut sheets—or computer paper into a printer.

Field. A section of a message or record. Each field is assigned to a different type of information, such as address, or retail price.

Field service. Staff who install and repair word processors out in the field (not in their home offices).

File. A collection of records, letters, text, or data—anything you would put in a file folder. Whatever you enter on your screen may get erased if you don't save it—and you save it by putting it in a file.

File name. The name assigned to a file. The system uses this name to retrieve the file.

Firmware. Memory circuits on the inside of the computer, which contain programmed general instructions for the computer. They are "firm" because they don't go away when you turn the computer off. See ***Hard wire.***

Fixed disk. A hard disk used to store programs and document files; it's fixed, because it remains in its cabinet and cannot be removed.

Flag. A signal—usually a 1 or 0, or a series of these bits in a particular place—indicating something about the message it accompanies.

Floating cursor. A cursor that can be moved anywhere onscreen to enter or change text. (Some machines limit entry to the bottom line.)

Floppy disk. A flat, square, somewhat flexible disk that is used for storage of programs and document files. Usually 8" or 5¼" square. Although floppies bend, they can't be bent too far without damaging them.

Floppy disk drive. The slot and mechanism you slip floppy disks into, to use them with your word processor.

Flow chart. A chart showing the way information flows through a company or program, either physically or logically.

Font. One style of type, in one particular size. The word comes from the days when all type was cast from hot lead, so print shops resembled foundries. "Font" and "foundry" derive from the French *fondre,* to cast. Now, of course, we use "cold type"—type composed photographically. But we still use hundreds of fonts that were first created in metal.

Footer. Any material you want to appear at the foot of every page, such as page numbers, names, dates.

Footnoting. Some word processors renumber and reposition your footnotes when you move around the referenced text; most don't.

Forced page break. If you have designed your document so that most pages have thirty lines, double-spaced, you can use a forced page break to make sure that the last page in Chapter One, with only three lines, ends up with white space at the bottom, so Chapter Two starts on a new page.

Format line. A line onscreen showing you how you've formatted the page—where margins are, for instance, and tab stops.

Formatted disk. A disk that has been prepared for use by a specific computer.

Formatter. The part of your word-processing program that organizes your text into the shape you want it printed in. Sometimes the formatter is a separate program you run after you enter the text.

Frame. An envelope for a message, on the analogy of a frame for a picture. The frame usually consists of a block of data, enclosed in special control characters, which warns the system that a message is coming inside of this frame. Sometimes people refer to the message, plus these control characters, as the whole frame.

Frequency. The rate at which a wave (of sound, say, or electricity) vibrates. If the cycle of beginning, rising, and falling away takes one second, we say that is a frequency of one hertz.

Frequency division multiplexing. A way of dividing up the available frequencies on a channel so that you can send different messages at different frequencies—in effect multiplying the number of channels. Abbreviated as FDM.

Full duplex. If you can send messages both ways on a line at once, that's full duplex transmission.

Full-page screen. A screen that can display somewhere around 55 to 70 lines of text at one time.

Fully formed characters. Most characters printed by a computer's dot matrix printer are fuzzy and incomplete, because they are just strings of dots. To get a fully formed character, you need to use a typewriter, or a letter-quality impact printer (one that uses a daisy wheel)—or, if you have a lot of printing and a lot of money, an ink jet or laser printer.

Function. A task your word processor can perform, such as inserting a word or moving a phrase. Also, in terms of the whole office, any major task accomplished there. For instance, in a personnel office, hiring a new person would be a function.

Functional design. The design of the functions of a word processor—creating what you can do and how you will be able to do it.

Function keys. Special keys that are pressed to activate word-processing functions. Sometimes they are separate keys, to one side or above the regular keyboard. Sometimes they are a combination of a special key (such as ALTERNATE, CONTROL, or ESCAPE), and a number or letter key. See also ***Alternate key, Control key, ESC.***

Gateway. A machine that sits between two networks, translating messages from one set of protocols to another. A protocol for translating protocols, serving as a gateway from one network to another.

Generalist. A person who performs a lot of different tasks, without being a specialist in any one. For instance, a traditional secretary is a generalist because she types, files, makes phone calls, sets up meetings, speaks for her boss, and keeps the books. By contrast, a word-processing specialist often only types.

General ledger. An accounting program that functions as your general ledger.

Generating. Creating. For instance, some word processors can look through your chapter headings and use them to generate a table of contents. Others take a list of words you provide and then look through the text, coming back with page numbers for each and every time the words appear—generating an index.

Ghost hyphen. A hyphen that you type into a word that might eventually have to be hyphenated. It's called a ghost because it's printed only when the word shows up at the end of a line, runs past the margin, and has to be broken to fit.

Glitch. A little problem—a weird inconsistency, a minor failure, a mistake in the way the word processor was designed.

Global. Any function that you can have done throughout the entire length of a document, rather than one line or page at a time, is considered "global."

Glossary. A collection of prepared definitions—or paragraphs—to be stored in memory and called up whenever you need to reproduce them, so you don't have to retype the material over and over again.

Go to. A feature allowing you to move your cursor forward or back directly by the length of one word, line, sentence, paragraph, or column.

Graphics mode. A mode in which daisy wheel printers can produce lines and drawings, rather than letters and numbers.

Half-duplex transmission. If you can send messages both ways on a line, but only one way at a time, that's half-duplex transmission.

Half-page screen. A screen that can display between 20 and 30 lines of text at a time—about half a normal single-spaced letter page.

Half spacing. The ability to move down half a line, rather than a whole line, and start typing again. Useful in mathematical formulas.

Handshakes. Procedures that two machines go through, establishing an electronic link.

Hanging. A program "hangs" when it stops. You can't type anything, and the text onscreen just sits there. The printer freezes.

Hard copy. A printed copy of the document.

Hard disk. A disk that is not "flexible," that cannot be easily bent. Sometimes such a disk is fixed in place, and cannot be removed from the drive that houses it; sometimes it can be removed. Used for document storage.

Hardware. The physical components of a computer or word processor, such as the keyboard, central processor, and video display screen.

Hard wire. To build a program right into the computer, so it cannot be taken out without disassembling the equipment—as opposed to software, which is not wired in at all, but read in from a disk each time you need to use it.

Header. A heading at the top of a page. Some systems let you define the headers once, then have the system pop them onto every page.

Help screen. A screen with advice to help you get out of difficulty. Some systems let you ask for help at any time; others just show you the help screen when they think that you've gotten yourself in deep trouble. Some systems don't help you at all.

Hertz. Cycles per second. A way of measuring the frequencies a particular circuit can carry.

High resolution. Clarity. Vendors boast that their system has high resolution, if letters look sharp and clear on a video display screen or printout.

Hot zone. An area near the right margin. When you type a word into it, you may find it goes past the margin, in which case you ask the system to break the word somewhere in that hot zone, as close to the margin as possible, inserting a hyphen and putting the rest of the word on the next line.

Human factors. What the engineers used to forget when they designed word processors. Now that vendors worry about human factors, we're beginning to see easier-to-read screens, friendlier buttons, more comfortable chairs.

Hybrid. A computer that can be used for both word and data processing.

Hyphenating. Putting in hyphens when the word processor breaks up words at the right margin, to create an even line of text there, as in a printed book. On cheap systems you do this yourself; more expensive systems do it for you.

Impact printer. All printers make an impact on paper. But this term has been applied only to printers that actually make a noise, thumping a key against a ribbon to slam ink onto the page, or spinning a daisy wheel full of characters, then ramming the right one against a ribbon to make an impression on paper.

Implementation specialist. A person who helps you decide which word processor will be right for your office—then helps you "implement," or install, it.

Index. In some systems, a list of what texts you have on a particular disk. Also, a function allowing you to create an accurate list of key topics with the page numbers where they appear.

Information processing. Handling information on your computer—whether that information is numbers or text.

Information system. A glorified word processor, one that has been expanded to let you handle calendars and worksheets. Or any computer system that lets you do calculations as well as prepare text.

Ink jet printer. Sprays ink onto the page. Very fast printer—and very expensive.

Input. Whatever you put into a computer, as when you type a word.

Input device. Any machine that helps you put information into the computer. Examples: keyboard, disk drive, modem.

Inquiry. A question you ask of the computer.

Insert. To put in. If you examine a sentence onscreen and realize that you forgot a word, a word processor allows you to insert that word easily in the right place.

Installation program. A computer program designed to help you get your word processor going for the first time—when you're "installing" it.

Integrated. A computer in which you can do both word and data processing, and transfer information back and forth from each program. For instance, you could bring totals from your General Ledger program over into your Annual Report document. But some vendors call their computers "integrated" even though the system can handle only one type of processing at a time, with no communication from one type of file to another.

Intelligent TDM. Time Division Multiplexing, a way of dividing up slowly arriving messages into short hunks, sending them at high speed down a line to another machine, which separates them out and dispatches them, at slower speeds again, to their recipients. It is called intelligent because this multiplexer also shifts the assignment of channels, so that a big-volume user can get through without fouling up anyone else.

Interactive graphics system. A computer system that allows you to draw charts or make pictures through interaction with its programs.

Interface. A connection, usually between two machines. Constantly misapplied to human beings, as when a salesperson says, "Let's get together and interface," meaning talk together.

Internal memory. The number of characters the computer in your word processor can remember at any one time. If you have a hundred-page document on a disk, the computer may not be able to look at more than twenty or thirty pages at a time. That's because it does not have much internal memory. Also known as **RAM**.

Inventory control. A computer program that monitors the products you have on stock, in the warehouse, and in your stores.

I/O. Acronym for Input/Output—those functions which let you put text in and get text out of your word processor.

ISX. Information Switching Exchange, a very powerful computerized switchboard from Datapoint.

IWP. International Information/Word Processing Association, a group of word-processing supervisors, operators, consultants, and others (1015 North York Road, Willow Grove, PA 19090).

K. Kilobyte, or 1024 bytes. Used to indicate the amount of room in memory or on a disk. For example, a word processor with a memory size of 64K can hold 64×1024 bytes of information, or about 64,000 characters.

Keyboard. The array of keys, buttons, bars, that you use to enter data in your word processor.

Keyboard buffer. A temporary storage area in the computer, holding characters as you type them in. This way, if you type faster than the computer can put the characters onscreen, it won't forget what you've typed, and when you pause for breath, it will catch up with you, drawing stored characters out of the keyboard buffer.

Keycap. The plastic top of the key; what you actually tap when you type. These can be removed, and replaced with new ones, if you get a new type element with a foreign language, special symbols, or math signs.

Kurzweil. Inventor of the Kurzweil Reading Machine, which can read books and translate them into speech so the blind can listen. Raymond Kurzweil also invented the Kurzweil Data Entry Machine, an Optical Character Reader (OCR) that can be trained to recognize new typefaces. (Before this, most OCRs were limited to one or two fonts.) After it has read a text, the machine translates it into codes your word processor can use, if you want to make changes to the material.

Laser printer. A printer that uses a laser to create many very fine dots on a page, so that the characters look almost as sharp as if they had been typed.

Lead operator. The best person operating a word processor, usually in a word-processing center.

Leased lines. A circuit of your own, leased from the phone company or someone else. Used to avoid the static caused by getting switched, switched, and switched again, on a regular long distance call. Important if you want to send a big volume of data at high speed, without many errors.

Letter merge. A function in which you merge an address from one list with a form letter, thus personalizing each message.

Letter-quality printing. Printing that looks like an executive's correspondence. Not the fuzzy gray letters that come out of a dot matrix printer—the kind you see on bills from the utility company. Usually, but not always, letter-quality printing comes from "impact" printers—regular typewriters or daisy wheel printers.

Link. Connection between two or more machines. There are several kinds of links—physical, logical, network. Protocols define the way to achieve these links.

List processing. A program that lets you create a document with a list of information, such as names and addresses, and then to use that list in other documents, or to rearrange the items in the list in new ways.

Load. To move a program or document file from disk into the computer's memory.

Local area network. Basis for a fully automated office, the local area network ties together office equipment within one or two buildings. It's distinguished from a wide area network, which may span three continents.

Locate. To find a phrase, title, page, or document within your files on disk or in the system's memory.

Log on. To sign into a system, often by typing in your name and password.

Loop. A way of arranging equipment along a local area network. Here the cable forms a loop, going through each terminal or node; messages can then make a complete circle.

Low-end system. The least expensive word processors—at the bottom of a vendor's line.

MagCard. A typewriter that stores text on magnetic cards.

Mainframe computer. A very large computer, capable of handling millions of characters every minute.

Maintain. To update a text once it has been created. Also, to keep a computer system operating.

Margin release key. A key that lets you move outside the margins you previously set.

Marker. A character that won't be printed, used to delimit some text. For instance, in some systems, if you want to move a paragraph, you put a marker at the beginning and at the end, indicating what you will move.

Megabyte (MB). A million bytes, or about a million charactrs.

Memory. What the computer remembers (internal memory) and what the disks recall (external storage).

Memory typewriter. A typewriter that remembers a few characters, or a few pages, then prints those out on command.

Menu. A list of tasks you can perform, offered onscreen.

Menu-driven. A word processor that shows you a menu with all the options open to you, then lets you pick what you want to do, is said to be "menu-driven."

Merge. To combine two or more texts to create a new combined document.

Micro. Microcomputer.

Microcomputer. A personal, or small-business computer with a microprocessor chip as its central processing unit.

Microfilm records. Records that have been reduced in size and stored on film.

Microprocessor. A small chip that functions as a central processing unit for a computer. Often inserted into the latest models of printers, copiers, facsimile machines, telephone switchboards, video display screens, and keyboards—to control their operation and to receive signals from other computerized equipment.

Microwaves. A way to send a signal, or boil an egg. Microwave radio can transmit 1000 to 15,000 million hertz (cycles per second)—but only along a line of sight.

Mini. A medium-sized computer, thought of as "mini" when all there were were gigantic mainframes. Larger than a personal computer, it can usually remember more and work faster.

Mnemonic. Helpful to your memory. For instance, when some vendors claim their commands are "mnemonic," they mean easy to remember.

Mode. In a word processor, functions are grouped into a general type, or mode: for instance, you might have an Edit Mode and a Print Mode.

Modem. A device that allows computers (which communicate in on/off pulses) to communicate over ordinary phone lines, which usually carry sound waves rather than on/off signals. There are several types: an acoustic coupler, for instance, has two rubber-circled holes to place the phone in—it's okay for slow messages, but static tends to creep in. Better are modems that plug directly into the phone line. As vendors add multiplexers (so the modem can divide one circuit into several different channels) and microprocessors (so the modem can give you a number of options), the price and the flexibility of modems increase.

Monitor. A video screen sold separately from the keyboard.

Mouse. A box that moves around on your desk, driving an arrow on screen. A pointing device.

Move. To take text from one place and put it somewhere else.

MSR. Marketing Support Representative—a salesperson.

MTST. Magnetic Tape Selectric Typewriter, an IBM Selectric that stores text on reusable magnetic tape.

Multipurpose OCR. An Optical Character Reader that can do more than just read a printed or typed text and translate that into codes your word processor will recognize. Features include some editing, reformatting, and correcting as you go.

Multitasking. Handling more than one person doing more than one different job at a time. Only sophisticated computers can cope with this.

Multiterminal. A computer or word-processing system with more than one terminal using the same processor.

Network. Any system that links together machines that transmit and receive information.

Node. The point at which information enters and leaves a network—for example, your video display screen.

Nonprinting comments. Comments you insert in a document on-screen but keep from being printed out.

Nonvolatile. Not erasable. Refers to memory in the computer that does not disappear when you turn the power off.

Number keypad. A ten-key pad, on which numbers are arranged as on a calculator, usually located to the right of the standard typewriter keys on the keyboard.

Object. In terms of the whole office, an object is what you work on—a whole application package, say. It might include half a dozen forms and some letters. Thus, any office procedure handles a number of objects.

OCR. Optical Character Reader, or Optical Character Recognition. Any machine that can read printed or typed copy, then turn that information into the codes used by the computer inside your word processor. See also **Multipurpose OCR.**

OEM. Original Equipment Manufacturer. But they don't really manufacture the original equipment: they modify it, repackage it, tinker with the programming, and then sell their adaptation to you.

Off hook. An indicator on a modem, showing that the phone is off the hook—that is, the modem is in the process of sending or receiving a message.

Office of the future. A general term for an office in which information can flow electronically from one word processor to almost any other office equipment and back.

Ohm. A way to measure resistance, in an electrical line. One ohm is the amount of resistance in a circuit in which the potential difference of one volt produces a current of one ampere.

Online. Immediately accessible to the computer, and to you.

Operating system. The program that actually operates the computer, when it runs "application" programs that apply computing power to particular tasks, such as word processing.

Operator. The specialist who operates a word processor. Usually refers to someone who just enters and revises text all day. Distinguished from a generalist—someone who does a job and happens to use a word processor to handle letters, or reports.

Optical character reader. See *OCR.*

Optical fibers. Very thin strands of glass that can carry short bright bursts of light, corresponding to the on/off impulses coming from a computer. A wide range of frequencies is possible, so these carriers will be able to transmit large volumes of information at the speed of light.

Optical scanner. A machine that can translate an ordinary photograph into a pattern of dots, so a printer can reproduce it.

Options. Features that do not come with the standard machine. Usually they cost more, and perform functions that most people don't bother with very often. But with the cheapest machines, almost anything you want to do turns out to be an expensive "option."

Order entry. A computer program that allows you to enter orders into your system, often generating bills, lading bills, and warehouse alerts.

Orientation. Some word-processing programs let you work within one line but give you a hard time moving around a page. That is called line orientation. Page-oriented systems tend to make it hard to handle movement around a long document. A document-oriented system lets you move freely within the whole document, no matter how long.

Original equipment manufacturer. See *OEM.*

Orphan. A single line left at the top of a page—most of its paragraph being back on the preceding page.

Output. Whatever a computer puts out, such as printed material.

Overlay. A technique used when a program cannot all fit into the computer's memory at one time. Some of the instructions remain out on the disk when not needed. When these instructions are activated, the computer calls them back from the disk and "lays them over" other information in memory.

Package. A program that can be purchased separately from your word processor.

Page break. A code indicating where you want a page to end. Usually the system will put the same number of lines on each page, but at the end of a chapter, you might want the last three lines on that page to end the page, so your next chapter will start at the top of the next page. So you enter the code to make a page break after the last line of the first chapter.

Paginate. To set page lengths and have the computer run through your text, dividing it up into pages and assigning page numbers as it goes.

Paragraph indent. A function that automatically indents for a new paragraph.

Parallel. A way of sending signals down 8 or 16 parallel wires at once. For fairly slow devices, this means you get more information across to another machine faster than you would if you just sent one bit after another down one line—serially.

Patch. A temporary or local change made in a computer program, to let it work in special circumstances, unforeseen by the programmer.

Payroll. A computer program that helps you keep track of your employees, and pay their salaries.

Peripheral. Any equipment attached to the central processing unit, but not part of it. Examples: a printer, your video display screen.

Personal computer. A small computer suitable for use by one person. (Larger computers serve hundreds of people at once.) By buying a special program, you can use a personal computer to do word processing.

Phone directory. You can put frequently called numbers in a computer's memory, keyed to a short phrase—say, the initials of the person you are calling. This way, you type in the initials, and the computer calls up the number right away. Often used in conjunction with automatic dialing, so the number comes up and the computer dials it. A feature in some modems.

Photocomposition. Setting type by projecting an image onto film, or photosensitive paper. Literally, a machine that allows you to compose with light. Produces "cold type."

Physical link. A protocol for making the physical connection between two machines.

Pica. A typeface that fits ten characters into an inch—larger and farther apart than elite.

Pie charts. Graphs drawn in the shape of pies, each slice showing a percentage of the whole.

Pin. A prong on a multiprong plug.

Pitch. A setting indicating whether the letters will be closer together, or farther apart.

Plotter. A machine that uses one or more pens to draw whatever the computer tells it to. Helpful for charts, graphics, portraits.

Presentation level. A protocol governing the way the system translates from digital codes (such as ASCII, or EBCDIC) into English, so that you can look at real words, not just 1s and 0s.

Preview. The ability to see text just the way it will be printed—before you actually send it to the printer.

Printer. The machine that types out your text. It takes coded impulses from your word-processing system and turns those into letters and numbers on paper.

Printhead. The device that does the actual printing on some printers. Examples: the type element on an electric typewriter; the daisy wheel.

Print queue. A line your document must wait in, until it gets its turn on the printer.

Procedure. In terms of the office as a whole, a procedure is a series of small tasks (the steps of the procedure), which aim to carry out one phase of a major office function—starting it, managing it, or concluding it.

Process. To manipulate. You process words when you enter them, rearrange and send them to the printer.

Productivity. A much-abused term, usually used to refer to the number of pages turned out each hour. Thus, by bringing in word processors, you can increase "productivity," if that's how you measure it.

Product line jobs. Jobs developing new word processors for a vendor.

Programmable key. A key that you can program, so that when you press it, the word processor carries out a function that otherwise might require a sequence of three or four keys. Speeds up your work, if you do a lot of something the designers didn't figure you'd use very often.

Programs. Computer programs that tell a computer how to perform functions such as word processing.

Prompt. A message from the word processor urging you to do something.

Proportional spacing. The ability to insert little spaces proportionally along a line so that by the end it stops right at the same spot as every other line—right margin justified. If you don't have proportional spacing, and you ask the word processor to justify your text, it will do so clumsily, putting a big space between the last two words, for instance.

Protocol. Agreed-upon convention for doing something. In communications, protocols define such things as how to make the electrical connection, how to send information through the channel, how to display the message.

Protocol converter. A machine that translates a message designed under one set of protocols so that a machine using a different set of protocols can understand it.

Queue. A line. You are in queue when your text is waiting behind someone else's to get to the printer.

RAM. Random Access Memory. A way of storing data so that you can lay it down and retrieve it randomly—which turns out to be much faster than if you have to go step-by-step through everything else on the disk before you get to what you need.

Reformat. To change the arrangement of the text—margins, indentations, spacing, for instance.

Refresh rate. The rate at which the image on your video display screen gets reestablished. If the refresh rate falls below 60 times a second, the image may shake and shimmy.

Renaming. The ability to change the name of a file. For instance, you may have started a file called "Wilson Proposal," containing your memos, letters, budgets, and draft proposals. Then when you get the Wilson job, you could change the name of that file to "Wilson Project."

Repeaters. Placed in the middle of a line, a repeater picks up a digital signal coming in, recognizes its 1s and 0s, and regenerates those, sending a brand-new signal along the line. (Different from an amplifier, which merely makes the old, degenerating signal louder—increasing the chance for error.)

Repeating keys. Some keys, when held down for more than a fraction of a second, repeat. Thus, on some word processors, all you have to do to get a row of periods is press down on that key for a few seconds.

Repeating last command. A function in which you just press a button, telling the machine to do again what you just told it to do. This saves keystrokes, since one command might involve as many as ten.

Request for proposal. A report specifying what kind of word processing you need, sent to various vendors, asking them to make you a proposal for meeting those needs with their equipment.

Reset. A button that lets you turn off the computer and turn it back on, instead of reaching around in back of the terminal to switch it off, then on again. Useful when you're changing programs and want to start again from scratch.

Resistance. The amount a given material resists electrical current passing through.

Resolution. Clarity of image. If it's sharp, it's high resolution.

Response time. The time it takes to get a response back from your word processor—or, if it's broken, from the repair people.

Reverse video. An image in which the screen's normal background color becomes the color of the character, and vice versa. Used to highlight text.

Right justification. Making the text line up evenly on the right, the way it does on the left.

Right justifying tabs. A tab stop usually helps you line the text up to the left of that position. But these tabs line the text up to their right.

Ring. A way of arranging equipment in a local area network. As with a loop, the cable is arranged in a rough circle. But here it does not pass directly through terminals. It goes through controllers, which decide whether or not a given message is addressed to their terminals.

ROM. Read-Only Memory. Memory that the word processor draws on to function; protected from you, it can be read from but not written over.

Rub out. To erase.

Ruler. A line on which you can set margins and tabs. Format line.

Satellite. A form of transmission in which we send signals up to the satellite, which then broadcasts them down across a wide area—half a continent, say. Can handle several thousand phone calls at once.

Save. To preserve something you've typed onscreen.

Scaling up. Expanding, in a network.

Scratch pad. A place in the computer's memory set aside for material you need to save for a little while, and then either erase or save on disk.

Screen. Video display screen, on which you can read your text.

Scroll. To roll the whole text up past the screen. The analogy is to an ancient scroll of pressed papyrus, in which text appeared on a continuous roll rather than cut pages.

SDLC. Synchronous Data-Link Control, protocol for controlling the flow of data, created by IBM.

Search. A function, allowing you to specify a particular word or phrase and have the word processor find it for you.

Search and replace. A function, letting you specify a particular word or phrase, have the word processor find it for you, then replace it with another entry.

Serial. A way of sending signals: one bit (or on/off pulse) right after another.

Service. Repair and troubleshooting, usually by the people who sold you the equipment, sometimes by independent technicians.

Session logic. A protocol setting up ways for you to log on to the system, hold a session with the computer, and log off.

Shared logic. A system in which several terminals share the basic logic of one central computer.

Sheet feed. A device to feed cut sheets of paper into the printer.

Shift. A key that lets you shift into capital letters, or back to lowercase.

Short-line seeking. A printer function: lets the printer skip over any blanks at the end of a line, to get quickly to the next piece of text it has to print. Saves time on long jobs.

Simplex. A mode of transmitting a message, in which you can only send signals one way.

Simultaneous. At the same time. Some systems let you print at the same time as you edit something else—that's truly simultaneous.

Single-user system. A word processor designed for one person only.

Small-business system. A computer and accompanying software designed to help a small business.

Smart terminal. A terminal that can do more than send or receive information from the central computer. It can do some processing, too.

Soft benefits. The benefits that cannot be exactly totaled up in monetary terms. Office automation can be justified in "hard" and soft terms. Improving morale might seem to be a benefit, but how much money does that save?

Software. The computer programs that tell the hardware how to process your words.

Software maintenance contract. A contract that allows you to receive all improved versions of the same program, as they become available.

Sort. A function, in which the system orders a list alphabetically, numerically, or some other way.

Specialist. In the transition from a traditional office to one with a word-processing center, a secretary who used to do a little of everything may end up being a specialist—just operating the word processor.

Spelling check. A function in which the system checks the spelling of every word against a dictionary, then highlights the words it doesn't recognize—some of which are mistakes, others just words that don't occur in its dictionary.

Stand-alone. A word processor that works without any other computers, terminals, keyboards, screens, printers—all by itself.

Star. A way of arranging the equipment in a local area network. A computer sits at the center; all messages go to it, then it redirects them to the recipients.

Status indicators. Lights or other signals that tell you the status of the machinery. For instance, a ready light.

Storage. The way you save your text: it could be on a magnetic disk, a paper tape, or a card. Storage media, then, include disk, tape, and cards.

Storing formats. Most systems store the format you used along with the text you arranged in that format. But some systems also let you store an oft-used format, without any text. That way, you can just call up your standard format, whenever you need it—rather than setting it up each time.

Strikeover. A character with a line through it. Used in legal documents to indicate what the attorney has omitted—so the other attorney can see what would otherwise be deleted.

Subscript. Text that gets printed slightly below the line.

Superscript. Text that gets printed slightly above the line.

Support. Assistance, such as repairs, maintenance, training, manuals, from the people who make or sell your word processor.

Switched phone lines. Regular phone lines. Your call goes directly to a local office, where it is switched to a trunk line; that line in turn leads to a series of other switches, until you reach another local office, which sends you to the person you're calling.

Symmetrical. A network is considered symmetrical when you can move easily from one computer program to another, without having to go through some intermediate process.

Synch. Synchronicity. When two machines are in synch, they both know when a message starts and stops, so neither misinterprets the signals.

Synchronous transmission. A form of transmission, usually faster than asynchronous. In synchronous transmission, the computers (or modems) at either end use a clock to establish a constant beat. So a message may consist of a clockbeat, a special pattern of bits announcing that a message is on its way, then a few thousand bits for your text, then another bit announcing that you've reached the end of your message. (Asynchronous transmission puts start and stop bits right after each character—filling the line with a lot of extra bits and slowing down the transmission of your text. It's not really *out* of sync—it's just in sync one character at a time. What is out of sync, in asynchronous transmission, is you: it's used when you aren't sending a steady stream of data, just a message now and then.)

Systems analyst. A person who analyzes entire systems—for instance, the way information flows through your office. Such analysis often leads to changes in the way work gets done, and prepares the way for some form of computerization—such as word processing.

Systems design. The activity of creating hardware and software that will help you carry out the various functions of word processing.

Systems house. A company that puts together systems, often using other people's equipment and computer programs, mildly modified.

T1, T2, T3, T4. Specifically conditioned phone lines, carrying millions of bits (on/off pulses) per second.

Tabs. Settings that allow you to press the tab key, and go quickly to a position in the middle of the page.

TDM. Time Division Multiplexing, a way of dividing up slowly arriving messages into short hunks, then sending them at high speeds down the line.

Telex. A way to send messages. You dial up Western Union, and send a message from your word processor; they transmit it to your branch office anywhere in North America, where it prints out.

Text editor. A program originally created to help programmers write and rewrite the short lines of programming code. It's not very helpful as a word processor if you write in units longer than 80 characters at a time.

Thermal printer. A printer that uses heat-sensitive paper. Employed mostly in calculators and cash registers.

Thimble. A type element that looks like a thimble. All the characters are around the outside. It bounces up and down and around, slapping against a ribbon, to make an inked impression on the paper.

Tickler file. A reminder file. When you hear about a meeting, you file that under the right day. Then each morning, you open to today's date, to find out what you have to do today. You can set these up on your word processor.

Time division multiplexing. See ***TDM.***

Time sharing. Sharing the central computer's time with lots of other people. Large computers operate so fast that they can listen to you, and handle hundreds of other problems at the same time, so that you don't feel you're being interrupted or slowed down.

Token passing. A way of passing control from terminal to terminal, on a local area network in the shape of a ring.

Top of page (or form). A mechanism for telling the printer where you consider the top of the page, or form, so that it always starts in the same place. Helpful when you use continuous paper, so that the printer doesn't print right over the crease.

Topology. In a local area network, a topology is the physical layout of the terminals, in relation to the connecting cables. For instance, in a loop, you have a cable circling through all the terminals, forming a complete loop.

Tractor mechanism. Prongs on a rubber or metal belt. These fit into the holes on conventional computer paper, and pull it through the printer.

Training. Instruction. Some vendors teach you how to use their machine; others leave that to you.

Transmission. A way of sending a signal—whether that signal is on/off electrical impulses, flashes of light, or microwaves.

Transport level. A protocol for sending messages from one network to another.

Tube. Video display screen, on which you can read your text as you write.

Turnaround time. The time it takes the computer to absorb what you've just said and to get back to you with the results. For instance, you type in the command to delete the last paragraph. The computer thinks about that for a few seconds, then agrees to do it. That's also known as response time. The phrase "turnaround time" also refers to the time it takes to get a document back from a word-processing center, or a remote computer center.

Turnkey. A system you can start using as soon as you take it home—without any complicated setup and installation.

TWX. You send your message from your word processor to a teletypewriter station, a machine designed to send text over long distances; from there it goes to Western Union; they route your message to another such machine in any other office in North America, where it prints out.

Type element. The type ball you see on a regular electric typewriter. All the characters are around the outside, and when you press a letter, the element spins around to slam the right one against the ribbon, making the character appear on paper.

Underline. To draw a line under the text.

Undo. To abandon a change you have just made, before the machine adopts it as final.

Update. To bring up to date. You do this to an old text—or to the program that runs the whole word processor.

Upgrade. An improvement in your word processor, often seen as taking you into a new level of performance.

User. That's you. Anyone who uses the system gets called this by the people who sell the equipment. To us, they're the vendors.

User-friendly. Jargon from the vendors, meaning that their word processor does not assault you with programming codes, difficult procedures, and threatening comments when you make a mistake.

Variable pitch. Ability to set characters up close together, or farther apart.

Vendor. The company that sells you your word processor or other equipment.

Verify. To make sure that your text has been stored correctly.

Vertical. Up and down. Some screens show only a few lines vertically, but others show 40 or more.

Videodisks. Recordings of TV, made on records; useful for storing up to 55,000 distinct TV pictures.

Virtual terminal support. A gateway processor from Nixdorf Computer. It makes your terminal look "virtually" the same as one on someone else's network, even if you both use different protocols.

Voice. When you talk on the phone, that's known as "voice traffic." So when you want to include actual conversations on an office network, those would be known as "voice messages," which can usually be stored at the other end, waiting for the recipient to return.

Volatile. A computer's memory is volatile—very changeable. If you pull the plug, it forgets.

Voltage. Electrical potential. A volt is the amount of force applied to a conductor with a resistance of one ohm, producing a current of one ampere.

What you see is what you get. Standard phrase heard from many salespeople, meaning that what you see onscreen is what you will get printed out. Not always true, no matter how many times they say it.

Widow. A single line left behind at the bottom of a page.

Window. Some systems imagine that the screen is a window, opening on the text.

Word-processing center. A central location handling word processing for many people throughout a company. Often staffed with specialists known as operators.

Word wrap. A function: as you type past the right margin, the word processor waits for you to finish a word, then snatches whichever word hangs over the edge, and puts that word at the beginning of the next line—in effect, wrapping your text around.

Work sampling. A technique for finding out how much time people spend on different tasks in the office—by wandering in and observing, at fixed or random intervals. You "sample" what people are doing.

Workstation. The place you work. At the least, this includes a keyboard and a video display screen.

WPS. Word-Processing Specialist, a salesperson, usually; sometimes, the person who helps you keep your system working, once it's installed. Often knows more about the machine than an average salesperson.

Index

Abandon changes, 42
Abbreviations in product list, 272
ABC Sales, 403–404
A. B. Dick, 274–77
Access, xix
Accounting, xx, xxiii, xxiv, 2, 3, 9, 161, 233, 243, 450
Action paper, 450
Acoustic coupler, 98, 450
Adding text, 24–25
Adjust, 450
Administrative Management, xix
Advance, 450
AES Data, 277–79
Aetna, 227
Air conditioning, 145–46, 149
Algo 2100, 279–81
Algorithmics, 279–81
Alignment, 450
ALOHA, 450
Alphanumerics, 450
Alpha plus, 277
Alternate character sets, 60, 83, 87, 264, 450
Alternate key, 62, 451. *See also* Function keys
American Management Association, 443
American Varityper, 281–83
Ampere, 451
Amplifier, 237, 451
Analog, 97, 236, 451
Analyzing work, 156–57
Anxiety, 151–52, 154–55
Apple Computer, Inc., xxiv, 60, 90, 132–33, 178, 283–85
Apple Pie Editor, 412–13
Apple Writer, 133, 283–85
Application, 73, 451
Application level, 245, 451
Applied Digital Data Systems, 285–87
Aquarius, 385–87
ARC, 235, 451
Architect, 9
Archives, 132
Archiving disks, 223
Arrow, 23–24, 32, 451
ASCII, 242–43, 451
Asian Computer Monthly, 442

Associations, 174, 443
Asymmetrical, 253, 451
Asynchronous, 77, 241, 255, 451
Atlantic Richfield, 226–27
AT&T, 226
Attached keyboard, 56
Attached Resource Computer (ARC), 235
Attributes, 58, 451
ATV Jacquard, 287–91
Audio monitor, 100, 452
Auto backup, 270, 452
Automated office, xvii–xx, 170, 226–58, 452
Automated answering, 452
Automatic dial, 100, 452
Automatic time stamp, 452
Auto save, 269, 452
Avon Products, 227

Background, 162–64
Backspace, 17, 42, 452
Backup of documents, 20–21, 222
Backup procedures, 222–23
Banking, xviii, xx
Barrister, 126
Baseband, 249, 255, 452
Basic Four Information Systems, 291–99
Baud, 240, 452
Baudot, 242, 452
Bell Telephone, 99
Bells and whistles, 452
Benchmark, 156
Benefits of word processing, xv–xvii
Bergerud, M., 441
Bidirectional printing, 452
Binary system, 453
Bit, 67–69, 72, 453
Bitmap, 453
Blinking, 59
Boilerplate, 219, 264, 446, 453
Boldface, 42, 59, 265, 453
Bookstore, 6
Booz, Allen and Hamilton, 70
Boss, xvii, xxiv, 3, 5, 150–51, 155–56, 230
Bottom, 18
Bps, 240, 453
Broadband, 249, 253, 453

482 ‖ INDEX

BSC, 453
Buffer, 101, 453
Bug, 453
Bundled, 74, 453
Burroughs, 226, 293-95
Burst mode, 250, 255, 453
Bus, 252-53, 255, 454
Business, word processing as, xvii-xxiv
Business Week, 442
Byte, 67-72, 453-54
Byte Magazine, 442

Cables, 246-51
Cado Systems, 295-97
Calculating, xix, 9, 37, 42, 159, 164, 170, 265, 454
Calendars, 81
Canada, 148, 152, 232
Canadian Data Systems, 442
Cancel, 42
Canned demonstration, 180
Capacitance, 454
Caps lock, 65
Careers, 434-40
Carriage return, 454
Carriers, 246-51
Cartridge disk, 72-73, 454
Catalog of documents, 45
Cat III, 295-97
Cathode Ray Tube. *See* CRT
CCITT, 243, 245, 454
Cecil, Paula B., 441
Center for Information Systems Research, 232
Centering, 32, 265, 454
Centers, word-processing, xx, 2, 5, 149, 480
Central Processing Unit (CPU), xx, 65-68, 457
Change case, 265, 454
Channel, 99, 454
Characters, 147, 454. *See also* Printers, Screens
Character display, 59
Character generator, 60, 454
Character set, 87, 454
Charts, 9, 226, 233
Check bit, 454
Checking spelling, 43
Checklists, 105-13, 141-43
Chiclet keyboard, 61
Chinese characters, 82
Chip, 65-68
Circuit, 248, 455
Clerk, xvii, xxiii, 4, 149
Closed network, 238
Closing a file, 18-19
Cluster, 2, 121, 245-46, 455
CMSA-CD, 252-53, 455
Codes, xxi, 255, 455
Coggshall, W. L., 232
Colleges, xviii, 8
Colored ink. *See* Plotters
Colors onscreen, 57, 60
Commands, 8, 455. *See also* Function keys, Control keys
Communications, 94, 96-101, 163-64, 167-68, 271, 455
Communications software, 79, 455
Compal, 297-99
Companies that sell word processors, 177-78
Company logo, 86
Compatibility, 99, 455
Competitive analyst, 438, 455
Components, 54-113, 455
Comprehensive Electronic Office, 405-406

Comptek, 126
Compucorp, 299-301
Compugraphic, 301-303
Computers, 6, 226, 234, 455
Computer processor, xx, 65-68, 455
Computer stores, 178
Computer World, 442
Concurrent printing, 455
Concurrent word and data processing, 128, 456
Configuration, 252, 255, 456
Connecting modems, 99
Connect time, 456
Conrath, David, 152
Consultants, xvii, xviii, 154, 174-75, 439
Contention, 252-53, 456
Continuous paper, 270, 456
Contrast, 57
Control of network, 251, 255, 456
Control characters, 77-78, 265, 456
Control keys, 62, 456. *See also* Function keys
Control key sequences, 134, 456
Controller, 251-53, 456
Conversion, 196, 456
Cooperation, 153
Copy, 263
Copying documents, 19-20, 27, 38, 149, 159, 163-64, 169-70, 233, 269, 456-57
Copying machines, 226, 229, 231
Corrections, 13, 16, 147, 159
Costs, xvii, xix, 9, 118, 125, 131, 135, 140, 162-63, 169
Courses, 443
CP/M, 131-33, 457
CPT, 60, 120, 177, 303-305
CPU, xx, 65-68, 457
Create a document, 14, 44, 457
Create a format, 44
Creative Computing, 442
Critical path diagrams, 9
Critical success factors, 156, 457
CRT, xix, 56-61, 457. *See also* Screens
CTRL key, 62, 457. *See also* Function keys
Cursor, 12, 14, 23, 28-29, 59, 76, 263, 457
Cursor keys, 62, 64
Customize, 457
Cut and paste, 11, 12
Cut sheets, 457. *See also* Printers

Dainoff, Marvin, 146
Daisy wheel, 85-86, 457
Data, xx, 233, 250-51, 457
Data base, xx, xxiii, 3, 8, 80, 233, 457
Data Cast, 442
Data General, 67, 226, 405-406
Data link, 457
Datapoint, 67, 235, 305-307
Data Pro, xviii, 261
Data processing, xxiv, 249
Data Processing Design, 406-408
Dataquest, 229, 232
Datasoft, 408-10
Data Terminals and Communications, 307-309
Dataword, 291-93
DBMS, 80, 458
Dead key, 458
Dealer, 458
Decentralized network, 251-52
Decentralized word processing, 458
Decibel, 92, 458
Decimal tabs, 44, 265, 458
Decision making, 153-71
DecMate Word Processor, 127, 178, 209, 315-17

DecWord/DP, 313–15
Dedicated circuit, 206
Dedicated word processor, xxiv, 114, 118–25, 458
Default, 458
Delete, 11, 12, 17, 24, 37, 44, 263–64, 458
Delta Data Systems, 309–11
Demonstrations, 11, 179
Density of disks, 70, 458
Descenders, 4, 59, 87, 458
Designer Software, 410–12
Desks, 146
Desktop Computing, 442
Detached keyboard, 458
Diagnostics, 458
Dictaphone, 311–13
Digital signals, 97, 238–39, 458
Digital telephone switchboards, 29
Digital Equipment Corporation (DEC), 66, 127, 176–78, 226, 313–17
Digital Research, 131–33, 457
Digitize, 238, 458
Directory, 2, 31–32, 45, 221, 270, 458
Direct sales, 177, 459
Disks: floppy, xxii, 2, 6, 8, 11, 19, 70–72; hard, 72–73; storage, 5, 69–73, 231, 459
Disk converter, 459
Disk drive, 13, 69
Display, xxii, xxiv, 40, 230, 459
Displaywriter, 178, 331–33
Distributed network, 253, 255, 459
Distribution of work, 162, 226, 231
Distributor, 459
Document, xix, 5, 13, 45, 459
Document analysis, 161–62, 459
Document standards, 218–19
Documentation, 5, 92, 191–92, 218, 459
Document index, 45
Document merge, 45, 459
Document-oriented systems, 75, 459
Document size, 75, 262
Doll, Dixon, 241
DOS, 459
Dot command, 78, 139, 265, 459
Dot leader, 459
Dot matrix printer, xx, 6, 83–84
Double density, 71
Double-sided disks, 71
Dow Jones, 243
Downey, Marty, 216–17
Down time, 197, 460
Drive, 20, 460
Dual display, 311–13
Dumb terminal, 460
Duplicate copy, 21
Durango, 126, 317–19

Ease of use, 115, 118, 123, 129, 134, 139
Easy One, 309–11
Easy Writer, 133, 414–17
EBCDIC, 243–45, 460
Edit, 11, 22–30, 32, 262, 460
Edit Pak, 387–81
Editor, 137, 460
Efficiency, 460
EIA, 243, 460
8100, 303–305
Electric typewriter, xviii, xix, xx
Electrical necessities, 206
Electronic mail, 170, 230–32, 235, 254, 460
Electronics Industry Association (EIA), 243–44, 460

Electronic Office Management and Technology, 442
Electronic typewriter, 9, 11, 114, 116–18, 240, 460
Electronic worksheet, 80, 460
Electrostatic printer, 84, 88, 460
Elite, 460
Elovitz, David, xvii
Emergency plans, 197
Emulation, 461
End of document, 18
End user, 461
Engineers, 1–2, 233, 437
Engraved keys, 62–64
Enhancement, 461
Enter, 15, 170, 254, 262, 461
Entry, 461
Environment, 148
Ergonomics, 57, 144–48, 461
Errors, 7, 147, 152
ESCAPE keys, 62, 461. *See also* Function keys
ET, 100n, 361–63
Europe, 147–48, 232
Evaluating word processing, 115–16
EW 100, 391–92
Execute, 30
Executive Secretary, 431–33
Executive workstation, 60, 461
Exxon Office Systems, 319–24
Eyestrain, 57, 60, 144–45
EZ 1, 399–40
EZ Type, 297–99

Facsimile machine, 226, 229, 234, 461
Fan-folded computer paper, 91, 461
FCC, 99, 461
FDM, 249, 461
Feasibility study, 154–71, 175, 461
Features, 259, 462
Federal Communications Commission, 99, 461
Feeder, 462
Fiber optics, 248, 255
Field, 462
Fielden, Rosemary, 441
Field service, 9, 196–97, 201, 462
Files, xxiii, 164, 169, 462
File names, 32, 269, 462
Filing, 6, 45, 149, 158–62, 170, 231
Find, 51, 231
Firmware, 73, 462
Fixed disk, 72, 462
Flag, 462
Flexible disks, xxii, 2, 6, 8, 11, 19, 69–72, 462
Flexibility, 115
Floating cursor, 76, 462
Floppy disk, 69–72, 462
Flow chart, 462
Font, 462
Footer, 47, 265, 462
Footnoting, 46, 265, 462
Forced page break, 265, 463
Ford, Henry, xvii
Form letters, xix, 3, 4, 22–27
Format, 13, 28, 44, 50, 77, 218, 234
Format line, 11, 14–15, 28–29, 463
Formatted disk, 71, 463
Formatter, 463
Forms, 7
Formulas, xix, 1, 46
Fortune Systems Corporation, 325–26
Fortune, 442
For:Word, 325–26

484 | INDEX

Frame, 245, 463
Freelancers, xviii, 215
French accent, 83
Frequency, 238, 240, 463
Frequency division multiplexing, 249, 463
Full duplex, 100, 248, 463
Full-page screen, 51, 463
Fully formed characters, 85–86, 463
Function, 11, 157, 161, 463
Functional design, 463
Function keys, 12, 18, 32, 62–64, 119, 134, 463
Furniture, 146, 205–206
Future Shock, xx

Gaffney, Carol, 152
Garbage on a disk, 71
Gateway, 246, 255, 464
Gauges, Louis, 166
General Electric, xviii
Generalists, 150, 464
General ledger, 464
General Mills, xviii
General Motors, xviii
Generating an index, 46, 464
German umlaut, 83
Germany, 152
Ghost hyphen, 464
Gibbs Consulting Group, xviii
Glare, xx, 145–48
Glitch, 464
Global, 464
Glossary, 46, 464
Goldfield, Randi, xviii
Gonzalez, J., 441
Go To, 29, 47, 464
Government: offices, xviii, 9; policies, 147
Graphics, xxii, 9, 60, 89, 234, 254, 464
Greek letters, 1, 60
Guide to word-processing systems, 259–433

Half duplex, 100, 248, 464
Half-page screen, 57, 464
Half spacing, 464
Hammer, Michael, 156
Handshakes, 464
Hanging, 464
Hannover, University of, 152
Hard copy, 30, 464
Hard disk, 69, 72–73, 465
Hardware, xxii, 54–104, 196, 465
Hardware upgrade, 195
Hard wire, 73, 465
Harmony, 153
Harris, Paul, 120
Hayden, 412–13
Hayes modems, 97
Headaches, 60
Header, 29, 47, 266, 465
Health, 57, 60, 144–48, 152
Hearing, 145–46
Heat, 145
Heimberg, Roslyn, 215–16
Help screen, 465
Hertz, 238, 247, 465
Hewlett Packard, 226, 327–28
Hidden costs, 201–203
Highlighting, 34
High or low intensity, 59
High resolution, 59, 89, 465
Honeywell, 226, 329–30
Hot zone, 465
HP Word, 327–28
Human factors, 465

Hybrid, 114, 125–31, 465
Hyphenating, 47, 266, 465

IBM (International Business Machines), xix, xxi, 66, 70, 123, 176–78, 226, 331–34
IBM Correcting Selectric, 116
IBM Displaywriter, 178, 331–33
IBM 5520 Information System, 333–35
IBM Mag Cards, 116
IBM Memory Typewriter, 213–14
IBM Personal Computer, 133, 178
IBM Selectric, 61, 119, 123
Illness. *See* Health
Image onscreen, 146–48, 231
Impact printer, 85, 465
Implementation specialist, 436, 465
Indents, 21, 28–29
Index, generating an, 46, 79, 266, 466
Information, xviii, 229–30, 254
Information processing, 120, 466
Information switching exchange, 235
Information system, 379–81, 466
Information Unlimited Software, 133, 414–17
InfoWorld, 442
Infowriter, 329–30
Ink jet printer, xviii, 84, 466
Input, 55, 70, 466
Inquiry, 466
Inserting, 24–25, 35–37, 47, 263, 466
Installation, 184, 193, 210–11, 466
Instructions to the computer, 73
Insurance, 3
Integrated, 466
Intel Corporation, 66
Intelligent Systems Corporation, 335–36
Intelligent TDM, 466
Intensity, 59
Interactive Graphics System, 234, 466
Interface, 88, 94, 98, 466
Interface Age, 443
Integrated Electronic Office, 235
Integrated word and data processing. *See* Hybrid
Internal memory, 466
International Business Machines. *See* IBM
International Data Corporation, xviii
International Information/Word Processing Association, 151, 443
Interviewing, 162
Inventory control, xxiv, 6, 467
I/O, 467
I/O devices, 70
ISX, 235, 467
Itek Graphic Systems, 337–39
IWP, 467

J100/200/300/500, 287–89
J425, 289–91
Japan, 48, 232
Japanese characters, 83
Job situation, 165–66
Jobs in word processing, 434–40
Jones, Lang, Wooton, Inc., xvii
Justifying text, 28, 47

K, 467
Keen, Peter, 232
Key to the list of word-processing products, 262–73
Keyboards, 12, 13, 30, 55, 61–65, 148, 235, 271, 467
Keyboard buffer, 65, 467
Keyboard layout, 61

Keyboard stickers, 63
Keyboard touch, 61
Keycap, 467
Keys for word processing, 61–65
Keystrokes—saving, 62
Kilobytes, 72
Konkel, Gilbert J., 441
Korean characters, 87
Kurzweil, Raymond, 103, 467
Kurzweil Data Entry Machine, 103
Kurzweil Reading Machine, 103

Laboratory for Computer Science, 157
Lanier, 120, 177, 339–42
Lanier No Problem, 216
LAN. *See* Local Area Network
Laser, 248
Laser printer, 84, 467
Lawyers, xvii, xviii, xx, 7, 233–34
Lazywriter, 133, 403–404
Lead operator, 215, 435, 467
Leased lines, 247, 255, 467
Leasing equipment, 200
Le Monde Informatique, 443
Letters (mail), xvii, xix, 4, 9, 35–36, 159, 169, 229
Letter merge, 266, 468
Letter-quality printing, xx, 6, 85–86, 468
Lex, 131, 417–19
Lexitron, xxii, 177, 371–73
Lexor, 119, 120, 343–44
Lexoritor, 119, 120, 343–44
Librarians, 8
Lights, 145–48
Line editors, 133
Line printers, 83–84
Lines, xix, 6, 158–61, 163
Line spacing, 266
Lines per page, 266
Link, xix, xxiii, 468
Linolex, xxii
Lisa, xxiv, 60, 91
List processing, 79, 468
Load, 70, 468
Local Area Network (LAN), 232, 238, 255, 468
Locating text, 25, 468
Log on, 468
Loops, 247, 252, 255, 468
Low-end system, 468
Lowercase, 4, 53

Macintosh, xxiv, 60, 91, 178
Magazines, 4, 442–43
Mag card, xxi, 468
Magna III, 276–77
Magna SL, 274–75
Magnetic media. *See* Disks
Magnetic tape, xxii, 11, 72
Magnetic Tape Selectric Typewriter (MTST), xxi, 470
Mail, 159–60, 230
Mail merge, 4, 79, 266
Mainframe computer, xix, xxii, 65, 226–27, 231, 251, 254, 468
Maintain, 48, 468
Maintenance of equipment, 9, 196–97, 201
Management of Word Processing Operations, 441
Managers, xvii, xxiv, 12, 145–46, 150, 171, 233
Manuals, xx, 5, 92, 191–92, 218, 459
Margins and tabs, 15, 28–29, 267
Margin release key, 266, 468
Marker, 468

Marketing, 30
Martin, Alexia, 234
Mass mailings, 79
Math packs, 79
MB. *See* Megabyte
McCabe, Helen M., 441
McGlaughlin, Dan, xix
MCS 8400, 301–303
Medicine, 2
Megabyte, 72, 468
Megadata, 345–46
Mellentin, William, 233
Memos, xix, 5, 9
Memory, xx, xxii, 68–69, 468. *See also* RAM, ROM
Memory typewriter, 114, 116–18, 469
Menu, 12, 13, 19, 23, 30–31, 469
Menu-driven, 469
Merge, 79, 266, 469
Micom, 367–69
Micro, 469
Microcomputer, xxiii, xxiv, 6–7, 60, 67, 114, 131–36
Microdata, 67, 347
Microfiche, 231, 235
Microfilm records, xviii, 232, 469
Micrographics, 234
Micromation, 132
Micropro, 131, 419–20
Microprocessor, 65, 469. *See also* Microcomputer
Microwaves, 247, 255, 469
Mini, 469
Mini-computers, 65–66
Mini floppy disks, 70
MIS Week, 443
M.I.T., 156–57, 232
Mnemonic, 469
Mode, 469
Modem, 9, 96–101, 239–42, 247, 469
Mohawk Data Sciences, 349–51
Molloy, Mary, 209–10
Monitor, 56, 469
Monitoring work, 151
Monroe, 351–53
Morale, 144–46, 150–55
Mouse, 91, 469
Move, 11, 32–33, 48, 233, 469
MSR, 179, 438, 469
MTST, xxi, 470
Multiple copies, 21
Multiplexer, 99, 248, 255
Multi-purpose OCR, 101–104, 470
Multi tasking, 170
Multi-terminal, 121, 125, 128, 470
Multi-user system, xxiv, 121
Multivision, 285–87

Naming documents, 219, 269
National Institute for Occupational Safety and Health (NIOSH), 145–46, 148
NBI, 120, 177, 353–55
NCR, 355–57
Network, 168, 229–33, 240–41, 251–58, 470
New York Times, 96
NIOSH, 145–46, 148
Nixdorf Computer, 67, 123, 246, 357–59
Node, 252–53, 470
Noise, 145–46
Nonprinting comments, 49, 267, 470
No problem, 341–42
Nonvolatile memory, 470
Norris, Charles, xviii

486 || INDEX

Northern Telecom, 421–22
North Star, 132, 359–61
Northword, 359–61
Number keypad, 64, 470

OA (Office Automation), xxi, 170, 227–58
Objects in tasks, 157–58, 163, 470
Objectives of office, 153, 168
Occupational hazards, 145–46
OC 8820, 351–53
OCR, 101–104, 234, 470
OEM, 137, 177, 470
Off hook, 470
Office, xvii–xx, 144–71
Office automation, xxi, 170, 227–58
Problems, 234–35, 242
Office equipment stores, 178
Office hazards. *See* Health
Office of the future, 470
Office procedures, 216–25
Office setting, 168–69
Office Systems Reports, 442
Off the shelf software, 131–35
Ofiswriter, 293–95, 400, 511
OHM, 470
Olivetti, 117, 361–63
Olympia USA, 363–65
Omega, 299–301
Omniwriter, 375–76
Omniword, 421–22
Online, 471
Ontel, 471
Open network, 238
OP 1/15, 365
Operating system, 71, 74, 471
Operators, 150, 434–35, 471
Optical Character Reader, 101–104, 234–35, 471
Optical fibers, 248, 255, 471
Optical scanner, xviii, xix, xx, 168, 471
Options, 471
Order entry, 471
Organizing documents on disk, 220–21
Orientation of word-processing software, 75, 262, 471
Original equipment manufacturer (OEM), 137, 177, 471
Orphan, 269, 471
Output, xvii, 471
Output device, 55, 70
Overlay, 128, 471

Package, 471
Page break, 40, 267, 471
Page-oriented systems, 75
Pages, xvii–xx, 5, 9, 168, 170
Paginating, 29–30, 39–41, 49, 472
Palantir, 410–12
Paper, xvii, xix, 6, 13, 21, 30, 159, 202
Paper handling, 91
Paragraph indent, 267, 472
Parallel, 241, 472
Para Research, 422–24
Para Text, 422–24
Paris, University of, 166
Parrot, 383–85
Paste, 12
Patch, 472
Payroll, 472
PBX. *See* Private Branch Exchange
Peachtext, 424–26
Peachtree Software, 424–26
Peck, Phyllis, 441

Perfect Software, 426–27
Perfect Writer, 426–27
Peripheral, 472
Personal computer, 60, 67, 234, 472
Personal Computer World, 443
Personnel offices, 7
Philips Information Systems, 367–69
Phone calls, 160, 164
Phone directory, 472
Phone lines, xvi, 3, 232, 235, 240, 247
Photocomposition, xviii, xix, 8, 93–96, 168, 233, 234, 472
Photocopying, xvii
Physical link, 472
Pica, 472
Picot, Arnold, 152
Pictures, 254
Pie charts, 472
Pins, 244, 472
Pitch, 21, 472
Pixel, 59
Plotter, 86, 472
Police, 2, 6
Pollution, 148
Popham, Estelle, 441
Poppel, Harvey, 170
Popular Computing, 443
Posture, 149
Prefix keys. *See* Control keys
Pre-installation training, 209
Preparing your office, 204–10
Pre-sales education, 191
Presentation level, 245, 472
Preview, 473
Printers, xviii, xix, xx, 2, 3, 4, 6, 8, 9, 21–22, 30, 49, 82–93, 145–46, 164, 168–69, 229, 234–35, 241, 473; character sets, 87; cost, 92; deciding on, 86–93; dot matrix, 83; ease of control, 91; electrostatic, 84; graphics, 89; ink jet, 84; laser, 84; letter-quality, 85–86; paper handling, 91; plotters, 86; quality of image, 86; reliability, 91; sound, 92; thermal, 84; using your typewriter, 85
Printhead, 92, 473
Printout, xvii, 40
Print queue, 270, 473
Private branch exchange (PBX), 229, 237, 250, 252
Procedure, 157–63, 170, 473
Process, 473
Processors. *See* Central Processing Unit
Productivity, 7, 144, 149–71, 473
Product line jobs, 437, 473
Professionals, xvii, xviii, xxiii, 12, 149, 437–48
Programmable keys, 268, 473
Prolink, 369–71
Prompt, 14, 473
Proofreading, xix, 435
Proportional spacing, 473
Proposals, 2, 3, 30
Protocols, 2, 243–46, 255, 473
Protocol converter, 245–46, 255, 473
Public relations, 39–41
Purchasing equipment, 199–200. *See also* Shopping

Quad density, 70–72
Quadriterk, 337–39
Questionnaires, 158–60
Queue, 270, 473

Radiation, 148
Radio Shack, 133, 428–29

RAM, 68–69, 474
Random Access Memory (RAM), 68–69
Raytheon, 371–72
Read Only Memory (ROM), 68, 475
Real estate, 7
Receive and send, 100
Reformat, 50, 268, 474
Refresh rate, 146, 474
Remembering multiple formats, 50
Remington, xxi
Removable disks, 72
Renaming, 19, 50, 269, 474
Renting equipment, 200–201
Repeaters, 239, 474
Repeating keys, 64, 474
Repeating last command, 50, 268, 474
Reports, xx, 2, 9, 230, 442
Request for proposal, 178, 474
Research before you buy, 172–76
Reset, 474
Resistance, 474
Resolution, 59, 474
Response time, 197, 474
Retail stores, 176, 178, 183
Reverse video, 58, 474
Revisions, xix, xx, xxii, 1, 7–8, 22–30, 32–41
Right justification, 268, 474
Ring, 252, 255, 475
ROM, 68, 475
Rothenberg Information Systems, 373–74
Royal Business Machines, 375–78
RS-232, 244
Rub out, 16–17, 475
Ruler, 11, 475

Sachs, Randi, xix
Salary survey results, 441
Sales cycle, 4, 171–84
Satellite, 240, 247, 255, 475
Sauer, Dotti, 213–14
Save, 475
Savin, 63, 379–80
Saving work, 27, 69, 231. *See also* Disks: storage
Savings, xix, 154, 162, 170
Scaling up, 253, 475
Schacter, Gerald, 119
Scientific Data Systems, 381–82
Scratch pad, 475
Screens, xxii, 11–13, 17, 30, 55–61, 144–48, 475
Scripsit, 133, 428–29
Scroll, 13, 17–18, 28–29, 51, 263, 475
Secretaries, xvii–xxiii, 1–3, 7–9, 12, 30, 35, 149–55, 162, 230
Sectors, 71
Security issues, 221
Select Information Systems, 132, 429–30
Selectric, xxi, 61, 116, 119, 123
Select word processing, 132, 429–31
Self-paced training, 192–93, 212
Send/Receive, 100
Serial, 475
Series 21, 349–51
Series 8000, 345–46
Service, 475. *See also* Support
Session logic, 245, 475
Seybold Report on Office Systems, 227, 442
Shared logic, 4, 121, 475
Shared resource, 121
Shasta Business Systems, 64
Shasta General Systems, 383–84
Sheet feed, 91, 270, 475
Shift, 51, 475

Shift lock key, 65
Shipping costs, 201
Shopping, 172–203
Short-line seeking, 475
Shows, 173
Shugart, 70
Shultz, M., xxi
Simplex, 248, 476
Simultaneous processing, 271, 476
Single-density disks, 71
Single-sided disks, 71
Single-user system, 120, 476. *See also* Stand-alone systems
Site preparation, 205
Skin problems, 145
Small Business Computers Magazine, 443
Small business xviii, 476
Smart terminal, 476
Sofsys, 431–33
Soft benefits, 476
Software: applications 73–81, 146–47, 476; bundled and unbundled, 74; definition, 73; licenses, 201; maintenance contract, 476; operating systems, 71, 74, 471; word-processing, 73–81, 115, 136–40
Sort, 52, 79, 268, 476
Sound, 145–46
Specialist, 476
Speed: of access, 235; of communications, 98; of printing, xix, 87, 168, 170; of processors, 67–68
Spelling check, 43, 79, 268, 476
S.R.I. International, 227, 233
Stand-alone systems, xxiii, 4, 120, 127, 476
Standard letter, 23–27. *See also* Boilerplate
Star, 252, 255, 476
Star Information System, xxiii, 58, 399–400
Starting up, 13
Statistics, 2, 5, 9
Status indicators, 100, 476
Stereo, 238, 240
Storage, xx–xxi, 11, 69–73, 476
Storing disks, 221
Storing formats, 268, 476
Strassmann, Paul, 228
Stress, 145, 149
Strikeover, 52, 268, 477
Subscript, 52, 269, 477
Superscript, 52, 269, 477
Supervision and management, 218, 433–36
Supplies, 202, 207
Support, 184–99, 477
Switchback, 230, 252
Switched phone lines, 247, 477
Symmetrical network, 253, 255, 477
Synch, 241, 477
Synchronous, 99, 241–42, 255, 477
Syntrex, 385–86
Systems analyst, xvii, 149–55, 437, 477
Systems design, 437, 477
System 7, 397–98
Systems House, 477
System 3000, 353–55

T1, T2, T3, T4, 240, 477
Table of contents, generating, 79, 266
Tabs, 28–29, 269, 477
Tandy. *See* Radio Shack
Tape, magnetic, xxii, 11, 72
Tasks, 157
TDM, 249–50, 478
Teacher, 5–6, 440. *See also* Training, MSR
Technical writer, 5, 438

488 || INDEX

Technology International, 387–88
Telecommunications, xxiii, 26
Telephones, 160, 164, 234–35, 249
Telephone lines, xviii, 226, 229, 232
Televideo, 132
Television, 229, 231–38, 240, 249, 254
Telex, 99, 478
Ten key, 64
Terminals, xx, 7, 56, 252–53. See also Keyboards, Screens
Texas Instruments, 389–90
Text editor, 137, 478
Text Wizard, 408–10
Thermal printer, 84, 478
Thimble, 85, 478
Third-party vendor, 136–40. See also OEM
Thursland, Arthur L., 441
Tickler file, 231, 478
Time, 153, 158, 163, 166–67
Time Division Multiplexing (TDM), 249–50, 478
Time sharing, 233, 478
TIPE, 990, 389–90
Titles, 32
Today's Office, 443
Toffler, Alvin, xx
Top, 18, 22
Top of page, 478
Topology, 252, 478
Toshiba, 391–92
Total office systems, 115, 140–41
Touch of the keyboard, 61
Tracks, 71
Tractor mechanism, 91, 478
Trade shows, xviii
Trainers, 436
Training, 153, 192–94, 201, 212–16, 478
Transmission, 97, 99, 231, 478
Transport level, 245, 478
Trouble-shooting, 194
TRS-80, 133
Tube, 478. See also Video display screen, Screens
Turnaround time, 478
Turnkey, 479
TWX, 479
Type element, 83–85, 479
Type fonts, 271
Typesetting, xviii–xx. See also Photocomposition
Typewriter, xviii, xxi, 5, 12, 13, 15, 16, 114, 116–18, 226, 240
Typing, 15, 149, 153, 161–62, 164, 167

Umlaut, 83
Underline, 53, 59, 234, 269, 479
Undo, 479
Unions, 147
United States, 148, 232
Update, xx, 148, 194–95, 202, 479
Upgrade, xxii, 124, 195, 202, 479
Uppercase, 4, 53
User, 144, 149, 479

User-defined keys, 50. See also Function keys, Programmable keys
User-friendly, 144, 479
User groups, 199

Variable pitch, 269, 479
Varityper, 281–83
Vector Graphics, 131, 393–94
Vendor, 177, 479
Verify, 270, 479
Vertical, 269, 479
Video disks, 234, 479
Video display screen, xxii, 56–61, 230. See also Screens
Videotape recorders, 234
View mode, 78
Virtual Terminal Support, 246, 479
Voice mail, 168, 231–32
Voice traffic, 250–51, 254, 480
Volatile, 68, 480
Voltage, 480
Vydec, 68

Wages, xvii, 434–440
Wang Laboratories, 67, 120, 123, 127, 177–78, 226, 234, 395–96
Wang Writer, 121, 178
Watching demonstrations, 179
Waterloo, University of, 152
What to read, 441–43
What you see is what you get, 76, 267, 480
Which word processor?, 443
White space, 39–41
Widow, 269, 480
Window, 17, 480
Wiring your office, 205
Word-11, 406–408
Wordmate, 347–48
Wordplex, 397–98
Word Processing, 441
Word Processing and Information Systems, 441
Word Processing in the Modern Office, 441
Word Processing: A Systems Approach to the Office, 441
Word Processing Concepts and Careers, 441
Word Processing in the Modern Office, 441
Words, 443
WordStar, 131, 133, 419–20
Word wrap, 15–16, 53, 262, 480
Work Measurement, 441
Work monitors, 151
Work sampling, 160–61, 480
Work Saver, 355–58
Workstation, xix, xxiv, 11, 30, 231, 480
WPS, 179, 480
Writers, xvii, 13, 438

Xerox, xxiii, 64, 176–78, 226–28, 240, 399–400; Xerox 800, 215; Xerox 820, 132, 178; Xerox 850, 215; Xerox 860, 215
XMark, 401–402

Your Future in Word Processing, 441